Inferno

The Devastation of Hamburg, 1943

KEITH LOWE

VIKING
an imprint of
PENGUIN BOOKS

VIKING

Published by the Penguin Group
Penguin Books Ltd, 80 Strand, London WC2R ORL, England
Penguin Group (USA) Inc., 375 Hudson Street, New York, New York 10014, USA
Penguin Group (Canada), 90 Eglinton Avenue East, Suite 700, Toronto, Ontario, Canada M4P 2Y3
(a division of Pearson Penguin Canada Inc.)
Penguin Ireland, 25 St Stephen's Green, Dublin 2, Ireland
(a division of Penguin Books Ltd)
Penguin Group (Australia), 250 Camberwell Road, Camberwell, Victoria 3124, Australia
(a division of Pearson Australia Group Pty Ltd)
Penguin Books India Pvt Ltd, 11 Community Centre, Panchsheel Park, New Delhi – 110 017, India
Penguin Group (NZ), 67 Apollo Drive, Mairangi Bay, Auckland 1310, New Zealand
(a division of Pearson New Zealand Ltd)
Penguin Books (South Africa) (Pty) Ltd, 24 Sturdee Avenue, Rosebank, Johannesburg 2196, South Africa

Penguin Books Ltd, Registered Offices: 80 Strand, London WC2R ORL, England

www.penguin.com

First published 2007
1

Copyright © Keith Lowe, 2007

Set in 12/14.75pt Monotype Bembo
Typeset by Rowland Phototypesetting Ltd, Bury St Edmunds, Suffolk
Printed in Great Britain by Clays Ltd, St Ives plc

A CIP catalogue record for this book is available from the British Library

ISBN: 978-0-670-91557-6

Inferno

Contents

Part Three – The Aftermath

Appendices

List of Maps

List of Illustrations

Section One

1 Churchill and Roosevelt at the Casablanca Conference, where the Combined Bomber Offensive was first agreed (US Army)
2 Sir Arthur Harris, Commander-in-Chief, RAF Bomber Command (Imperial War Museum)
3 Major General Frederick L. Anderson, commander US VIII Bomber Command (US Air Force)
4 Hitler arrives at Hamburg's airport on one of his many pre-war visits (Archiv Erna Neumann)
5 Karl Kaufmann, Hamburg's gauleiter and a loyal disciple of the Führer (Studio Schmidt-Luchs)
6 Göring (left) was head of the Luftwaffe, but it was Erhard Milch (right) who ran the show. Chief of Air Staff Hans Jeschonnek (centre) shot himself shortly after the bombing of Hamburg (Private collection)
7 Colin Harrison: 'One minute I was a schoolboy, next minute they called me a man and put me in an aeroplane.' (Private collection)
8 Bill McCrea: 'When we were detailed on the first Hamburg raid we thought, "Now we'll see what it's *really* like!"' (Private collection)
9 Doug Fry (centre), hours before he was shot down at the end of July 1943 (Private collection)
10 Baptism of fire: Ted Groom and pilot Reg Wellham's first operation was the firestorm raid of 27 July (Private collection)
11 Hamburg before the war. Narrow streets like this allowed fires to spread rapidly (RAF Museum)
12 The bright lights of the Reeperbahn in the 1930s (Denkmalschutzamt Hamburg)

Section Two

Section Three

Introduction

He who fights with monsters should look to it that he himself does not become a monster. And when you gaze long into an abyss the abyss also gazes into you.
Friedrich Nietzsche[1]

In his eyewitness account of the Hamburg firestorm and its aftermath, Hans Erich Nossack admitted to feeling a mixture of awe and elation whenever he saw the fleets of British bombers flying over the city. Despite his natural fear during an air raid, he often found himself willing the bombers on, almost hoping for the opportunity to witness a truly catastrophic event. Rather than going to the shelter he would stand spellbound on his balcony watching the explosions rising above the city. He did not blame the British and American airmen for the havoc they were wreaking, but saw it rather as the inevitable expression of man's urge to destroy – an urge that was mirrored in his own morbid fascination. That this fascination was accompanied by revulsion, both at what was happening before him and at his own emotions, did not lessen the power of his darkest cravings.[2]

There is a sense in which the whole of the Second World War can be seen as a battle between these dark cravings – the human urge to destroy – and the desire to keep such instincts in check. From the victors' point of view the war has often been portrayed as an almost mythical struggle by the 'free' world to rein in the destructive urges of Hitler's regime. And yet the Allies were just as destructive towards their enemies as the Axis powers ever were – necessarily so, since destruction is the very business of war. The tragedy of this particular conflict was that both sides should so completely abandon all restraint, until there was no way out of the war but by the total devastation of one side or the other.

Nowhere is this more apparent than in the bomber war. Each side began bombing with relative caution – especially the British, who promised early on that all bombing would be confined to strictly military objectives. Each side gradually descended into varying degrees of what the Germans called *Schrechlichkeit* ('frightfulness') – the deliberate terrorizing of civilian populations. And each side accompanied their bomber raids not only with increasingly bloodthirsty calls for the utter destruction of their enemy, but with jubilation whenever that destruction was partially achieved. The uncomfortable elation experienced by Nossack at the bombing of his own city was merely a token of what was happening across the whole of Europe.

At the end of the war, when things had returned to 'normality', both sides tried to distance themselves from these events. This denial of the past has been most pronounced in Germany, where it seemed that the only way the population could cope with the horrors they had witnessed was to pretend they had never happened. In 1946, the Swedish journalist Stig Dagerman described travelling through the moonscape of Hamburg on a train: despite the massive expanse of ruins not a single other passenger looked out of the window. Dagerman was immediately identified as a foreigner precisely *because* he did so. The story is an apt metaphor for the way Germans have collectively avoided looking at the ordeal they experienced. Until recently, few German authors have been willing to engage emotionally with the subject because to do so would open too many wounds. The peculiar mix of collective guilt for being a part of a nation that unleashed war upon the world, and anger at the heartlessness of their own treatment – so that they were simultaneously both perpetrators and victims of atrocity – has made it much easier to turn away and pretend that life continued as normal.[3]

In Britain and America there has been a corresponding avoidance of the consequences of our bombing war. We know all about what it was like for our airmen, and the bravery they displayed in the face of formidable German flak and fighter defences is a strong part of our collective folklore. Triumphant films have been made about it, such as *The Dambusters*, or Hollywood's *Memphis Belle*. There are countless books about the airmen's experience – about the stress of waiting at dispersal, the nerves of the long flight into battle, the terror of flying through flak, or even of being shot down by fighters. That is as it should be – those were the things we did, and it is important that we remember them. But after the bombs have been dropped, and the surviving bombers have returned home, the story tends to end. What happened on the ground, to the cities full of people beneath those falling bombs is rarely talked about; even when it *is* discussed, it is usually only in terms of the buildings and factories destroyed, with a cursory mention of civilian casualties. We, too, like to pretend that nothing terrible came of those bombs. (I am talking here about our *collective* consciousness – the airmen themselves are among the few of us who seem to have thought about it, understood what they were doing, and either come to terms with it or made a conscious decision not to try to square the impossible: there was a war on, and they know what we don't, that war is a terrible thing out of which *no one* escapes looking good.)

The one exception to this rule, of course, is Dresden. The disproportional amount of attention Dresden gets is our one act of contrition for the destruction we rained on the cities of Germany. There are various reasons why this city has become the emblem of our guilt – it was truly beautiful, the scale of its destruction over just a few days was awe-inspiring, and since it occurred towards the end of the war many people have wondered with hindsight whether it was not an unnecessary tragedy. All this is worthy of discussion, but it does not excuse our forgetfulness about other cities in Germany. What about Wuppertal, Düsseldorf and Berlin? Berlin suffered more bombing destruction in terms of area than any other city in the war: almost four times as much as Dresden.[4] And what about Hamburg? Just as many people died in Hamburg as in Dresden, if not more, and in ways that were every bit as horrific.

In continental Europe the destruction of Hamburg is regarded as a defining moment in the Second World War. It happened eighteen months before Dresden, at a time when much of Germany was still confident of final victory. It was a far greater shock to the system than Dresden was, unleashing almost a million refugees across a nation that had still not quite accepted the consequences of bombing. Those refugees brought with them tales of unimaginable horror: fires hot enough to melt glass, a firestorm strong enough to uproot trees and hurl them into the flames, and rumours of 200,000 people killed within a few days and nights (although, in fact, the total was more like 45,000).

I have been consistently surprised by the general ignorance of these facts among my own countrymen. In the two years I spent writing this book I came across few people outside the world of military historians who knew that Hamburg had been bombed at all, let alone the sheer scale of the destruction that took place. On the Continent the bombing of Hamburg is a byword for horror, yet in Britain few people know it happened. In North America, too, there is widespread ignorance of the basic facts, although to some extent America's geographical and emotional distance from Hamburg excuses this. Even those who have heard of the Hamburg firestorm are generally unaware of its ghastly human consequences.

The main purpose of this book is to put that right. My intention is to convey the events as they appeared at the time, not only to the British and American airmen who fought their way across the skies of Europe, but to the people of Hamburg who became the victims of their bombs. Hamburg was a handsome and prosperous city before it was destroyed: in the first few chapters, I will explain some of the city's history, and try to re-create the atmosphere in this Hansestadt in the years leading up to 1943. It is only by knowing what was there before the bombing that we can truly appreciate what was lost – both physically and psycho-logically. I have also devoted several chapters to the immediate and long-term aftermath of the firestorm because it has never been adequately described before, in Germany or abroad. The effect of the catastrophe on the German people, and on Germany itself, was far-reaching, and continues to cause controversy today.

The second purpose of this book is to try to correct the erroneous belief that war is somehow a glorious or heroic under-taking. During the course of my research I interviewed dozens of bomber veterans, and they are unanimous on this point: there is nothing glorious about sitting in a Lancaster or a B-17 bomber for upwards of five hours, in the freezing temperatures of the upper atmosphere, waiting to find out if you will return home safely. At best it is dull, at worst it is terrifying: the rare moments of exhilaration are insignificant when compared to this.

There is nothing glorious about being bombed, either, as the British learned during the Blitz when more than 40,000 British civilians were killed. The most infamous German raid was on Coventry, where local industries, civilian houses and historic build-ings in the centre of the city were devastated. In their collective imagination this is what British people believe it must have been like for the Germans – a little like Coventry, or perhaps slightly worse. It is a false impression. What happened in Essen, Bochum, Düsseldorf and the other cities around the river Ruhr was like two years of Coventrys, night after night after night. Coventry suffered only a single major bombing raid; Essen was bombed on a much larger scale, twenty-eight times. Hamburg is on another level altogether. What happened there is more accurately compared to Hiroshima or Nagasaki.[5]

Until recently America did not know what it was like to be bombed at all. Geographically remote from any hostile neighbours, the USA has always enjoyed almost total immunity from air attack,[6] and until a few years ago its people had never been seriously threatened. The shock was therefore all the greater when a group of Al Qaeda terrorists flew two commercial airliners into the World Trade Center on 11 September 2001. The sheer horror of this action still consumes Americans with righteous indignation – and so it should – but tragic as this event was, it was essentially only the destruction of a handful of buildings. True, almost three thousand people perished, but imagine the sense of awe, of shock, if the whole of Lower Manhattan had been destroyed. Imagine an area from the tip of the island all the way up to Madison Square

consumed by a *single* fire, and the rest of the city as far as Central
Park reduced to rubble. What would have been America's reaction
if the death toll had not been 2,800, but ten or fifteen times that
number? Imagine eight square miles of the city without a single
building left standing – mountains of rubble as far as the eye can
see, corpses littering the streets, the smell of decay pervading
everything. This was what happened in Hamburg in the summer
of 1943.

★   ★   ★

This book would not have been possible without the help of scores
of Allied ex-airmen and German civilians who consented to be
interviewed. Their willingness to share their diaries and to rake
over painful memories from more than sixty years ago has been
humbling, and I can only thank them for the patience with which
they answered my questions. I am aware that there is something
distasteful about some of the questions I was obliged to ask, especially in the specific details I demanded. Indeed, when interviewing
people who lived through the firestorm I often found myself
experiencing a mixture of emotions similar to that described by
Nossack as he watched the bombers fly over his city – excitement
at the prospect of gathering good material, a perverse hope that
their descriptions would become even more graphic, and a faint
sense of shame at the inappropriateness of my enthusiasm. Writing
about catastrophe (or, for that matter, reading about it) is not
the same as experiencing it, and there is inevitably something
voyeuristic about examining someone else's misery in this sort of
detail. I hope, therefore, that this book will not merely convey my
own uncomfortable fascination with the terrifying stories those
people told me, but also the lingering revulsion they have communicated to me at the human cost of war.

There is no space here to list the scores of people and institutions
on both sides of the Atlantic who have helped me over the past few
years. Many are named in the Acknowledgements (pages 471–2),
but that cannot do justice to the enormous contribution they
have made, or their selfless enthusiasm for my project. There are,

however, a handful of people who deserve special mention. First and foremost I am deeply indebted to Mirko Hohmann and Malte Thießen for sharing their knowledge of the German sources, and for looking after me on my various trips to Hamburg. Paul Wolf was a huge help in gathering elusive American material; and Sonia Stammwitz helped with the translation of some of the denser German documents, as did Jenny Piening and Sylvia Goulding. I am also tremendously grateful to my editors Eleo Gordon and Lisa Drew: without their support this book would never have been started.

Lastly I must thank Liza and Gabriel for giving me a reason to leave my study each evening, and lock away the terrible stories and photographs that have been my companions by day. Several years of research into some of the most frightening events of the twentieth century have taught me not to take their presence for granted.

Keith Lowe, 2007

Author's Note

According to the old adage, Britain and America are two nations divided by a common tongue, and nowhere was this more apparent than in the different terminology that the two air forces employed to describe the same things. To avoid confusion I have used British terminology to describe the British 'operations', and American terminology to describe their 'missions'. For a comparison of different terms, please see Appendix D (pages 367–8).

On the whole I have used German sources to describe the German experience, but on one or two occasions I have turned to existing English translations out of necessity. For those who are interested in further study, there are substantial notes at the end of this book (pages 401–58) – but this should not be necessary for the general reader.

PART ONE
Hamburg

1. City on the River

Wherever there's trade, there tread Hamburgers.
Hamburg saying, mid-nineteenth century[1]

The city of Hamburg lies on the banks of the river Elbe in northern Germany, about sixty miles from the coast of the North Sea. In truth, it is not a hospitable place to found a city. Situated on a fluvial plain, most of the ground is little better than marsh, and it is prone to flooding. Ever since the area was first settled the city fathers have fought a constant battle against the storms and tides that regularly cause the waters of the river to rise and break their banks. The threat extends far beyond the city boundaries. For mile after mile the earth lies flat, perhaps rises a little, then is flat again, providing scant protection from the whims of the river. In times of flood the entire area becomes submerged: farmland, docklands, parks, city streets and houses are ruined. When eventually the water subsides it leaves behind it a blanket of silt covering city and countryside alike, reducing everything to a dull, muddy uniformity.

There is nothing to protect the city from the weather either. No mountains infringe on the curve of the horizon, or provide a break to the prevailing winds rolling in from the North Sea. The moist sea air produces huge banks of cloud, which smother the region for most of the year, bringing frequent rain and occasionally sleet and snow. In winter, if the wind changes direction and blows in from the Baltic, temperatures plummet and drift ice appears on the river. Even in summer the nights can be cold and wet, and the temperature rarely reaches the highs that other parts of Europe experience.

The element that dominates the city is water. The river Elbe is its lifeblood, linking it to the North Sea and trade routes across the globe. A second river, the Alster, was dammed in 1235 and has formed two large lakes right in the city centre. To the east, elaborate networks of canals creep like tentacles into the city's warehouse and workers' districts. To the south, in the midst of the Elbe, lies a series of islands that have been linked together over the centuries into a vast complex of docks and waterways: this is Hamburg's harbour, one of the largest ports in the world, and the foundation of the city's considerable prosperity.

Apart from its harbour, Hamburg is an unremarkable place. Unlike Dresden, which lies a couple of hundred miles upstream, it has never been considered a jewel, and its architecture is generally functional rather than ornate. Its city churches have none of the scale and grandeur of other German cathedrals, like that at Cologne. There are no palaces or castles here, like those in Berlin, Potsdam or Munich; in fact, the grandest houses the city has to offer are the upper-middle-class villas along the Elbe Chaussee. The city boasts more bridges than Venice, but that is where the comparison ends, and not even its most enthusiastic citizens would pretend otherwise. Few pleasure boats travel the city's canals, hardly any of the buildings are more than sixty years old, and the sound of voices and footfalls is drowned by the noise of traffic flowing down the six-lane dual-carriageways that scar the city in all directions.

Even before the Second World War, Hamburg was never really considered a destination for sightseers: the historic centre of the city was not particularly historic, since most of it had been destroyed by fire less than a century before. The few tourists who came to this part of Germany generally preferred the picturesque centre of nearby Lübeck. Neither is it considered a city of culture. Hamburg did not have a university until after the First World War, and while the Musikhalle and the Hamburg Opera are much admired by the middle classes, the city has always been better known for the more low-brow pleasures to be found on the Reeperbahn in the St Pauli district.

To their credit, the people of Hamburg have never much cared about the lack of superlatives connected to their city: they are proud of what they have, and unconcerned about what they do not. They are a tough, practical people, accustomed to dealing with challenges and to making the best of any situation that Fate might throw at them. Over the past two centuries they have seen their city ravaged in turn by epidemics of cholera, famine, economic recession, unemployment and, of course, by flooding. The town centre has been destroyed by fire not once but four times – despite the huge quantities of water that dominate the city's open spaces.[2] In the face of such a history it is little wonder that there are so few ancient architectural gems.

However, the lack of grand monuments in the city cannot be blamed entirely on natural disasters: it is also the result of an inherent reserve that has deep roots in the city's mentality. For more than eight hundred years Hamburg has been a place of merchants, and the centuries have carved it into a middle-class rather than an aristocratic city. The town centre is dominated by the towers of that most bourgeois of German buildings, the *Rathaus* (or town hall). It sits before a large piazza, where Adolf Hitler once addressed a crowd of more than twenty thousand, overlooking the great Alster lakes. The streets around the *Rathaus* are filled with exactly the kind of buildings one would expect in a city of merchants: shops, office buildings and, a little further south, the warehouse district of the Speicherstadt. The only towers to break the skyline, apart from those of the *Rathaus*, are the spires of the city's five main churches.

As for the rest of Hamburg, it is generally a green, pleasant place to live. To the west of the city are the tree-lined boulevards of Eimsbüttel, Eppendorf and Harvestehude, with their tall, elegant apartment buildings and rows of flower-filled balconies. To the north, the leafy suburbs of Winterhude, Barmbek and Alsterdorf cluster round the huge Stadtpark. Further north still, in Ohlsdorf, the greenery conceals the largest cemetery in Europe: four square miles of gravestones among well-tended gardens.

The working-class districts have traditionally been confined to the east of the city, in suburbs like Hammerbrook, Hamm,

Rothenburgsort and Billbrook. Here, low-rise apartment blocks
have always crammed in high concentrations of people within easy
commuting distance of the docks and warehouses. There is nothing
– not a building, not a tree, not a lamp-post, not even a street sign
– that is more than sixty years old. In some areas even the people
have moved away. In Hammerbrook, for example, there are few
apartments, only offices and warehouses, garages and depots. After
office hours, the only human beings that walk along Süderstrasse
are prostitutes trying to attract the attention of a passing car. In the
smaller streets even those signs of life are missing, and the whole
area lies silent.

⋆   ⋆   ⋆

While the historic centre of the city might lie on the north shore
of the Elbe, it is the harbour that is its true heart. The industrial
landscape here is vast and impressive, and has a savage beauty
unparalleled by any other place in Germany. Formations of cranes
stretch as far as the eye can see, towering above the warehouses
and the dry docks of Hamburg's ship-building companies, like the
silent regiments of some huge mechanical army. The many-
coloured blocks of transport containers rise in mountains from the
quayside, dwarfing the trucks and railway trains that come from
all over Europe to collect them. Their reflection stains the grey
waters of the Elbe with every colour of the rainbow.

   When the population of Hamburg gathers each May at the
Landungsbrücken to celebrate the official birthday of the harbour,
they are not merely giving thanks for the wealth that floods through
its gates. The harbour is more than just a source of jobs and
economic prosperity: it has provided Hamburg with its identity as
a city of trade. Because of it, Hamburg has been known for
centuries as Germany's gateway to the world.

   According to tradition, the harbour was founded more than
eight hundred years ago, in 1189, when the Emperor Frederick
Barbarossa granted Hamburgers the right to duty-free trade all
along the Elbe from the city to the sea. With such an advantage
over their neighbours, the city's merchants soon built Hamburg

into a major trading centre. By 1242 the city was powerful enough to draw up an agreement with nearby Lübeck, thus forming the template for the Hanseatic League. This alliance brought them major trading partners right across the region – not only in Germany, but also in Bruges, Amsterdam, London and even as far away as Novgorod – making this marshy, watery city one of the wealthiest in Europe.[3]

By the sixteenth century Hamburg was nothing short of a huge, city-wide storehouse, holding vast quantities of goods for resale throughout Europe. Tall warehouses stacked with grain, oil, salt and beer rose beside the narrow canals and waterways that carried the tide of commodities into the heart of the city. The more expensive goods, such as honey, fine wines and amber, were stored on the higher floors to keep them safe from the floodwaters of the Elbe, while the lower floors were reserved for cheaper items, such as fish or lumber. With the discovery of the New World, local merchants who had made themselves rich by trading in cloth or foodstuffs were soon trading in precious gems and metals, saltpetre, coffee, tea, tobacco and exotic spices. One of the most lucrative cargoes was that of peppercorns, which Hamburg's spice traders brought back in sackloads from the Orient. Even today, the wealthier citizens of Hamburg are still occasionally called *Pfeffersäcke* ('peppersacks') – a derogatory nickname for fat-cat businessmen.

The city's residents lived in similarly tall houses, rising above the squalid streets like warehouses of humanity, storing workers for use in the busy port. In such cramped conditions hygiene was impossible, disease was rife, and life expectancy short. Despite the ubiquitous waterways, fire was a very real danger. In 1284 the entire city was completely destroyed by a huge fire that, according to tradition, left only a single building standing. In 1684, after a series of smaller fires, a second conflagration destroyed 214 houses. Nearby Altona also suffered a major fire in 1711, followed by the deliberate burning of two-thirds of the city by Swedish troops two years later.[4] After each catastrophe, the city was rebuilt with houses even taller and more densely occupied than before.

Among this jumble of homes and warehouses there were also small islands of industry – tanneries, weaving houses, potteries, breweries and shipbuilders. Some of the city's most important industries were brought here by outsiders. Hamburgers learned the art of sugar refining from the Dutch, and by the early 1600s Hamburg was one of the world's biggest exporters of refined sugar. Dutch immigrants also brought the velvet and silk trades to the city. The French brought new baking techniques, and *Franzbrötchen* are still something of a city speciality. Greenlanders brought their skill in extracting oil from whale blubber, and set up a district of workshops in Hamburger Berg (now St Pauli): the glut of train oil they produced meant that the citizens of Hamburg could afford to put lanterns along the major streets, making this one of the first cities ever to have street lighting.[5]

As a maritime power, Hamburg has always teemed with foreigners, and the face of the city seems to have changed with every new influx of immigrants. It was not only the sailors and adventurers who settled here, drawn to Hamburg along the world's trade routes in search of a better life: refugees came too. While the rest of Europe was persecuting its religious minorities, Protestant Hamburg tended to extend a cautious welcome to anyone who brought in new money or new trades. In the sixteenth century Jews from Spain and Portugal settled there after being expelled from their own countries, and built one of the largest Jewish communities in Europe. Dutch Calvinists found safety from the Catholic armies of Philip II, and came to dominate the city's foreign trade. Later, Huguenots would flee there after the purges in France, as would aristocrats after the French Revolution. Hamburg fast became one of the most cosmopolitan places in Europe, a Renaissance Babel where English gentlemen and French princes knocked shoulders with Finnish sailors, Brazilian rubber merchants, and the countless migrants from Mecklenburg and Schleswig-Holstein who flocked there to take a tiny share of the city's considerable fortune.

★   ★   ★

Hamburg has always been like this: hardworking, multifarious and quick to embrace new ideas. Throughout its history, the only constant has been change. Buildings rise, are demolished by fire or flood and rebuilt; whole suburbs are regularly created and destroyed. The population comes and goes from all over the world, creating distinct communities that flourish for a few generations then disperse once more as they are integrated into the whole. This is natural to Hamburgers, and continues to this day.

Even the river is not constant. Before the Second World War, parts of it silted up and caused problems for the ever-larger ships that travelled in and out of the harbour with the tides; specialist pilots had to guide them to the safety of their berths. Sometimes whole islands of silt would form in the centre of the river; for months, or even years, they would give the illusion of solidity, before the waters rose once more and they were swept away towards the sea.

2. The Anglophile City

I am the enemy you killed, my friend
Wilfred Owen[1]

Through its trade links, Hamburg has developed associations with many countries over the centuries; but two relationships are particularly interesting, especially when considering the events of the Second World War. Hamburg's connections with Britain and America go beyond that of mere trading partners: somehow those two English-speaking nations have found their way beneath Hamburg's skin. This is particularly the case with the British – or, more specifically, the English. Even during the height of the war Hamburg still thought of itself as an anglophile city, and it was not until the dreadful events of July 1943 that Hitler's propaganda minister was able to note with wry satisfaction that the city was at last learning to hate its English cousins.[2]

Hamburg's ties to England were deep-rooted and remain close to this day. As part of the Hanseatic League, the city has been trading with London since the thirteenth century. The first English company to set up a permanent office in the city was the Merchant Adventurers Company in the sixteenth century. It was followed by other English merchants, trading wool and fine English cloth for continental wine, linen and timber, and by 1600 Britain had established itself as a significant trading partner.

As Britain's power grew, it became increasingly important for Hamburg to maintain a good relationship with its neighbours across the North Sea. This was not always easy. For example, in 1666 when Dutch men-of-war attacked British merchant ships in the Elbe, the British blamed Hamburg for allowing the warships passage, and insisted on compensation. The lawsuit between them continued for four years, but when Britain eventually threatened reprisals against the city there was nothing the burghers could do but resort to the centuries-old tradition of buying their way out of trouble. There was no question of Hamburg standing its ground: the city had only two warships at the time, which it used for escorting convoys, while the British navy consisted of 173 ships, equipped with 6,930 guns.[3]

Hamburg's precarious relationship with Britain blundered on, with various minor mishaps along the way, until the end of the eighteenth century. Then, in the 1790s, the city unwittingly found itself embroiled in a dispute between France and Britain, and its relationship with both countries rapidly degenerated. The dispute centred round Napper Tandy, the leader of the ill-fated Irish revolt against the British, who had fled to Hamburg in 1798 with three of his comrades. The British legation demanded that Hamburg hand over the rebels, but the French envoy objected, arguing that to do so would be a violation both of Hamburg's neutrality and of international law. France was at war with virtually the whole of Europe at the time, including Britain, and would not tolerate any action that could be considered pro-British.

After a month of negotiations over the prisoners, Britain finally threatened military action. To emphasize the point, she seized several ships sailing under the Hamburg flag, and stationed a block-ade at the mouth of the Elbe. Left with no choice, in 1799 the Hamburg authorities handed over the prisoners. The French, under Napoleon, were furious at what they saw as a betrayal of Hamburg's neutral status, and immediately set up a complete embargo of goods traded from the city. In the end Hamburg was allowed once again to buy its way out of trouble, by paying the French Republic a huge four million livres in compensation. But Napoleon remained angry, and vowed to bring the city of Hamburg to heel.[4]

Finding itself on the wrong side of Napoleon turned out to be one of the biggest mistakes in the city's history. Ever since the fourteenth century its policy of strict neutrality had been respected, by and large, by the nations of Europe. As a consequence, it had managed to avoid the many wars that had repeatedly devastated other cities in the region over the past four hundred years. But Napoleon was determined to build an empire, and had no intention of allowing this city state to continue trading with his enemies, regardless of whether they did so under a neutral banner or not.

The first stage of Hamburg's downfall occurred in 1801, when the Danes, who had allied themselves to the French, finally occupied the city. Their intention was only to disrupt British trade, and they stayed for only two months, but it emphasized Hamburg's powerlessness in the face of a sizeable army. It also showed what the French and Danes thought of the 'neutrality' of Hamburg's relationship with the British. Five years later, after defeating the Prussians at Jena–Auerstadt, Napoleon himself marched on the city, and on 19 November 1806, three thousand French troops entered Hamburg.

In truth, Napoleon was not much interested in Hamburg: it was merely a pawn in a much larger game with the British, his other major enemy. Almost the first thing the French did after invading the city was to confiscate all British property, and to burn British wares in a huge bonfire on the island of Grasbrook. City merchants were told to declare all profits made by trading with Britain, and all correspondence with France's enemy was banned. The British responded by blockading the entire European continent, cutting off Hamburg from all foreign trade.

The city was to remain in French hands until May 1814, when Marshal Davout finally surrendered to the British/Prussian allies. By this time Hamburg was ruined: its once hugely profitable trading houses were bankrupt, its banks out of business, its industries destroyed and its population on the brink of starvation. Hamburg's ancient talent for rebuilding and reinventing itself out of every disaster had been stifled, and for a while it seemed as though the city would not recover. But help was on its way, and from an unlikely source. After contributing to the city's downfall, Britain came to Hamburg's rescue. In the following years dozens of British firms opened branches in Hamburg, providing much-needed jobs for the people. Penniless Hamburg merchants became commissioning and transport agents for the British, and within a short time the port was trading once more. The city was grateful. It was this era, more than any other in Hamburg's history, that laid the foundations of the city's love affair with Britain that continues to this day.

The following decades reflected the new balance of control in the city, as trades opened with British markets in mind. The first steamship to drop anchor in Hamburg's harbour was British, and by 1825 there was a regular passenger service to Britain. This was followed by trade services to several British colonies and protectorates, such as Sierra Leone and Zanzibar, and in 1851 Godeffroy and Woermann began the city's first ever trade service to Australia. The world was once again unfurling before Hamburg, but it was a world in which Britain was the undisputed superpower.

While trade increased exponentially in the decades after the Napoleonic Wars, the vast majority of the ships that anchored in the harbour were British. In 1835 only 14 per cent flew the flag of Hamburg.[5] This did not change until after 1850 when Hamburg became a major centre of shipbuilding in its own right, and giant German shipyards, such as Blohm & Voss and Howaldtswerke, began to transform the south shores of the Elbe into a centre of industry. New freight companies were also founded, such as Ferdinand Laeisz's Flying P Line and the Hamburg-Amerikanische Packetfahrt-Actien-Gesellschaft (HAPAG), which was soon to become the biggest shipping company in the world.

Despite this renaissance of German trade and industry there remained a distinctly British atmosphere in Hamburg until the Second World War. Hamburg's relationship with Britain was not merely economic, it was personal. After centuries of trading with one another, wealthy patricians from Hamburg often sent their sons to England to spend half a year or so among the English, and many personal friendships stretched across the North Sea. They were not confined to the rich city merchants – tradesmen, students and even dock workers had close relationships with their counterparts in Britain.[6] There were links with the English at all levels of Hamburg society, and by the middle of the twentieth century

Hamburg was universally known in Germany as 'the anglophile city', which would appear painfully ironic after the events of 1943.

*   *   *

Hamburg's relationship with America was of a very different nature from that with Britain. If Britain had treated the city rather paternally in the years after the Napoleonic Wars, America treated it more like an equal partner: right from the start, each side saw the other as an unmissable opportunity to get rich quick. While Hamburg's relationship with Britain had taken centuries to mature, that with America was virtually love at first sight. Within just ten years of opening formal relations in 1783, America had overtaken the Mediterranean as a trade destination; within fifty years it had overtaken most of Hamburg's traditional partners. From now on, the city would increasingly turn away from its European brothers and sisters, and devote much more effort to its new relationship across the Atlantic.

Like most other countries, Hamburg did not have any kind of association with the American states before 1783, for the simple reason that they were a British monopoly so trade with them was effectively closed. After America won its independence, however, the city of Hamburg was among the first to send the fledgling nation its best wishes, and to propose a trading relationship. Within a short time, Hamburg merchants, like Voght & Sieveking, were sending ships across the Atlantic with their holds full of Westphalian and Silesian textiles, and returning with all those commodities that had proved so lucrative for British traders over the preceding decades: rice, sugar, cocoa, coffee, cotton and, of course, tobacco.

The links between Hamburg and America were based on the huge volumes of trade that passed between them, but over time a more personal side to the relationship evolved. In the second half of the nineteenth century one of the city's biggest exports to the USA was not ceramics, textiles or glassware but people. America was opening up as a land of opportunity, and thousands of Germans were emigrating there each year in search of a better life – many of them Hamburgers.

Despite the great wealth of certain sections of the community on the Elbe, poverty was rife among the lower classes,[7] and for many in Hamburg's slum districts the temptation to start afresh on the other side of the Atlantic proved irresistible. It was not a decision that was made lightly. Travelling to America was a desperate business, and conditions during the long sea voyage were comparable to those in eighteenth-century slave ships. Travellers would be crammed into a dark hold with barely anything to eat and only half a pint of water to drink each day. There was little sanitation, no doctors, and after seventy days at sea it was not uncommon for diseases like typhoid or cholera to have claimed up to a fifth of the passengers. For those who survived, conditions on the other side of the Atlantic were often only marginally better than those they had left at home, but a large proportion did find a better life, and the letters they sent back were enough to inspire yet more people to make the journey.

By 1866 more than fourteen thousand people were travelling each year from Hamburg to America. They came from all over northern Europe – even from as far away as Russia – and many from Hamburg itself. A faster, more reliable steam service now navigated the route, and companies like HAPAG were growing rich on the hopes and dreams of this constant stream of emigrants to the USA.[8] Later on, even members of the middle and upper classes made the voyage across the Atlantic, but on luxury cruise liners. By the turn of the twentieth century, the biggest passenger ships could make the crossing in under six days. There was even talk of flying Zeppelins across the ocean, and Hamburg was a major centre of Germany's growing aircraft industry.[9]

By the early 1900s not a single community in northern Germany was untouched by emigration to the United States. At the outbreak of war in 1914, the German population of the United States was so large that the Canadians were induced to take precautions against the possibility of cross-border attacks.[10] In Hamburg almost everyone had friends or relations in America – after all, the majority of northern European emigrants to the United States had embarked on their journeys from that very port.

It was this personal relationship, more than any volume of trade, that bound the two peoples together: Hamburg and America had, quite literally, become family. When the USAAF flew over the city in July 1943, more than a few American airmen could trace their ancestry back to Hamburg. Their grandparents or great-grandparents had passed through the port on their way to America, and now, as descendants of those emigrants, the young men were returning to destroy the city that had been their gateway to a new life.

★   ★   ★

But we are running ahead of ourselves. Before we become embroiled in the catastrophic events of 1943, it is necessary to explain a little about how those events came about in the first place – not least because Hamburg remains firmly in the centre of the story. For that we must turn our focus not merely to the beginning of the Second World War, but to the end of the First, for it was in 1918, in the dockyards of Hamburg and Kiel, that some of the most potent seeds of the Second World War were sown.

3. City of Rebellion

All that is solid melts into air, all that is holy is profaned, and man is at last compelled to face with sober senses, his real conditions of life, and his relations with his kind.
Karl Marx[1]

At the outbreak of the First World War Hamburg was no longer recognizable as the small city that had been invaded by Napoleon just a hundred years before. The industrial revolution had transformed it into a metropolis for the region: it was now the second biggest manufacturing centre in Germany after Berlin, and the third largest port in the world after London and New York. The constant influx of immigrants had brought the population to more than a million, and forced the city to expand well beyond its medieval city walls. Whole new suburbs had been built to house its workers, while others had been demolished to make way for a brand new warehouse district, the Speicherstadt. It was home to a wide variety of heavy industries – not just shipbuilding, but engineering and electrical companies, oil refineries, asbestos factories, as well as coffee-roasting plants and rice mills – and one of the most prosperous places in the whole German Reich.

After four years of fighting, however, virtually all of this had been ruined. Not only had the city sacrificed forty thousand of its young men to the trenches, but the rest of the population was starving. The British blockade of the German coastline had caused shortages across the country, but in Hamburg this was compounded by the effect it had on the city's economy. Trade kept Hamburg working, and once starved of it the city fell apart: industries failed, food and fuel became desperately scarce, and the people increasingly angry with the military regime responsible for their hardship. The atmosphere of Hanseatic conservatism that had characterized the city for hundreds of years was rapidly replaced by radicalism, and strikes and protests erupted all along the lower reaches of the Elbe.

Things came to a head in November 1918, shortly before the Armistice was signed, when Admiral Hipper ordered his ships out on one final desperate attack on the British Grand Fleet. The sailors at the naval bases of Kiel and Wilhelmshaven saw this as a pointless suicide mission, and promptly mutinied. The uprising spread quickly across northern Germany, and on 5 November workers at several of Hamburg's shipyards voted to strike in sympathy with the sailors. At first the city council managed to pacify them, but that evening ten thousand workers attended a meeting of the radical Independent Social Democratic Party (USDP) and agreed to hold a general strike throughout the city. During the night groups of sailors occupied key strategic positions in the city – the Elbetunnel, the main station, the union buildings and the city barracks – and even boarded torpedo boats in the harbour to disarm them. The following morning a crowd of some forty thousand workers and soldiers marched on the General Command in Altona, and effectively seized power over the whole of the Hamburg area.[2]

By the time Germany accepted the Allies' armistice terms on 11 November, Hamburg, with many other cities, was already in the hands of revolutionaries. The consequences were enormous. In later years, when order had been restored, many Germans would come to remember the end of the war not as a time of defeat at the hands of the Allies – after all, the Allied armies had never reached German soil – but as a period when their country had collapsed from within. With the passing of time, they began to believe that they had not lost the war at all, but had merely been betrayed by their own people: as the German general Paul von Hindenburg said, his army had not been defeated, but 'stabbed in the back'.[3]

In reality, the November revolution had little or no effect on the outcome of the war, which had already been lost. Nor was it a particularly violent revolution. The transfer of power from the old élite to the new republic was relatively peaceful – it was not until well after the war was over that the real problems began. During the winter of 1918–19 the well-ordered society that Germans thought they knew seemed to vanish. In the face of drastic food and fuel shortages, crime levels soared. Violence became increasingly common, inflation spiralled out of control, and transport difficulties made German lives thoroughly miserable.

In Hamburg there was a complete breakdown of the social order. Gangs roamed the city, and there were frequent gun battles in the streets after dark. One British observer witnessed a particularly brutal scene at around this time. Leslie Hollis was a Royal Marine stationed in Hamburg as part of a force brought in to oversee German war reparations in the city, when he found himself caught up in the chaos.

Communist riots under a man named Spartacus had broken out in the city. The weak German government was powerless to restore order. Disgraceful scenes were witnessed. People suspected of being war profiteers were paraded naked round the city in tumbrils, the womenfolk being allowed the dignity of girdles of dead rats. I remember a deplorable scene by the beautiful Alster Lake in the centre of the city. The Spartacists had captured some of their political opponents. They were thrown into the lake and told to swim for it. As soon as they had reached a distance of imagined safety they were shot from the shore. We were powerless to act because this was a domestic affair. Retribution for the Spartacists was very swift.[4]

By April 1919 food was so hard to come by that people began breaking into shops and storehouses to feed themselves. On one occasion some two thousand men tried to storm a warehouse on Markusstrasse, and had to be fought back by policemen under the cover of machine-gun fire. Police stations came under attack by gangs trying to obtain firearms. On 23 June, after learning that one of the city's factories had been manufacturing products with rotten meat, thousands rioted in the streets, looted shops, and even tried to storm the town hall. Hamburg was in a state of virtual siege, and relative order was not properly restored until General Lettow-Vorbeck's Freikorps occupied the city in July and imposed martial law.[5]

In such an atmosphere, it is not surprising that political extremism gained a strong foothold in the city. When so much of the city was going hungry, groups from the far left felt they had a perfect right to plunder stockpiles of food and fuel in the city's warehouses. Conversely, groups on the far right were in favour of extreme measures to bring the looters under control. The Freikorps, for example, had no compunction about suppressing real or supposed threats to the government in an extremely brutal and bloody manner. Originally set up to bolster the police, the Freikorps was a volunteer military organization that was often little better than a coalition of vigilante groups: it was a magnet for disaffected youth and bitter ex-soldiers, and served as a training ground for many who would reappear as Nazis in the following years.[6]

However, the extremist group with by far the largest following in Hamburg was the Communist Party. Political groups of the far left had a long history in the city. While the union movement had been fighting for important labour reforms in the second half of the nineteenth century, there were always more radical wings that believed the only way for workers to win a fair deal was to seize power. With the revolution of November 1918 they finally had their way, and ruled the city for several months as the Workers' and Soldiers' Council. After the election of 16 March 1919, they handed power back to the city parliament, but there were always radical groups who wanted to seize it again, and it was not long before they tried. On 23 October 1923, at around five o'clock in the morning, hundreds of Communists attacked Hamburg police stations in a desperate attempt to gain control of the city by force. Led by Ernst Thälmann, the uprising centred on the workers' suburbs of Eimsbüttel, Barmbek, Schiffbek and Bergedorf. In the end they failed, but not without much loss of life on both sides: seventeen policemen and sixty-one Communists were killed in the fighting, and a further 321 people were wounded. In the aftermath of the rebellion almost a thousand people were arrested.[7]

*   *   *

In the following years the atmosphere in Hamburg began at last to calm down. Although Ernst Thälmann retained his seat in the Hamburg parliament, the Communists never came close to ousting the more moderate Social Democratic Party (SPD), and the traditional conservatism of the Hanseatic temperament gradually reasserted itself. Slowly but surely prosperity returned to the city. Despite the severe restrictions of the treaty of Versailles,[8] Hamburg's firm links with Britain and America gave it access to capital on favourable terms, and the city recovered much more quickly than the rest of Germany. By the end of the 1920s company business was flourishing once more, and the average worker was back to earning pre-war wages. While a current of radicalism still flowed beneath the surface, an air of relative contentment had returned to the city.

Unfortunately this period of relative stability came to an end during the winter of 1929–30 when the whole world was plunged into an economic slump. As global prices went into free-fall, and exports shrank to almost nothing, Hamburg's fragile economy began once more to collapse. Within two years unemployment had reached almost 40 per cent, and political radicalism returned. The only difference was that this time it was not the Communists who attracted the protest vote. Radicalism in the 1930s would wear an altogether different face.

4. The Rise of the Nazis

Clear the streets for the brown battalions, clear the streets for the
Storm Trooper . . .
1930s Nazi Party song[1]

In the summer of 1930 an event took place in Hamburg that would soon become a local legend. On 19 August about two hundred people gathered at the 'Am Stadtpark' beer hall in Winterhude to attend an election meeting of the Nazi Party. It was an impressive turnout for a minority party. Ever since the recession had taken hold, the Nazis had been enjoying increasing support in Hamburg, and people came from all different sections of society. They were expecting speeches – the usual anti-Semitic, anti-Marxist, anti-liberal invective – followed by a debating session, then perhaps a drink in the adjoining pub before they went home to bed. That night, however, there had been rumours that the local Communist Party were planning to disrupt the meeting. As a consequence the arriving audience was greeted by bands of Nazi storm troopers, who had been called in to 'protect' the meeting in case of a fracas. As the audience took their seats unease hung in the air.

The meeting started without any disturbance, and for a while it looked as though the rumours were unfounded. But at nine o'clock the door of the beer hall flew open and a large man entered, claiming to be a member of the 'Red Front' – a militant wing of the Communist Party. He was followed by a long chain of others: 'Tall chaps; fists of iron; splendid men. The best of the Hamburg Communist Party.'[2] Fifty or so of these 'Red Marines' took their seats in the audience, and a similar number went to stand in a corner at the back of the room, beside an open window.

At first their presence did little to disrupt the meeting, and the speeches went ahead. The trouble began during the question-and-answer session, when the chairman challenged the visitors to announce whether their presence was peaceful or not. He was answered by a flying beer glass, which smashed on the wall behind him. Within moments a storm broke loose across the room. Communists and Nazis attacked one another with whatever weapons came to hand: knives, glasses, bottles, even chairs. In panic, most of the audience fled for the door, but some stayed to join the storm troopers in a desperate battle. An old man used his cane to strike repeatedly at the Red Marines and when it broke he picked up a chair leg and used that instead. His white beard was soon flecked with blood.

The Communists outnumbered the Nazis almost two to one, and they also had a large mob outside who were trying to break down the door. Despite this, the Nazis forced them into a corner, and one by one the Red Marines fell. Of the hundred or so men who had interrupted the meeting, at least eighty were battered to the floor, and those remaining were eventually forced to escape through the open window at the back of the beer hall.

At last the police arrived, with emergency medics, and cleared everyone out. While the crowd outside was being dispersed, the victorious Nazis regrouped on the banks of a nearby river, and congratulated themselves on a job well done: they were convinced that they had won the fight because they had the stronger ideology, and therefore the stronger will, the greater strength, the wilder courage. They eventually marched, singing and celebrating long into the night. The battle they had just fought would soon pass into Nazi myth as a vital stepping-stone in the party's long struggle to win power in the city.

While this beer-hall brawl in fact had little or no significance in the Nazis' rise to power in Hamburg, the episode says a great deal about how they saw themselves. From the very beginning, the National Socialist German Workers' Party (NSDAP) was imbued with a sense of struggle against a hostile world. They saw the Communists as a particular threat because they were one of the few groups that actively fought against them, but they could also see other more subtle dangers. Practising Christians exercised an insidious control over the minds of the German people because they respected the passive virtues of humbleness and forgiveness. Foreign immigrants polluted German blood, just as Communists polluted German minds, and the Jews threatened to enslave the ordinary German worker in perpetual bondage to capitalism. All of this was not only tolerated but encouraged by corrupt and spineless politicians, who were little more than puppets to foreign governments and a sinister conspiracy of world Jewry. The Nazis believed themselves besieged on all sides, much as they had been that night in the Am Stadtpark pub, and the only way to save themselves, and Germany, was through violence.

The beer-hall battle was one of the most common images seen in Nazi propaganda. It was a microcosm of what they believed was necessary throughout the whole of Germany: a violent blood-letting to dispatch the myriad enemies of the people, and to purge the nation of weaklings. That the Nazis were almost always out-numbered in such stories was an important part of the myth, and reflected a fundamental flaw that would eventually lead to their downfall. In the years to come senior Nazis came to believe that they would *always* triumph, no matter what the odds against them, provided they maintained a fanatical belief in the strength of their cause.

★   ★   ★

At the beginning of the 1930s the NSDAP had already done far better than most people ever thought possible. For more than a decade it had been a minority party, with little appeal to anyone outside its core fanatical audience. But with Germany reeling in the aftermath of the Wall Street crash, the Nazis began to appeal to a much wider spectrum of people. The country now had over six million unemployed workers – 121,000 in Hamburg alone, or almost 40 per cent of the working population[3] – and an increasingly desperate electorate cast about for someone to blame. The Nazi Party was there to provide the answer. Its long list of scapegoats began with its enemies inside the country – Communists, Jews, liberals – and ended with the international community who had crushed Germany beneath the heel of the Versailles treaty at the end of the First World War. Hitler's invective against all these groups, which had seemed petulant when the country was in recovery, now attracted enormous popular interest.

The success of the party in Hamburg was perhaps most surprising of all. For decades the city had been a stronghold of *left*-wing politics, with the most serious challenge to the moderate Social Democrats coming from the German Communist Party (KPD). In fact, in 1928 Hitler's NSDAP had just three seats on the city council, representing only a tiny proportion of the vote. But Hamburg was hit particularly hard by the stock-market crash. The city had borrowed heavily from America during the 1920s, and when American banks called in their debts a host of companies was forced into bankruptcy. Those that survived suffered terribly at the fall in international trade. With unemployment so high, the city's expenditure on welfare also spiralled out of control.

A disillusioned electorate turned away from anyone associated with the administration that had got them into such a mess. The party they turned to was the Nazis, whose three seats on the city council grew to forty-three in under three years. By 1932 they had fifty-one seats, which made them the strongest voice on the council.[4] What was happening all over Germany was also happening in Hamburg: a switch in the balance of power so rapid it was breathtaking. As Victor Klemperer, a university professor in Dresden, wrote in 1933:

it's astounding how easily everything collapses . . . Day after day commissioners appointed, provincial governments trampled underfoot, flags raised, buildings taken over, people shot, newspapers banned, etc. etc. . . . . And all opposing forces as if vanished from the face of the earth. It is this utter collapse of a power only recently present – no, its complete disappearance (just as in 1918) – which I find so staggering.[5]

There is a strong view that Hamburg never truly supported the Nazis, despite their victory. The Nazi vote was always several points below the national average, and the other main parties remained strong until the bitter end.[6] However, if general voters in Hamburg did not take to Hitler in quite the same way as they did elsewhere, those who supported the Nazis were particularly zealous. Actual membership of the Nazi Party was much higher here than the national average,[7] and brawls like those in the Winterhude beer hall were relatively common. It was as if the very strength of the opposition served only to increase the Nazi Party's siege mentality.

As Hitler's power grew, Hamburg won something of a reputation for fanaticism, especially when it came to persecuting other political parties. Even before the Nazis had come to power, storm troopers had already murdered one of the KPD councillors – Ernst Robert Henning was shot in 1931. When civil liberties were suspended in February 1933, Hamburg was one of the first authorities to round up Communist Party functionaries and throw them into prison. This was soon followed by the arrest of Social Democrats, trade-unionists and other opponents of National Socialism, many of whom were later either executed or sent to concentration camps. In the coming years 1,417 men, women and teenagers from Hamburg would be executed for political reasons – twenty of them former members of the city parliament.[8] Even members of the Nazi Party were not safe. In June 1934, during the 'Night of the Long Knives', dozens of Hitler's political opponents within the local Nazi Party were murdered as part of a nationwide purge. The violence of the Hamburg beer hall had expanded to a concerted campaign of brutal control on a national level.

Hitler gained overall control of the national parliament after the elections of 5 March 1933, when the NSDAP seized 44 per cent of the vote. He was quick to consolidate power. With many of his opponents already under arrest, within three weeks of his election victory he had bullied the Reichstag into passing the 'Enabling Act'. This infamous piece of legislation, officially entitled the 'Law for the Lifting of Misery from the People and Reich',[9] gave him the right to bring in emergency legislation whenever he felt it necessary, without having to refer to Parliament. This effectively granted him absolute power.

Over the next four months he systematically dismantled all opposition to Nazi rule. All other political parties were dissolved, and a law was passed making their re-formation illegal. Trade unions associated with the SPD were banned in May. Newspapers and radio stations that did not agree with the Nazi position were banned, and replaced with Nazi propaganda organs. In Hamburg, which had more newspapers than any other city in Germany, this had a substantial effect: on 29 April the *Hamburger Echo* was put out of business, quickly followed by the *Hamburger Nachrichten* and the *Hamburgische Correspondent*. Even though the Hamburg city council had complied enthusiastically with almost everything the national government had asked of it, the Bürgerschaft itself was dissolved on 14 October. From that day until the end of the war, absolute power over the whole city passed to the hands of the Nazi gauleiter and Reich governor Karl Kaufmann.

Over the following months and years the tendrils of Nazi control reached into every area of life in Hamburg. Books that displeased the Nazis were burned on the Kaiser-Friedrich-Ufer, and works by ostracized artists, such as Ernst Barlach, were removed from Hamburg's public collections. People in positions of power or influence were replaced with Nazi sympathizers, not only in the city parliament but in police stations, hospitals, schools, and even private businesses. During the course of 1933, 10 per cent of commissioned police officers were dismissed for political reasons.[10]

To ensure that the Nazi message was spread as widely as possible, organizations were set up to cover every area of German life. To replace the banned trade unions, the Nazis set up their own equivalent, the Deutsche Arbeitsfront. Weekend holidays and acceptable cultural activities were organized for the people by Kraft durch Freude ('Strength through Joy'). Boys were encouraged to join the Hitler Youth, and girls to join the League of German Girls. While membership of those organizations was supposedly voluntary, it effectively became compulsory as the years went on.

The brave new world of Nazism was felt most keenly perhaps in schools and colleges. Wiebke Stammers, who was a schoolgirl in Hamburg at the time, remembers vividly the changes that took place: 'We no longer had religious lessons. They disappeared from the timetable . . . And we had instead what was laughingly called *Lebenskunde*, which was all about the party and the history of the Nazi Party, the life story of Hitler, all the people in the party, where they came from, what they'd done. It was terribly boring.'[11] Gradually her schoolbooks were replaced with new editions that complied with Nazi ideology: history books propagated the 'stab in the back' myth of the First World War, geography textbooks described Germany's need for *Lebensraum* by expanding her borders, and biology textbooks emphasized the ideas of racial purity, struggle for survival, and self-sacrifice for the good of the race.[12] When her headmistress refused to join the Nazi Party, she was sacked and replaced with somebody more compliant to the regime. Likewise, two of her teachers were fired after being denounced by pupils for making anti-Nazi comments in class. Two of her classmates were expelled because they did not join in with the denunciation. What happened to all those people in later years is unknown, but it is certain that, at the very least, they would have been watched carefully by the authorities.

Underlying the actions was the unspoken threat of violence against anyone who did not agree with Nazi ideology. Those who did not fit into the standard Aryan mould were in particular danger. Committed Christians, handicapped people, Gypsies, homosexuals, foreigners: in a cosmopolitan city like Hamburg there were seemingly endless targets for persecution. Even teenage jazz enthusiasts found themselves on the wrong side of the authorities. When American phonograph records were banned early in the war, scores of swing fans in Hamburg were rounded up and sent to the youth concentration camp at Moringen. Their crimes? Sexual promiscuity, dancing 'like wild creatures' to 'Negro music', and deliberately speaking English, which was also banned at the beginning of the war.[13]

The first people to suffer, however, were undoubtedly the city's Jews. Shortly after the Nazis came to power a national boycott of Jewish businesses was declared. Despite intimidation from Nazi vigilantes, many Hamburgers defied the boycott – but the message was clear nevertheless. Six days later, on 7 April 1933, a law was passed banning Jews from the civil service. This was soon followed by similar laws prohibiting them from working in the legal and medical professions, the media, the performing arts and the army. In 1935 the infamous Nuremberg Race Laws were passed, depriving Jews of citizenship and forbidding marriage between Aryan Germans and Jews.[14] Once again, the background to this anti-Semitism was one of constant low-level violence. Random acts of brutality against Jews in and around Hamburg accumulated, and there were incidences of policemen standing by while Jewish shopkeepers were assaulted. The net result was a culture of fear and helplessness in much of the city, but particularly among Hamburg's Jewish community. They could sense what was coming: those Jews who could afford it, and were able to gain visas, fled to other countries. Within two years of the Nazis coming to power a quarter of the city's Jews had emigrated.

For those who stayed behind the final proof of their helplessness was not long in coming. On the night of 7 November 1938, in response to the murder of a German diplomat by an expatriate Jew, Joseph Goebbels orchestrated the nationwide pogrom that came to be known as Kristallnacht. During the course of just twenty-four hours more than a thousand synagogues across the country were either vandalized or burned to the ground. Jewish cemeteries, like that at Altona, were vandalized, Jewish homes were set alight, thousands of Jewish shops were looted and their windows smashed, and nearly a hundred people were murdered. Approximately thirty thousand Jewish men were rounded up and sent to concentration camps. Afterwards, in a final absurd insult, Germany's Jews were ordered to pay a collective bill of one billion Reichsmarks to the government to cover the cost of the damage to their own property.[15]

While most Germans were shocked by the pogrom, few dared to speak out against it. Hamburg, to its credit, was one of the only places where such vandalism was openly condemned. In their 'Reports on Germany', the exiled Social Democrats claimed that:

The broad mass of people has not condoned the destruction, but we should nevertheless not overlook the fact that there are people among the working class who do not defend the Jews . . . If there has been any speaking out in the Reich against the Jewish pogroms, the excesses of arson and looting, it has been in Hamburg and the neighbouring Elbe district.[16]

Those who spoke out against the Kristallnacht pogrom were taking their lives into their hands: the judicial authorities in Hamburg were notoriously harsh when judging political dissidents.[17] However, while Hamburgers might have been unusually vocal about the atrocities they had seen, few people translated their outrage into action. As one Hamburg woman wrote in her diary shortly afterwards, while the persecution of the Jews had 'inflamed all decent people with anger', there was depressingly little that any of them did about it:

For me nothing was more devastating than the fact that nobody, not even those who opposed the régime most vehemently, stood up against this, but remained passive and weak. I cannot stress these facts too strongly. It was as if we were caught in a stranglehold. And, worst of all, one even gets used to being half throttled; what at first appeared to be unbearable pressure becomes a habit, becomes easier to tolerate; hate and desperation are diluted with time.[18]

Once the battle against the enemy within was under way, Hitler turned his attention to the enemy without. The treaty of Versailles at the end of the First World War had considerably reduced Germany's power, and imposed severe restrictions on its armed forces, and limited rights to defend its borders. As the main architects of the treaty, Britain and France were considered responsible for Germany's humiliating status, although the whole League of Nations was implicated. One of Hitler's first actions on the international stage, therefore, was to pull out of the Geneva Peace Conference, in October 1933, and withdraw from the League of Nations.

In direct violation of the Versailles treaty, Germany now embarked on expansion of its armed forces. In March 1935 the German government shocked the world by revealing the existence of the Luftwaffe, a branch of the Wehrmacht (armed services) that had hitherto been banned. A year later Hitler broke the terms of Versailles once again by marching his troops into the Rhineland on the border with France. His borders secure, he now reintroduced the conscription of men into the army, and embarked on a huge four-year plan of rearmament. It was becoming increasingly difficult to believe that such measures were meant only for Germany's defence, and many suspected that Hitler was actually inviting a reaction from the rest of the world. In the words of Hermann Goering, Hitler was 'preparing the German economy for total war'.[19]

Given its shipping links and huge manufacturing capacity, it is unsurprising that Hamburg now became important to the Nazi regime's plans. In 1936, military contracts suddenly poured into the city's shipbuilding companies – so much so that HAPAG lodged a complaint that its military commitments were making it fall behind on orders for merchant and passenger ships. Other shipping companies also worried that they were becoming far too dependent on the German Navy for business.[20]

The up-side to the story was that rearmament provided Hamburg's ailing industries with a much-needed tonic. Until now the city had gained little from the change of regime. While the rest of Germany had started to recover as early as 1934, unemployment in Hamburg was still high. The entire Lower Elbe area had always depended on international trade, and Hitler's policy of restricting imports in favour of German-made goods had had a disastrous effect on the city's trade and shipping industries. Rearmament, however, brought jobs and money to Hamburg. New businesses were set up, all devoted to preparation for war: oil refineries, engine factories and aviation engineering works. The need for huge amounts of raw materials also increased trade, particularly with Scandinavia.

Hitler had big plans for Hamburg. For centuries it had been

surrounded by satellite towns, many of which had worked in direct competition with the city, but on 1 April 1937 this was to change: Altona, Wandsbek, Harburg and twenty-eight smaller munici- palities were consolidated into a single industrial and administrative giant that would become known as Greater Hamburg.[21] With this single action the city became hugely more efficient. It also doubled in size overnight, and its population increased by 41 per cent to 1.68 million.

In keeping with the city's new status, Hitler drew up grand plans for a new Kongresshalle, a 250-metre high *Gauhaus*, and a road bridge to span the Elbe.[22] The Hamburg–Lübeck *Autobahn* was completed in 1937, and the clearance of the slums in the Neustadt was also carried out as a priority – ostensibly under a programme of housing reform, but actually because the area was a hotbed of Communist resistance to the Nazi regime. The impor- tance of Hamburg's position to the new Reich was underscored by the fact that Hitler visited this city more than any other during his time as leader of the Nazi Party.[23]

As Hamburg churned out warships and U-boats, the Reich Chancellor was busy provoking the world towards conflict. In March 1938 he marched his troops into Austria to 'encourage' her people to vote for an *Anschluss* (or 'union') with Germany. (At the same time he transported more than ten thousand Austrian guests to Hamburg to attend the launch of the troopship *Robert Ley* – a rare example of his use of the carrot as well as the stick.)[24] A year later, in defiance of an agreement made with Britain, Hitler's tanks rolled into Czechoslovakia. A pattern was emerging: Germany was turning on her neighbours one by one.

During his last major visit to Hamburg in February 1939, Hitler hinted that such actions were only the beginning. At the launch of the battleship *Bismarck* he explained that his ultimate aim was 'the future eradication of the enemies of the Reich, now and for all time'.[25] The festive atmosphere of a launch was a long way from the beer-hall brawls that had characterized the early years of the Nazi Party, but the themes in Hitler's speech were the same. Several years on, the Nazis were obsessed with enemies of the

Reich, which still appeared to outnumber Aryan Germans on every side.

When Germany invaded Poland on 1 September 1939, the 'enemies of the Reich' stepped forward. Two days after Hitler's accumulated weaponry began to pour towards Warsaw, France and Britain picked up the gauntlet and declared war on Germany.

The violence of the beer hall had at last expanded to its logical extreme: the treaty of Versailles was dead, extremism was taking over Europe, and the entire continent was spiralling inexorably downwards into a vast, all-encompassing war. At the centre of it all the Nazis, surrounded by enemies, were outnumbered, but fanatically certain that the strength of their ideology would see them through to ultimate victory, whatever the odds against them. Like the staunch defenders of the Nazi election meeting in Winterhude in 1930, the forces of the Fatherland would carry on fighting until there was no one left to fight. For Germany this would result in six years of increasing hardship, followed by the agony of defeat and disgrace. For the city of Hamburg, whose 'Red Marines' had long since been battered into silence, it would result in almost total annihilation.

5. Hamburg Prepares for War

Truly, I live in dark times!
Bertolt Brecht[1]

Despite the eagerness with which the Nazis seemed to embrace conflict, there was little enthusiasm for war among the rest of the German population, especially in Hamburg.[2] The city had never done well out of war, and the memories of the hardships created in 1914–18 were still relatively fresh in people's minds. Mathilde Wolff-Mönckeberg summed up the feelings of many when she wrote in her diary that she and everyone she knew was in 'absolute despair' at the outbreak of war. 'We were convinced that immediate and total annihilation would follow.'[3]

Many in the city's Nazi administration seem to have shared her fears. Throughout its history Hamburg had been vulnerable to attack from the sea and the surrounding land. Now it faced a brand new danger: a threat from the air. Unlike many other towns closer to the French border, Hamburg had never suffered from bombing between 1914 and 1918. This did not mean that its citizens were unacquainted with the overall concept: in fact, the opposite was true – the city had been a centre for German aviation even before the First World War, and many of the zeppelins that bombed British cities had been based in airfields around Hamburg.

Now, to combat this new danger from the air, city officials immediately set about creating a system of civil protection unlike anything Hamburg had seen before. The first thing they did was to launch a programme of strengthening the cellars of houses and apartment blocks throughout the city, to protect them from the possibility of blast bombs. However, it was soon realized that there were not enough to go round. The soggy, waterlogged soil upon which Hamburg was built meant that whole districts were devoid of cellars – the high water table of the Elbe floodplain would have swamped them – so in these areas extra air-raid shelters were built. Even before the war there were some eighty-eight public air-raid shelters in Hamburg, but by April 1940 this had risen to 549. A year later there were 1,700 shelters, splinter-proof buildings and bunkers across the city, with room for at least 230,000 people.[4]

The city authorities quickly recognized that the main threat from bombing was fire. While high-explosive bombs caused terrible damage to buildings, it was localized. Fire from incendiary bombs, however, could destroy whole areas of the city. They set about training an army of firemen and air-raid wardens in every suburb. In theory, each block had its own fire officer. The railway authority alone had almost 1,500 firemen, and 15,000 fire-watchers kept a look-out over the port area. More than seven hundred sand boxes were placed in streets and squares, and measures were taken to ensure that a water supply would be available if the mains should fail. New wells were dug, water carts requisitioned, and containers built. In Blankenese the cellars of two derelict buildings were converted into huge water tanks, which could be called upon in times of emergency.[5]

Everyone in Hamburg knew how quickly a conflagration could spread if it was allowed to get out of control: they had learned about the Great Fire of 1842 at school. In the early part of the war, the entire population set about removing anything flammable from the place in their buildings that was most vulnerable to falling bombs – the roof. They cleared their attics of personal belongings and all superfluous woodwork, such as partitions, was removed. Businesses fitted their buildings with incendiary-proof ceilings, and firewalls were set up, especially in the harbour area, to stop fire spreading.

Finally, in an attempt to throw enemy bombers off target, a city-wide programme of camouflage was put in place. Stations were masked so that they would look like ordinary buildings from above; oil depots were hidden; wharves were disguised to look like insignificant parts of the riverbank. The whole of the inner part of the Alster Lake was hidden beneath a fake reconstruction

Hamburg and its defences, 1943

0	1	2	3 miles

0	1	2	3	4 kms

* Heavy flak positions
* Light flak positions
■ Barracks/military bases
(H) Military airfields

N
W	E
S

River Alster

LOKSTEDT
EPPENDORF	WINTERHUDE
HOHELUFT	BARMBEK
HARVESTEHUDE	UHLEN-	WANDSBEK
BAHRENFELD	EIMSBÜTTEL	HORST	EILBEK
ROTHERBAUM
FLOTTBEK	Alster	BORGFELDE
ALTONA	Lake	HAMM
OTTENSEN	ST GEORG	HORN
NEUSTADT
ST PAULI	ALTSTADT	HAMMERBROOK

River Elbe
STEINWARDER	ROTHENBURGSORT
KLEINER	BILLBROOK
GRASBROOK
VEDDEL
Norder Elbe
WILHELMSBURG

Süder Elbe

HARBURG

of the city centre, complete with imitation streets and false buildings. The idea was that British bombers aiming for the *Rathaus*
might mistake the reconstruction for the real thing, and drop their
bombs harmlessly into the lake.

As a consequence of all this activity, Hamburg was probably
better prepared for catastrophe than any other city in the world.
There was shelter of some description for just about everyone, and
by 1942 the entire population had been trained in methods of fire
control. In the words of the then chief of police, 'As far as Air
Protection was concerned, everything that it was humanly possible
to do was done.'[6]

★   ★   ★

Yet whenever the sirens rang out above the city streets it was
impossible to feel completely safe. Everyone knew the drill. First
the *Kleinalarm* would sound, warning that hostile aircraft were in
the area, and that everyone should get ready to take cover. Then
a second alarm would be sounded: fifteen rapid four-second wails
from the sirens. As soon as this *Fliegeralarm* was heard, everyone
should take shelter immediately: they had just twenty minutes
before the first bombs fell. On arrival at the bomb shelter they
would have to show their *Platzkart* to the shelter supervisor, and
make their way to their own allocated seat. Here they would wait
– sometimes for several hours – until it was safe to leave.

Although Hamburg was not attacked until May 1940, and the
raids even then were fairly ineffective, the sound of the siren was
enough to strike fear into the hearts of all who heard it. Eva
Coombes lived in Hamburg during the early years of the war, and
remembers being in a state of almost permanent anxiety:

You always had the siren. There were two kinds of siren – the warning
siren and then the proper one. When the warning siren was heard I was
the first one racing at high speed down the staircase into the cellar. And
I was shaking with fright . . . I always used to say I had a nervous
breakdown – I couldn't have done, because I was much too young for
it – but I was absolutely terrified of the bombing.[7]

In the early days, the damage caused by bombing was minimal compared to the disruption the air-raid alarms inflicted. Night after night, particularly in the summer months, people had to drag themselves from their beds to take shelter, then return to their rooms to snatch a few more hours' sleep before daybreak. Frustratingly, most of the alarms were false: the bombers changed course, or flew past Hamburg to bomb Kiel, Lübeck or some other city nearby. The British got into the habit of flying 'nuisance raids' over Germany for the sole purpose of keeping people awake at night, which often caused more disruption than the bombs did. In his diary, Hitler's propaganda minister recorded his regular irritation at 'the absurd fact that ten nuisance planes drove fifteen to eighteen million people out of bed'.[8]

By the end of 1940, Hamburg had already had more than two hundred air-raid warnings,[9] most of them in the middle of the night, and the authorities were having to adopt strategies to cope with people's chronic lack of sleep. Children were allowed to come to school late on mornings after an air-raid warning, or perhaps even miss school altogether. In the end, a scheme known as the *Kinderlandverschickung* was set up to evacuate them to safer areas in the interior of the Reich, and tens of thousands of children were sent to schools in places as far away as Bavaria. They stayed away until the following year, when a decrease in the regularity of raids allowed them to filter back to the city.

Adults were not accorded nearly such considerate treatment. They were required to turn up at work no matter how little sleep they had had the night before, and there were severe punishments for absenteeism. With so many men away at the war there were serious labour shortages, and lack of sleep was no excuse for shirking. In fact, as the war progressed, many were required to work even longer hours: in January 1942, for example, the standard working week for public officials was increased from forty-six to fifty-eight hours, and vacation periods all but disappeared. Early in 1943, after much resistance, women were also conscripted for war work.[10]

★   ★   ★

With no holidays, longer working hours and sleep deprivation at epidemic levels, grumbling became a part of life: 'the soul moving its bowels', as Goebbels called it.[11] A tired, grumpy population was much more likely to complain about all the other hardships it had to endure: rationing of food, fuel and tobacco, clothing shortages, travel restrictions, and the ubiquitous queues that meant shopping trips always lasted for hours.

Soon the luxuries of 1939 were only a distant memory. Before the war, Wiebke Stammers would always cut away the fat from her meat: 'I remember my mother's favourite saying, "May God forbid it, but if war ever broke out again you would be going down on your hands and knees to eat it. And you would eat anything." And I said, "I would rather starve than eat fat." . . . It never occurred to me that it would ever come true – but she was right.'[12]

In fact, the conditions suffered by the people of Hamburg were not nearly as bad as those endured by the British during the first half of the war. But many people remembered the disastrous food shortages of the First World War, and were constantly worried by the spectre of famine. In desperation, large numbers turned to 'hamstering' – making trips to the countryside to buy extra rations on the black-market. In the words of Wiebke Stammers, 'Many a diamond ring went to the country to buy food.'[13]

While most people simply got on with life and tried to make the best of things, for some the constant restrictions were too much to bear, and their grumbling became increasingly subversive. Else Baker clearly remembers her father, who was a Hamburg docker, openly criticizing Hitler: her mother was constantly asking him to lower his voice, for fear that he would be overheard.[14] Likewise, whenever twelve-year-old Hannah Kelson complained, her parents would silence her, saying, 'For God's sake, don't let anybody hear that!'[15]

They had good cause to be concerned. The Sicherheitsdienst (SD), the security service of the SS, had informers in all walks of life, and reports on individuals who criticized the regime went all the way to the top.[16] The authorities were troubled by the small pockets of resistance that were appearing across the country, such as the White Rose movement in Bavaria (which also had members in Hamburg), and various Communist groups in Berlin. In Hamburg the swing movement was gaining in popularity, and there had been incidences of 'swing youth' waylaying members of the Hitler Youth and beating them up.[17] Unsurprisingly, the Nazi regime could not tolerate this, and the movements were violently suppressed.

★   ★   ★

By the middle of 1943 there was little good news to be had in Germany about the war. German troops had suffered their first heavy defeats in Russia, at Stalingrad and Kursk, and Rommel's troops had been ejected from the coast of North Africa. While the Nazis and their allies still controlled mainland Europe and huge areas of Russia, some people in Hamburg realized that the tide was turning.[18]

The relative lull in the bombing war between July 1942 and July 1943 was no consolation.[19] With raids increasing in other parts of Germany, the Hamburg authorities sensed that it was only a matter of time before the war would return to their doorstep. As the Hamburg chief of police wrote in a report, all of the air-protection services maintained the highest level of preparedness in the run-up to July 1943.[20] Their only mistake, if there was one, was to assume that when the great attacks came they would be similar to those that had gone before.

It appears that the population felt much the same way. Although they feared the next attack, most people believed they had done everything they could to protect their homes – they would deal with each raid as it came. With hindsight, their concerns seem petty: they grumbled about losing sleep because of the air-raid warnings; they sent their children to the countryside, but grudgingly, as a precaution; at night they worried that an attack might damage their roof, or blast their windows, or that a direct hit might destroy their home altogether. However, it never occurred to them that their entire city was at risk. The worst they could imagine was that they might be killed, or perhaps someone close to them.

By day, it was easy to forget that there was a war on. The city had not been bombed during daylight hours since 1940 – why should that change now? – and the fighting was hundreds of miles away. People went about their business as they always had done. The sun was shining – it was a glorious summer – and the streets were filled with children making the most of their vacation.

On the afternoon of 20 July 1943 Fredy Borck was playing in the courtyard of his apartment block in Rothenburgsort when he heard an aeroplane above. Suddenly propaganda leaflets rained out of the sky: 'We didn't dare touch [them], because it was said they might be poisoned. So we ran to the house and brought fire tongs and coal shovels, and used those to pick them up. We weren't supposed to read them either, but we did. It was an appeal to the people to leave the city immediately, because we were to be the next bombing target.'[21]

A debate ensued among the family as to what they should do. They had a shack in Krümmel near the coast that they could go to, but there was no guarantee of safety there – a large munitions factory stood nearby, which might easily be an alternative target for Allied bombers. Besides, Fredy's grandmother refused to leave the city. So they decided to stay, saying 'It would not be so bad,' and Fredy went back out into the courtyard to play. The sun shone, scorching the city for the rest of the week, and still the war seemed hundreds of miles away.

Darkness Falls from the Air

6. A Brief History of Bombing

Give us something to destroy . . .
Don't despise us; we're heralds and prophets.
Primo Levi[1]

The one thing that could not be said about the horrors created by the Combined Bomber Offensive is that they were unforeseen. At the beginning of the twentieth century, while most of the world was still celebrating the advent of powered flight as a thing of wonder, there were many who worried that mankind was not yet responsible enough to wield such power peacefully. Their fears were crystallized in 1908 by H. G. Wells, whose hugely popular novel, *The War in the Air*, described the possibility of a world war in which aerial bombing campaigns would destroy every major city and bring about 'universal social collapse'.[2] His fictional descriptions of the bombing of New York make uneasy reading for anyone acquainted with the effects of British and American bombs in 1943:

They smashed up the city as a child will shatter its cities of brick and card. Below, they left ruins and blazing conflagrations and heaped and scattered dead . . . Lower New York was soon a furnace of crimson flames, from which there was no escape. Cars, railways, ferries, all had ceased, and never a light led the way of the distracted fugitives in that dusky confusion but the light of burning.[3]

Over the next few years, such predictions became increasingly common. When Italian aviators fighting in North Africa dropped the world's first aerial bombs on Turkish troops in 1911, there was general dismay that the genie had been let out of the bottle.

Reports in English newspapers claimed that such bombing would revolutionize warfare. Gustaf Janson, a Swedish writer, described how aerial bombardment would one day see entire cities 'burnt, blown to pieces in explosions, annihilated, exterminated'.[4] Across Europe, the popular imagination was fired with images of a man-made Sodom and Gomorrah.[5]

At the time, however, such ideas were still fantasy – fairy stories to frighten children. Powered flight was in its infancy, and not a single country was capable of delivering the mass of machines necessary to produce such devastation. The few occasions before 1914 when aircraft were used to drop bombs only seemed to demonstrate how ineffective they were. For example, after the initial excitement over the Italian bombing of Libya died down, most of the world's press dismissed it as pointless. The German correspondent for the *Berliner Tageblatt* claimed that the results had been virtually nil, and that Italian aviators had had very little effect on the war. A French military observer reported that the bombs he had seen produced no casualties and no damage. Many fell into the sand without exploding, and those that detonated produced only a small and harmless blast. More importantly, the Turks did not appear in the least bit frightened by the experience.[6]

Yet the idea that aerial bombardment could be used as a devastating force persisted in the popular imagination and in the minds of military theorists. The image of Sodom and Gomorrah seemed to tap something deep within human nature: not only the nightmare of being on the receiving end, but also the dream of being able to wield such irresistible power oneself. Soon military thinkers across the world were weaving their own fantasies: most seemed to think that bombing would end up saving lives by making wars shorter and more decisive. Some went so far as to claim that the threat of bombing would eventually bring peace and order to the world.[7]

The outbreak of the First World War destroyed all such benign theories for good. The first bombings of the war were isolated affairs, but it was only a matter of time before those separate attacks were grouped together into full-scale bombing offensives. It was the Germans who first embraced bombing as a strategic weapon.

France was attacked regularly, especially Paris, but it was Britain that received the full shock of the German air offensive. The idea was to attack British ports, stations, arsenals, factories – anything that contributed to the British war effort – methodically and incessantly. Most of the early raids came from zeppelins, which were able to fly incredibly long distances without having to stop and refuel, but at the same time German manufacturers were developing the world's first effective long-range bomber aeroplane – the twin-engined Gotha.

The effect on the civilian population was dramatic. For centuries Britain had been an island fortress, protected from the rest of Europe by the English Channel, but in a few short years the advent of powered flight had rendered the country defenceless. When the first bombs began to fall during the First World War there were scenes of panic in all of the areas affected. Rates of absenteeism in factories and offices rocketed in the days after an attack, and the quality of the work done by those who turned up was vastly reduced. Skilled workers in armaments factories made a much greater number of mistakes in precision work in the days after an air raid. In Hull, women and children fled the city at the first sound of the alarm and spent night after night huddled in sodden fields outside the city. As one commentator observed, exposure to the cold must have caused far more harm than the few bombs dropped from the Zeppelins.[8]

Worse was to come with the arrival of the Gothas, flying in broad daylight and strewing bombs as though the country had no defences. On 25 May, a formation of planes bombed a crowded shopping arcade in Folkestone, killing ninety-five people and wounding 260. Two weeks later they attacked London, killing 162 civilians, including sixteen children in an infant school in Poplar. It was the first of seventeen attacks on the city by Gothas.

By the end of the summer of 1917 the British government began to worry that the increased intensity of air raids was having a disastrous effect on morale. An emergency committee, set up under the chairmanship of Jan Smuts, decided that there were only two ways to counter the German attacks. First, the air force should be made independent of both the army and the navy, so that it could respond specifically to the air threat. Second, and most important, the fight should be taken back to the Germans. According to Smuts, the way to total victory over Germany was to launch a massive air campaign on German cities; if not now, then certainly in the near future: 'The day may not be far off when aerial operations, with their devastation of enemy lands and destruction of industrial and populace centres on a vast scale, may become the principal operations of war, to which the older forms of military and naval operations may become secondary and subordinate . . .'[9] The Prime Minister, David Lloyd George, backed up this prediction with a solemn promise of revenge for the damage the Germans had caused in London: 'We will give it all back to them, and we will give it to them soon. We shall bomb Germany with compound interest.'[10]

In accordance with the findings of the Smuts Report, the Air Ministry set about creating the world's first independent force of aeroplanes and airships – the Royal Air Force, which finally came into being on 1 April 1918. Five weeks later one of the most influential men in the history of air power, Brigadier-General Sir Hugh Trenchard, was appointed to command an independent force of British bombers in France. His brief was to attack every German railway junction, airfield, factory and iron foundry within 150 miles of his airbase at Nancy. Since most of these targets were in heavily built-up areas, bombing them would have the added effect of undermining civilian morale.

The new commander of the independent bombing force took to his task with gusto. Trenchard was well known among the British establishment for his tremendous efficiency and enthusiasm for air power. Known affectionately as 'Boom', because of his booming voice, he was a man of strong opinions who had a talent for finding and nurturing gifted subordinates. His many disciples included the future leader of Bomber Command in the Second World War, Arthur Harris, and the American prophet of air power, William Mitchell, who regularly sought Trenchard's help and advice in 1917 and 1918.

According to Trenchard, the aeroplane was almost exclusively a weapon of attack, and any use of aircraft to defend against enemy bombers was at best useless, and at worst recklessly wasteful. In 1917 when two squadrons of fighters were withdrawn from the Western Front to defend London he was greatly angered, and argued that the British were merely playing into German hands by diverting men and equipment away from the one place where they were most useful. The destruction the Germans were wreaking on British and French cities had to be borne until the RAF's own bomber attacks on Germany threw the enemy on to the defensive. Trenchard recognized the limitations of bombers in the First World War, but saw their future potential, particularly in the breaking of enemy morale.

As Trenchard began his bombing campaign on the towns of western Germany, the traditional British restraint over the fate of non-combatants became a thing of the past. There is no question that this policy was sanctioned by the government. In September 1918 the air minister, Lord Weir, wrote to Trenchard: 'If I were you, I would not be too exacting as regards accuracy in bombing railway stations in the middle of towns. The German is susceptible to bloodiness, and I would not mind a few accidents due to inaccuracy.' Trenchard's reply showed no squeamishness for the fate of civilians: 'I do not think you need be anxious about our degree of accuracy when bombing stations in the middle of towns. The accuracy is not great at present, and all the pilots drop their eggs well into the middle of the town generally.'[11] For Trenchard, the main use of bombers was in breaking the morale of the German people. As he said after the war, 'The moral effect of bombing stands undoubtedly to the material effect in a proportion of twenty to one.'[12]

The seeds sown by the German zeppelins and Gothas in 1917 had grown into a full-blown policy of indiscriminate destruction: 'area bombing' had been born. The only blessing for German civilians was that the policy was short-lived. On 11 November 1918 the armistice agreement was signed, and the towns of Germany were spared any further bombardment. However, the spectre of strategic bombing had been released, and would return twenty years later to haunt the entire European continent for six long, devastating years.

*   *   *

The advent of strategic bombing marked a huge change, not only in the way wars would be waged in the future but in the concept of what constituted warfare. Whereas in the past the devastating effects of war had been confined to a relatively small area – the immediate 'battle zone' – now aircraft could leapfrog armies and bring destruction to areas hundreds of miles behind the front lines. Since aircraft could go anywhere, the battlefield had grown to encompass entire nations. Moreover, their targets were no longer specific factories or arsenals, but 'the morale of the people'. Generals on both sides used these new weapons to take the fighting to the heart of their enemy's cities, and they did this for the simple reason that now, at last, they could.

It is easy to condemn the actions of people like Trenchard, or the German zeppelin commanders who ordered the bombing of London and Paris, but the opposing sides were waging what the French quickly called '*la guerre totale*',[13] and there was a dreadful but undeniable logic to their actions. When an entire nation's resources are backing the prosecution of a war, why should a military commander draw any distinction between the soldier at the front and the civilian in a factory that produces weapons? Shortly after the war, studies on air power appeared across the world, and almost all agreed on this point: there was no longer any difference between civilian and soldier. When farmers grow food for the army, miners produce their raw materials, railway workers bring them to the front, and women and children provide soldiers with comfort while they are on leave, all these people become legitimate targets. In an era of total war there can be no holding back, because any action that produces a knock-out blow to the enemy will potentially save the lives of tens of thousands. This logic drove the military strategy of the time.

After the dreadful waste of all the static, defensive land battles of the past four years, air power soon began to be seen as the perfect way to restore movement to warfare. It was the offensive weapon *par excellence*, striking suddenly and giving the enemy no time to parry the blow by calling up reinforcements. It was also cheap. In the face of widespread cuts in defence spending after the war, Trenchard was able to keep the fledgling RAF intact simply because it was so much cheaper to police the British Empire with a bomber force than it was to launch expeditions by the army on the ground. Trenchard's vision was to create a long-range bomber force with which Britain could maintain her empire and keep her European neighbours at bay, much as she had done with her navy for most of the previous two hundred years.

However, as theorists like the influential Giulio Douhet pointed out, Britain did not rule the air as she did the sea. Not only that, but air power was fundamentally different from sea power: aeroplanes were not limited in scope or direction of movement, and now even the heart of the British Empire itself was vulnerable. London, 'the great metropolis until now rejoicing in her inviolability', could be attacked just as easily as anywhere else.[14]

That fact was not lost on the population of London, which still remembered the panic caused by the 1917 Gotha attacks. During the 1920s and 1930s a succession of lurid novels appeared in which the bombing of London produced swarms of refugees like 'human rats',[15] or where in the post-apocalyptic ruins of the city 'the people lived on the rats and the rats lived on the people'.[16] Films like the 1936 science-fiction movie *Things to Come* showed how bombing would be used in a global war that would eventually destroy civilization throughout the world. The opinions of the professionals were no more reassuring. In 1923 J. F. C. Fuller warned that the dropping of poison gas on London might injure as many as two hundred thousand people in half an hour, and 'throw the whole city into panic'.[17] Douhet was even more graphic in his predictions, and claimed that bombing a city like London would result in 'a complete breakdown of the social structure', which would inevitably lead the people to rise up in revolution against their own government.[18]

All these various prophets of air power singled out London in their descriptions because at that time the British capital was still by far the most powerful city in Europe, and also the one most protected by natural barriers. If London were vulnerable, how much more vulnerable must every other European city be? As a consequence, fear of bombing was fairly universal throughout western Europe between the wars. Even Canada and the USA were not immune to such anxieties, despite their geographical remoteness from any enemy – as was demonstrated by the faintly absurd air-raid scares in Ottawa and New York during the last year of the war, and again in 1942.[19] But it was only in Britain that such concerns reached virtual hysteria. By the 1930s even the most enthusiastic champion of bombing, J. M. Spaight, was forced to admit to a widespread pessimism among his contemporaries, who foresaw 'a fate comparable to that of Sodom and Gomorrah' for British cities.[20]

As the Second World War approached, the predictions became more and more gloomy. In 1937, the military theorist Sir Malcolm Campbell wrote the following account of the likely outcome of an air raid on London:

First would come hundreds of aeroplanes . . . each carrying up to a thousand small incendiary bombs. These would be dropped at a rate of one every five seconds, and each machine would leave a string of fires in its wake. If all the fire-fighting appliances in the country were concentrated in the one place, they would not be able to cope with a tenth of the fires that would rage over the whole area attacked. Even if they could, hard on the heels of the fire-raisers would follow fleets of heavy bombing machines, dropping their loads of high-explosive bombs on a city already virtually fated to destruction by fire. And as if that were not enough, then would come other fleets of aircraft to drench the flaming ruins with poison gases. Unless the people could take refuge in safety below ground, the casualties in a city like London must amount to a million or even more, while the material damage would be simply incalculable. The picture is not over-drawn – it is what inevitably will happen to a country which fails to take the elementary precaution of making itself strong enough to hold what it has.[21]

When such a premonition is extended beyond just one city to ten, twenty, fifty cities, it is no longer a vision of Sodom and Gomorrah. It is a vision of Armageddon.

It must be stressed at this point that not everybody believed that such destruction was inevitable. There had been many and varied attempts to ban bombing ever since the first Hague Peace Conference in 1899 but, as is so often the case with such conferences, the proposals were always rejected by too many of the countries that really mattered.[22]

In one famous instance, in March 1933, the peace conference at the League of Nations took up the question of firebombing. Poison gas had already been banned in 1926 because its uncontrollable nature threatened the lives of innocent civilians; it was argued now that fires caused by incendiaries were every bit as uncontrollable as gas when dropped on city targets, so should also be banned. Everyone agreed, and for a while it looked as though firebombing would indeed be banned. The conference was already working out the practical details when, in October that year, the newly elected Adolf Hitler walked out and withdrew from the League of Nations. Without Germany, the ban meant nothing. Ironically, Hitler's action had ensured the death of hundreds of thousands of his own countrymen.[23]

*   *   *

Over the next few years the whole world rearmed itself, and rapidly sank back into the quicksand of war. It is difficult now, even with hindsight, to see how another world war could have been avoided after the Nazis took power in Germany. Repeated attempts to mollify Hitler at the negotiating table proved a waste of time: the entire doctrine of the Nazi Party was centred on preparing for war.[24] By 1937 the newly formed Luftwaffe was rehearsing its tactics with the bombing of republican towns like Guernica in the Spanish Civil War. In the spring of 1938 Hitler annexed Austria. In 1939, despite frantic British attempts at appeasement, he marched into Czechoslovakia. In September he invaded Poland, followed by Denmark, Norway, Holland, Belgium and France. In just under ten months Hitler and his allies had taken control of virtually the whole of mainland Europe.

Despite all the dire predictions of the 1930s, the war in the air was fairly restrained until this point. At the outbreak of hostilities President Roosevelt had appealed to both sides to renounce the 'bombardment from the air of civilian populations and unfortified cities', and both sides had hastened to agree.[25] Neither wished to provoke the ire of the world's greatest industrial nation.

The British in particular promised that they would 'never resort to the deliberate attack on women and children and other civilians for purposes of mere terrorism',[26] and for a long time they kept their promise. During the six-month lull between the invasions of Poland and Norway, the RAF took serious losses in coastal raids on the German Navy: these were completely unsuccessful because they were forbidden to attack ships when they were at their most vulnerable – in port – because of the possibility of hitting civilians. During the battle for Norway air crew were instructed not to use any bombs, just their machine-guns to avoid hitting innocent bystanders.[27] For all Britain's refusal to ratify international agreements on bombing, she began the war with admirable, if somewhat unrealistic, restraint.

With the exception of the bombing of Warsaw in 1939, Germany exercised similar control. It made no sense to destroy the cities and industries of the countries she wanted to occupy, and Hitler had no intention of provoking America into renouncing its neutrality. In any case the Luftwaffe was overwhelmingly a *tactical* air force – it confined its activities mostly to the battle zone, by dive-bombing and strafing opposing troops. The *strategic* bombing they carried out was generally directed at the destruction of enemy airfields and transport links, not civilian populations.

The change came during the invasion of the Low Countries in May 1940, when the Germans surrounded the Dutch port of Rotterdam. The general in command of the 39th Panzer Korps told the Dutch defenders that unless they capitulated immediately the city would suffer 'complete destruction' by German bombers.[28] The following day, when negotiations between the two sides broke down, the Luftwaffe was dispatched to keep the general's promise. Soon a hail of bombs was falling on the heart of the old city, setting large areas on fire. Later it became apparent that the Dutch garrison had surrendered before the air strike had taken place, but the order to recall the bombers came too late to save the city. That evening, while the houses still burned, the German Army entered Rotterdam just as they had entered Warsaw, unopposed.

The bombing of Rotterdam had sealed the Wehrmacht's success in Holland, but it was a propaganda disaster for Germany. Over the next few days reports appeared across the world claiming that as many as thirty thousand civilians had been killed (although in reality the figure was more like a thousand).[29] Outraged, the British lifted some of their restrictions on bombing military targets inside Germany. On 15 May, the day after Rotterdam was bombed, Churchill sent ninety-nine bombers to attack rail and oil installations east of the Rhine. A few days later thirty were sent to attack the Blohm & Voss shipyards in Hamburg – the first of 213 attacks on the city. While a handful of bombs did hit the shipyards, in the darkness most fell in residential areas around the Reeperbahn, and thirty-four people were killed. The German press immediately hailed it as a 'ruthless terror attack on the civilian population'.[30]

So began Britain's strategic bombing campaign against Germany: a long-term systematic effort to destroy all German rail links, oil installations, airfields, armaments factories, metal foundries, stockpiles of raw material – in fact, anything of military value. Hitler responded, predictably, by ordering his air force to prepare for a full-scale air offensive against Britain, as a reprisal for the attacks on Germany and as preparation for a cross-Channel invasion of the British Isles. The battle for mainland Europe was over. The battle of Britain was about to begin.

★　　★　　★

Britain was the last piece in Hitler's jigsaw of western Europe, and his generals set about trying to conquer it in much the same way as they had conquered the rest of the continent. Their first task was to achieve command of the air, which meant destroying as many Royal Air Force planes and airfields as possible. Only after they had gained complete air supremacy would a cross–Channel invasion be possible.

When the Luftwaffe made their first bombing sorties over Britain in June 1940, an atmosphere of relative restraint still surrounded the bombing war. Hitler explicitly forbade his air force to attack London and other cities, partly because he had promised not to make war against women and children and partly because he wanted his forces to concentrate on the targets that mattered.[31] At first the Luftwaffe attacked in daylight, but when German losses began to mount they were forced to switch to night attacks.

This was where both sides finally lost what was left of the mutual restraint with which they had started the war. In the dark, the German bombs increasingly missed their intended targets and fell on residential areas; then, on the evening of 24 August 1940, a dozen German bombers veered off course and accidentally dropped their bombs on central London. In retaliation, Churchill immediately ordered his bombers to attack Berlin. Although the raid caused little material damage it infuriated Hitler, who told a mass rally about ten days later, 'If they attack our cities, we will simply erase theirs.'[32] In reprisal for the Berlin attack, he ordered Hermann Goering to stop attacking purely military targets and concentrate on London.

There has been speculation that Churchill ordered the attack on Berlin deliberately to provoke this response in his enemy. The RAF was under serious threat at the time, and it was only after the Luftwaffe switched to area bombing that it could recover. If this was the case, then it was an expensive gamble. London suffered seventy-one major raids during the Blitz, and twenty thousand men, women and children lost their lives.

Attacks on towns across Britain soon followed. In November the Luftwaffe destroyed Coventry, and Hitler was so impressed that he coined a new verb, *coventriren* – 'to coventrate'. Over the next six months the Luftwaffe attempted to 'coventrate' Birmingham, Liverpool, Manchester, Sheffield, Portsmouth, Plymouth, Bristol, Swansea, Cardiff, Glasgow and Belfast. Britain responded by targeting places in Germany where the centres of industry were surrounded by densely populated residential areas. The idea was that even if the factories were not destroyed, the homes of those who worked in them would be. If this was not officially a policy of 'area bombing', in practice that was exactly what it was. The pinpoint targeting of specific installations was simply not possible: from 15,000 feet, in the dark, it was considered accurate if an aircraft bombed within five miles of its aiming point. On 12 December 1940 the British government gave up all pretence when Winston Churchill ordered the bombing of Mannheim: for the first time the British had designated the city as the target, rather than anything specific within it. As the British official history of the bombing war points out, with the advent of such area bombing, 'The fiction that the bombers were attacking military objectives in the towns was officially abandoned.'[33]

It was an almost exact copy of what had happened in the First World War: a few piecemeal attacks, leading to a German offensive on Britain, and gradually the initial restraint exercised by both sides was whittled away to nothing. The only difference between the two wars was in scale. On 17 September 1940 alone the Luftwaffe unloaded more than 350 tons of bombs on London – more than the total dropped on the whole of Britain throughout the First World War. By the following April, they were able to drop more than a thousand tons of high explosive on the British capital in a single night. During the nine months of the Blitz more than forty thousand British people were killed, and a quarter of a million homes destroyed, leaving three-quarters of a million homeless.[34] All the terrifying pre-war predictions were beginning to come true.

And yet, in one respect, the prophets of air power seemed to have got it wrong. Contrary to the message preached by all the theorists before the war, the morale of the British people was not broken by the ordeal they had been through. If anything, they had become more determined, and their response to the bombings was vengeful rather than fearful. Politicians clamoured for retaliatory strikes against German cities; their speeches were echoed in the newspapers, which were filled with indignant leader columns requiring the RAF to fly to Berlin and give as good as Britain was getting.[35]

As Hitler turned his attention to Russia, and the raids on Britain petered out, the leaders of the bruised and battered RAF were given the space they needed to plan their revenge. The air force was still too weak to take the fight to the heart of the Reich, but it was obvious that Britain was now in the war for the long term. Over the next eighteen months the RAF would build its strength to create the most formidable bomber force the world had yet seen. Just as she had in the First World War, Britain now set her sights on a huge bombing campaign to destroy the German infrastructure. The only difference was that this time there would be no armistice to save the German people from British wrath.

To carry out this bombing campaign, the Air Ministry looked for a new commander-in-chief to lead Bomber Command. The man they settled on was an experienced and determined airman named Sir Arthur Harris. Over the next three years he would preside over the greatest, most systematic destruction of population centres the world has ever known, and in the process would become one of Britain's most controversial war figures. The climax of his reign, when the world began to believe that his air force might even win the war single-handedly, was the bombing of Hamburg.

7. The Grand Alliance

. . . they have sown the wind, and they shall reap the whirlwind
Hosea 8:7[1]

Air Chief Marshal Sir Arthur Harris took over the reins of Bomber Command at the end of a very low period for the RAF. For the previous six months the RAF staff had been suffering a serious crisis of confidence: their insistence that 'the bomber will always get through' had proved wrong, their accuracy when they did get through was appalling, and their losses had been heavy.[2] In two years of bombing they had not even dented the German war economy – although they did not yet know how truly ineffective they had been – and they had killed only as many Germans as they had lost in air crew. One British defence scientist of the time calculated that only a single German died for every five tons of bombs dropped – a hopeless waste of resources even if one agreed with the brutal realities of area bombing.[3] Critics of Bomber Command were appearing throughout the British establishment. Even Churchill was sceptical about bombing: 'Its effects, both physical and moral, have been greatly exaggerated,' he said in September 1941. 'The most we can say is that it will be a heavy and I trust a seriously increasing annoyance' to the Germans.[4]

By the spring of 1942, however, this was beginning to change. Brand new planes were rolling off the production lines, such as the Avro Lancaster, which could carry twice the load of almost any other bomber in existence, and the De Havilland Mosquito, which could fly higher and faster than even most German fighters. New radio technology was being developed to improve navigation, and new bomb-sights were being produced to improve the RAF's appalling accuracy record. To accompany these changes, the RAF had been on a massive recruitment drive, transferring men from the other armed forces, and drafting some from previously reserved occupations to swell its ranks for the years to come.

So, when Harris first arrived at Bomber Command Headquarters in High Wycombe many of the problems that had plagued his predecessors were already well on the way to being solved. What was needed now was a determined leader, capable of making wise use of the formidable weapon in his hands. It is easy to see why Harris was chosen for the job: while his wisdom might sometimes have been called into question, not even his fiercest critics would have accused him of lacking determination.

Arthur Harris was born in Cheltenham, in 1892. His father, who was a civil servant in the British Raj, always wanted him to go into the army – which the young Arthur Harris was dead set against. After a series of arguments, he left home at the age of sixteen and travelled to Rhodesia (now Zimbabwe) where he tried his hand at farming, gold mining and driving horse teams. It is ironic that after all this he should have joined the army anyway, but six years later, at the outbreak of the First World War, that was what he did. In 1915, after taking part in the fight for German West Africa, he made his way back to Britain and joined the Royal Flying Corps – then part of the army – and began a lifelong relationship with aeroplanes. Over the next twenty years he flew everything from night fighters to flying boats. He ended the First World War as a major, with the Air Force Cross, and went on to command squadrons of bombers in some of the furthest-flung outposts of the empire under Trenchard's Air Control scheme. Eventually, in 1933, he returned to England and worked his way through the ranks of the Air Ministry, until he became Commander-in-Chief of Bomber Command mid-way through the Second World War.[5]

By all accounts Harris was a forceful man, possessed of almost boundless energy and a bluntness that verged upon rudeness. He despised the other armed services, and was fond of saying that the army would never understand the value of tanks as a replacement

for the cavalry until they could be made to 'eat hay and shit'.[6] He
had a dry, cutting sense of humour, and did not suffer fools gladly.
After the bombing of Pearl Harbor he was called by a friend in
New Jersey who wanted advice on how to defend his factory
against incendiaries. Harris told him to get a long-handled shovel
and throw any out of the window – then went on to say that he
should wrap it up and send it to Harris, who 'would eat it and
every incendiary bomb that fell on America in the war'.[7] His
aggressive nature was reflected in the way he drove. Late one night,
while racing his Bentley between London and High Wycombe, he
was stopped by a policeman who reproached him: 'You might
have killed somebody, sir.' Whereupon Harris replied, 'Young
man, I kill thousands of people every night!'[8]

Harris made few friends, but those he had remained loyal to
him throughout their lives. The Chief of Air Staff, Charles Portal,
had been his friend for years, as had many of his subordinates –
particularly Robert Saundby and Ralph Cochrane, who had first
served with him in Iraq in 1922, and Don Bennett, who had served
with him in a flying-boat squadron at the end of the 1920s. His
plain speaking also made him friends in the American air force,
especially General Ira Eaker, who shared many of the same problems when it came to dealing with the other armed services. Most
importantly, however, he inspired a fanatical devotion among the
air crews who served under him, many of whom vociferously
defend him to this day. To them he was known as 'Butcher' Harris,
or 'Butch' for short – a man who would always get the job
done, however distasteful it might seem to others, and whose first
concern was to provide his men with the right equipment and
resources to do their job.

Harris was a staunch disciple of Trenchard, and firmly believed
that if enough concentrated misery could be inflicted on the cities
of Germany over the next eighteen months the Nazis would be
compelled to surrender. One of his first actions after taking command was to appear on a newsreel in which he said, in clipped
tones, 'There are a lot of people who say that bombing cannot
win the war. My answer to that is that it has never been tried yet.

We shall see.'[9] He had no qualms about area bombing, and remained unapologetic about it to the end of his life. 'If the Germans had gone on using the same force for several nights against London,' he said, after the war, '. . . the fire tornado they would have raised would have been worse than anything that happened later in Hamburg, and the whole of London would have gone as Hamburg went.'[10]

Right from the start, Harris's aim was to attack the very heart of the Reich: Berlin, the capital city; Hamburg, the centre of shipbuilding and trade; and the Ruhr valley, Germany's industrial heartland. But the RAF was not strong enough yet to make a serious impact on such heavily defended targets, so he concentrated instead on demonstrating to the world what British bombers were capable of once they were deployed in force. The aim was threefold: to quieten the critics at home, to show support for the Russians, and to demonstrate to the Germans what lay in store for them if they continued the war.

The targets he picked were two medieval cities on the Baltic coast of Germany: Lübeck and Rostock. Both seem to have been chosen for their vulnerability rather than their strategic importance: their crowded wooden buildings were highly flammable, and would provide a perfect opportunity for Harris to test his belief that the incendiary, rather than high explosive, was the most efficient means of destroying a city. As Harris said, the closely packed Hanseatic town of Lübeck was built 'more like a fire-lighter than a human habitation', and when 234 aircraft firebombed it on 28 March 1942 60 per cent of the old city was consumed.[11] More than a thousand people lost their lives in the worst single attack on a German city so far.

A month later, a series of similar attacks was launched on Rostock, which again destroyed about 60 per cent of the city centre by fire. As German propaganda minister Joseph Goebbels stated in his diary, community life had come to an abrupt end: 'The situation in the city is in some sections catastrophic.'[12] Later Harris justified the attack by pointing to the Heinkel aircraft factory on the outskirts of the town, but the real victory was psychological. While the British had failed to make any real impact on major targets, like Berlin or the cities of the Ruhr, they had proved their worth against smaller targets. Here, at last, was a demonstration to the world that the power of the RAF was on the rise.

The destruction of Lübeck and Rostock was merely a taste of things to come. On 30 May Harris launched the first thousand bomber raid of the war. The target was originally supposed to be Hamburg, concentrating as many bombers in one attack as the port normally saw in a year, but the city was temporarily reprieved when the weather over the German coast deteriorated, and the target was switched to Cologne. That night 1,046 aircraft took off for the north Rhineland, and within a few hours had dropped 2,000 tons of bombs on the city. An estimated 3,300 houses were destroyed in the attack, along with thirty-six factories, and 469 people were killed, most of them civilians. Twelve thousand separate fires raged through the city, the gas mains exploded, the water mains were severed, and all transport systems were put into such disarray that the disruption was still felt months later.[13] But, most importantly, the RAF had achieved a major propaganda success. The magic figure of a thousand bombers was far greater than anything the Luftwaffe could achieve, and when Britain was falling behind their enemy in every other arena of the war this was an important morale boost for her people.

★   ★   ★

A second morale boost occurred later in the summer of 1942, when the Americans entered the fray. The USA had officially joined the war shortly after the bombing of Pearl Harbor at the end of 1941, but she was by no means ready for it. Like her British allies, she had been slow to arm. While Germany had been rapidly building her air force since 1935, and Japan likewise throughout the 1930s, it was not until 10 July 1940 that Roosevelt convinced Congress to spend an extra $5 billion on war production. Slowly the world's greatest industrial giant began the long process of building her army's air force. By the time the Axis powers declared war against America in December 1941, she was producing some

26,000 military aeroplanes per year, compared to Britain's 20,000 and Germany's 11,000. Even so, without experienced crews to fly them it would take eighteen months before the Americans could deploy in force over the skies of northern Europe.

The overall commander of the United States Army Air Force (USAAF) was Lieutenant-General Henry 'Hap' Arnold, the son of a Pennsylvanian doctor. Arnold had learned to fly before the First World War when he joined the Aeronautical Division of the US Army Signal Corps, and at one point had even held the world altitude record. Throughout the First World War he ran the army's aviation schools, and rose steadily through the ranks until, in 1938, he became head of the Army Air Corps.

If Butch Harris was an uncompromising commander, Hap Arnold was positively severe. He drove his staff relentlessly, and is reputed to have given one officer such a dressing-down that he slumped dead over Arnold's desk from a heart-attack. Impatient, austere, unceasingly demanding, he would rarely tolerate any form of failure or delay, regardless of whether there was a good reason for it or not. However, like Harris, he was widely respected as a man who got things done, and he had many friends within the air force. Also like Harris, he proved shrewd in his choice of subordinates, and surrounded himself with brilliant and energetic people like Carl Spaatz, Ira Eaker and Fred Anderson.

By the time of the Hamburg raids, Arnold's representative in Britain was Ira Eaker, commander of the US Eighth Air Force. The contrast between Arnold and Eaker was stark. While Arnold was brusque, Eaker was thoughtful and likeable, and spent many years conducting what amounted to public relations for the USAAF. He was a highly educated man, and had attended Georgetown University, Columbia University, and the University of Southern California. Despite their differences in character the two men seem to have got on well, to the extent that they were able to write three books on military aviation together.

Early in 1942, Eaker was dispatched to Britain to set about creating an organization capable of taking the fight to Germany. From the beginning he and his entourage were welcomed by the

British, who immediately handed over several airfields for their use. There has been some suggestion that British friendliness in those early days was governed by ulterior motives, and that what they really wanted was to assimilate the fledgling USAAF into a combined air force firmly under British control. However, it seems much more likely that they were simply glad to accept a new ally, and willing to pass on as much help and advice as was necessary to get them operational as soon as possible. And their help was considerable: the RAF immediately shared its radar and communications systems, as well as vital intelligence; British Spitfires were put at the USAAF's disposal, both for fighter escort and to carry out weather reconnaissance; fuel trucks and other equipment were donated to US air bases; US airmen were given places on RAF training courses; British resources were used to help build new air bases, and the list goes on.

Relationships between the two forces, especially in the upper levels of command, were remarkably harmonious. When Eaker first arrived in Britain he lived with Harris and his family, and often brought gifts and toys from America for Harris's young daughter. He also regularly attended Harris's 'morning prayers' at Bomber Command Headquarters, when Harris and his staff chose the following night's targets. To some degree, therefore, the RAF and the USAAF were working as a combined force from the outset. But from an official point of view, the RAF and the USAAF were, and would remain, completely separate forces, each with their own priorities and methods.

Five weeks after Harris's thousand-bomber raid on Cologne, American airmen were ready to make their first operational flight over mainland Europe. On 4 July six USAAF crews, flying in borrowed planes, accompanied a squadron of British bombers on a daylight raid against German airfields in Holland. It was a baptism of fire: two of the six American planes were shot down by flak, while a third's starboard engine was blown to pieces and barely managed to limp home. Nevertheless, a point had been made. The Americans had arrived in Europe.

Six weeks later a dozen American bombers made their first

independent attack of the war, this time flying their own planes –
the formidable B-17 'Flying Fortresses' of 97th Group. Their target
was the Rouen–Sotteville railway marshalling yards, to the west of
Paris. As the formation crossed the English Channel, one of the
lead planes was carrying General Eaker, and it is proof both of the
strength of American enthusiasm and their unshakeable faith in
their aircraft that such a high-ranking commander was allowed
to fly on this earliest of missions. Fortunately he, and all of the
American air crews, returned safely late that afternoon – although
two Spitfires in the British fighter escort were shot down.

The Americans had a different philosophy from the British.
While the RAF had been forced to fly by night to avoid casualties,
just as the Luftwaffe had been earlier in the war, the Americans
were determined to conduct their bombing in daylight. There
were two reasons for this. First, they were morally opposed to the
bombing of civilians – at least in Europe – and strongly believed
that bombing in daylight, when they could see their proper targets
clearly, would result in fewer unnecessary casualties.[14] Second, they
were convinced that daylight bombing would be far more effective.
Unlike the British, whose bombing precision had barely improved
since the First World War, the Americans had developed the highly
accurate Norden bombsight, which allowed them consistently to
drop bombs within fifty feet of a practice target from a height of
four or five miles above the earth.[15] There was a saying in the
USAAF that their aviators could drop a bomb into a pickle barrel
from 30,000 feet: when their accuracy was so good, it made perfect
sense to pinpoint their efforts on exact targets, rather than waste
their bombs over large areas by night.

To start with, Harris, Portal and even Churchill objected to
the American insistence on daylight attacks, largely because they
thought the whole policy was doomed. It was one thing to hit a
practice target in the clear blue skies of California, but a different
thing altogether to find a specific building in the centre of a
German city, especially when that city might be shrouded in the
thick cloud of a European winter, and defended by both Luftwaffe
fighters and walls of predictive flak.[16] The Americans refused to be

swayed, and it took them until the second half of 1943 to come to the painful realization that, in the absence of a long-range fighter escort, their terrible losses in the skies over Germany would be too heavy to bear.

But all that was in the future. For now the policy of daylight bombing seemed to be successful, largely because the Americans confined their fledgling efforts to targets in western France or the Low Countries, where they could still be accompanied by fighters. By the end of 1942 the Americans had flown more than 1,500 sorties in twenty-seven operations (missions), and lost only thirty-four aircraft – a loss rate of just two per cent. American optimism was so high that in August 1942 Ira Eaker confidently predicted that he and Butch Harris together would be able 'completely to dislocate German industry and commerce and to remove from the enemy the means for waging successful warfare' as early as the middle of 1943.[17] When the two leaders were finally to join forces in the bombing of Hamburg, his prediction would almost come true.

★   ★   ★

Right from the beginning the British and American air forces had worked closely together, and their co-operation was formally sealed when British and American military and political leaders met in Casablanca in January 1943 to plan a combined air offensive against Germany. Since the Allies were not yet strong enough to attempt an invasion of mainland Europe it was decided that the only way to carry the fight to the Axis powers was to increase the bombing campaign. Indeed, if the Allies were ever to attempt an invasion, it was essential that they first achieved air supremacy over the Germans.

To this end, the Combined Chiefs of Staff issued a directive to Air Marshal Harris and General Eaker, ordering them to begin demolishing a range of German targets: submarine yards and bases, aircraft production, ball-bearing factories, oil and rubber plants, and military-transport systems. They were also required to undermine German morale, as the preamble to the directive made clear: 'Your primary aim will be the progressive destruction and dislocation of the German military, industrial and economic system, and the undermining of the morale of the German people to a point where their capacity for armed resistance is fatally weakened . . .'[18] The plan was to subject Germany to a round-the-clock bombing campaign on a vast scale. RAF Bomber Command would continue their campaign against the cities by night, while the US Eighth Army Air Force would attack specific military targets by day.

The coming year would be very different from anything that had gone before. Attacks would be bigger, more widespread, and they would be repeated again and again until the destruction was total. Over the next six months the Americans built up their air force from eighty or so operating planes to a force of well over three hundred, and accumulated vital combat experience over targets in northern Europe. The British, meanwhile, began a relentless offensive against the industrial cities of the Ruhr. In March they hit the Krupps armament factory in Essen, causing severe damage to buildings and machinery. In May they devastated Dortmund and Wuppertal in quick succession, especially the latter, where a miniature firestorm consumed most of the city centre. In June they attacked Düsseldorf, starting fires that raged over forty square kilometres – twenty military installations were hit, seventy-seven companies put out of business, and 140,000 people were made homeless.

Germans all over the country noticed the increasing intensity of the bombing, and gossip flew from one city to the next. Wild estimates of the death tolls circulated: in Dortmund, they said, fifteen thousand people had been killed (the figure was actually around six hundred), in Düsseldorf seventeen thousand (in reality it was twelve hundred) and in Wuppertal twenty-seven thousand (actually 3,400).[19] Worse than the numbers being touted were rumours about how people had died. Tales were told of victims being turned into living torches by the phosphorus bombs, or becoming stuck in the melted asphalt of the roads. Such rumours certainly reached Hamburg, but few who lived there truly believed that the same fate lay in store for their city. When British reconnaissance planes dropped leaflets claiming that Hamburg would be next, no one heeded them: even those Germans who thought the Nazis were doomed believed that Hamburg would be left largely intact, because the British and Americans would need the town and its harbour later on.[20] Besides, propaganda leaflets had been dropped throughout the war, and few people paid much attention to them.

But Hamburg would indeed be next. Even while Dortmund and Düsseldorf were still reeling from their attacks, Harris issued an operations order in which he stated his intention 'to destroy Hamburg': 'The "Battle of Hamburg" cannot be won in a single night. It is estimated that at least 10,000 tons of bombs will have to be dropped to complete the process of elimination. To achieve the maximum effect of air bombardment this city should be subjected to sustained attack.' Moreover, having learned that fire was the best weapon, Harris ordered that most of the bombers should carry 'maximum economic incendiary loads' to saturate the fire services of the city.[21]

Harris expressed the hope that the Americans would join in with the bombing of Hamburg, but it was not up to him to make that decision. Until now the USAAF had never bombed a target that the British had bombed the previous night – it was deemed too dangerous – and 'round-the-clock bombing' had been merely a theory, not a reality. But the Americans also had their eye on Hamburg. The city contained many targets that they considered high priority, including aircraft-parts factories and submarine builders. US planes had tried to attack the city at the end of June, but had been forced back by heavy cloud. Now, weather permitting, they would be all too happy to join the RAF, and when General Eaker issued the order to attack the Blohm & Voss shipyards on the banks of the Elbe, Hamburg's fate was sealed.

It must be said that not everyone on the Allied side was happy about this new target. Shortly before the attack took place Sir Henry Tizard, the brilliant academic who was responsible for creating the British radar network, wrote to the Prime Minister expressing his misgivings about the proposed series of raids. He was an outspoken critic of many aspects of British bombing policy, and doubted that the war could ever be won by bombing alone. He was particularly unhappy about the prospect of destroying Hamburg, a city that he believed was essential to keep intact so that it could be used to administer Germany after the invasion: 'Hamburg is anti-Russian, anti-Prussian and anti-Nazi. It may well be soon, if not already, anti-war. Apart from submarine construction and shipping, generally it is not industrially important. It is a centre of commerce rather than of production. It is a very important port and might therefore be much more useful to us alive than dead.'[22]

Churchill did not agree, and neither did the Chief of Air Staff. In a strongly worded rebuttal, Sir Charles Portal pointed to the numerous industrial, chemical, transportation and engineering targets within the port. 'It seems abundantly clear that Hamburg is much more than a dormant centre of peace-time commerce,' he said, 'and, if so, I certainly do not think we should refrain from bombing it.'[23]

Tizard's suggestion was rejected: the bombing of Hamburg would go ahead as planned. The final piece of the jigsaw was a codename for the series of attacks, and the one they eventually settled upon was 'Operation Gomorrah'. The symbolic implication of the title was clear: God's power to rain down fire and destruction upon the earth now lay in man's hands, and was being wielded in what the British establishment saw as just retribution for the damage that the Luftwaffe had caused during the Blitz.

8. The British Plan

Technology is making gestures precise and brutal, and with them men.
It expels from movements all hesitation, deliberation, civility.
Theodor W. Adorno[1]

On the morning of 24 July 1943, Air Chief Marshal Sir Arthur
Harris arrived at Bomber Command Headquarters in High
Wycombe at his usual time of 9.00 a.m. At the base of a large
grassy mound, guarded by sentries, was a doorway that led to the
enormous underground Operations Room. Harris made his way
into the bunker, and took his seat at the desk in the midst of the
room. Behind him a huge board listed the available crews and
aeroplanes, squadron by squadron, while on either side were great
wall maps of Europe and a target priority list of dozens of cities
and objectives. Around the table stood a dozen or so others:
Harris's deputy commander-in-chief, Sir Robert Saundby; the
meteorological officer, Magnus Spence; the senior air staff officer
and his deputy; naval and army liaison officers; and various representatives of Intelligence and Operations. That day an American
VIP was also present: Brigadier-General Fred Anderson, the commander of the USAAF's bomber force in Britain.

The routine at Bomber Command HQ was well established.
Normally there would be a brief report of the previous night's
operations, followed by a weather report from Spence. Apart from
Harris, Spence was probably the most important man at the meeting, and his reports on the movements of various weather fronts
across Europe were essential when it came to choosing the following night's targets. Having listened to his summary, Harris would
select two or three and, with a hasty shuffling of folders and photographs among his staff, the possibilities would be laid out on the

table before him. There was rarely any discussion over what the target should be: Harris ran the meeting, and the decision was unequivocally his. After he had examined the folders, he would make a final decision, and the meeting would draw rapidly to a close. Harris would return to his office, and his subordinates would set about putting the operation in motion.[2]

That morning, however, everyone knew what the target was likely to be – weather permitting. The attack on Hamburg had been scheduled for two days now, but had been cancelled twice because a bank of heavy cloud was moving south towards the city. Now, as Spence laid out the weather charts on the table and began to explain the conditions, it became evident that the weather was at last good enough to go ahead. Harris studied the charts, then gave the order to proceed as planned. Moments later he rose from the chair, leaving the other members of the team to telephone through his decision to the Pathfinder Force, the bomber groups, the army, the navy and Fighter Command. General Anderson would take the news back to the USAAF headquarters at Wycombe Abbey. Operation Gomorrah was on.

⋆   ⋆   ⋆

The plan had been outlined in detail two days before, on the morning of 22 July, when the operation was first ordered.[3] In theory it was fairly simple. Every available aircraft from bomber squadrons across the country would take off between about ten o'clock and ten thirty that night. They would fly to specific points along the coast, and merge together into one huge stream of bombers flying across the North Sea. About eighty miles from the German coast they would converge on a single point, where they would turn in a tight flow, and fly down towards Hamburg. (The bomber stream never flew directly towards the target, for fear of giving away their destination to German radar stations.) At exactly one o'clock on Sunday morning, the Pathfinder aircraft would drop red and yellow target marker flares over Hamburg to indicate the aiming point. Two minutes later the first crews would start dropping their bombs.

Because of the sheer number of planes taking part in the raid, they were to attack in six waves of 100 or 120 bombers each.[4] Each wave would have an average of about eight minutes to clear the target, which meant that there would be fifteen or sixteen bombers passing over the aiming point every minute. The most important thing was to achieve as much concentration as possible, so that the whole of the area around the aiming point was saturated with bombs. Then the fire services would be overwhelmed, and unable to prevent massive conflagrations springing up. To avoid the bombing becoming unfocused, more Pathfinders would continue to mark the target – this time with green target indicators – after the attack had begun. If the bombers could not spot the red markers, they were to aim at the greens. Having released their loads, they were all to return home on a roughly parallel course.

Such plans were easier ordered than executed. Even an undefended target could be difficult to find in the darkness of night, and in the past the RAF had often bombed the wrong parts of a city, or even missed it altogether. To prevent such disastrous wastefulness, British scientists had developed a range of electronic navigational aids. The most important of these for medium to long-range targets, like Hamburg, was called H2S. It worked a little like an airborne radar device, except that instead of transmitting high-frequency pulses into the surrounding sky it would direct them at the ground. By plotting the echoes on the screen of a cathode-ray tube, it was possible to get a rough picture of the ground below, even through heavy cloud. The system was still in its infancy, and the picture it gave was sometimes so fuzzy as to be useless, but it was particularly good at picking up built-up areas surrounded by water. Hamburg would therefore be relatively easy to identify: the wide river Elbe, and the distinctive lake in the centre of the city would provide an unmistakable outline.

The second major difficulty was the strength of the defences, both on the way to Hamburg and over the city. The whole coast of Europe was guarded by squadrons of German night fighters. As soon as a formation of bombers came within a hundred miles of mainland Europe, the German long-range 'Freya' radar would pick them up and the defences would get ready for action. Once the bombers came within thirty miles or so, a second, short-range, radar system called 'Würzburg' would be able to direct night fighters towards the bomber stream. The 'Würzburg' system was extraordinarily effective for its time. Using one radar set to pick up an individual plane, a second set could guide a night fighter to within a few hundred yards of his quarry. The pilot would then be able to engage his own 'Lichtenstein' radar, and home in for the kill. The only drawback of the system was that each radar station could direct only one interception at a time. That was why the British had evolved the tactic of concentrating all their bombers into a tight stream: if they could push as many planes as possible through a single point, the German defences would intercept only a handful before the majority had gone past unscathed.

It was not only German night fighters that were directed by radar. The Reich had flak defences that stretched all the way from the sea to Berlin and beyond, and they, too, were radar-controlled. As soon as RAF bombers appeared over a city like Hamburg, radar-controlled searchlights that were a slightly different colour from all the others – usually an intense bluish beam – would begin to hunt them down. Once the blue master-beam had locked on to a British bomber, all the other searchlights would join it, creating a huge cone of lights with the hapless aeroplane at its apex. Thus lit up, the plane would have to dive violently to escape the force of German flak batteries intent on blowing it out of the sky.

Another problem was predictive flak. Using their radar screens, the German defenders could plot the height, speed and direction of flight of any one of the British bombers. They could then predict exactly where the aeroplane would be in the time it took the flak shells to fly 20,000 feet into the air, and direct the flak batteries accordingly. The only way for a British pilot to avoid this was to zigzag and corkscrew across the sky – which, when the sky was full of other aeroplanes, greatly increased the chances of a collision. When a crew were about to release their bombs even this course of evasive action was denied them: if they were to hit the target they were obliged to fly straight and level for a full minute before the bombs were released and they could think about escaping. Only when the photoflash had gone, marking the place they had bombed on an intelligence photograph, could they turn tail and head away from the hail of flak.

Hamburg had some of the most formidable flak defences in Germany. Not only was there a ring of batteries on the outskirts of the city, but four massive gun towers stood in the centre and the port. The heaviest guns were capable of firing a pair of 128mm shells twice a minute, each weighing 26 kilograms, to a range of 45,000 feet vertically into the sky.[5] If an aircraft received a direct hit from a shell like this it spelled disaster for the crew inside – if not immediately, then during the long flight over the North Sea on the way home. Even if an aircraft was not hit, the threat of the incredible firepower exploding around them could seriously unnerve a crew, and cause them to drop their bombs early and off-target.

Given the importance of the target and the strength of Hamburg's defences, Harris was determined to use every advantage he could to make sure the operation succeeded. By the summer of 1943 Germany's radar-controlled defences were causing intolerable casualties, so Harris began to press the Prime Minister to authorize the use of a new secret weapon that would jam German radar. Codenamed 'Window', it consisted of bundles of paper strips coated with metal foil on one side. When the bundles were dropped down the flare chute during the flight over Germany they would disperse, and as the strips floated to earth they created a false 'blip' on German radar screens. With thousands of false readings it would become impossible for the operators to tell where the real bombers were – at a stroke, all of their defences would be rendered useless.

Until now the device had never been used because the Ministry for Home Security was terrified that Germany would copy it and use it against Britain. However, by 1943 the threat of a new Blitz by the Luftwaffe was unlikely, so on 15 July Churchill gave Harris the go-ahead. Ironically, the Germans already knew of the principle behind Window – their own version was called Düppel –

but the German Chief of Air Signals, General Martini, had prevented its use because, he, too, was afraid of the consequences if
the British ever copied the idea.[6] Over the coming week Martini's
worst fears would come true.

Since Window only worked on the Würzburg and Lichtenstein
frequencies, the bombers would also use two other devices:
'Mandrel', which interfered with the German long-range Freya
radar, and 'Tinsel', which jammed German radio frequencies by
transmitting the sound of the aircraft engines to drown the voices
of the pilots and their radar controllers.

This, then, was the British plan of attack for what would become
known as the battle of Hamburg. As Harris made his way back to
his office, his deputy, Air Vice Marshal Sir Robert Saundby,
remained in the Operations Room to organize the practicalities of
the raid. First he telephoned Air Vice Marshal Don Bennett, head
of the Pathfinder Force, which would lead the operation. After
discussing the precise route to and from the target with him,
Saundby set about organizing the other details of the attack: bomb
loads, take-off times, aiming points and so on. Only after every
detail had been precisely established would he and the rest of the
staff retire to their own offices in the base at High Wycombe. For
the rest of the day, department by department, the devastation of
Hamburg was carefully prepared.

9. The First Strike

I know death hath ten thousand several doors
For men to take their exits
John Webster, *The Duchess of Malfi*[1]

At air bases across the eastern half of England it was a beautiful summer's day. Clear blue skies and bright sunshine had brought most of the young men from their quarters early, and for the first few hours of the day they passed the time in whatever way suited them best: reading, sharing cigarettes outside their quarters, or playing cricket on the wide-open spaces of the aerodrome. There was an atmosphere of expectancy in the air: operations had been cancelled for two days in a row, and if they were cancelled again there would be the chance of a day out in one of the local market towns. They could dash for the bus to York or Nottingham, Lincoln or Cambridge or even take a train to London. They might perhaps catch a matinée at the cinema, then have a quick meal before they joined the many other servicemen at one of the pubs or Saturday-night dance-halls. For those with wives or girlfriends, it would be a chance to spend valuable time together; for those without, it would be an opportunity to meet some of the local girls. Unlike those in the other armed services, the men in Bomber Command were not quite so restricted by the discipline of barrack duties, and when they were not on operations their time was generally their own. It was a good life for a young man – as long as he remained on the ground.

The cancellation of the previous two operations, both on Hamburg, had been frustrating for everyone. Thursday had been particularly bad. Many crews had taken their aeroplanes to the end of the runways and were about to take off when the trip had been cancelled. Some had already swallowed caffeine pills or benzedrine, dispensed by the station medical officer, to keep them awake during the long flight across the North Sea and back. It was too late to get to any of the local towns to blow off steam, so those who could had made their way to the village pubs to counteract the action of the drugs in their system with alcohol. Others settled down in the mess, or tried to get an early night. Even those who hadn't taken the MO's 'wakey-wakey' pills often found it difficult to sleep. Having geared themselves up for action throughout the day, they found it difficult to let go of all the accumulated anxiety. They knew that any cancellation of operations was only a temporary reprieve: if they didn't fly on their first, tenth or twentieth operation tonight they would only have to do it tomorrow or the day after.

While most of the young airmen relaxed in the morning sunshine, a few, usually the skippers of the aircraft, would make their way to the station office to hear the results of the morning's 'group tie-up' with Bomber Command Headquarters. Others would go to the messes, where the battle order was pinned to a board whenever operations were on. When they discovered that 'ops' were indeed on, there was a general sigh. There was no indication of what the target would be, but the fuel loads designated for each plane were the same as yesterday so it was probably Hamburg again. There would be no chance of a trip to Betty's Bar, or the Snakepit, or the Windmill Theatre this Saturday night. Reluctantly, they headed back out on to the airfield to relay the news to their air crews on the grass.

Once a crew knew that ops were on, a change came over them: the frivolity of a cricket match would be replaced with an air of purpose – they had a job to prepare for. They would leave off what they had been doing and make their way out to where their planes were standing, round the perimeter of the airfield. Here, trains of bombs would be arriving, ready to be fused by the station armourers, then loaded into the planes. That morning something else was waiting for them too: stacks and stacks of brown-paper parcels, piled up on the runway beside each plane. Many of the men were used to taking propaganda leaflets on a raid, but this was different. Unable to contain their curiosity some of the men opened the packages, but what they found inside perplexed them. Each package contained nothing but bundles of paper strips – about fourteen inches long and an inch wide – silver on one side, black on the other. Speculation about what they might be was rife. 'We couldn't make head nor tail of it,' said Harold McLean, of 427 Squadron. 'One chap peed on it to see if it reacted. It didn't.'[2]

While the airmen were puzzling over the packages, the ground crew – the 'erks', as they were affectionately known – were busy checking the aircraft. After a while the airmen climbed into the machines to join them. No matter how curious they might be about the enigmatic parcels, there was work to be done on the plane – equipment to be checked, mechanisms to be tested. This was the machinery on which their lives depended, and few crews neglected their preparations for a night on ops. The gunners would oil their guns, and perhaps realign them so that they converged at the right point. The bomb-aimer would check his instruments, as would the wireless operator and the navigator. Then, perhaps, the pilot and the flight engineer would take the machine up for a quick air test, to make sure it was flying smoothly, before returning to base for lunch and the long, slow wait till dusk.

That afternoon was a nervous one for many. Until briefing in the evening there was nothing to do but hang around and try not to think of the night that lay ahead. They were barred from leaving the base, so there was no chance of distracting themselves with a trip to the local village. Instead they would take to their quarters and try to catch an hour's sleep, or lie on the grass in the bright summer sunshine, gazing across the airfield at the petrol bowsers pumping fuel into their aircraft, at the erks cycling round the perimeter track, or the WAAF drivers bringing bomb trains to the hangars. Many airmen describe feeling strangely divorced from all the purposeful activity that surrounded them during the long hours of the afternoon, as if it had nothing whatsoever to do with them. And yet, subconsciously, they were aware that it had everything to do with them – that they, indeed, were the reason for it. It was impossible to forget that in a few hours' time they would be taking off in those huge, forbidding machines, and the peaceful English afternoon would be transformed to a nightmare of flak and fighters in the skies over Germany.

Experienced airmen would try to avoid thinking of what lay ahead, and distract themselves with games of chess or football, or by laughing at the latest buffoonery of Pilot Officer Prune in *Tee Em* magazine. It was best not to think of all the narrow escapes of previous sorties over the cauldron of Essen and the other cities of the Ruhr valley. And yet the thought inevitably surfaced: perhaps tonight their luck would run out. Bomber Command losses were running at almost five per cent at the time – in other words, one in every twenty planes on any given night would not come back. A standard tour was thirty operations. It did not take a mathematician to work out that the odds of finishing it alive were stacked against any airman.

For inexperienced crews the prospects were even worse: there was always a far higher proportion of losses among those who were on one of their first five operations. Brand new crews, or 'sprogs', as they were known, would have felt especially nervous about what lay ahead. All the training in the world could not prepare a young man for the stress of combat, and many were worried about how they might react. If a pilot panicked or a gunner froze at the wrong moment, it might mean not only his own death but that of his crewmates. It is important to remember that many airmen were still in their teens when they began flying – the average age of a new recruit into the training schools was twenty one – and many viewed their first operation as an important rite of passage into manhood.[3] At this stage of the war they were aware that a significant number would be blown out of the sky.

At last, around five o'clock, the men were called. The crews would filter into the briefing room and take their places in the rows of chairs, some talking and joking to take their minds off the night ahead, but the majority gazing quietly at the board at the end of the room, curious about what lay beneath the sheet that covered it. Once the door was closed behind them there would be a roll-call, and then the officer in charge of operations – usually one of the flight commanders, but occasionally the commanding officer (CO) – would pull down the cover to reveal the target map. Across the room men would crane forward to see where the red line of ribbon on the map led to. For the benefit of those at the back, the officer would declare, in a loud, clear voice, 'Your target for tonight, gentlemen, is Hamburg.'

For many crews there was a sense of at least partial relief on seeing the target. After numerous flights to the Ruhr, where the defences were second only to those at Berlin, it would make a welcome change: the flight to Hamburg was mostly over the North Sea, so there was less chance of being caught by flak on the journeys in and out. On the other hand, in some squadrons Hamburg was as notorious as anything the Ruhr could offer. In 57 Squadron, for example, Hamburg had a particularly bad reputation. They had not attacked the city since March, when the CO, Freddie Hop-croft, and his crew had almost been killed. Ever since then the CO had briefed other targets with the words, 'Now, boys, the defences are nothing like as good as Hamburg's, so you should be all right.' After several months of this the strengths of the Hamburg defences had gained near-mythical status, and to learn that they were flying to the city naturally filled 57 Squadron crews with trepidation.[4]

After a general briefing by the CO, describing their route, the time of attack and so on, a variety of other officers would take the stage. The meteorological officer would advise on weather conditions over the target and on the journey in. The armament officer would detail bomb loads, and the signals officer would brief them on what radio countermeasures they would use. Tonight, for the first time, the ground stations would be transmitting average windspeeds (or 'Zephyrs', as they were codenamed) to all the crews at regular intervals to help with navigation.

Eventually the intelligence officer took the stage. He com-manded the men's attention far better than the others because he told them where the danger spots would be on the outward flight and why they were going after this particular target. Hamburg, he explained, was not only a major hub of manufacturing, it was also Germany's main centre of submarine production. If they could knock the city out of the war it would deal a blow not only to the Germans at home but to their effort in the battle of the Atlantic.

That day, however, the intelligence officer had something else to tell them. Once he had finished his normal spiel, he explained the secret behind the brown-paper packages that the crews had seen being loaded into the aircraft earlier. The silvery strips inside the parcels were called Window, he said, and they were a new and simple measure designed to confuse German radar defences.

'You will already have been told how to drop Window,' the intelligence officer continued; 'it has been worked out as carefully as possible to give you maximum protection, but there are two points which I want to emphasize strongly. Firstly, the benefit of Window is a communal one: the Window which protects you is not so much that which you drop yourself as that which is already in the air dropped by an aircraft ahead. To obtain full advantage, it is therefore necessary to fly in a concentrated stream along the ordered route.

'Secondly, the task of discharging the packets of Window will not be an easy one. You are hampered by your oxygen tube, intercom connections, the darkness and the general difficulties of physical effort at high altitudes. Despite these hardships, it is essential that the correct quantities of Window are discharged at the correct time intervals.'

He went on to explain that Window was considered so important that the Air Ministry was already developing machines to ensure a steady flow from the aircraft. In the meantime, however, it was up to the airmen themselves to maintain a 'machine-like regularity' when dropping the bundles down the flare chute.

'When good concentration is achieved,' he continued, 'Window can so devastate an RDF defence system that we ourselves have withheld using it until we could effect improvements in our own defences, and until we could be sure of hitting the enemy harder than he could hit us. The time has now come when, by the aid of Window in conserving your unmatched strength, we shall hit him even harder.'[5]

During briefings the intelligence officer was often a figure of fun. Whenever he claimed that an operation would be a 'piece of cake', or that the route out to a target would be free from flak, he was greeted with jeers from the more cynical airmen. Today, however, his speech was greeted by a respectful silence. While some of the old hands privately doubted that a few bundles of silvered paper would protect them from the ferocity of the German defences, most crews seemed to accept the speech at face value. The secrecy that had so far surrounded the new device had obviously impressed them: this was not merely intelligence guesswork but something that had been worked out scientifically. Most of the airmen knew enough about radar to recognize its limitations; that it could be jammed by clouds of foil strips seemed plausible. Only time would tell.

Then the CO took the stage once more and asked if anyone had any questions – but by now they had been well briefed, and few had anything to ask. He told them to synchronize their watches, wished them luck and left the room.

As the men filtered out of the main briefing room there was no time to talk about the unusual speech they had heard, even if it had been seemly to do so. Many had now to go to shorter, specialist briefings, to make sure that all the minutiae of their duties were fixed firmly in their minds. Navigators would be given the exact route to and from the target, along with details of turning points, the winds they were likely to encounter and so on. Wireless operators were told which German frequencies they would be jamming, and reminded to listen out for the 'Zephyr' transmissions, while bomb-aimers were informed of what colour target indicators they would see, and which were the right ones to bomb.

It was only when all the crew members came together for their flight meal in the mess, at around seven o'clock, that they were able to discuss the forthcoming operation. By now, though, most were tired of it, and wanted to talk about something else. The only mention of the job that faced them would come in typical

RAF gallows humour: they would shake their heads and run a
finger across their throats to imply that another crew would be
shot down. The anxious questions of new crews would be greeted
with callous replies: 'Oh, I wouldn't worry about *that*. You're not
going to make it tonight anyway . . .'⁶ As they collected their trays
of bacon and eggs, beans, tomatoes and even fruit juice – rare
luxuries in British civilian life in 1943 – some would use their sense
of impending doom to flirt with the girls behind the counter, and
entreat them to give them extra-large helpings. After all, they'd
say, this might be their last meal. It wouldn't do to die on an empty
stomach: the least the kitchen staff could do was to fatten them
up, like lambs for the slaughter, before they went out into the
hellish skies over Germany.

★   ★   ★

After their meal, the men made their way to the flight offices to
pick up their parachutes and don their flying gear. They would
empty their pockets of everything personal – even the stub of a
cinema ticket could give away important intelligence if they were
captured – then fill them with everything they might need: escape
kits, foreign currency, perhaps a penknife for emergencies, and the
all-important flying rations to stave off hunger on the way home.
The gunners and bomb-aimers looked strangely inflated: wearing
several layers of jackets, including an electrically heated one, it was
a miracle that they fitted into the confined spaces of the gun turrets.

As the crews waited for the trucks to come and take them to
dispersal there was much laughing and joking – but the station
staff, who had seen hundreds of air crews fly off never to return,
knew it was all bluff. Even the most *blasé* airmen were exhibiting
nerves, and each of the many different ways they found to fight
down their fear had its own poignancy. Some lay on the grass,
smoking pipes and gazing out into the dusk. Others flirted shame-
lessly with the WAAF drivers who came to pick them up, snatch-
ing a last opportunity to speak with a woman before taking off
into the unknown. For the many New Zealanders, Australians and
Canadians among the crews it sometimes helped to talk about their

homes, thousands of miles away on the other side of the world. Superstition was rife. Some men were laden with lucky charms and dolls; when they lost or forgot one, they might fall into a blind panic. Many slavishly followed a little ritual as they prepared themselves – always wishing their crew members luck with the same words, always buttoning their coats in the same order, always taking the same seat in the truck to where their plane was waiting for them, huge and silent in the dusk by the perimeter track.

Out on the airfield, with half an hour to go before the engines were started, the airmen's anxiety mounted still further. For Bill McCrea this was the worst time. Surrounded by the smell of kerosene and engine oil, the grey-blue mass of the aeroplane looming over him, there was nothing left to dispel his rising nerves:

You had to hang around at dispersal, and talk to the ground crew. That was very, very bad. We'd talk about anything, anything at all. Anything apart from what you had to do – the job. Sometimes I felt physically sick . . . It wasn't what was happening at the time that was the problem. Whenever anything happened you could fight it, you had things to do. It was the thought of what *might* happen – that was the worrying thing.[7]

As the sun was sinking over the horizon, the crews indulged in their last ritual of the evening – relieving their bladders against the huge wheels of the aircraft – then climbed into their positions inside. The pilot and flight engineer would run up the great Merlin engines in the correct order, one by one: 'Starboard inner: contact.' A press on the starter button, and the engine would roar into life. 'Starboard outer . . .' With all four engines running, the pilot and flight engineer checked the oil pressure, tested the throttles and magnetos for each engine. The navigator spread his maps, and the gunners crammed themselves into the turrets that would be their cages for the next six hours. On a signal from the flight engineer, the ground crew would pull away the wooden chocks from in front of the wheels and the aircraft would start to taxi round to the dispatcher's caravan, where groups of WAAFs had gathered to wave goodbye to each plane as it headed off down the runway.

A green light was flashed as the signal for take-off – radio silence was imperative, even now, in case the Germans got wind of the impending attack – and, with a roar, the first of 792 Lancasters, Stirlings, Halifaxes and Wellingtons took off into the gathering dusk.

Kenneth Hills, a bomb-aimer with 9 Squadron, remembers this moment as the most nerve-racking of all: 'Taking off was always a sobering moment, bearing in mind what a tyre burst would do for you when you were full of high explosive and 100-octane fuel, bumping down the runway, seeing the perimeter hurtling at you, waiting for the lift-off which seemed endless, then suddenly you're clear, no bumps, no tyre burst, just a lovely sound from the Merlins, and you're on your way.'[8]

The first plane to leave the ground was Sergeant P. Moseley's Stirling of 75 (New Zealand) Squadron at 9.45 p.m. He was soon overtaken by the faster Lancasters of the Pathfinder Force, who would be leading the attack. Of the hundreds of planes that headed down runways across England that evening, only one failed to take off; forty-five more would return to their bases with technical difficulties – an average figure for this time in the war.

For those who were left on the ground, take-off was always an impressive sight. 'About twenty yards away we could just discern a vast dinosaurish shape,' wrote one American observer on a similar night, as he watched the last of the stream of planes leaving the airfield.

After a moment, as if stopping to make up its mind . . . it lumbered forward, raising its tail just as it passed us, and turning from something very heavy and clumsy into a lightly poised shape, rushing through the night like a pterodactyl. At this instant, a white light was flashed upon it and a Canadian boy from Vancouver who was standing beside me, put down its number and the moment of departure. It vanished from sight at once and we stood staring down the field, where in a few seconds a flashing green light announced that it had left the ground . . .

A great calm settled over the place as the last droning motors faded out in the distance and we all drove back to the control room where staff hang onto the instruments on a long night vigil . . . I went to sleep thinking of the . . . youngsters I had seen, all now one hundred and fifty miles away, straining their eyes through the blackness relieved only by the star-spangled vault above them.[9]

An hour later, just after 11.00 p.m., the last of the huge fleet of aircraft took to the air. The battle of Hamburg was about to begin.

★   ★   ★

Once each plane was airborne everyone's nerves subsided. Each member of the crew had a job to do, and there was a sense of relief that the operation was finally under way. In the cockpit the pilot held the controls in both hands, wrestling the aircraft up into the sky, while the flight engineer advanced the throttles for one side or the other, to correct any swing that had developed after take-off. Flying a four-engined heavy bomber in 1943 was a physical business, and required brute strength, especially when taking off or landing.

Behind the pilot and the flight engineer, curtained off from the cockpit, the navigator sat, sideways on, at his table. Charts and log books were laid out before him, lit by a small Anglepoise lamp as he took his first reading of the night. 'First course, Skipper, 032 degrees,' he bellowed, through the intercom. It was difficult to hear one another over the deafening noise of the aircraft engines, and the men often had to speak loudly and clearly to make themselves understood.

Just behind the navigator, separated by banks of equipment, sat the wireless operator. Unlike the other members of the crew, he often spent the flight in his shirtsleeves: the Lancaster's heating system had a hot-air outlet right beside him and he was the only member of the crew to stay warm throughout the trip. Beyond him was the main spar, which in the Lancaster was a waist-high wall of metal between the two wings – and beyond that were the stacks of Window, piled up next to the Elsan chemical toilet, ready to be dropped down the flare chute. A narrow ladder led up to the turret, where the mid-upper gunner scanned the sky above for the possibility of intruding German night fighters.

The final two members of the crew sat in the extremities of the plane. In the nose, beneath the cockpit, the bomb-aimer faced downwards, with nothing but a sheet of Perspex between him and a drop of thousands of feet to the ground. At the very back the 'tail-end Charlie' – the rear gunner – had nothing to look at but the fading glow of the sunset on the western horizon. Separated from the rest of the crew, he faced a lonely night. It was cold too: it was all too easy to mistake a smudge on the glass for an approaching night fighter, so the rear turret had a square section cut out of the Perspex in front of the gunner's face, called a 'clear-view panel'. The rear gunner was literally flying with a window open. At 20,000 feet temperatures could fall to −30°C and lower, and even his electrically heated suit could not always take the edge off a chill like that. Besides, some rear gunners either did not wear their heated suits or did not plug them in because they found the warmth made them drowsy. Rear gunners were often the only members of the crew to spot an approaching night fighter, and when the long dreary night could be interrupted in a split second it was better to remain alert, even if it meant shivering in Arctic temperatures.

★   ★   ★

There were four main types of British bomber in use at this stage of the war. The newest and most effective was the Avro Lancaster: a huge, sleek machine capable of flying to Berlin and back laden with over six tons of bombs. Its long, cigar-shaped fuselage was punctuated by five Perspex blisters, through which its crew would constantly scan the skies for attackers. Four Rolls-Royce Merlin engines along its wings could carry it to a height of 22,000 feet and above, and at speeds of 266 m.p.h. The Lancaster was unquestionably the best night bomber of the Second World War.

Slightly bigger and more temperamental in the air was the Handley Page Halifax. With a ceiling of 20,000 feet, the Halifax was relatively safe from flak, but its blind spot beneath the back of the aircraft made it vulnerable to fighters coming from behind and below. Despite its impressive ceiling, and top speed of over 275 m.p.h., it could carry only just over half the bomb load of a Lancaster.

The Short Stirling was often described as a 'gentleman's aircraft': it was easy to handle, and capable of absorbing an enormous amount of punishment before it succumbed to flak or fighter fire. Without the waist-high spars that the Lancaster had in its interior, it was also relatively easy to escape from – which was fortunate, because its lamentable ceiling of only 16,000 feet made it the first target of all the German flak batteries. There are tales of Lancaster and Halifax crews cheering when they heard that Stirlings would be accompanying them on an operation, because they drew German fire away from the higher-flying machines.

The last type of aeroplane that flew to Hamburg that night was the twin-engined medium bomber, the Vickers Wellington. This unfortunate aircraft was virtually obsolete by this stage in the war, and seemed to combine all the worst drawbacks of all the four-engined 'heavies'. It was slower, smaller, and had fewer guns to defend itself. It flew at a similar height to the Stirling, but could carry less than half its bomb load. Seventy-three of these aeroplanes had taken off for Hamburg that evening, with a further twelve tasked with minelaying in the Elbe estuary and dropping propaganda leaflets over France.

For the first part of the trip, the main force would also be accompanied by a small force of light bombers: eleven De Havilland Mosquitos would follow them across the North Sea, then peel off to attack alternative targets in Kiel, Lübeck, Bremen and Duisburg. These additional targets were merely diversions, designed to keep the Germans guessing about the main force's true destination.

At first glance such diversionary missions looked extremely dangerous for the crews concerned: bombers are like herd animals – safe in numbers but vulnerable when they venture out alone. If one considers that the Mosquito was made only of plywood, and usually had no defensive armament, then those four diversionary raids looked like a suicide mission. However, Mosquitos were so fast, and capable of flying at such extreme altitudes, that they were virtually untouchable. All would return unscathed to England the next morning.

This, then, was the force that took off from airfields across

England on 24 July. Its first task was to climb as high and as quickly as possible – the higher they were, the safer. As they did so, they set course for their crossing points on the English coast: 4 Group and the Canadians of 6 Group headed towards Hornsea, 1 and 5 Groups made for Mablethorpe, on the coast of Lincolnshire, while 3 Group and the Pathfinders of 8 Group headed for Cromer, in Norfolk.

Over those seaside towns all the separate squadrons in each group would merge into a wide stream heading out to sea. For those in the vanguard it was possible to make out many of the other aircraft filling the sky around them. By now it was well after ten o'clock, but with double summertime bringing the clocks forward two hours the sky was still fairly light, especially to the north and west. For those coming later it was already too dark to make out any of their fellow aeroplanes. Only the occasional blink of green and red navigation lights told them that they were not alone, but as they headed out to sea even those lights were extinguished, rendering almost eight hundred aircraft virtually invisible in the night.

As they made for the darkness of mainland Europe, the atmosphere inside each aeroplane was professional, businesslike. Each member of the crew was left to perform his duties in his own way. In general, strict radio silence was observed, and crews did not speak to each other on the intercoms unless there was something important to report. The only sound was the constant drone of the aircraft engines as they continued to climb as high as they could go, but in the thin, warm air of summer many aeroplanes struggled to reach their operational ceilings.

Leading the bomber stream were the Pathfinders of 8 Group. Behind them, spreading back over almost two hundred miles, was the rest of the force. They were heading to a point about eighty miles from the German coast – 54°45N, 07°00E – where the three separate streams of bombers were to merge into one, then turn towards the south-east and their target. The lead aircraft had already been in the air for two and a half hours. They turned at about twenty past midnight and headed towards the German coast on a bearing of 103°.

RAF route on the
night of 24 July 1943

Route to Hamburg
Route-markers
Aircraft shot down

Ten minutes later the flight engineer in each of the leading aircraft climbed over the main spar into the back of the plane and began to drop the first bundles of Window.[10] The crews had been provided with stop watches and told to throw the bundles down the flare chute at exactly one-minute intervals. The bundles were supposed to disperse into small clouds of paper that would float harmlessly down through the air. In practice, however, the 'machine-like' efficiency called for at the briefing often ended up being a little more chaotic. Sometimes the Window would blow back into the aircraft, filling the air in the back of the plane with metallized paper strips. Once or twice the bundles did not open properly and the solid packets hit other bombers, ripping off aerials or even breaking through the Perspex of a gun turret.[11] Even when the Window dispersed properly, it often blew up on to the mid-upper turrets of the aeroplanes, obscuring the gunner's view. One side of the paper was covered with a black coating that easily rubbed off, and after fifteen minutes or so the plexiglass on the mid-upper turret was so smudged and blackened that the gunner there was effectively blinded. The black coating also came off on the man tasked with throwing it from the plane; many bomb-aimers and flight engineers soon looked like chimney sweeps, covered from head to toe with soot.

Despite the various mishaps, though, most of the crews managed to drop the bundles of metal strips according to plan. As they ploughed on towards the German coast they had no idea whether or not the new device would work, and gradually they became anxious once more. In less than half an hour they would be over Hamburg, and the real test of their new tactics would begin.

★   ★   ★

By now the Germans knew the RAF were coming. A long-range Freya radar station near Ostend had picked up the first aeroplanes heading across the sea at around eleven o'clock, and the defences had been plotting the course of the bomber stream ever since, waiting to see where it turned before committing their night fighters to action.[12] By half past midnight, shortly after the first

planes in the bomber stream had turned towards Hamburg, the
night fighters of several airfields were airborne. Since Hamburg
was now a possible target, at 12.33 a.m. the order was given to
sound the Fliegeralarm sirens.[13]

In 1943 Germany had the most impressive defences of any
country in the world. First came the infamous Kammhuber Line
– a belt of interlinked night-fighter 'boxes' that stretched the length
of the European coast. Each box had its own fighters, which would
patrol that box only, ensuring an evenly spread defence across the
whole line. Hamburg in particular was protected by more than a
dozen airfields.[14] Closer in, there were belts of searchlights, and
dozens of heavy-flak batteries (see Map 1, p. 36). It was a formidable
set-up, and the whole structure was now on high alert, waiting for
the British to arrive.

As the bomber stream approached the coast, it was being
watched closely by the head of the German 2nd Fighter Division,
Generalleutnant Schwabedissen, in his headquarters at Stade airfield. Housed in a giant bomb-proof bunker, Schwabedissen's
central combat station was the nerve-centre of all the defences in
north-west Europe and was a true triumph of German technology.
One of only five control centres in the country, it was nicknamed
the 'Battle Opera House', or the 'Kammhuber Kino', because of
its resemblance to a cinema. Inside, dominating the huge control
room, there was a gigantic frosted-glass screen, about fifty feet
wide, inscribed with a map of Germany. On to it were projected
spots of light, which represented all of the different aeroplanes in
the sky at any one time – white spots to show the enemy planes
approaching, green spots for the German night fighters, and illumi-
nated details of their height, position and direction of flight.

Even the Luftwaffe's commander of fighters, Adolf Galland,
found this feat of technology impressive:

The whole was reminiscent of a huge aquarium lit up, with a multitude
of water-fleas scuttling madly behind the glass walls. Each single dot and
each change to be seen here was the result of reports and observations
from radar sets, aircraft-spotters, listening posts, reconnaissance and

contact planes, or from units in action. They all merged together by telephone or wireless in this centre, to be received, sorted, and within a few minutes transposed into transmittable messages. What was represented here on a giant map was a picture of the air situation . . . with about one minute's delay.[15]

In front of this huge map, on rising steps like those in an amphitheatre, fighter-control officers (*Jägerleitoffiziere*) were seated in several rows, ready to direct their night fighters by radio into the hunt. Above them, on a raised balcony, Generalleutnant Schwabedissen and his staff conducted the battle against the Allied bombers in an unhealthy fog of cigarette smoke, his voiced orders rising above a symphony of ticking teleprinters, humming ventilators and the urgent murmur of telephone operators across the room.

Tonight everyone was watching the screen as avidly as any cinema audience. Schwabedissen had already ordered his night fighters to scramble, and scores of green T-shapes were making their way across the frosted-glass map. Ahead a mass of white dots was making its way towards the German coastline. But something was wrong: while the front of the bomber stream still appeared to be moving forwards, the tail end remained static on the map – it was as if the RAF bomber force was expanding before their eyes.

Up on the balcony, Schwabedissen demanded to know what was going on, but nobody could give him a straight answer. Nervous telephone operators were engaged in urgent conversations with radar stations throughout north-west Germany. The messages they were getting back were always the same. It was impossible: there appeared to be not merely hundreds of bombers approaching but *thousands* – too many for the radar screens to cope with. Some radar sets appeared to have stopped working altogether: instead of registering single, distinct 'blips' on their screens they showed nothing but a general fuzz, as if the bombers were approaching in a solid wall several miles wide.

In the air, the situation was just as confused. Night-fighter pilots who had been following instructions from their fighter-control officers now found themselves being sent round in circles. When it became clear that something was wrong with the ground radar, they began to rely on their Lichtenstein sets – but they, too, were beginning to show false readings, as one German fighter pilot, Wilhelm Johnen, recalled:

It was obvious that no one knew exactly where the enemy was or what his objective would be. An early recognition of the direction was essential so that the night fighters could be introduced as early as possible into the bomber stream. But the radio reports kept contradicting themselves. Now the enemy was over Amsterdam and then suddenly west of Brussels, and a moment later they were reported far out to sea in map square 25. What was to be done? The uncertainty of the ground stations was communicated to the crews . . . No one knew where the British were, but all the pilots were reporting pictures on their screens. I was no exception. At 15,000 feet my sparker announced the first enemy machine on his Li [airborne Lichtenstein radar set] . . . Facius proceeded to report three or four pictures on his screen. I hoped that I would have enough ammunition to deal with them! Then Facius suddenly shouted: 'Tommy flying towards us at a great speed. Distance decreasing . . . 2000 yards, 1,500 . . . 1,000 . . . 500 . . . He's gone.' 'You're crackers, Facius,' I said jestingly. But I soon lost my sense of humour, for this crazy performance was repeated a score of times.[16]

No matter where the pilot flew he made no contact with any bombers: they disappeared, like phantoms, as soon as he approached. Window, it seemed, was having exactly the effect that the British desired.

★　　★　　★

As the leading British Pathfinder aircraft crossed the German coast near Heide, they began to drop the first of their yellow route-maker flares. The idea was to give the bomber stream, which was still spread out all over the sky, a single point to fly through – that way they would be a far more concentrated force as they arrived in Hamburg. However, it was not only the RAF bombers who

saw the flares: a handful of German night fighters in the area
spotted them too. In the absence of anything else to help them find
the bomber stream, they headed towards the light. One managed to
shoot down a Halifax, which fell in flames and exploded over the
sea. A few minutes later a second Halifax was attacked, but this
time the rear gunner returned fire at once, and the German plane
fell, eventually crashing into the ground near Flensburg.[17]

It is easy to summarize such events in a few words, but combat
like this was a desperate affair, especially for British bomber crews.
After more than two hours of silence, a burst of fire could appear
from the darkness and kill seven men in an instant. Crews that
were shot down rarely saw it coming. If they did, a short burst
from one of the gunners was sometimes enough to scare off the
enemy – an alert bomber crew could be just as deadly as the
night fighters, as the combat over the German coast that night
demonstrated. Usually it was the rear gunner, with his clear-vision
panel at the back, who saw the danger first. He would broadcast a
warning to the pilot on the intercom: 'Fighter on the port quarter
– corkscrew port!' The temptation to turn away from an attacker
was strong, but the trick for survival was to turn *into* him so that
he could not follow. Then, for the next thirty seconds or so, the
bomber pilot would have to throw his aircraft about the sky,
hoping that he had dropped out of his attacker's line of sight. As
long as he kept flying in a spiral motion then his enemy would not
be able to keep his guns trained on him for more than an instant.
A minute later the bomber would be back on course, with nothing
to show for the experience but the mess of charts and instruments
that had been thrown off the navigator's desk, and the faint smell
of fear in the aircraft.

That night there would be very few such incidents. Most of the
German night fighters remained tied to their 'boxes', unable to
locate the bomber stream amid the confusion. The aeroplanes
continued unmolested across the coast, and down to their next
turning point above Kellinghausen, a few minutes north-north-
west of Hamburg.

Some of the crews dropped propaganda leaflets on German

towns along the way. More would drop leaflets later, either over the target or on the way home. Leafleting was an unpopular pastime in the higher levels of Bomber Command, and staff officers joked that its only effect was to supplement German civilians' rations of toilet paper. (They were only half joking: when middle-class Hamburg housewives were reduced to cutting squares of toilet paper from biscuit wrappers, this important commodity was in short supply.)[18] Tonight's leaflets showed a picture of RAF bombers flying over the burning streets of Dortmund, with the caption '*Die Festung Europa hat kein Dach*' ('Fortress Europe has no roof'). To press the message home, one or two airmen emptied the contents of their urine bottles on to the leaflets before dropping them out – a petty act of contempt to add to the injuries they were about to inflict.[19]

Eventually, after almost three hours in the air, the navigators of the leading Pathfinders recognized the outline of the city on their H2S sets: they had arrived. As they began their final approach to Hamburg, the crews of more than seven hundred bombers braced themselves for the onslaught of flak and searchlights they expected to encounter above the most heavily defended target in northern Germany. But the nightmare never materialized. There were fifty-four heavy and twenty-six light flak batteries defending the city, and twenty-two searchlight batteries,[20] but they were all reliant on the same 'Würzburg' radar sets that were being disrupted so efficiently by Window. In some cases the battery commanders could hear the drone of aeroplanes in the sky above them, yet when they turned to their radar operators for confirmation the response was the same as before: instead of clear, distinct pulses showing where the aircraft were, the radar screens were a mass of flashing zigzag curves, making it impossible to distinguish anything specific. Some batteries began to shoot random, unaimed barrages into the sky; others remained silent. Hamburg's defences had been blinded.

For some of the more experienced bomber crews, the sight that greeted them when they arrived over the target was a dream come true. 'Under normal circumstances the searchlights kept a fairly accurate pinpoint on any aircraft,' says Leonard Cooper, a flight engineer with 7 Squadron (Pathfinder Force), 'but on this occasion they were just waving around all over the place.'[21] Ted Edwards, a pilot from 100 Squadron, was equally impressed: 'We were quite amazed to see the searchlights just weaving around the countryside over enemy territory. They hadn't got a clue where we were.'[22]

For those sceptics who had doubted that Window would work, it was a moment of revelation. 'They said that Window was going to upset the German radar when we went in, but we more or less said, "Oh, *yes*?"' remembers Leonard Bradfield, a bomb-aimer with 49 Squadron. 'But when we actually got there it was *happening*! We were absolutely delighted.'[23] He continues:

It was absolutely fantastic. We came up the Elbe and could see the river quite clearly. The radar-controlled blue master searchlights were standing absolutely upright and the white ones were weaving around, just search-ing. There were no night fighters because they were all in their boxes waiting to be given the vectors. The flak was just in a block over the target . . . It was the only time on any bomb run I was able to have 20 seconds completely unimpeded, without being stalked by the flak.[24]

It is important to note that although the flak was fired blindly, the sheer number of shells aimed into the air meant that several aircraft in the vanguard of the attack were hit. Later on two planes would be shot down, with no survivors.[25] Not everyone managed to escape the searchlights either. Gordon Moulton-Barrett, who was on his first operation as a 'second dickie' pilot, remembers seeing a Lancaster coned by lights: he watched as the aircraft dropped vertically downwards, falling 10,000 feet in a matter of seconds, before pulling out of the dive and disappearing once more into the safety of darkness. To the impressionable Moulton-Barrett it seemed like a brilliant, death-defying manoeuvre, and he had to suppress the urge to applaud.[26] For the Lancaster and its crew, however, it had been a matter of survival: a steep dive was the only way to escape a cone of searchlights.

With just a few minutes to go before zero hour (0100), the

Pathfinders were sizing up the dark city below them. As previously mentioned, the plan was to drop three different kinds of markers for the main force to aim at: yellow target indicators (TIs) to start with, at Z–3, along with flares to light up the city for the subsequent planes; red ones next, aimed visually, between Z–2 and zero hour; and green ones to back up the reds for the rest of the raid. In the event, things did not go quite according to plan. While the marking began exactly on time, led by a Lancaster of 83 Squadron, many of the first group were eight or nine minutes late. Without their flares to light the city, many of the next group did not drop their red TIs at all. Fortunately for the city centre, those that did fall were fairly spread out. There were four main groups: some fell in the Baaken dock area south of the river, near the Grasbrook gas-works, another group in the east of the city, between Wandsbeker Chaussee and Hasselbrook railway station, and two more salvos in the west, in Altona.[27]

For the few minutes before the bombs began to fall, the skies over Hamburg were lit by a spectacular firework display – a prelude to the coming bonfire – as the beautiful pyrotechnic candles cascaded out of each TI and floated gently to earth. The Germans called the TIs *Tannenbäume* – Christmas trees – a homely term that described their beauty, but not their terrible purpose.

As the bright lights drifted down the first Lancasters of the main force made their bombing runs. The aircraft were effectively in the hands of the bomb-aimers now. As the target was sighted, the navigators would hand over responsibility to the bomb-aimer, who would guide the pilot to the correct point directly over the red glow of the TIs. Leonard Bradfield remembers the run-in clearly:

It was a brilliant night. You could see the ground absolutely crystal clear. You could see the outline of the city, and you could also see where the markers had gone down . . . To bring her up in line directly over the target took some twenty seconds straight and level. Then we let the bombs go. We had the 4,000-pounder as usual, and we had four 1,000-pounders, one of which was on a delayed action. Then we had the ninety-four-pound thermite incendiary bombs. Owing to their light weight we had to drop them quite early in the sequence. But the 4,000-pounder was the master – you could really feel the 'cookie' go. I'm talking in terms of under half a minute from the first to last being dropped . . . We then had to fly another twenty seconds for our photo flash to fall so it could take a photograph of where our bombs landed.[28]

It was this brief period over the aiming point that was the most nerve-racking for most crews. A minute could seem like a lifetime when the crews were obliged to fly straight and level, a perfect target for the flak guns below. The bomb-aimer would direct the pilot by shouting above the drone of the engines: 'Left, left . . . steady . . . bombs gone!' The leap of the aircraft as the heavy 4,000-pound 'cookie' fell away was echoed by a leap of hearts into throats – and as soon as the photo flash had gone the pilot would veer away from the immediate danger area and head for the darkness beyond. But tonight, with the city's defences in such disarray, even this most hazardous of times was relatively safe. As one pilot recalls: 'I remember thinking, it's going to be great from now on, for the rest of my tour! You could see other Lancs silhouetted against the fires all just going steadily on, whereas in the past people would have been weaving quite madly. Everyone seemed to have come to the same conclusion: from now on it was going to be easy.'[29]

During the next hour, more than seven hundred planes would pass over the west of the city, and many pilots reported seeing the sky filled with planes. In such circumstances the danger of collision was very real, and many crews had to endure the horror of seeing bombers flying directly above them, bomb doors open, about to drop their load. Tonight, fortunately, no one was harmed by a fellow bomber – but one Stirling collided with a Ju88 night fighter as he dived to avoid a searchlight. Geoff Turner and his 75 Squadron crew managed to limp home, but the night fighter was almost certainly finished. It turned on its back and fell headlong towards Hamburg, to be recorded later as a 'probable' victory to the British crew.[30]

⋆   ⋆   ⋆

Between one and two o'clock in the morning of Sunday, 25 July, 2,300 tons of bombs were dropped on to Hamburg, a new and frightening world record for a single attack. A lot of the weight was made up of huge high-explosive bombs: 8,000-pound 'block-busters' and 4,000-pound 'cookies', but it was undoubtedly the incendiaries that did most damage. The fires started by the first waves made it easier for the later waves to find their way to the target, and those in turn stoked the fires further. A total of 350,412 individual incendiary bombs fell in and around the city, starting countless fires – again, a new world record.[31]

The official British intelligence report of the time announces such figures with a certain pride, which was certainly echoed in the hearts and minds of most of the crews who took part in the attack. Once they had dropped their bombs and turned away to the south of the city, they had the opportunity to see the results of their work. The comments they noted in their log books afterwards were almost always the same: 'Good trip', 'A very good prang', 'Very nearly perfection'. Scores of crews in the latter stages of the attack reported seeing very large explosions in the docks. By the time the last Halifaxes of 6 Group had dropped their bombs, the whole of the west of the city had become 'a mass of raging fires with black smoke rising to 19,000 feet'. Crews in the final wave reported the merging of all the separate fires into 'one large conflagration spreading over the whole city'. It was so huge it could be seen by British Mosquitos flying on dummy attacks over Duisburg, 140 miles away.[32]

It is easy to begrudge these men their feeling of pride at the destruction they were wreaking, but it is foolish to be surprised by it. Their job was to wage war, and tonight they had done their job well. For many it was nothing new. They had seen similar scenes over Dortmund, Wuppertal, Cologne and Essen. They had seen the war from the other side too, in London, Coventry, Sheffield, Plymouth and many other cities across Britain. For most of the young men in the bombers, tonight was a logical extension of all that had gone before – the concept of 'an eye for an eye' expanded to the scale of whole nations. And we must remember that

RAF bombs dropped on Hamburg
on the night of 24 July

the crews were not only British. The Polish airmen in Bomber
Command had a reputation for being particularly bloodthirsty,
revelling in any opportunity to avenge the rape of their homeland.
Canadians, Australians, New Zealanders and South Africans, who
had never seen an attack on their home soil, were there for reasons
that were more vague: a principle to be upheld, or a sense of
loyalty to the Empire and 'home country'. Many had joined up as
volunteers simply for the excitement of flying. Their only thought
now was to get home safely to their beds, one day closer to their
next period of leave, and one operation closer to the magic total
of thirty.

Mixed with their satisfaction was relief that the main part of the
job was over, as they headed back into the safety of darkness. But
their relief was misplaced: this was perhaps the most dangerous
time of all. Silhouetted by the fires behind them, their guard down
because of the natural complacency that follows such bursts of
adrenaline, they were easy targets for night fighters. And now, at
last, the night fighters were arriving. Once the attack on Hamburg
had begun, many fighter controllers had abandoned their radar sets
and told their crews to head straight for the city. Some had seen
the fires and flown in on their own initiative. By half past one in
the morning, the skies on the way out of Hamburg were becoming
far more dangerous than they had been going in.

The more disciplined crews would not drop their vigilance for
a moment. The skipper would return to zigzagging the plane, and
warn the gunners not to look into the fires below for fear of losing
their night vision. Navigators would set course along the designated
route, roughly parallel to the route in, to take advantage of the
safety provided by the bomber stream. Flight engineers and bomb-
aimers, their job done, would return to dropping bundles of
Window down the flare chute, lest they lose the advantage they
had gained over the enemy radar. And the wireless operators would
continue broadcasting 'Tinsel', the sound of their engines, on
the German frequencies to block out any radio communication
between their rivals in the air.

However, not all crews were quite so disciplined. Nervous and inexperienced pilots ignored the laid-down route and made a bee-line straight for the coast. It was an understandable temptation, particularly for those new pilots and navigators who had never experienced flak before. Some rear gunners could not help staring, mesmerized, into the inferno on the ground behind them, only to find that when they did tear away their eyes they were effectively blind in the darkness. Some crew members lit cigarettes, which they would puff between breaths on their oxygen masks, while others would open their flying rations with a yawn, exhausted by anxiety.

Almost half of that night's casualties were shot down by night fighters on the journey home – and of those, most had been off track. Without the benefit of thousands of bundles of Window to mask their movements, they had been located by German radar and summarily dealt with. Some, like the crew of Flight Officer J. S. Cole, were lucky to escape. After being picked up by search-lights over Cuxhaven on the coast, Cole was attacked by a Messer-schmitt Me109 – a day fighter – but was able to dive away without being hit.[33] Likewise Sergeant S. Grzeskowiak was on his first operation when his Wellington was attacked by a Junkers Ju88 night fighter. He managed to escape after being hit, but was leaking petrol all the way home, and eventually had to crash land at Trusthorpe in Lincolnshire. Those crews lived to tell the tale, for now at least.[34]

Others were not so lucky. Wallace McIntosh, a rear gunner with 207 Squadron, saw a Lancaster 'blazing like hell' a thousand yards away as a German fighter came in repeatedly to attack it. As the plane fell out of the sky he saw five parachutes open, but the Lancaster's rear gunner, obviously trapped inside the plane, carried on firing till the end. 'I have never seen such bravery,' McIntosh recalls. 'The poor bugger was still sitting there firing away and the fighter went back in to have another blast at him, with the gunner still defiant, and the Lancaster blew up.'[35]

For the vast majority of crews, however, the journey home was as uneventful as the journey in. By four o'clock in the morning the first of the Pathfinders had already landed at their bases, and the main bomber stream was crossing the coast into England. This was the last moment of danger for the RAF crewmen. For some of those who had been hit by flak there would be an emergency landing at an unfamiliar airfield. There was always the chance that returning planes could be attacked by German intruders, but the biggest fear was the possibility of ground fog, which could make landing hazardous. Tonight, at the height of summer, the likelihood of that was not great – but even in clear conditions it could be dangerous landing in the dark. Despite the wealth of his experience, the CO of 83 Squadron, John Searby, collided with a Lancaster of 156 Squadron as the two came in to land at Warboys. Fortunately both aircraft landed safely.

After taxiing back to their original positions on the airfield, the crews would emerge from their planes, grinning with relief. Transports would take them to the station buildings where they would be ushered in for debriefing. Blinking in the light, and glad of the chance for a cup of tea and a smoke, the men would sit down at a table with the intelligence officer to tell their stories. Every aspect of their trip was noted: the effects of Window, the weather conditions over the target, how easy it had been to spot the target indicators, how extensive the fires in the city and so on. If they had been attacked by enemy fighters, or seen anything unusual, special care was taken to record the details. Only when this process was over were the men allowed to have breakfast and go to bed, exhausted by their long night in the air. For many the whole process would be repeated the following night: in the war over northern Europe the summer months were all too short, and Bomber Command had to make use of every crew it could while conditions allowed.

★ ★ ★

That, then, was the pattern of a single night in the life of the Bomber Command crews – a typical operation made extraordinary by the introduction of a new weapon. Window had been a phenomenal success, and would continue to save the lives of RAF airmen for the next six weeks, before the Germans were able to counter its effects. Many crews have since thanked their luck that they were flying in the summer of 1943, because they were able, during that brief period of relative safety, to clock up enough operations to finish their tour. This simple, radar-jamming device had secured their future.

As they made their way to breakfast, however, few were thinking of the future. Six hours of heightened senses and intense emotions had left them worn out, and every one was now ready for bed. Their reward for the night's efforts was a huge meal of bacon and eggs – as much as they could eat – but as soon as it was finished they returned to their quarters. Some were so exhausted they were unable even to undress before they fell into bed.

While they slept, the day was only just beginning for everyone else at the station. Out on the airfield the erks were already hard at work to repair any damage to the squadrons' precious aeroplanes. Intelligence staff were developing and analysing the bomb photographs taken by each, and collating the information in a report for Group Headquarters. Their reports today would be upbeat. Despite a fair amount of 'creepback' over the countryside to the north-west of the city – a phenomenon caused by successive crews dropping their bombs marginally early – it was plain that the bombing had been very concentrated in certain areas, and a great deal of damage had been caused.

Over the next few days reconnaissance planes would fly high over Hamburg taking daytime photographs of the damage to enhance the intelligence reports, but even now, with what they knew already, the atmosphere at airfields across the country was optimistic. Casualties had been low (only twelve planes missing out of 792), and it seemed to many that a new era in the bombing war had begun.

Few could have guessed where this new era would lead.

10. The Devastation Begins

The fronts draw nearer, the nights grow longer . . . the Luftwaffe is
helpless, German cities are defenceless . . . Each night brings the threat of
devastation closer. It is only a question of time.
British propaganda leaflet, 1943[1]

To claim that the people of Hamburg had no inkling of what was about to befall them on the first night of Operation Gomorrah would not be quite true. Most had heard of what had happened to the cities of the Ruhr over the preceding months, and while German radio and newspaper reports were deliberately vague on the details, the city's anxious housewives allowed their imaginations to fill in the gaps. Rumours abounded. People told each other furtive stories about factories and houses being blown sky-high, men and women rushing frantically for the rivers, their clothes on fire. Some claimed that the British had deliberately targeted the cathedrals at Cologne and Aachen in an attempt to destroy German heritage. Others swore that when the Americans bombed Kiel and Flensburg they had dropped fountain pens and other everyday articles filled with explosives.[2]

The Allies did whatever they could to fuel such fears. BBC broadcasts to the continent became progressively more triumphant in tone.[3] British and American planes dropped hundreds of thousands of leaflets on northern Germany, many of which fell on Hamburg. These gave a variety of lurid statistics about what had happened to other German cities, and went on to imply that the people of Hamburg would be next to feel the devastating bite of the bombs.[4]

Despite all this, however, many people refused to believe that the bombers were heading their way, for the simple reason that they did not *want* to believe it. After four long years of fighting they were sick of war, and some even hoped that the Allies would hurry up and invade so that the whole thing could be over quickly.[5] More rumours claimed that the Allies were being deliberately lenient on Hamburg because they would need the city when they invaded.[6] Regardless of everything that had happened since 1939, Hamburg was still largely an anglophile city: many people could not bring themselves to believe that their friends and allies of the past 150 years would ever have the will to inflict such suffering on them.[7]

Besides, the city had not been targeted properly for four and a half months. What few alarms there had been recently had all proved false. Despite constant warnings from the authorities to remain alert, while the skies were clear and the sun shone, it was easy to pretend that they were safe from attack.

*   *   *

Were it not for the war, the day before the bombers arrived would have been idyllic. It was a hot Saturday in July, and the whole city seemed to have come outdoors to enjoy the sunshine. Hamburg had been experiencing an unusually lengthy spell of glorious weather, and the long, warm days reminded people of peacetime. Now that the school holidays had begun the city's many parks were thronging with children playing *Völkerball* or *Kippel-kappel*, and the open-air swimming baths at Aschberg and Ohlsdorf were filled with teenagers splashing and calling to one another as they dived from the railings. Down by the Elbe, off-duty workers rolled up their trousers and strolled through the shallow water, or rested on the river's sandy banks beneath the trees. Old couples walked arm in arm along the Alster, or sunned themselves on their balconies and in their gardens. In the absence of any air raids the atmosphere in the city was fairly calm, perhaps even relaxed. A gentle breeze blew in off the river, caressing the spires of the churches, while those in the city streets below went about their everyday business undisturbed.[8]

Despite the shortages, there were still plenty of ways to relax in the city. At the beginning of July the famous Althoff Circus had been in Wandsbek, delighting children with a combination of clowning and breathtaking acrobatics. Lovers of horse-sports were looking forward to the Preis von Deutschland at Farmsen Race-course, and the Hitler Youth were holding their area champion-ships in canoeing. In the evenings there was also a wide variety of entertainment. A Hungarian dance orchestra had been playing in the Orchideen Café, and Strauss's *Die Zigeunerbaron* was on at the Volksoper on the Reeperbahn. The cinemas showed a variety of escapist films, mostly adventure movies or romances such as *Der dunkel Tag* (*The Dark Day*) and *Du gehörst zu mir* (*You Happened to Me*).[9]

There was double summertime in Germany, as there was in Britain, so it stayed light in the evenings almost until ten o'clock. As the fleet of RAF bombers took off across the North Sea, many Hamburgers were coming out of the cinemas and theatres. Others were still finishing their evening meal, or sitting out on their balconies to enjoy a cool drink before bedtime. Those who didn't have to get up for work on Sunday celebrated the end of the week with friends or family, perhaps even with sons or husbands on leave from the front, but towards midnight most of the city was turning in. It was hot and sultry, so many people had dragged mattresses out into the courtyards to sleep in the open air.[10] As they lay looking up at the bright stars above them, the war seemed far away.

Awake or asleep, the whole city was brought back to reality when the quiet of the night was broken by the sound of sirens. The noise did not produce panic – in fact, it was greeted with little more than weary sighs. The alarms had already gone off once that night, at around nine thirty, but they had been cancelled ten minutes later. Now, at half past midnight, people expected a repeat performance and many rolled over to go back to sleep. Hamburgers were used to sirens: in the previous three years they had endured no less than 318 air-raid warnings, the vast major-ity of which were false alarms. Even the actual attacks they had experienced – 137 in total – were mostly fairly minor, especially during the past twelve months.[11] Familiarity had bred complacency.

In Lokstedt, in the north-east of the city, Wanda Chantler was struggling to wake a room full of women and convince them to come to the air-raid shelter. She was a twenty-year-old Pole who worked in a forced-labour camp packing cans of fish for soldiers at the front. As first-aid officer at her barracks, she was obliged to go to the shelter, but few of the others would join her.

First of all there was a great big howl of sirens. And the girls all said, 'Oh, it's like this every night – nothing will happen.' They went off so often, those sirens: we sometimes got them twice a night. We all got so fed up, particularly those that were on the day shift, because they had no sleep – the planes never came in the daytime, they always came in the night. But these girls said, 'We're not getting up. Nothing will happen.'[12]

Reluctantly, she and five other women trudged down to the makeshift underground shelter on the other side of the compound – a move that probably saved her life.

Elsewhere, other Hamburgers were showing similar reluctance to go to the shelters. Hannah Kelson was fourteen, and had a typical teenager's response to any suggestion that she should leave her bed just because the RAF might be coming: 'Let them come, I don't care.'[13] For some it was the conditions in the bunkers kept them away. Martha Bührick, a fifty-seven-year-old teacher who lived in Barmbek preferred to sit on a stool in the doorway of her bathroom rather than go to the 'community bedlam' of the air-raid bunkers.[14] Some of the shelters were uncomfortable because people brought as much as they could carry 'just in case' – not only jewellery and important papers, but suitcases, pet dogs, cats and even chickens.[15] It is not surprising that many wanted to avoid the shelters unless it was absolutely necessary.

There were other reasons to stay above ground: a raid on the city could be a spectacular event, and many Hamburgers admit that they often stood in their doorways or on their balconies during an attack to watch the progress of the bombs. The novelist Hans

Erich Nossack recorded watching some women on the roof of a neighbour's house applauding as a British plane, caught in search-lights, was shot down.[16] Civilians have always turned out to watch battles from a supposedly safe distance – however, as Nossack makes clear, the true reason that they watched was not to see the battle in the sky but the unfolding destruction of their city. 'I had one unequivocal wish,' he says. 'Let it get really bad!'[17]

Tonight Nossack was not on his balcony to witness events: he was on holiday in the countryside, just to the south of the city. Like many others he was unmoved by the sound of the sirens. It was the noise of aeroplanes humming overhead that snapped him into action.

I jumped out of bed and ran barefoot out of the house into this sound that hovered like an oppressive weight between the clear constellations and the dark earth, not here and not there but everywhere in space . . . One didn't dare take a breath for fear of inhaling it. It was the sound of eighteen hundred aeroplanes [*sic*] approaching Hamburg from the south at an unimaginable height. We had already experienced two hun-dred or even more air raids, some of them very heavy, but this was something completely new. And yet there was an immediate recog-nition: this was what everyone had been waiting for, what had hung for months like a shadow over everything we did, making us weary. It was the end.[18]

In the centre of town many others were also beginning to realize that this was the full-scale raid they had been dreading. State Secretary Georg Ahrens was now broadcasting a warning over the radio on all channels: 'Go immediately to your air-raid shelters! Enemy bombs may drop within the next three minutes!'[19] Soon the streets were busy with people making their way to the public shelters. There was still plenty of time, but they ran anyway, out of a desire to get a good place in the bunker and genuine fear for their lives.

For those who were late, further confirmation arrived of what lay in store for them. Cascades of bright red and yellow marker bombs, and later green ones too, fell over the city, filling the night with a miraculous glow. For one woman at least, on fire duty at one of the city's department stores, the *Tannenbäume* were a sight she would never forget: 'I stood there looking out of the hatch at the wonderful sky. This was something one would otherwise never see . . . The whole sky above Hamburg alight – prettier, much prettier than a firework display.'[20]

Sixteen-year-old Gotthold Soltwedel, who was serving as a flak helper on the huge flak tower in the centre of town, also saw it:

I can still remember the first 'Christmas trees' exactly. Dazzling coloured flames hung over us on little parachutes; and likewise on the ground, in the middle of the Heiligengeistfeld, colourful incendiaries lay as markers for the bombers. I can also still hear the first bomb howling down. It was very near. As if on command we charged away from the guns and into the entrance of the bunker, knocking our *Leutnant* to the floor in the process. He screamed at us dreadfully and called us cowards.[21]

By now there were very few people out in the open – even the majority of fire wardens had taken cover, coming out intermittently to conduct quick patrols of the buildings. Earlier in the year, Goebbels had discussed with Hitler the idea that fire wardens should be stationed on the roofs of houses during air raids so that they could combat incendiary bombs as soon as they fell, but he soon realized that this would cause too many casualties.[22] In general, only official observers and those manning flak batteries were around to see the sheer mass of marker bombs, incendiaries and the spectacular explosions of the 4,000-pound 'cookies' and 8,000-pound 'blockbusters'.

From his flak battery in the north east of the city, Rudolf Schurig had a panoramic view of the unfolding situation:

We soon saw anti-aircraft fire at eight o'clock, and then they were there: direction Eimsbüttel, Altona. The first *Tannenbäume* fell there, a glowing green hail of fire, which was to mark the target for the following aircraft. And suddenly the sky above that district was as light as day. A large number of bright parachute flares, which ignite very low down and slowly drop, lit up the district as if it were an enormous freight depot, lit by many flood lamps. Here the first anti-aircraft shells were fired, the first of our new artillery. How it thundered! . . . At each volley we had a feeling of security. We would show the Tommies what it meant to attack Hamburg, our Hamburg![23]

Things started to go wrong when the effects of the RAF's new radar-jamming device, Window, took hold. As Rudolf Schurig was soon to discover, his earlier sense of security had been misplaced:

Everything seemed to be going well, as we had practised in exercises and battle hundreds of times. But suddenly our radar apparatus stopped working. This happened regularly to this highly sensitive machinery, and would quickly be fixed; in the meantime we would switch to the neighbouring battery. But they were unable to give us any information, as their radar was also broken . . . It was then confirmed that none of the radar in Hamburg was functioning; we did not yet know why . . . A paralysing terror began to creep over us. We felt like someone who has been given a rifle to defend himself, but who is blindfolded at the same time.[24]

For Johann Johannsen, who was manning a flak battery in Altona, things were even worse. Altona was directly beneath the RAF marker flares, and was about to receive the full force of the bombs.

High above us we could hear the drone of the enemy machines. Suddenly countless flares were above us, so that the whole city was lit up in a magically bright light . . . With incredible swiftness the disaster was suddenly upon us. Before and behind our battery heavy chunks of metal were striking. Howling and hissing, fire and iron were falling from the sky. The whole city was lit up in a sea of flames! With dogged fury we remained at our guns, exposed to the raging force of the attack. Everyone looked for something to hold on to, so as not to be hurled down by the pressure of the exploding bombs. Every now and then I cast another look over towards my house. I skipped a breath – a column of fire shot up high – everything was in flames![25]

Johannsen was in the unenviable position of being able to see his house from the flak position. Bound by duty to remain at his post, he was powerless to react when he saw his home on fire: the best he could do was to pray that his family had not been killed and continue firing at the enemy. In any case, with bombs raining around him there was plenty to occupy him here. Moments later he was startled by a terrible howling above him, and an incendiary bomb hurtled down exactly between his two flak guns: it crashed through the roof of the building and set fire to the fourth floor below. Despite injuries to his hands and face from exploding shards of glass, Johannsen was still not given permission to leave his post and check his family – the flak battery needed all the men it could get. Despite physical pain and mounting anxiety he remained at the guns until after the all-clear was sounded.

*   *   *

For some who were sheltering in bunkers and cellars, things were almost as terrifying as they were for those outside. The difference was that while the flak gunners at least had a role to play, those in the shelters could do nothing but sit and wait. The tension and uncertainty that built up over several hours became almost unbearable.

Hiltgunt Zassenhaus had been studying for her university exams at home when the alarms went off. She lived in the north-west of the city so the bunker where she and her family took shelter was beneath the flight path of the bombers as they approached. At the beginning of the attack the shelter was virtually empty, and there was space to relax and reread a letter from her brother Björn. 'Then came a sudden flicker of the lamps, a roar, an explosion. Was it inside or outside? The light went out. My pocket torch fell to the ground. The pram rolled towards me, set in movement by the shaking of the bunker. I jumped up. The light flickered a couple of times – then another explosion – and all was dark. I fell on my knees, my head in my hands.'[26]

The sound of the bombs was terrifying, but it was perhaps even more frightening when the bomb was so close that it was no longer audible. As another woman who lived through this series of raids explains, the bombs became truly terrifying when one stopped hearing and started to *feel* them. 'Whenever a person hears a "singing" or "whistling", it doesn't matter if he is in a cellar or in a living-room, the impact of the bomb is some distance away. But woe betide you if you can feel the air pressure blast on your ears (very unpleasant); then the bombs are falling directly in the vicinity. One hears no booming, nothing, only this terrible blast of air pressure.'[27]

In Hiltgunt Zassenhaus's bunker one such wave of pressure blew the internal cover off the ventilation shaft, and the iron doors of the bunker groaned under the strain. The girl cowering inside was paralysed with fear. Once it became obvious that this was a full-scale attack, scores of other people arrived, desperate to escape the nightmare in the streets. Within a short time Hiltgunt's bunker was overflowing with shocked and frightened people: 'One explosion followed another. Suddenly from outside a despairing hammering on the bunker door – wild screams tore the night. Someone opened the door, and the crowd fell in like the possessed; they screamed to one another and struggled for breath, and the block walls echoed with the howling of children and the wailing of women. Over all droned the voice of Herr Braun [the bunker warden]: "Calm down! We have space for everyone!" '[28] Beneath the seemingly endless explosions Hiltgunt lost all sense of time and, in the pitch darkness, all sense of space. She was aware only of the heaving mass of humanity around her. 'Crammed together in the darkness, we became just a single mass of bodies, and at each explosion we swayed with the shaking bunker walls.'[29]

On the first night of bombing the conditions inside some bunkers were appalling. Many of the structures were little more than a series of narrow tunnels in the ground, with wooden benches along their concrete walls. Even the larger, overground bunkers were often extremely cramped. They became so overcrowded that sometimes they were reserved exclusively for women and children, while some over-zealous bunker wardens also excluded foreign workers. There were simply not enough places to go round.

Paul Elingshausen, who witnessed the bombing that night, was shocked by the air-raid shelters. After trying, and failing, to save his house from the hail of incendiary bombs, he eventually joined his wife and two young children in the nearby bunker.

Imagine around a thousand people crammed into the small rooms, a real heat inside, sweat running down our bodies, the bunker full of smoke from outside, not a drop of water to drink, no food and no light. The electricity went straight away. Torches were all flat; the few tallow candles were soon finished. And the whole time there was such an atmosphere; outside the bombs roared, often so close that the bunker shook. Can you imagine this with women and babies?[30]

Despite the conditions, few complained. They were aware that the alternative – to weather the storm outside – was infinitely worse. Occasionally those near the doors would hear reports on what was happening outside as those on fire duty returned with messages for the bunker warden. In general, no news was good news. Fire wardens rarely beat on a shelter door unless it was time for everyone to evacuate the shelter.

★   ★   ★

Descriptions of what it was like to be in the streets at the time of the bombardment are rare, for the simple reason that few were foolish enough to risk it. With more than thirteen hundred tons of high-explosive bombs falling on the city, there was the strong likelihood of being caught in the blasts. Also, incendiary bombs struck the ground at high speed, and the most fearsome spilled liquid phosphorus as they landed. There was also the threat of being hit by falling masonry.

Wanda Chantler was one of the first to discover why it was so important to seek shelter during an air raid. She was sitting in the makeshift earth bomb shelter with the handful of women she had managed to rouse from their beds earlier when 'Suddenly a gust of wind blew the door in. There was a terrific noise. It was like a winter's night when the wind comes howling through the door and through the window, and you sit in the kitchen hoping it will go away – that sort of noise. And this wind blew our wooden door right open and we were exposed to a terrific blast of hot air. Until then we didn't hear the bombs falling. We didn't even *know* they were falling.'[31]

The blast knocked Wanda off her feet, and the other girls had to help her up. Shaken by the explosion, they huddled in the open doorway wondering what to do. Since their shelter no longer seemed to provide much protection they decided to venture back across the compound to see if the other women were all right. But as soon as they stepped through the door they saw that 'The barracks was not there. It just was not there. I looked, and then I looked down, and it was all in a heap. That was all that was left of the barracks . . . We stood, the six of us, and we didn't know what to do.'

Numbed by shock, they did not move for a while, but eventually they were drawn to the rubble that had once been their sleeping quarters by cries: 'It was light, you could see everything, because it was burning, because the firebombs were falling down as well, and the phosphor bombs. We saved lots of girls, but some of them died. We just kept pulling them out of the rubble. There were bits of flesh everywhere. Bits of flesh. And there was one arm, just an arm, sticking out of the debris. One hundred and twenty-three girls died that night.'

Throughout Hamburg, similar destruction was being wreaked on countless other streets and houses. While those who had sought shelter in the larger public bunkers were generally safe, many more people had hidden in the cellars of the larger houses. When one of these received a direct hit, or caught fire, those in the cellar often found their exit blocked by rubble or flames. In such cases they could only escape by breaking through to a neighbouring cellar in the hope that there might still be a way out.

Sometimes the only option was to run through the fires, the most terrifying choice of all. Although he was only a small child at the time, Klaus Müller remembers doing exactly that. He lived with his parents and grandparents, who owned a milk shop on Marthastrasse, right in the centre of one of the worst-hit areas, and was sheltering with his family in a cellar beneath his grandfather's apartment. As the bombing subsided, it became apparent that the whole house was on fire, and that the only way out was through a burning passageway into the inner courtyard. Fortunately, Klaus's grandfather had kept several milk churns filled with water in their cellar for just such an emergency. 'As a small child one remembers everything as being far larger – it was probably only a few metres – but it was an inferno. The entire entrance was filled with flames . . . My grandfather and the other men poured ten milk churns of water into the passageway, and this created a small path through which we could pass.'[32]

As he and the rest of the group escaped through the inner courtyard to the street outside, they found the whole of Martha-strasse on fire – not only the houses but the asphalt on the road. Beyond, they could see Bellealliancestrasse and the Eimsbüttler Chaussee where there was a small park, which would be safe, but to get to it they had to run along the pavement beside the burning road. It was only twenty metres, but by the time they got there Klaus's clothes were alight – his parents had to beat out the flames, then carry him to safety in the park.

A few streets away, nine-year-old Liselotte Gerke was sheltering in a cellar on the Eimsbüttler Marktplatz. The street was home to a large tram depot, and tonight a line of stationary trams was nose to tail along the centre of the road. As Liselotte came out of her shelter she saw that while her side of the street was relatively untouched by the bombs, the opposite side was burning, and scores of people were trying to cross the road to escape the flames. But the trams were in the way, and there wasn't time for them all to clamber into the cars and out the other side. The next day, when she and her friends went out to investigate the damage to the trams, she stumbled on a pair of small, charred corpses. 'This was the moment the war started for me. It was the first time I had ever seen anything like it.'[33]

*   *   *

Descriptions like these are merely snapshots of what people experienced that night. The bombs spread over the entire west of the city, and in many places to the east and south. Tens of thousands of people were affected, and since the bombs were indiscriminate, women and children found themselves caught up in the fire and explosions just as frequently as the city's workforce, who were the ostensible target of the attack. Even political prisoners and forced labourers such as Wanda Chantler were affected. Terrifying though their ordeal was, however, the bombing raid was no worse than many others that had taken place in other parts of Germany. Despite the widespread destruction, most people escaped with their lives, and even their belongings, intact. Hamburg had not yet been made special by its ordeal – it was just another name on the long list of towns that had suffered heavy bombing raids.

That said, the death toll was extraordinarily high. Early estimates claimed that about fifteen hundred people died during this raid – far more than in any other previous attack on the city – and tens of thousands more were now homeless.[34] For a city that had made such a huge effort to ready itself for an attack like this, the figures represented a crushing defeat.

According to the official police report on the disaster, the performance of the emergency services had been exemplary, but in the heat of battle it was inevitable that many of the drills that had been practised so often did not go according to plan. Hans Brunswig worked in the technical division of the Hamburg fire service, and noted that some of the Nazi Party volunteers did not follow the drills properly, and were content to muddle through.[35] Many eyewitnesses on the night say the same thing: Erwin Garvens, for example, noted in his diary that it was almost impossible to put out the fires in his neighbourhood because of a lack of leadership and direction. While the women co-operated admirably, many men, particularly the soldiers on leave, were quick to abandon burning buildings to their fate.[36]

To be fair, however, the huge destruction in the city, including the severing of many water mains, made it almost impossible for even the best-trained fire-fighters to do what they were supposed to do. Paul Elingshausen, the deputy air-raid warden of his block, spent almost two hours fighting the fires in his and the neighbouring houses before he finally gave up:

There was no running water, the Tommies had smashed the waterworks first. The small amount of water we had on the ground was quickly used up, and we had to abandon house after house. Finally Dr Wilms's house caught fire, and I, as deputy air-raid warden, stopped fighting the fire, since there was neither sand nor water, and the flames were already licking the side of our roof. We started to save what could be saved . . . I had all of fourteen minutes to rescue the most important things, some clothes and other stuff . . . One cannot imagine how fast fire is, and how easily it can cut off your escape route; this is why I also gave up, no matter how much I would have liked to have this or that. And so I stood below with what little stuff I had, and was forced to watch, full of impotent anger, as our beloved building burned.[37]

The British tactic of dropping a combination of high-explosive and incendiary bombs had worked: while the incendiaries started the fires, enormous explosions kept the local wardens away from them until it was too late. Further bombs on timer fuses continued to hamper the fire service into the next morning. The gas and water mains had been cut, and so had electricity supplies, making many pumps useless. Just as problematic was the damage to telephone lines. In order to direct the emergency effort, the control room of the Air Protection leader had to be in communication with all the affected areas – but while they were swamped with calls from the south and east of the city, the worst-hit areas in the west were unable to inform them of how bad things had become. As a consequence, early on at least, the fire service was directed to

the wrong parts of town. Once the mistake was discovered, the
fire chief had no choice but to send out motorcycle dispatch riders,
some of whom perished in the chaos. Officers on reconnaissance
were often forced to take long detours and were unable to report
back for several hours. Things became even more difficult when
the control room was engulfed in flames, and its staff were compelled to evacuate to another building.[38]

Early that Sunday morning the city's gauleiter, Karl Kaufmann,
was compelled to declare a state of emergency. Immediately the
running of the city came under stronger Nazi Party control, and
the SS were sent out to make sure that fire-fighters continued the
effort to extinguish fires throughout the day. Kaufmann's worst
fear was that the RAF would return the next night to stoke the
fires, in which case it was essential that Saturday night's conflagrations were put out by dusk on Sunday. In the event it proved
impossible. Even after fire services from all of the nearby towns
had been drafted in to help, many fires raged for days. In some
areas the fires were so huge that they were not extinguished for
several weeks – many households had already bought their winter
supplies of coal and coke, and when they caught fire it was next
to impossible to put them out.[39]

⋆ ⋆ ⋆

Once the all-clear had sounded, the flak batteries stopped firing.
Unable to pinpoint the attacking aeroplanes, the best they had
been able to do was put up an unaimed barrage in the hope that
they might score a few hits. When they stopped, the barrels of the
guns were glowing with the heat of the firing. Rudolf Schurig,
the officer in command of the heavy flak battery at Steilshoop,
claimed afterwards that his battery alone had shot 547 rounds into
the sky on that night.[40] In total, about fifty thousand rounds of
heavy flak were discharged into the heavens.[41] For all that, only
a single Wellington had been shot down over Hamburg, and a
Halifax of the Pathfinder Force seriously damaged.[42]

Now that the firing had stopped, the flak helpers were free to join the emergency effort in the streets. In Altona, the wounded Johann Johannsen was finally given permission to stand down by his battery commander. He went immediately to look for his family. As he hurried through the burning streets he narrowly missed being blown to smithereens by a high-explosive bomb: even though the RAF planes had returned home, explosions were still going off throughout the city, partly because numerous bombs had timer fuses, and partly because chemicals caught fire in factories. By the time Johannsen reached his house, he was a bag of nerves:

Everything was in flames: houses, vehicles, trees. Burning phosphorus dripped from the roofs. Around my house it was empty of people – apparently they were sitting in the cellar even though the house was ablaze. I hurried into the stairwell, where glowing sparks were already coming down, and then in two, three leaps was down in the air-raid cellar. On my question, 'All Ok?', I discovered that my son and another person who'd been sheltering in the cellar had broken through a wall cavity into a neighbouring cellar.[43]

As he gathered up his family and took them through the streets to safety, the suitcase he had rescued from the cellar caught fire, set alight by a 'huge rain of sparks . . . pouring down over everything'.[44]

Across Hamburg people were emerging from their shelters to be greeted by chaos. After several terrifying hours below ground, Rolf Arnold clearly remembers his first sight of the devastation that was unfolding outside his Harvestehude home:

As we left the cellar after the regular tone of the all-clear siren, the first window in the stairwell presented us with a view over the courtyard towards Harvestehude: a terrible picture – everything we could see was on fire. Grindelberg was burning on both sides, and the facing parts of Oberstrasse, Werderstrasse, Brahmsallee, Hansastrasse and Hallerstrasse – they were all burning. It was a complete sea of flame.[45]

Just across the Alster in Winterhude, the picture of destruction was similar, as Mathilde Wolff-Mönckeberg recorded in her diary shortly afterwards:

Back in our flat we stand on the balcony and see nothing but a circle of flames around the Alster, fire everywhere in our neighbourhood. Thick clouds of smoke are hanging over the city, and smoke comes in through all the windows carrying large flakes of fluttering ash. And it is raining in torrents! We go into the road just for a moment at three thirty a.m. In the Sierichstrasse several houses have collapsed and fire is still raging. The sight of the Bellevue is dreadful, and the Mühlenkamp is nothing but glass and rubble. We go to bed completely shattered.[46]

The huge fires across the city were so numerous that they sparked off a number of unusual meteorological events. To begin with, the massive heat had created strong winds. Johann Johannsen claims he had to struggle against 'a frightful storm, caused by the heat'.[47] Liselotte Gerke remembers her aunt telling her the next day that she was unable to fight her way through the wind to the shelter at Osterstrasse station, and had to go to the one at Emilienstrasse instead.[48] And then, amid all the wind and fire, another phenomenon occurred: it started to rain.

The full effect of these events could only be seen clearly from a distance. Professor Dr Franz Termer, director of the museum of ethnology, was watching the city burn from his home in Hochkamp in the far western suburbs:

I will never forget the view over burning Hamburg. On a wide horizon, from north to south, a single fiery glow; above this, while we had a clear starry sky over us, an enormous cloud whirled and billowed upon itself over the city, reaching to the sky with sharp, threatening edges. I was reminded of a volcano eruption, and, to strengthen this, the phenomena it caused were similar to an eruption. Because of the hot air, which rose and then cooled and condensed in the upper atmosphere, a downpour fell over Hamburg from the 2,000–3,000-metre high cloud of smoke . . . In Hamburg the rain mixed with the ash and created a thick black mud, as we know of volcanic eruptions – a mixture that covered everything, distorted people's faces and matted their hair. I personally saw such creatures on the following day.[49]

★   ★   ★

As Sunday dawned Hamburg was wreathed in thick black smoke. Perversely, the morning seemed darker than the night before: at least then the people had had the fires to see by, but under the smoke there was nothing to light the streets. Night had become day, and day night, as Pastor Schoene of the Christuskirche in Eimsbüttel noted: 'By the morning everything was wrapped in black smoke, which was so thick that at nine o'clock in the morning it was still too dark to see anything indoors. Not until eleven o'clock did it become lighter, so that one was able to see what time it was. At three in the afternoon the sun appeared like a small ball shining through the smoke cloud.'[50]

The houses and their coal stores were burning and so were numerous warehouses, storing everything from timber and grain to margarine.[51] The municipal gasworks was ablaze, and in Barmbek three thousand litres of ethanol exploded in a liqueur factory.[52]

The billowing smoke was blown by the prevailing winds eastwards across the city. When Ilse Grassmann woke up in her Uhlenhorst apartment, she recorded in her diary the eerie effects of this huge cloud: 'The sun has no power today. It is already midday and it still hasn't managed to pierce through the layer of smoke and ash. An indescribable radiance: a wan, yellow light gives everything a feeling of unreality that is beginning to seem oppressive.'[53]

Mathilde Wolff-Mönckeberg, who lived a little further north, noted: 'There is no proper daylight the following morning, the town is so shrouded in smoke. The sun cannot fight its way through, but looks like a bloodshot eye on to the devastation. It remains like that all through the day; the smell of burning is all pervading, so are the dust and the ash. And the siren never stops.'[54]

Her husband, Emil, walked into the city to see what had happened, and when he returned, 'He was full of sad tales. His beloved cigar shop no longer existed, his favourite luncheon place,

Michelsen, destroyed, huge devastation at the Gänsemarkt, a direct hit on the Opera, Eimsbüttel and Grindel wiped off the face of the earth.'[55]

In fact, the scale of the damage was beyond anything that anyone on the ground could yet imagine. In Eimsbüttel whole streets had been destroyed, with post offices, schools, churches, the tram depot, the police station and Schlump railway station. In Altona the damage included numerous factories and council offices, the military hospital, an electricity sub-station, the county courts, the police headquarters and barracks, and the old town hall.[56] Although no area was quite 'wiped off the face of the earth', the damage in the west of the city was extensive, and the dispersed nature of the bombing meant that not a single area of central Hamburg was unaffected. The effect on morale was devastating.

Wanda Chantler had spent most of the night doing what she could to help the wounded and dying in her forced-labour camp, even stepping through the barbed wire to help rescue a German family whose house on the other side of the street had been hit. After a long night she returned to the rubble. Exhausted and confused, she wanted to see if any of her few belongings had survived the destruction, and was particularly concerned about her Latin grammar book, which she had been studying in the evenings:

I should have taken it with me in my pocket when the warning sounded, but it was so hot that night that I didn't put my coat on. So I'd lost my grammar, and I was looking for it in this terrific light from the fires. And there, in the debris, were five eyes on a plank, looking at me. Just five people's eyes. And I said 'Go to sleep,' and started crying. Five eyes on a plank. I said, 'Go to sleep, I'll come back.' But when I came back they were not there.[57]

Over the coming week, the forced labourers of the Lokstedt fish-canning factory were abandoned by the authorities, forgotten among the mounting devastation. Wanda and many of the other surviving prisoners considered escaping – the barbed-wire perimeter fence of their camp had been blown down, and the guards were caught up in the wave of chaos that had swept the city. But since they had nowhere to go most stayed where they were, waiting for someone to tell them what to do.

A few days later Wanda was in the factory dining room that had become their makeshift dormitory, arms flailing, striking out at anyone who came near her. When she had been restrained, she was diagnosed as having suffered a complete nervous breakdown, brought on by the shock of the horror she had witnessed. To this day she is haunted by the memory of five eyeballs on a plank amid the debris of her barracks. There could be few more stark images of the reality of modern warfare.

★   ★   ★

On the afternoon of Sunday, 25 July, Gauleiter Karl Kaufmann announced that nobody would be allowed to leave the city without special permission – and thereby ensured the deaths of thousands in the coming days.[58] Certain that what had happened was merely the beginning of something much larger, those who had strings to pull did so now. However, even those who won permission to leave often found it difficult to do so because the train network had been severely disrupted. Those who had cars drove to safety, perhaps using petrol they had set aside for such an emergency.[59] Parents who could afford to do so sent their children to friends or relatives outside Hamburg. Some of the homeless, the *Ausge-bombten*, were evacuated to other parts of northern Germany in specially commissioned army lorries while others were forced to find shelter where they could in the city.

The majority of Hamburgers had nowhere to go, and no means of transport in any case. Thousands of people were involved in emergency operations and could not leave the city because they were desperately needed – there would be no let-up for several days. The rest had to stay and go to work as normal: without permission to leave it would have been impossible to find work, shelter or rations elsewhere.

The people of Hamburg did what the people of Essen, Bochum, Cologne, Warsaw, London and many other European cities had done before them: they gritted their teeth and got on with life as best they could. Although they expected another attack, nobody could have predicted what was about to befall them. The raids that were yet to come would be unparalleled in history.

11. The Americans Join the Fray

There is many a boy here today who looks on war as all glory, but,
boys, it is all hell
General Sherman[1]

The people of Hamburg did not have to wait long for the second strike. The Allies had been talking about 'round-the-clock bombing' ever since the Casablanca Conference in January: now, for the first time, it was to become reality. Even as the British bombers were arriving home, American planes were being prepared for a follow-up attack. Hamburg would be given just fifteen hours to recover before the bombs fell again.

There were lots of sound reasons as to why the Americans were keen to attack the city again so soon. For a start, the staff at the USAAF bomber headquarters knew that the RAF had jammed German radar the night before, and they hoped that the chaos this had caused would give American crews a better chance of getting in and out alive. More importantly, they hoped their bombers would do greater damage by attacking immediately: a sudden daylight bombing would keep the city in disarray and cause even more damage when it was least able to cope. Hamburg's fire-fighters could not be in two places at once: while they were putting out fires in the west, US bombers would drop their bombs in the south, in Hamburg's harbour district.

The man who made the decision to bomb Hamburg that day was Brigadier-General Frederick L. Anderson, Jr, the head of the Eighth Air Force's VIII Bomber Command. Anderson was one of Hap Arnold's 'wonderboys', an energetic thirty-seven-year-old who had seen rapid promotion over the past few months. In mid-May he had been given command of 4th Bombardment

Wing, but was only there for six weeks before he was promoted to his present job. By all accounts he was an enthusiast for long-range strategic bombing and when, later in the war, it looked as though precision bombing might be failing, he was not averse to the idea of area bombing instead.[2] He was certainly interested in the way the British were conducting their bomber war: that night he would board an RAF plane bound for Essen to see for himself what area bombing looked like.[3]

Anderson regularly attended Sir Arthur Harris's planning sessions. RAF Bomber Command Headquarters was only a ten-minute drive from his own headquarters at Wycombe Abbey, and it seemed prudent to learn at first-hand what his British partners would do that night before he planned his follow-up for the next day. So, when Harris had placed his finger on the map at Hamburg on 24 July, Anderson was present. Later that morning he had held a meeting with his own staff officers at which he, too, chose Hamburg as his target. Unlike Harris, however, Anderson specified exactly which buildings they were to aim for. Out of all the possible targets in the city, he picked two: the Blohm & Voss shipyards, in the south of the city, and the Klöckner aero-engine factory, in the south-east. According to the latest directive from the Combined Chiefs of Staff, they were two of the highest priority targets in Germany.[4]

Anderson's staff knew that this mission would be their toughest yet. The USAAF had tried to attack the city only once before, exactly a month ago, and that mission had ended in disaster. The Germans had jammed their navigational aids, and the weather had been so cloudy that most of the American planes had been unable to find each other, let alone the target. They had only got as far as the German coast before the Luftwaffe had arrived in such numbers that they had been forced to turn back. Eighteen planes had been shot down. As the 303rd Bombardment Group's group leader had said in his official report afterwards, the mission had been 'futile'.[5]

The American planners were determined not to let the same thing happen again. First, they checked the weather: there was no point in attempting an attack on Hamburg if the target was covered with cloud. The forecast was for clear skies – but to make sure, a reconnaissance flight was sent to Heligoland early on the day of the attack. When it returned with reports of perfect conditions, the raid was given the go-ahead.[6]

The air-force staff then devised a plan to confuse the Germans, and give their own crews the best possible chance of reaching the target and getting back safely. Hamburg was not the only city they would bomb, so it was important to co-ordinate all the different attacks to make sure they complemented each other. It was also important to conceal their true targets until the last possible moment: once the Germans knew where they were heading they would be able to lie in ambush.

Three separate forces would fly. The first was bound for the Heinkel aircraft factory at Warnemünde, on the Baltic coast. This wing would fly out towards Germany, but while it was still over the sea it would suddenly turn northwards, as if it were heading for Denmark. The idea was to draw the German fighters out of their airfields too early, so that by the time the Americans actually crossed the coast they would be forced to return to their bases to refuel.

The second force was smaller – just three bomb groups, or about sixty planes – and was bound for the U-boat yards at Kiel. It would fly across the North Sea with the Warnemünde wing, and also turn northwards, then suddenly switch back on itself. Again, this was designed to confuse the Germans, conceal the true aim and draw out the Luftwaffe fighters too early.

About forty minutes behind those forces there were two combat wings, bound for Hamburg. The first was to bomb the Blohm & Voss shipyards, while the second was to attack the Klöckner aero-engine factory. By this time, so the planners thought, the Luftwaffe would be back at their airfields refuelling, thus giving the Hamburg force time to get to the target relatively unmolested. After the city had been bombed, both combat wings would join up with the Kiel force, and they would fly home together. By now the Luftwaffe would be back in the air, and it was safer to fly

The American Plan
25 July 1943

- - - - 6 Bomb Groups to Warnemünde
——— 6 Bomb Groups to Hamburg
········ 3 Bomb Groups to Kiel

DENMARK

North Sea

Heligoland

Kiel

Warnemünde

N
W · E
S

Cuxhaven

Frisian Islands

Wilhelmshaven

Hamburg

Emden

Elbe

Cromer

HOLLAND

Bremen

GERMANY

Lowestoft
Southwold

Diversion raids

Amsterdam
Schiphol

Hanover

0   50   100 miles

0   50   100   150 kms

in larger numbers. The Hamburg and Kiel wings would look out for each other on the way home.

The final piece of the jigsaw was a pair of diversionary flights, well to the south. A small force of fighters and light bombers would attack occupied Holland and northern France, making believe that they were the main danger. The idea was to hold down German fighters in these areas, and prevent them reinforcing the defences in northern Germany.[7]

It was an ambitious plan, fraught with danger. If the various diversions did not work, the planes bound for Hamburg would find themselves the focus of all the combined fighter defences of Germany, Holland and northern France. If either the Warnemünde or the Kiel force aborted its mission the Hamburg force would be isolated, and if the Hamburg and Kiel forces failed to meet up on the way home they would be more vulnerable to attack. The USAAF was taking a huge gamble in splitting up its force into four smaller units: unless the plan worked perfectly, any one of them might end up facing the full force of the Luftwaffe alone.

That the Americans believed they could attack a target as strong as Hamburg with a divided force, in broad daylight, without fighter cover, was perhaps an indication of how green they were. It is important to remember that, for them, this was still early in the air war, and they had not yet had a chance to learn from their mistakes. General Anderson had been at his post for a mere three weeks, and his staff had planned only a handful of missions to Germany on this scale before. The bomber groups were just as inexperienced. None of the six groups that took off for Hamburg that afternoon had even existed when America joined the war, and four had been in England for a matter of weeks.[8] In the past eight months they had been created, trained, transported across the Atlantic, accommodated in a foreign country and thrown into the thick of the air war. By any standards, this was a baptism of fire.

It is easy to criticize the naïvety of their plans, but they had not yet had the opportunity to accrue long years of experience as the British had. That they were able to bomb Germany at all in the summer of 1943 is little short of a miracle.

*   *   *

The RAF watched the Americans plan their missions with a degree of curiosity. Despite superficial similarities, it had become obvious by now that the USAAF was a very different air force from the RAF. The contrasts existed at every level – strategic, tactical, even down to the design of the aeroplanes. In the end it boiled down to one basic difference: the British bombed by night, but the Americans bombed by day.

I have already touched on some of the practical and ethical reasons why the USAAF was determined to fly bombing missions in daylight, but that they believed they could succeed in this hazardous enterprise, at which the British, and the Germans before them, had been forced to give up, was down to the quality of their planes. While the British and Germans had tried to fly through swarms of enemy fighters in outdated, poorly equipped bombers, the Americans had something much more suited to the job: the Boeing B-17 – easily the best daylight heavy bomber of the Second World War.

The B-17 was not nicknamed the 'Flying Fortress' for nothing. It was equipped with bullet-proof windows round the rear gunner's position, armour plating throughout, and it bristled with machine-guns. The B-17F, the model in operation during July 1943, had up to sixteen .50-calibre Browning machine-guns: four in the nose, two in the tail, four on the roof, two in the belly, and two on either side in the waist. When it was under attack, every member of the ten-man crew, except the two pilots, had something to shoot with. And, most importantly, unlike the bombers of other nations, the B-17F had no blind spots.

A single American bomber was therefore a pretty formidable opponent for any fighter. However, unlike the British at this stage of the war, the Americans did not fly one by one but in groups of twenty or so, in close formation. Each group of twenty would be accompanied by two others: one group would fly in the lead, the next slightly higher and to one side, and the last slightly lower and to the other side. Any German fighter pilot who dived through the middle of a formation like this was either extremely brave or extremely foolhardy: with anything up to a hundred guns firing at him, there was little chance that he could have escaped unscathed.

To protect it from flak, the B-17 had been built to fly at heights of 30,000 feet and higher. This was 5–6,000 feet higher than a pilot of heavy bombers in the RAF could dream of. It flew at speeds of just under 300 m.p.h., which, again, was considerably faster than any RAF heavy bomber. True, it could carry less than half the bomb load of a Lancaster, but the Americans reasoned that they did not need to carry such huge numbers of bombs. Their philosophy was built on dropping a few accurately placed bombs on specific targets – not, as with the RAF, on plastering the whole area with bombs. They were happy to sacrifice their bomb capacity for the ability to fly higher, faster and more safely than any other air force in the world.

The only problem with the theories was that they didn't quite work – at least, not yet. No matter how high or fast the American bombers flew, they were no match for the German fighters, and probably would not be until the introduction of long-range American fighter escorts later in the war. The USAAF was certainly not strong enough to commit to several targets at once, and seriously underestimated the strength of the Luftwaffe. Their British counterparts warned the Americans of what they would face and could not understand why they refused to listen. To the British, it looked as though the USAAF was determined to repeat the mistakes they themselves had made.

The late Pierre Clostermann, one of the Allies' greatest fighter aces in the Second World War, once described to me the first time he ever saw a USAAF officer: he was wearing a cowboy hat, a revolver on his hip and 'swaggering like he had just stepped out of the Wild West'.[9] The American air force at that time was brash, confident in its abilities to the point of arrogance, and determined to live by its own rules. Eventually the brashness would be vindicated – indeed, many have argued that it was only by forcing the Germans into a long-term, daylight gun battle that the Allies finally gained air superiority – but in the meantime some harsh lessons had to be learned.

★   ★   ★

If there were close links between the RAF and the USAAF at command level, there were fewer between the airmen. The Americans had separate air bases, and rarely had the opportunity to meet their British counterparts. When they did meet, however, there was a strong mutual respect between them. Walter Davis, of 91st BG, remembers a conversation he had in the summer of 1943 with an RAF man he met in a London pub. The British airman insisted on buying him a drink with the words, 'You wouldn't catch me going over Germany in daylight!' In reply, Davis simply said, 'Well, you wouldn't catch me going over there in the dark!'[10]

To a certain degree, Davis was being generous to his RAF drinking partner. Of the two air forces, the RAF men unquestionably had the better deal – at least at that stage of the war. Of course, the Americans did not have to take off or land in the dark, they had their squadron colleagues around them as they flew, and they could see danger coming. But without the cover of darkness they were little better than sitting ducks, and their rigid adherence to formation flying meant that when the guns started firing they could not take evasive action. As one US veteran cogently put it, 'We were ordered to fly in an aluminum crate, carrying two thousand gallons plus of 100-octane gasoline, with a six-to-eight-thousand-pound bomb load, in tight formation, straight and level, while people shot at us.'[11]

With tactics like that, life expectancy in the US Eighth Air Force was not high. The airmen knew this – it was one of the first things they learned when they got to Britain. For example, Samuel Fleming was told as soon as he arrived at Molesworth air base that there was no way he would get through his tour alive: 'What it boiled down to, according to the guys keeping score, was this. In 1943 and 1944, the average life span of an Eighth Air Force bomber and crew was fifteen missions. The assigned tour of duty for crew members, however, was initially twenty-five missions, and later increased to thirty and finally to thirty-five missions . . . One did not have to be a brain surgeon to figure out one's odds of finishing a combat tour.'[12]

Joseph Mutz was similarly demoralized when he arrived in Britain. He had been slightly delayed on his journey across the Atlantic, and got to his base a few days after most of the men with whom he had trained. One of the first things he did was to look up a friend, only to find that he had already been shot down. It was impossible not to come to the conclusion that the same fate awaited him. 'I had a rock in my stomach, and I just knew that we were never going to make it. Just *couldn't* make it. I even went as far as writing my brother. I told him what to do with my insurance money.'[13]

This was not what these men had signed up for. Most had joined the air force because they thought it would be better than serving in the infantry – they had been warned about the dangers of the trenches by their parents, some of whom had experienced the horrors of the First World War. But it was now beginning to look as though they had made the wrong choice. While the bulk of the infantry were still safe at home, and would not see action for almost another year,[14] American airmen were dying in droves. Nor were they safe from some of the more gruesome aspects of war, as anyone who experienced a direct hit on his plane soon discovered. Scott Buist, a USAAF gunner from New Brunswick, remembers having to pull the remains of his crewmate from the ball turret after it had received a direct hit. 'We had to pull him out, an arm, a leg, pieces, his head; I put his head in the basket . . . This was a kid that I slept next to.'[15]

Perhaps the operative word there is 'kid'. Almost all the men who flew B-17s during the Second World War were in their late teens and early twenties. Most had never been outside the United States before, yet now they were thousands of miles from home, fighting a foreign war for the sake of a noble principle. Many were lonely, and desperately missed their friends and family at home. They were all, to some degree, scared of the task that lay ahead. But they were determined to do their best, if only for the sake of their pride.

Those were the men who would bomb Hamburg during the afternoon of 25 July 1943. They faced the combined dangers of flak, fighters, mechanical malfunction, extreme cold and lack of oxygen. More than 1,200 would take off. A hundred and fifty would not return.

12. The Luftwaffe Strikes Back

No plan survives contact with the enemy.
Field-Marshal Helmuth von Moltke[1]

When the crews turned up for briefing on the morning of 25 July none knew what lay in store. For weeks now, unpredictable banks of cloud over northern Europe had prevented the USAAF planning any missions to Germany, and most of the men hoped it would stay that way – at least until they had finished their tours. Over the past month they had concentrated on targets in France and the Low Countries, mostly airfields and aircraft factories. Raids like this were the 'milk runs' that every airman hoped for when he attended a briefing: a relatively short trip across the English Channel, often with fighter escorts to keep him safe.

However, there were signs that things were about to change. A week ago some had been detailed to attack a synthetic-rubber factory in Hanover – a mission that had been called off at the last moment due to bad weather. Then, on the previous day, they had made their first trip to Norway – easily the furthest any of them had flown on a mission. There had been little or no opposition along the way, but that was not the point: the men were getting the message that nowhere in Europe was beyond them. So, as they gathered in the briefing rooms at their various bases that morning, there was tension in the air. They knew that it was only a matter of time before they were sent somewhere truly dangerous.

The ritual at briefing was pretty much the same as it was for the RAF. There was the same blackening of windows and locking of doors, and the same false bravado as the young men talked or joked away their nerves. And, just as in RAF briefings, all eyes were drawn to the large board at the end of the room, hidden behind a curtain. It showed the information they were all eager to receive: a map of Europe marked with a ribbon showing their route to the target and back.

When the men had taken their seats, and the windows had been covered, the briefing officer stepped on to the platform, and the room descended into an uneasy silence. Without ceremony, he pulled aside the curtains on the target map. Philip Dreiseszun, who attended the 381st BG briefing in Ridgewell, remembers this moment with particular clarity. 'Then came the moment of revelation! The board cover was removed as we heard the words, "Gentlemen, the target for today is Hamburg!" A stunned silence gave way to utterances of dismay and alarm.'[2]

Nobody liked flying to targets in Germany, but today the crews had real cause for concern. They knew that Hamburg was one of the best-defended cities in Germany – they had been told so a month ago at their last briefing on that target. Those who had flown on that unfortunate mission knew what could go wrong – especially the men of the 379th BG, who had lost six crews that day. Even those who had not been around at the time had probably heard about it: it had been one of the USAAF's most disastrous missions to date.

As the men shifted uncomfortably in their seats, the briefing officer outlined the strategy behind the day's mission. The target for 379th, 303rd and 384th BGs was Blohm & Voss, the most important U-boat manufacturer in Germany. For the 91st, 351st and 381st BGs, the target was the Klöckner aero-engine factory. The Luftwaffe had been stepping up production of fighter planes in recent months, and it was imperative that the Allies should stop them – the lives of American airmen depended on it.[3]

After his opening statement, the briefing officer outlined the specifics of the mission: the route they would be taking, the sort of weather they could expect and so on. But the information every man in the room was waiting to hear was what sort of opposition they should anticipate. Of course, when it came, the news was only what they expected. Fighter opposition would be fierce, so it was essential that all groups did their utmost to stay in tight

1 Churchill and Roosevelt at the Casablanca Conference, where the Combined Bomber Offensive was first agreed.

2 Sir Arthur Harris, Commander-in-Chief, RAF Bomber Command.

3 Major General Frederick L. Anderson, commander of US VIII Bomber Command.

4 Hitler arrives at Hamburg's airport on one of his many pre-war visits. He never returned once war had broken out, despite appeals for a morale-raising tour after the city was destroyed.

6 Göring (*left*) was head of the Luftwaffe, but it was Erhard Milch (*right*) who ran the show. Chief of Air Staff Hans Jeschonnek (*centre*) shot himself shortly after the bombing of Hamburg.

5 Karl Kaufmann, Hamburg's gauleiter and a loyal disciple of the Führer.

7 Colin Harrison: 'One minute I was a schoolboy, next minute they called me a man and put me in an aeroplane.'

8 Bill McCrea: 'When we were detailed on the first Hamburg raid we thought, "Now we'll see what it's *really* like!"'

9 Doug Fry (*centre*), hours before he was shot down at the end of July 1943.

10 Baptism of fire: Ted Groom and pilot Reg Wellham's first operation was the firestorm raid of 27 July.

11 Hamburg before the war. Narrow streets like this allowed fires to spread rapidly.

12 The bright lights of the Reeperbahn in the 1930s. Scenes like this were impossible during the black-out.

13 The heart and soul of Hamburg: the docks and shipyards were the main reason the city was such an important target.

14 False streets and buildings were floated on the Alster lake in an attempt to disguise the city centre. This camouflage caught fire during the bombardment, adding to the inferno.

15 Secret weapon: a factory worker cuts strips of 'Window' to the right length.

16 RAF ground crew prepare bombs before loading them into a Stirling bomber.

17 Hamburg from the air on the night of 24 July. The centre of the picture shows the Neustadt on fire, with bombs spreading back towards Altona at the bottom.

18 Streaks of flak over Hamburg. Without radar to guide them, flak gunners were forced to fire blindly into the sky.

formation. And the flak would be almost continuous from the moment they crossed the coast. The briefing officer was particularly clear on that, and told the men that Hamburg alone would have ninety-eight heavy AA guns trained on them. (As formidable as this sounded, there were actually at least three times more than that.) He advised the men to take evasive action wherever possible: 'If you are able to observe the flashes of the AA guns,' he said, 'it will take the shell twenty to thirty seconds to reach you.' That was the moment for the whole formation immediately to shift height and direction.[4]

The men listened in silence, trying to take in the statistics and instructions. As one veteran from 384th BG remembers the dread in the room was almost palpable: 'There was definitely an air of apprehension about this briefing. It's always stuck in my mind that, after the target had been revealed, every navigator in the group prepared a course for the nearest friendly country. Sweden, I think it was, on this day.'[5]

What Philip Dreiseszun remembers most clearly is the reactions of his crewmates. Some were downright despondent, but once they had all had time to digest the news, the main emotion seemed to be grim determination:

Our bombardier, James H. Houck, gloomily expressed feelings of foreboding. The rest of us, I believe, were in a state of numb awe, of mixed feelings of fear and wonder, and facing unknown qualities in ourselves. How would we react in confrontation with the might of the German Luftwaffe and the formidable anti-aircraft fire we surely would meet? The bonds, fortunately, that held a crew together were a subconscious factor in helping us set individual concerns aside long enough to concentrate on the tasks that lay ahead.[6]

⋆   ⋆   ⋆

After lunch the crews went to get their gear: rations, escape kits, flight clothing, parachutes. Just as the RAF had done the evening before, they milled around nervously, some cracking jokes, others communing silently with themselves as they waited for the personnel carriers to take them out to their planes. The only difference was that this was not taking place at twilight but in the hazy sunshine of a hot summer's day. By the time the trucks came, everyone was overheating, particularly the gunners in their heavy, wool-lined suits. Out at dispersal they would busy themselves inside the plane, but once everything was ready they would shelter in the shade of the wings, leaving off their flight jackets until the last possible moment as they waited for the signal that it was time to go.

It was not until after one o'clock that they climbed on board and the B-17s' engines roared into life. Edward Piech flew as a bombardier with the 351st BG during this time, and remembers the thrill he always felt as the line of bombers prepared to leave the ground: 'There was a green flare and then the first, the lead ship would take off. And then a few seconds after that each one, one by one, lined up in a column . . . I will never forget the sound of those B-17s taking off. They just sort of leave a thrill up and down my spine: no matter where I am and I hear those sounds, I can't escape from it. It is actually, to me, a beautiful sound.'[7]

As the planes took to the air, the first task was to gain height and assemble into formation. This sounds simple, but in fact it was one of the day's most problematic tasks. Slotting each plane into its correct position in the formation was time-consuming – it could take an hour or longer to get it right.[8] Veteran Donald Hillenmayer explains:

These airplanes climbed at the rate of five hundred feet a minute when they are fully loaded so to get up to, say, twelve thousand feet to form, that's pretty close to half an hour just to get there . . . So, the lead crew, he's up there, starts to circle and here comes the second plane and he cuts him off and gets into formation. Here comes the third one, he cuts them off, he gets into position. Now, you do that, say, eight or ten times . . . It took us an hour and a half to form.[9]

This was only the start of the problem. Once each individual group had arranged themselves into the proper formation they had to find each other so that they could fly together across the sea. The combat wing bound for Blohm & Voss assembled without much trouble, but the Klöckner wing had major problems. The 91st BG, which was supposed to be leading two of the other groups, was unable at first to find either in the haze. In desperation, the lead plane made the whole group circle back over England, firing flares to attract attention to themselves. In this way they eventually picked up the low group in their formation (the 351st BG), but the high group (the 381st BG) was still nowhere to be seen. It was only after the formation leader gave up and set course for Germany that they spotted the 381st BG ahead. This group doubled back to fall in behind the leaders thus losing more time.[10] After all the delays the wing was in a woefully ragged formation, and it was still struggling to close up two hours later as it crossed the German coast.

While all these complicated manoeuvres were going on, there was little that the crews could do but sit and wait. Conditions inside the B-17s were far from comfortable, especially for those in the extremities of the plane. They were climbing to an altitude of between 26,000 and 30,000 feet: at these heights the temperature regularly drops to less than −40° C, and despite wool-lined boots and electrically heated suits it was not uncommon for airmen to come home with frostbite. 'The warmest I ever flew on a mission was thirty below zero,' says Albert Porter Jr, who served as a ball-turret gunner later in the war, 'and the coldest was close to sixty below. When we finished the mission, the whole front of our outfit was solid ice from the condensation of your breath.'[11]

Flying at any altitude above 10,000 feet meant they were all reliant on oxygen, for which they plugged their face masks into one of the plane's central outlets, but spare bottles were stowed throughout the plane in case of emergency. These could make the difference between life and death. If the crew's air supplies were cut off, a lack of oxygen to the brain (anoxia) would lead eventually to unconsciousness. It was important to react to any cut in oxygen immediately − after a minute or two, the airmen would be unable to perform even the simplest task. The worst thing about anoxia was that those affected often did not realize it. As their reactions slowed they often believed they were behaving normally, and by the time they were fumbling with the oxygen bottles it was too late – they were incapable of saving themselves. Experienced airmen kept a constant watch on their fellow crew members to make sure that everyone was conscious.

Of all the members of the crew, those who were under the most constant stress were the pilot and co-pilot. They might not suffer the cold, like the gunners at the back, because the cockpits were heated, but the pressure of holding the bomber in close formation with twenty other aircraft for several hours on end was physically and mentally exhausting. The other members of the crew – the navigator, the wireless operator, the bombardier – were also obliged to undergo prolonged periods of intense concentration. They had to keep a constant log of their position in case anything went wrong, and all crewmen were supposed to keep a look-out for fighters whenever they were not otherwise engaged.

Of the 123 planes that took off for Hamburg that afternoon fourteen were forced to turn back, mostly because of mechanical malfunctions. Unlike the British night bombers, who often got away with flying to a target and back on just three engines, many B-17 crews were understandably reluctant to fly over German territory in anything but a fully functioning machine. After the fourteen had returned to base, the remainder of the force continued their climb. It was imperative that they attained their bombing altitude before they reached the European coast.

As they rose through the haze they found themselves flying in the deep azure of the infinite sky. Soon even the haze melted away, and they were left with the perfect flying conditions they knew as CAVU – 'ceiling and visibility unlimited'. For a short while the heavens seemed a peaceful place: there were no enemy fighters to worry about just yet, and nothing broke the eternal blue but the vapour trails of a hundred Flying Fortresses. Perhaps some of the crew took a few moments to sit back and admire the view. Others swapped jokes and teased each other over the intercom in voices that were just a little too loud or too merry, but as

USAAF route over Hamburg, 25 July

— Routes of Bombardment Groups

Fires from previous
night still burning

•••• Area obscured by smoke

Areas hit by US bombs

Klöckner
factory

Norder Elbe

WILHELMSBURG

Neuhof
power station

381st
B.G.

91st
351st
B.G.s

379th
303rd
384th
B.G.s

Alster
Lake

Blohm & Voss
Shipyards

Howaldtswerke
shipyard

River Elbe

Süder Elbe

HARBURG

3 miles

4 kms

N
E
W
S

they approached the coast of Europe they lapsed into silence, as all eyes concentrated on combing the heavens for the tell-tale glint of German metal.

★   ★   ★

The lead group of bombers first sighted the German coast at around four o'clock. As the navigators searched for landmarks to pinpoint their position, everyone else watched the surrounding sky. It was not long before they found what they were looking for: the distant dots of fighter planes rising to meet them. As they approached the mouth of the river Elbe, at about 4.15 p.m., the first German fighters attacked, half-heartedly at first, as if they were merely testing the Americans. But gradually the Luftwaffe was appearing in greater numbers, hovering at the edges of the formations, waiting for a chance to pounce on any B-17 that strayed even slightly from the rest. 'You always had the feeling you were in a chicken coop,' said a veteran of those raids, 'and the fighters out there are foxes or weasels.'[12]

Darrell Gust was a navigator on one of the 303rd BG's Flying Fortresses. In his position behind the bombardier in the nose of the plane, he could see exactly what went on around the formation:

We were hit by swarms of fighters as soon as we crossed the coastline. These guys were *eager*! Maybe twenty to thirty miles from the target, I looked out of the window over my navigator's table and saw an Me 109 sitting out there out of range, but apparently flying the same course we were, and maybe 200 to 300 yards below our formation. I knew that fighter pilots sometimes did this, kind of looking us over. Then they would suddenly zoom up and ahead of us, positioning themselves for a 180-degree turn and a nose-first attack on the B-17 formations.

I thought, 'this bastard is up to no good and I'll keep my eye on him.' He just kept flying parallel to us, but he seemed to be getting closer. He finally edged in to what I estimated to be about 700 to 800 yards. I grabbed the 0.50-cal above my navigator's desk and gave him about 15 to 20 rounds. I could immediately see my tracers going behind him. I corrected my aim and gave him a burst of about 30 rounds. Suddenly, there was a plume of white smoke emerging from the Me109, and he started to drop in a vertical dive. I called to S/Sgt Virgil Brown, our tail gunner, that I had nailed an Me109 and asked him to keep his eye on it. He said he saw it go straight down and crash behind us.[13]

This was probably the first casualty of the day, an Me109 from III/JG26 (i.e. III Gruppe of Jagdgeschwade 26 – see Appendix D): it crash-landed at Stade airfield, but the pilot escaped unhurt. Two more German fighters from this *Gruppe* alone were also forced to land with combat damage in the next few minutes.[14] It was a good omen for the Americans, but there was still a long way to go.

It might not have seemed like it to the bombers in the van-guard of the mission, but the American plan was working quite well. While the skies appeared to be bristling with German fighters, there were far fewer than there might have been. The force bound for Warnemünde, which had approached northern Germany some forty minutes earlier, had succeeded in drawing many Luftwaffe planes into the air too early, and several Me109s and FW190s that might have been there to greet them were now refuelling at their airfields. The diversionary raids in France and Holland had also worked: at least two Luftwaffe *Staffeln* were sent from Schiphol and Woensdrecht airfields to deal with the attacks, which might otherwise have been sent northwards to defend Hamburg.[15] (A *Staffel* was roughly equivalent to a British flight or an American squadron, although the comparison is slightly contrived. See Appendix D.) In fact, the only part of the American plan that had not seemed to work was the attack on Kiel. The three bomb groups in this wing had had such a hard time finding each other, and were so dispersed across the sky, that the wing leader had been forced to call off the mission. They had returned home without dropping a single bomb on German soil. Neverthe-less, the other deceptions had done their job: not a single American bomber was shot down before it reached the target; and while the Blohm & Voss wing might have had to deal with German fighters, the Klöckner wing, which came in about fifteen or twenty minutes behind them, had a virtually free run into Hamburg.

However, the German fighters were only one part of the formidable Hamburg defence line: there was nothing the Americans could do to deceive the flak guns. Indeed, as they flew through the clouds of exploding shells, there was little any of them could do to avoid being hit. Ironically, the tactics they relied on to keep themselves safe from the fighters also made them vulnerable to flak. A single B-17, weaving back and forth more than five miles above the ground, would have been an impossible target for the flak gunners. A group of twenty, forced to fly relatively steadily so that they could keep together, was a much bigger target. After the failures of the previous night, the German flak gunners must have relished the opportunity to take their revenge.

Many American aviators feared flak far more than they did fighters. Walter Davis, who was flying a plane in the Klöckner wing, was one: 'You could *see* the fighters. And we had gunners on our airplane. Whereas you can't see the flak – you don't know when it's going to come. You can see it exploding, but you can't dodge it . . . And they had so much of it over there . . .'[16]

The anti-aircraft fire began before they even reached the German coast: two flak ships in the Elbe estuary opened up on them. A short time afterwards, when the batteries of Cuxhaven also started to fire, the flak became accurate and intense – 'So thick you could get out and walk on it,' according to Davis. It carried on virtually uninterrupted for the next twenty minutes, but it was not until they reached Hamburg that it became really bad. 'When we were going in to Hamburg it looked like there was a big black cloud over the city. Actually it was the smoke from the flak coming up.'[17]

This was far worse than anything the Americans had experienced before. The flak bursts seemed to create an impenetrable curtain before them, and they had no choice but to fly straight through it. As they approached the city they saw flashes in the air as the shells exploded – red or pink explosions, followed by small clouds of brown or black smoke, like thousands of firecrackers filling the sky. Some airmen found the sight mesmerizing. But there was never any doubt about the danger they were in. Some of the planes were thrown about by the sheer force of the exploding shells. According to the men of the 381st BG, flying in the Klöckner wing, the anti-aircraft fire was 'the most intense we have ever seen'.[18]

It took the Americans just twenty minutes to fly from the coast to the outskirts of Hamburg, but they were under fire for the whole journey. By the time they reached the city many had holes in their wings and fuselages, a handful had even lost an engine. Worse still, they were taking casualties. In the lead group of the Blohm & Voss wing, the *Judy B* had taken a vicious blow to the side of the cockpit. Lieutenant Charles Bigler, the nineteen-year-old co-pilot, remembers what happened:

It was five minutes before our bomb run over Hamburg. A Nazi fighter came in straight on my side and knocked out my oxygen. A shell glanced on the back of my seat and hit the pilot's back. He slumped over and I tried to keep him up with one hand and hold the ship with the other. If I had let him slump I would have been unable to control the ship. We made our bomb run with me driving with one hand.[19]

The pilot, Willis Carlisle, had died instantly. For five minutes, without any oxygen to sustain him, Charles Bigler held the dead man up, only calling for help once he had completed his bomb run. Over the next hour a desperate struggle ensued as the bombardier and the top turret gunner tried to get oxygen to Bigler, and at the same time remove the body of the dead pilot. Although he was under continual attack from German fighters, and falling almost 25,000 feet, Bigler somehow got the *Judy B* home – he was so exhausted by the ordeal that he had to be carried from the plane by the station medics.

This was probably the most dangerous time for the Americans. If they wanted to drop their bombs correctly they had no choice but to stay in formation and fly straight and level towards the target. Evasive manoeuvres to avoid the flak were prohibited because even a small deviation could send the bombs off course. During this critical couple of minutes, they were effectively sitting ducks. Even after the bombs had gone they were obliged to keep straight

and level until they had taken their target photographs. Only then could they follow the group leader in his gentle weave across the sky to avoid the flak.

However, that day there was another problem, one that had not been anticipated. As they approached the target it became clear that it was not only the sky that was filled with smoke, from the flak shells: there was smoke across the ground too. Some of the American airmen assumed that it must be a deliberate screen, set by the Hamburg authorities to obscure the city centre. As the 303rd BG's group leader said to the press office when he returned home: 'There must have been a million square miles of smoke screen.' (In his official report he reduced this claim to about fifty square miles.) As a consequence, he went on, 'the bomb results were unobserved'.[20] Others, like the ball gunner of 384th BG's *Doris Mae*, thought that the Americans must have unwittingly created the screen: 'The preceding group's bombs had sent up a lot of smoke. If they hit the target, we did too for I followed our bombs right down into the centre of the mess.' Unknown to this eyewitness, there had been no previous group: the 384th BG was the first to drop its bombs.[21]

In fact, the smoke was coming from the fires started by the RAF the night before. It is ironic that the success of the British raid threatened to prevent the Americans following it up, but that was what happened. A westerly breeze was blowing thick black clouds across the target area, making it almost impossible for the Americans to see where to drop their bombs. The Blohm & Voss shipyards were on the edge of the huge smoke cloud, but the Klöckner factory was in the middle of it, so it began to look as if neither wing would find its target. In an effort to salvage the mission, two of the Klöckner groups decided to head for Blohm & Voss instead, in the hope that it might be easier to see. The third group, the 381st BG, was still too far behind the leaders to realize what they were doing and carried on with their planned route above the smoke.

So it was that five Bombardment Groups, instead of three, headed towards the U-boat yards on the banks of the Elbe. They still did not know whether or not they would be able to bomb it, and for a short while the mission hung in the balance. But as the bomber formations made their final approach, by a piece of great good fortune a gap opened in the smoke clouds. Blohm & Voss was still obscured but the quays and buildings of Howaldtswerke, one of Hamburg's other shipyards, were clearly visible. As they got closer the smoke began to close over the target area once more so, without wasting any time, the 384th BG opened their bomb bay doors and unleashed 44,000 pounds of incendiaries on the dockyards. They were followed at roughly one-minute intervals by the 379th, the 303rd, the 351st and the 91st BGs, dropping wave after wave of high-explosive and incendiary bombs on to the buildings below.[22]

Meanwhile, the 381st was still struggling to keep up with the rest of the force. Unable to see what the other Klöckner groups had done, the group leader decided to cut the corner off the designated route to save time, but as he flew across the south of the city he and his group found themselves alone. From there on he stuck to the planned route, heading eastwards over the smoke, but it soon became obvious that he would never find the Klöckner factory – the smoke was too thick. With the mission looking like a lost cause, the group held on to its bombs and decided to seek out a target of opportunity on the way home. They settled on the railway marshalling yards at Heide, which they bombed at ten past five, half an hour after the other groups had got rid of their loads. Then they hurried to close up with their fellows for the hazardous journey home.

By now all six groups were looking more than a little ragged. Of the 123 Flying Fortresses that had started out this afternoon, fourteen had aborted the mission before even reaching Germany, almost half of those that remained now had flak damage of some sort or another, and many more had been hit by cannon fire from the ever-present fighters.[23] Those American planes with major damage were now in serious trouble. If an engine had been hit, or any of the vital controls, it would become more and more difficult for the pilot to keep up with the others. And stragglers knew that they would face a doubly dangerous journey home: not only would they be the first to be targeted by the German fighters, but they would have to face those attacks alone.

★　　★　　★

As the bombers struggled to stay close together the Luftwaffe appeared in force around them. Fighters from Heligoland, which had been first to contact the invading force, had refuelled and were coming in for a second attack. They were joined by others from Deelen, Husum, Jever, Nordholz and Oldenburg.[24] Some American groups reported seeing as many as a hundred, two hundred or even three hundred fighter planes over the next hour or so. At times they seemed to fill the sky, attacking in waves from every conceivable angle; there was nothing the Americans could do but abandon all other duties and man the guns.[25]

With such huge numbers of fighters coming in at them, it was only a matter of time before the Flying Fortresses started to go down. Survivors of the two Hamburg wings unanimously claimed that the German fighters were far more ferocious than usual, pressing home their attacks with terrifying determination.[26] The Luftwaffe had not yet learned that the best method of attack was to dive at the bombers head on, and break up the formation – but this happened anyway. The largest number of attacks came from below at the rear, and in general they were not by single fighters but by groups of three or four at a time.

The lower groups took the brunt of this ferocity, particularly the stragglers. The worst hit was the 384th BG, which by now was limping on with several disabled planes, their normally tight formation looking more and more ragged as the afternoon wore on. Some individual planes in this group were attacked more than twenty times, yet somehow, miraculously, stayed airborne.[27] Others could not take the punishment. Brad Summers was one of the co-pilots with 384th BG:

Before we got to the target we had one hit, knocked all the glass out of the top turret. The engineer, who managed the turret, I think his oxygen mask protected his face quite a bit. There were some little splinters in his neck and shoulders, but he went back to his gun. He couldn't put his head out because of the wind blowing through the turret, so he huddled over down inside trying to [aim] by the tracers (the gun sight was also destroyed), which is not a very accurate way to shoot . . .

We proceeded on and got several other hits. I recall seeing a flash out of my window and I looked and there was a rip in the skin on the top of my wing. It must have been about eight or ten feet long, opened about four or five inches wide. The skin was peeled back where apparently a 20mm shell from a fighter plane had gone in and ripped it out. As I looked, I saw another hole open up. The only thing I could figure was, an 88mm shell had gone right through the wing without exploding.[28]

It was around this time that the tail gunner had a direct hit on his turret. The concussion from the explosion lifted and threw him into the body of the plane, but he crawled back to see if the tail guns were intact. One was still working, so he went back to firing it until a second direct hit blasted him through the doorway again. This time his guns had been blown out of the back of the aircraft. With no top turret, and most of the back of the plane blown away, Summers's Flying Fortress had become an easy target for the fighters. First an aileron went. Then some hits in the tail knocked out the trim tabs so that Summers had to lean forward on the stick to hold down the nose of the plane. Finally the stabilizer was blown away, leaving the two pilots powerless to fly the plane. There was nothing to do but bail out. Summers continues:

I hooked my parachute on and I got my hat. I put that on, then I decided, well, heck, I'd probably lose it anyhow, so I threw it away and got a bail-out oxygen bottle . . . I don't know why all these silly thoughts went through my head, like wanting to get my hat, but anyway, I was beginning to feel the effects of the lack of oxygen – anoxia, we called it – getting a bit lightheaded . . . I decided I'd better get out of there right away. I just did a somersault right out the door and down I went.[29]

Summers fell several thousand feet before he pulled the ripcord of his parachute, and only did so when he thought he might pass out. One of the waist gunners was not so lucky – he was killed in his position by flak. And Kenny Harland, the valiant gunner who had carried on shooting despite having his top turret blown apart, died when he hit the ground. Everyone else survived to become prisoners-of-war. That they did, and that they had so much time to bail out, is testament to the sheer strength of the B-17 Flying Fortress under punishment.

Some of the planes from the other groups were having just as tough a time. Philip Dreiseszun was a navigator in 381st BG when the full force of the German fighter formations attacked:

The enemy swarmed at us from all directions. Our gunners, Houck [the bombardier] and myself were all firing; new belts of ammunition were hurriedly installed as rounds were expelled . . . Our plane lurched, shuddering heavily as 20mm shells tore through the fuselage and Plexiglas windows. Houck spun around from his front firing stance, sinking to our little deck in a sitting position. I was slammed against the worktable but felt no pain. The attack ended, and I turned my attention to Houck. Above his chest-pack parachute was a gaping hole which spurted blood . . . I prayed for some sign of life; there was none.[30]

When the bail-out order came, Dreiseszun agonized over whether he should push his dead comrade out of the plane with his parachute on so that he could be recovered for burial once he reached the ground. But, reasoning that the parachute might get caught on the tailplanes and endanger the rest of the crew, he decided eventually to leave him where he was. He pulled the cord on the emergency hatch, kicked open the door and leaped through it into 27,000 feet of cold space and nothingness.

I let myself fall free in the awesome quiet. I estimated about 2000 feet and then pulled the ripcord. The 'chute jerked violently as it unfurled, buffeted by the strong wind at that altitude. The leg straps tightened painfully in the groin area. On seeing the 'chute unfold, I knew I was a goner! It was full of large holes, small holes and many tears. How it kept me afloat . . . I'll never know. During the attack, a 20mm shell had evidently made a direct hit on my parachute . . . The final 6000–7000 feet were like a free fall. I hit the ground with such a jarring impact, it felt like every bone in my body had shattered. I lost consciousness.[31]

When he came to a German soldier was sitting on him, searching him for weapons. He was lucky. Two of his crewmates who had landed nearby were killed by a mob of angry civilians. The tail gunner went down with the plane. The other five members of the crew survived to become prisoners-of-war.

A pattern was emerging in the Luftwaffe's attacks. First the fighters picked off the stragglers – those planes that were already crippled by flak and earlier fighter attacks. Then they concentrated on the planes at the back of the formation – most of the B-17s lost had started off at the back. And, finally, once one or two of the smaller formations were under strength (and therefore had fewer guns with which to defend themselves), the fighters came in to finish off the rest.

It was this last point that proved particularly devastating. While some bomb groups made it home relatively untroubled, others suffered attack after attack all the way across Germany and most of the way across the North Sea. Of the three bombardment groups in the Klöckner wing, for example, two only lost a single plane on the way home. The third, which had been severely depleted from the outset when seven of its planes had aborted their mission, received the full brunt of the German storm. This group, the 381st, lost three planes on the way home – and all three were in the same squadron, Dreiseszun's 532nd.

The story was the same for the Blohm & Voss wing. The twenty-one planes in the lead group suffered just fifteen attacks and lost two planes, both stragglers. The high group was attacked nineteen times, and lost one plane out of twenty – again, a straggler. The low group (the 384th BG) was attacked *eighty* times – more than twice the number of the other two groups put together.[32] It

Attacks on 384th BG, 25 July

High Squadron

Lead Squadron

Low Squadron

Key:

Missing

Abortive

Attack by fighter from
11 o'clock and 6 o'clock

lost seven planes that afternoon, six from the same squadron, the 544th, which was all but wiped out.

The reasons for this loss were simple: the low squadron of the low group was the most vulnerable place to fly in the entire formation, and was often nicknamed 'Purple Heart Corner' or 'Coffin Corner' because of the disproportionate number of planes that were shot down there. After they had come through Hamburg, 544th Squadron had been under relentless attack for forty minutes, and four of the seven planes were now struggling to keep up. They were picked off mercilessly by the German fighters. Once the squadron was down to three planes it was easy prey: the fighters came in again and again until two more had been shot down. The only plane left struggled upwards to fall behind the lead formation, but it had to suffer nine more sustained attacks before the fighters left it alone.

It goes without saying that every one of those stricken bombers went down fighting. Of the ten men in a B-17 crew, eight had guns to fire, and they did so until the bitter end. The pilot would only give the order to bail out once all hope was lost. He would switch on the automatic pilot, then he and whatever crew were still alive would don their parachutes and leap from the plane; with the automatic pilot in control, the empty plane would often fly dozens of miles further before it crashed. Some abandoned B-17s drifted as far as the Frisian Islands and the borders of Holland – seventy or eighty miles from where their crews had left them.

Sometimes the pilot would lower the landing gear before bailing out, in what was effectively a signal of surrender. At this stage in the war there was still an unofficial code of chivalry among aviators of all nations: if an American bomber lowered its wheels, the German fighters would stop firing and either escort the damaged plane to an airfield or circle it as the airmen dropped, one by one, in their parachutes. This admirable arrangement was spoiled later in the war when, according to USAAF legend, one bright spark had the idea of using the system to lure the Germans closer, then open fire on them. From that moment on, disabled American planes were given no quarter.[33]

The final B-17 to go down that afternoon was flown by Thomas Estes – one of the last surviving planes from the low squadron of the low group. The crew had been under attack for well over an hour, and had already watched several of their squadron comrades go down. They had seen at least one man drop from a stricken plane without a parachute, his arms and legs thrashing as he fell.[34] They had fended off so many attacks that the tail gunner and the ball-turret gunner had run out of ammunition: they had been reduced to tracking their attackers with empty guns in an attempt to make it look as if they were still firing. As the crew told the story later, the assault had been ferocious: 'They came in pairs, attacked down, slashing along our left side . . . They totally disregarded our fire and pressed their attacks to within a hundred feet of our plane.'[35]

By the time Estes's plane was out over the sea he was barely able to fly it. Three of the engines had been hit, the left wing tip was shattered, and the oxygen supply to the top turret had been knocked out. When 20mm shells blasted a gaping hole in the nose the bombardier and the navigator were thrown back into the tunnel by the explosion, which ripped off their helmets and oxygen masks. Both men struggled back to their guns, but it was no use: the Flying Fortress was going down into the sea.

When this happened Staff Sergeant George Ursta was manning the ball turret, waving his guns at the attacking fighters to make believe he was still firing. He picks up the story:

I was still tracking ships when I heard an explosion and saw the number-two engine smoking. I called up the pilot and asked him if it was a good idea to get out of the ship at this time. He said I should leave the ball turret and I went up to the radio room. I saw that the gang all had 'chutes on so I put mine on ... The engineer came back and told us that we didn't need any 'chutes as we were going to ditch, so I took my harness off and threw it out of the window. The engineer started throwing out ammunition and I helped him, and we both took the right-hand gun and threw it out ... After that we were told to go into the radio room and find good positions so we wouldn't upset after we hit the water. I just sat there with my eyes closed and said a little prayer.[36]

As they glided inexorably downwards the bombardier, David Davis, put his head out of the escape hatch at the top of the radio room to see how close they were to the water. Unfortunately, as he was doing so six Focke-Wulf 190s came in at the plane head on, and the pilot was forced to dive to avoid them. Davis was thrown through the top hatch and only managed to prevent himself falling out of the plane by clinging to the fuselage. The others in the radio room scrambled up to the hatch and did their best to pull him back in, but there was nothing they could do. After it had fallen 5,000 feet, the plane levelled off and Davis was at last flung back into the radio room. Brute strength, and not a little luck, had prevented him being sucked out into the empty sky.

A few minutes later the B-17 hit the water. Even now the fighters continued to attack: as the shaken crew clambered out of the sinking plane 20mm shells continued to burst on the wings and the water around it. One of the fighters doubled back to make another pass, but when the pilot saw the life-rafts self-inflating he turned for home. That was the last any of the crew saw of the battle of Hamburg.

After the sharp dive, many of the crew believed that their pilot, Thomas Estes, had been killed. In fact, he was dazed but alive – he was the last to get out of the plane before it sank. The ball-turret gunner saw him crawl out of the side window of the cockpit and hauled him on to the life raft.

Miraculously all ten crew men had survived the ditching. They spent two nights trying to keep their dinghies afloat, which had been peppered with holes by exploding flak fragments, and were picked up eventually by a Danish fishing-vessel and brought back to the English coast. Against the odds, they had lived to fight another day.

*   *   *

German fighters carried on harassing the American planes halfway across the North Sea. Some, such as the Focke-Wulfs of I/JG I from Husum airfield, were on their third sortie that afternoon. As the Americans flew further out to sea they were eventually attacked by night fighters too – a group of twin-engined Me110s from Leeuwarden. That German fighter controllers would send these cumbersome night fighters into battle shows how committed they were to finishing off as many B-17s as they could. Night-fighter crews were not properly trained to attack formations of Flying Fortresses, and their machines were not nearly so able to zip away, should they be caught in the overlapping fields of American fire.

The radar operator of a night fighter explains what he saw as his pilot steered the Me110 towards the American formation:

It was the first time I had seen Boeings from the air. From five or six kilometres away, they looked like a great heap, like a great swarm of birds. You couldn't see individual planes, only those at the front. We had been told that the Americans were very dangerous, that each plane had eighteen guns. We only had these little slow night fighters. When we saw a bomber at night, there was a feeling of joy but, in the day, it was a strange feeling because you knew that, instead of shooting at only one bomber, many bombers would now be shooting at us.[37]

Nobody expected night fighters to attack a full formation of B-17s, but their controllers had explicitly instructed them to keep a look-out for American stragglers.[38] Their only real advantage was that of surprise: if they headed out in front of the formation they would be hidden by the brightness of the evening sun, which by now was shining right into the American gunners' eyes. Eventually they spotted a B-17 in the high squadron of 303rd BG that was lagging slightly behind the others and came in to attack.

Their tactics worked, but only to a degree. It was common for some of the gunners to rest easy around this time – they would take off their oxygen masks for a smoke or a few bites of the Hershey chocolate bars they kept among their flying rations. The Americans were indeed caught off-guard – their official reports refer to this last combat of the day as a 'sneak attack' – but their superior fire power was enough to keep the Me110s at bay. Indeed, they even managed to shoot down one of the German fighters – flown by Leutnant Eberhard Gardiewski and his radar operator Friedrich Abromeit. Both of the Me110's engines were hit, and it crashed into the sea some twenty miles off the Dutch coast. The crew were eventually picked up by a British motor torpedo boat and brought back to England. It was the final encounter of the day: with their fuel running low, the other German fighters were recalled to their airfields in Germany.

★   ★   ★

The Flying Fortresses did not get back to their various bases until after seven thirty that evening, more than six hours after they had taken off. Battered and short of fuel, many had difficult landings – the final challenge in a mission beset with problems. Several planes were so short of fuel that they had to land at alternative airfields. Even those who made it back to their own did not have an easy time. One of 303rd BG's planes, the *Yankee Doodle Dandy*, almost crashed at Molesworth airbase. The pilot found himself caught in

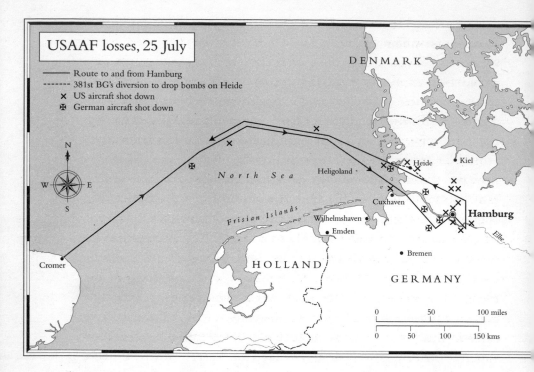

USAAF losses, 25 July

——— Route to and from Hamburg
------ 381st BG's diversion to drop bombs on Heide
✗ US aircraft shot down
✠ German aircraft shot down

DENMARK

North Sea

Heligoland

Frisian Islands

Wilhelmshaven

Emden

Cuxhaven

Heide

Kiel

Hamburg

Elbe

Bremen

HOLLAND

GERMANY

Cromer

N
W   E
S

0   50   100 miles
0   50   100   150 kms

the prop wash of another B-17 while he was coming in to land, and the sudden turbulence tossed the plane around in the air until one of its engines ran out of fuel. As it plummeted towards the ground disaster was averted when the engineer, Stan Backiel, had the presence of mind to raise the landing gear, giving the pilot just enough lift to pull the plane back up again.[39] *Yankee Doodle Dandy* came round again and this time landed perfectly.

A few minutes later the last of the B-17s joined it on the ground. Their hazardous mission, the seventy-sixth in the history of VIII Bomber Command, was now officially over.

At each airfield, the station commander and his staff stood out in the dying evening sunshine and anxiously counted the planes in, just as they had counted them out six hours ago. They were not the only ones waiting to welcome the men home. The ground crews, who were particularly attached to the aeroplanes and the crews, were anxious to see that both had returned safely. Most had a long night's work ahead, trying to patch up the aircraft so that they could be used again in the morning. Intelligence officers were also standing by, ready to debrief the men and note down what had happened on today's troublesome mission. Those airmen who had not flown were eager to find out what they had missed. And at one or two of the airfields newspaper men from Associated Press and United Press were ready to record the immediate impressions of the exhausted crews as they climbed out of their battered B-17s.

However, the station medics were first on the scene. There were casualties in many of the planes that had returned. For example, the radio operator of *Yankee Doodle Dandy* had run out of oxygen while manning the ball turret, but the battle had been so frantic that no one had been able to come to his aid for over half an hour. By the time they got him back to base he had swallowed his tongue, his eyes were frozen shut, and he was virtually blue from lack of oxygen. The co-pilot was also injured: as he was coming back to help his crewmate, the base of the top turret had revolved violently, crushing his foot in the mounting. Both men would be nursed back to health over the coming days and weeks, and the radio operator, Richard Grimm, went on to earn a DFC later in the war.[40]

The crew of the *Judy B* were in even worse trouble when their plane came to a halt at Kimbolton airfield. Their pilot was dead, their co-pilot badly disabled after his ordeal in the air, and two other crewmen were almost unconscious from lack of oxygen. At Ridgewell, the home of 381st BG, there were two more cases of severe anoxia, and two men from 384th BG had to be hospitalized at Grafton Underwood because of wounds they had received.

They were the lucky ones. Of the 123 crews that had started out that afternoon, fifteen had failed to return. As the survivors were driven back across the airfield to the debriefing rooms they could see for themselves how many planes were missing. Later, when they gathered for a meal, the empty seats spoke far more eloquently than any statistics. At Grafton Underwood the atmosphere was particularly sombre: seventy faces had vanished from the mess hall during the course of an afternoon.

That night most of the men went to bed early, too exhausted to consider anything but sleep. Some were issued rations of whisky to calm their nerves, and perhaps cheer them a little. Others were offered sleeping pills to help them shut off the effects of adrenaline.[41] They were emotionally and physically worn out.

They needed their sleep. Every one of those bomber groups was scheduled for another maximum effort tomorrow, and most of the men would be up before sunrise to repeat the performance.

13. The Americans Again

They know that if a flaming bullet comes through their gasoline tank it immediately becomes a burning torch and they are gone. They know that if a wing is torn off there is the same result. They know that a dozen fatal things may happen any time, and that if they fall two hundred or twenty thousand feet, existence is at an end . . .
Billy Mitchell[1]

While the men of VIII Bomber Command slept, American intelligence officers worked late into the night analysing the information they had gathered during the various debriefing sessions. The statistics did not look good.[2] To start with, fourteen of the planes bound for Hamburg had abandoned their mission before they had reached the German coast. That represented more than 11 per cent of the total force: an unacceptable figure. In the case of the wing that had been supposed to bomb Kiel the *entire* mission had been called off because they had been unable to assemble into a safe formation. If the average is taken for all the American forces bombing that day, more than a quarter of the B-17s had turned back before reaching Germany. Something had to be done about this problem, and soon: every plane that aborted its mission merely increased the risk of failure, and worse, for those who carried on.

The loss rate was even more worrying. Fifteen planes out of 123 had been shot down: that was 12 per cent of the total force detailed for Hamburg, and nearly 14 per cent of those who flew over the city. Losses like those were unsustainable. Half a dozen similar missions, and the entire American bomber force would be wiped out.

Another concern was the number of planes returning home damaged. Sixty-seven planes had been shot up, nine so badly that they could barely fly. To make things worse, twenty-three planes had been damaged by their own squadron companions. This was probably inevitable – the Americans flew in such close formations that it was sometimes difficult not to fire at each other – but, nevertheless, the loss rate was bad enough without adding to it by friendly fire.

Over the coming weeks the USAAF would do their best to overcome these problems. They would introduce 'Splasher' radio beacons to help their bomb groups find each other before they left the English coast – that way there would be less chance of them having to abandon their mission because of an inability to assemble properly. They would insist on ever-tighter formation flying to reduce the risks of being attacked by German fighters. But in the end nothing they suggested could hide the fact that they were outclassed in the skies over Germany. No matter how formidable a group of Flying Fortresses was, it was no match for the combined forces of heavy flak and swarms of Me109s.

The final piece of the intelligence picture was perhaps the most discouraging. After all the losses they had suffered, it seemed that only 60 per cent of the planes had bombed anywhere near the target. Seventy-three crews had dropped their loads on or near the docks in Hamburg, another thirteen had bombed the railway marshalling yards at Heide; the rest had been either shot down, had aborted, or dropped their bombs elsewhere. Of all the statistics, this one had to improve most urgently. If the bombers were not hitting their targets there was little point in flying to Germany in the first place.

Needless to say, these figures were highly confidential, and did not become public knowledge until long after the war. There was, however, one set of numbers that was advertised as widely as possible: the statistics for how many German fighters had been shot down. American claims for the day were huge: thirty-eight destroyed, six probably destroyed, twenty-seven damaged.[3] Some bomb groups had suffered terrible casualties, but with scores like those they could at least console themselves with the thought that they were giving as good as they got.

The only problem with the figures was that they were fiction. It is understandable that the American airmen believed themselves so successful: any German fighter that dived through a formation might have ten B-17s firing on it at the same time, and if it went down every one of those B-17 crews would claim the victory. In the end, however, it was still only one fighter shot down, not ten. German records give an idea of how inflated American claims could be. They suggest that only six fighters were shot down by B-17s *in total* that afternoon, and a handful damaged.[4] That is less than a sixth of the number claimed by the USAAF. American intelligence officials suspected this, but they let the numbers stand because they served as a much-needed morale boost to their men. At this stage in the war they needed it.

★   ★   ★

As morning dawned on 26 July, the USAAF crews assembled once again for a briefing on the day's target. They did not know it yet, but they were at the beginning of a seven-day rollercoaster that would come to be known as 'Blitz Week': almost two thousand sorties on twenty-three towns and cities across northern Europe.[5] Today was the third maximum effort in a row.

The Americans had a policy of resting one squadron in every group for each raid, so only a few of the men flying on the twenty-sixth would have been on all three of those missions. However, two-thirds of that day's force had been through yesterday's ordeal. Those men had had only five hours' sleep, and were still recovering from the battering they had received over Hamburg; it goes without saying that they were hoping for an easier target now. They were to be sorely disappointed. Not only were they going back to Germany, but their mission was the same as the one that had just decimated them. Their exact targets would also be the same: the Klöckner factory and the Blohm & Voss shipyards.

It is impossible to imagine the dismay, not to mention the sense of *déjà vu*, that some of the men must have felt as the curtain opened on the target map. However, there were some major differences from the briefing yesterday. For a start, the wing that was to fly on the shipyards today was the one that had been detailed for Klöckner yesterday, and vice versa. The wings themselves would be organized differently too: today the 381st BG would lead the Blohm & Voss wing (with the 351st and 91st BGs in the high and low positions); and the 303rd BG would lead the Klöckner wing (with the 379th and 384th BGs in the high and low positions). It was important to spread the responsibility so that the newer groups would have an opportunity to prove themselves and the established groups would get a rest. They would be flying a route similar to yesterday's, with the difference that they would turn southwards after hitting the target, rather than northwards, and head for the North Sea by flying between Bremen and Oldenburg.

That day's Hamburg raid was, again, just one part of a bigger plan involving several attacks on German territory. Three other combat wings would attack a rubber factory in Hanover and, just as on the previous day, one was supposed to fly a feint off the German coast to draw the fighters from their airfields prematurely. There would again be a series of diversions over northern France and the Low Countries by a force of light bombers under fighter escort. Each of the various combat wings and diversionary forces would aim to cross into Europe simultaneously, but at different points, in the hope of splitting German defences.

The American planners had done all they could to protect their forces. Now it was up to the individual crews. It was a tired and apprehensive group of men who left their various briefings and made their way to their planes. Unlike the day before, they now knew *exactly* what was waiting for them in the skies over Germany. Some were plainly demoralized, which might have influenced events later that morning.

★   ★   ★

The two Hamburg wings took off at around 9.00 a.m. into the hazy sunshine of another warm summer's day. They were in trouble almost immediately. While one wing managed to assemble without too much difficulty, the other was a shambles from the start.

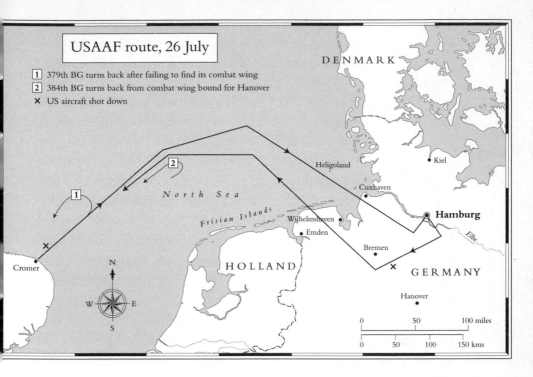

USAAF route, 26 July

1 379th BG turns back after failing to find its combat wing
2 384th BG turns back from combat wing bound for Hanover
✕ US aircraft shot down

DENMARK

North Sea

Heligoland

Kiel

Cuxhaven

Frisian Islands

Wilhelmshaven

Hamburg

Emden

Bremen

Elbe

HOLLAND

GERMANY

Cromer

Hanover

N
W   E
S

0   50   100 miles
0   50   100   150 kms

The 303rd BG, which was supposed to be leading the Klöckner wing, failed to find either of its two accompanying groups, although it came across several unidentified formations of B-17s. Eventually the 303rd BG leader, Major William Calhoun, gave up looking for them and fell in behind the Blohm & Voss wing.[6]

Meanwhile, the 379th BG spent half an hour wheeling and dispersing with various other groups of planes over the English coast but eventually gave up looking for its leaders and returned to base. The other missing group, the 384th BG, ended up following one of the Hanover wings most of the way across the North Sea, then turned back. It would have been possible for it to bomb Hanover instead of Hamburg, but the group leader was worried that, unlike his group, the formation he was following might be equipped with long-range fuel tanks. Given the possibility of the entire group running out of fuel over the sea on the way home, he took the sensible decision to abandon the mission. So it was that only four bomber groups, rather than six, approached Hamburg.

Thirty-nine planes had turned back because they had been unable to form up properly.

However, they were not the last planes to drop out. The number of abortive flights, which had so concerned VIII Bomber Command Headquarters the night before, was escalating. In the 303rd BG, five planes aborted their mission – a quarter of the number dispatched. In the 351st BG, nine planes turned back, and in the 91st BG, eleven – just over half. In fact, of the 121 Flying Fortresses that took off for Hamburg, only fifty-four reached the target. Just one of the sixty-seven planes that turned back did so because of damage caused by German defences.[7]

One might be forgiven for asking what could have caused such a phenomenal drop-out rate. It was normal for there to be a few engine problems in any mission, but the number of technical malfunctions for the Hamburg wings that day was twice what it was on any of the other wings. Some of the excuses for turning back were woolly at best: engines that were running a little rough, an erratic turbo, loose fittings on a pilot's oxygen hose and so on. A few of the reasons given appeared to be outright inventions. For example, one 351st BG crew claimed that they had returned because of a malfunction in one of the supercharger regulators, but when the station mechanics investigated they were unable to find anything wrong. The number of 'pilot illnesses' that occurred frankly defies belief. The only real explanation is that many of those who had experienced the previous day's ordeal could not face the thought of going through it again. They had simply lost their nerve.[8]

The four bomber groups that approached Hamburg around midday on 26 July were so badly depleted that they were in serious danger. Had the defences been anything like as ferocious as the day before they might have suffered even worse casualties. But they were lucky – most of the German fighters had been deployed further south to tackle the B-17s that were flying on Hanover. While those wings were attacked mercilessly, the Hamburg force was allowed to fly across Germany relatively unmolested. That is not to say there were no fighters around – on the contrary, thirty or forty were waiting for the Hamburg force as it crossed the coast – but unlike yesterday they seemed happy to sit back and wait for the flak to do its work, then pick off any stragglers later. Fortunately for the Americans, however, the flak did not do nearly as much damage as it had the day before, and almost the entire force reached the target and returned without sustaining any serious damage.[9]

Once the four bomber groups had arrived at the city, the next challenge was to find their targets. This was easier said than done because, once again, the docklands were immersed in clouds of smoke. Unlike yesterday, however, most of this smoke was not caused by the fires in the city: instead it was a deliberate screen produced by German smoke pots on the ground. This time the Hamburg smoke-screen units had not been caught unawares; much of the panic in the city had died down during the last twenty-four hours and they had had time to prepare for the coming bombers. Blohm & Voss was completely obscured, as were several other areas of the city. In the event, the Blohm & Voss wing chose to attack Howaldtswerke again, as they had yesterday, because this target was clearly visible beneath them. They scored several direct hits on the shipyard, as well as on the MAN diesel engine works.[10]

The 303rd BG wisely chose not to attempt an attack alone on the Klöckner factory, but instead flew over the Neuhof power station, just south of the targets the other bomber groups were striking. One of its bombs scored a direct hit, putting the plant out of action for more than two weeks – probably the single most important effect of the raid. This group then fell back in with the other bomber formations and turned southwards for the long journey home.

Unlike the RAF raid two nights previously, which had lasted almost an hour, this bombing run took just a minute to execute. There were so few planes, and they were flying in such close formation, that as soon as the lead bomber had dropped his bombs the rest of the formation were able to follow suit. More than 126 tons of incendiaries and high explosive fell in the minute between 11.59 and midday, and then it was over. This was exactly the way precision bombing was supposed to go: the all-important dock

American bombs on
Hamburg, 26 July

areas received dozens of direct hits simultaneously, but apart from those who were in the area at the time, most of the civilians in Hamburg barely knew that the bombing had happened.

*   *   *

The journey home was potentially even more dangerous than the previous day's withdrawal flight. Their route would keep the Americans over German territory for almost twice as long, and by flying between Bremen and Oldenburg they would attract the attention of both flak and fighters all the way out. It had been a calculated risk on the part of the planners: the Hanover forces would also be flying through this area, and the USAAF were gambling that the Luftwaffe would not be able to attack both forces in great numbers. In the event, it was the Hanover wings that continued to suffer the brunt of the German storm. The Hamburg group was barely bothered at all – since the formation had held up to the flak remarkably well, it was merely escorted out of German territory by a fighter force that was unwilling to do much beyond hover at the edges waiting for stragglers.

In the end, only one B-17 was unable to keep up with the others – an unfortunate plane called *Nitemare*, piloted by First Lieutenant James W. Rendall Jr, which had been hit by flak on the way into the target and on the way out.[11] With two of its engines on fire, it was only a matter of time before it was forced to drop away from the formation. German fighters lost no time in dealing with it, attacking the plane three and four abreast. The radio operator was killed by their machine-gun fire, and the B-17 was so badly damaged that there was no option for the rest of the crew but to bail out. The ball-turret gunner did so, but his parachute failed to open and he died when he hit the ground after a fall of 26,000 feet. The navigator and bombardier reached the ground safely, but were shot while trying to escape shortly afterwards. They died from their wounds in hospital. The rest of the crew survived to become prisoners-of-war. *Nitemare* crashed near Nindorf, ten miles south-east of Rotenburg.

While the stricken plane was making its long descent to the

ground, something unusual happened in the skies above. As the fifty or so remaining bombers were making their way back to the coast they were joined by nine strange B-17s, which tried to slot themselves into the American formation. They had none of the usual markings of an American plane, such as the call and identification letters, and their waist-gun windows were closed. When one tried to join 351st BG the other crews became suspicious and fired a few warning rounds at it. It turned immediately and headed back into Germany. Presumably they were captured planes that the Luftwaffe hoped to slot into the American formation either to gather intelligence or to attack it – German records for that day are somewhat patchy and do not mention what they were hoping to achieve. Whatever the case, the strange B-17s turned away after the Americans had crossed the coast and returned to Germany, accompanied by two twin-engined fighters.[12]

There was only one other loss for the Hamburg force. On the way home a second plane from 91st BG ran out of fuel and had to land in the sea. Its pilot, Lieutenant Jack Hargis, took the plane down gently, and the crew got into their dinghies without much trouble. They were eventually brought home by an RAF rescue launch (which also had to tow home the two Walrus seaplanes that had originally come to rescue them, but which were unable to take off again due to rough seas).

The Hamburg wings had been incredibly lucky. Their loss of just two planes and one crew made this one of the cheapest bombing raids the Eighth Air Force had ever flown over Germany. The wings that had flown to Hanover that day were not so lucky. Like the Hamburg force on the previous day they had attracted most of the German fighters, and sixteen B-17s had been shot down. A further six had been lost by a wing that never made it to Hanover, but bombed Wilhelmshaven, Wesermünde and a convoy off the Frisian Islands. The huge losses took the shine off the Hamburg 'milk run': the loss rate was still 12 per cent of the effective planes, well over twice what was considered sustainable.

Over the coming days such losses continued. On Wednesday, 28 July, twenty-two American planes were shot down over Kassel and Oschersleben. Another ten were lost on Thursday, and twelve more on Friday. By the end of the week eighty-eight Flying Fortresses had gone, with another dozen so badly damaged that they had to be scrapped. Nearly nine hundred American airmen were dead, wounded or missing. The following weekend VIII Bomber Command retired to lick their wounds, and for the next two weeks the American B-17s ceased flying. Despite some good bombing results, including those at Hamburg, their attempts to make their mark in the skies over Germany had only left them depleted and demoralized. This was one battle that the Luftwaffe seemed to have won.

14. The Eye of the Storm

First the left and then the right! . . . But he's held to his feet, held to the ropes,
looked to his corner in helplessness!
Clem McCarthy[1]

The attacks by the USAAF on 25 and 26 July shocked Hamburg. The city had not seen a daylight raid since the beginning of the war, and it had certainly never seen American planes fly over it: that formations of Flying Fortresses were now daring to approach Hamburg in broad daylight suggested that Germany's enemies felt a new confidence.

Despite their losses in the air, the Americans had been able to do considerable damage to the port. The Blohm & Voss works had suffered quite badly, with severe hits on the construction, the ship-fitters' and engine-erecting shops, the boiler-house, power station, foundry and tool stores. Two of the dry docks had also been heavily damaged. In the Howaldtswerke factory several furnaces were now out of action, as were the shipbuilding and machinery sheds, and the diesel engine works. The USAAF had also scored direct hits on the power station at Neuhof, the oil stores beside Rosshafen and many of the nearby railway sidings.[2]

While none of this would have directly affected most people in Hamburg, the effect on their morale is incalculable. They were still seriously shaken by the Saturday-night bombing, and that they would now have to endure daylight attacks as well was alarming. Rudolf Schurig was out in the centre of Hamburg when the alarm went off for the first American raid, and remembers how frightened everyone suddenly was: 'The sirens sounded once more – the *Fliegeralarm*. Terror and dismay played across people's faces all over again. Women grabbed their children, men grabbed their wives, and they hurried to the nearest air-raid shelter where whole crowds were gathering. I have never seen the people of Hamburg running in such panic because of an air-raid siren!'[3]

Hiltgunt Zassenhaus remembered sheltering the next day during the second American attack. In the shelter everyone was even more nervous than usual because of the destruction they had already witnessed:

Shortly after ten we heard a distant hum over the clouds; the sound came nearer, became a roar. The sirens had failed, but the doom-laden drone in the heavens was warning enough. We hurried down to the cellar of the Institute. Professors, students, women and children, men in blue work overalls, covered with dust from labouring in the debris. The room had no windows. The power had failed. We stood pressed up close to one another in the dark and listened to the noise outside. It sounded like they were attacking the harbour. Then there was a crash nearby. We huddled together in breathless silence. Even the children said nothing.[4]

It was the incessant nature of the attacks that made them so difficult to bear. By attacking so soon after the British raid, the Americans had seriously hampered the rescue effort – and since the entire city was engaged in putting out the old fires there was nobody to deal with the new ones caused by the B-17s. To make things worse, the RAF had sent six Mosquito bombers to Hamburg on Sunday night, and again on Monday, with the sole purpose of causing as much nuisance as possible. After what had happened on Saturday night, nobody was taking any risks, and the entire city had huddled inside its air-raid shelters for several hours on both nights. Among their obvious material woes, the whole population was now suffering from severe sleep deprivation.

It was not until Tuesday that the people of Hamburg got any peace. In the lull that day, the city authorities were finally able to get a clear picture of the damage that had been done. It was not a pretty one. Worst hit were the areas around Altona and Eims-büttel in the west of the city where whole districts had been burned to the ground. Barmbek was also fairly heavily damaged, and the port area on the south shore of the Elbe had been hit by all three raids in succession. With the damage to power lines, and the destruction of Neuhof power station, electricity was now limited. The gas and water mains had been breached in countless places, which hindered the fire services' efforts to extinguish the fires. The transport systems in the worst hit areas were now non-existent, although the main train lines in and out of the city were still functioning. There was major disruption to the telephone network within Hamburg, and after the destruction of the long-distance exchange in Rotherbaum all lines to the rest of Germany were defunct.[5]

Almost all of the fires had been brought under control, which had required a Herculean effort. However, according to Hamburg's chief of police, by the evening of Tuesday, 27 July, there were still fifty large fires burning across the west of Hamburg, and a further 1,130 smaller ones that the fire-fighters had been unable to put out. Despite heavy reinforcement from other northern German fire units, the sheer number of fires had been overwhelming. At the height of the crisis eighty-seven kilometres of street frontage had been ablaze in the west of the city alone. There were several *single* fires that covered an area of four square kilometres or more: such conflagrations were simply too big to deal with. The best the firemen could do was put out smaller outbreaks at the edges, and stop the blaze spreading. By nightfall on 27 July, almost every fire-fighter in Hamburg was still working in the west of the city. Most had had no rest and little food for three days. But the situation, broadly speaking, was stable.[6]

★   ★   ★

With the fires under control, the heavy pall of smoke that had smothered the city all day on Sunday began to disperse. Hiltgunt Zassenhaus described the scenes of utter devastation she encountered as she walked into the university on Monday morning to attend her physics exam:

Along the way furniture was piled up outside the burning houses. Cushions and mattresses were singed, mahogany scratched and scorched. Their owners sat beside them, as if they were waiting for removal vans. But no vehicle could have come along the torn-up streets; and where the streets were clear cars and lorries drove through at top speed. Their vibrations sent a trembling through the broken walls; façades crumbled together and blocked off one street after another.[7]

The threat of falling façades was not the only danger she encountered as she tried to pick her way through the city:

Rubble blocked the streets, so we had to go round it; we climbed over broken walls and charred wood, one after another, like a line of ants . . . 'Watch out!' shouted a voice from the side of a mountain of rubble. 'There are unexploded bombs all over here!' But in blind indifference the crowd continued. What was the point of closing off the way? There were unexploded bombs everywhere. Each step back was just as dangerous as each step forward.[8]

Because of the widespread destruction to electricity cables and gas and water mains, even those living outside the worst-affected areas found their lives beset with difficulties, as Dr Franz Termer described in a letter to a friend at the time:

Organization has quickly fallen apart. A shortage of bread is now beginning to take hold. One cannot cook, there is no gas as yet; one can only wash sparingly as there is no water in our homes. We cook at a neighbour's house – she has an electric oven. We have the advantage that on one of the plots in our road there is a pump in the garden, to which the entire neighbourhood traipses. My wife pushes the pram with water containers, I carry buckets.[9]

In devastated districts the daily journey to the water hydrant was not only depressing, it was downright dangerous. Just south of the Hagenbeck zoo a coal depot on Steenwisch was still ablaze, as was a floor-polish factory that had suffered a direct hit. The

178 *Inferno*

LOKSTEDT
EPPENDORF
HOHELUFT
HARVESTEHU
EIMSBÜTTEL
ROTHERBA
BAHRENFELD
ALTONA
OTTENSEN
NEUSTAD
FLOTTBEK
ST PAULI
Norder Elbe Three mile limit
Blohm & Voss
Shipyards
STEINWÄRDER
Köhlbrand
Howaldtswerke
shipyard
WILHELMSBURG
N
W E
S
1 mile

Damage caused by British and
American bombers, 24–26 July 1943

STERDORF

WINTERHUDE

BARMBEK

WANDSBEK

UHLENHORST

EILBEK

Alster
Lake

HOHENFELDE

ST GEORG

BORGFELDE   HAMM

HORN

LTSTADT

HAMMERBROOK

KLEINER
RASBROOK   ROTHENBURGSORT

BILLBROOK

VEDDEL

▪ ▪ ▪ ▪ ▶   Path of British bombers, 24 July

▶   Path of American bombers, 25 & 26 July

△   Aiming point for British bombers

■   Buildings totally destroyed by bombs

polish was flowing down the road: residents had to step barefoot through the hot liquid to get water from the hydrant on the other side of the road.[10]

There were other blows to morale. Thousands of people's homes had been destroyed, but so had the places where they worked, shopped, or spent their leisure time. In all the cutbacks ordered by Joseph Goebbels after his proclamation of 'Total War', Germany's cinemas and theatres had remained unrestricted, because the Nazis recognized how important they were for keeping up people's spirits.[11] Now many of Hamburg's best-loved theatres lay in ruins. The Opera House in St Pauli was completely burned out, as were parts of the Staatstheater, and the front of the Thalia-Theater in the town centre had been seriously damaged by a bomb that had exploded opposite. Many cafés and dance-halls, such as the Trichter dance-hall in St Pauli, were now little more than rubble. Even the theatre museum in Altona had been destroyed.[12]

One of the most poignant episodes in this tragic period involved the famous Hagenbeck zoo, which was hit in the British attack on Saturday night. Four keepers died during the struggle to put out the fires, and five more were killed when the zebra house received a direct hit. But it was the animals that suffered most. A hundred and twenty large animals were lost during the night, along with countless smaller ones. When an 8,000-pound blast bomb landed near the big-cat house several of the occupants escaped: two jaguars and a Siberian tiger had to be shot the next morning. All the big cats that stayed inside burned to death in the fire.

In the zoo's official report the writer's weariness is plain:

Everything that was not burned down was destroyed by explosive bombs: the main buildings, both restaurants, the cattle sheds, the deer and goat house, the aviary, the walkways and superintendent's house, the zebra stalls, the ticket office, the country house opposite the main entrance, the business yards, the baboon enclosure, the monkey bath, the Rhesus monkey enclosure, the aquarium. The remaining buildings were partially destroyed by fire and explosion, and have been provisionally repaired by hand.[13]

Curiously, none of the animals was driven wild by its experiences, and few tried to escape from their broken cages and enclosures – it is probable that they were every bit as shocked as their human counterparts. There were a few exceptions: some of the monkeys escaped into the surrounding area, and a stallion used his new-found freedom to play with a circus mare, even though he had lost an eye.

In the following days, the animals were either rounded up or shot. The most valuable beasts were put on to a train to be transported to safety in Bavaria. They never made it. While their train was in sidings in the east of the city it was caught in the next air raid, and the animals perished.[14]

The city's spiritual institutions did not fare well either. In destroying the city's churches, the RAF had succeeded where Hitler had failed. Christuskirche on Holstenplatz was a wreck, as was St George's church to the east of the Alster.[15] The huge Gothic Nikolaikirche was so badly damaged that Hamburgers to this day swear that it was the main aiming point of the British attack. The claim is without basis: the RAF Pathfinders were told simply to mark the area between the Alster and the river Elbe, and could not possibly have made out the spire of the church from 20,000 feet in the dark. But the church was, and is, such a potent symbol for the city that it was easy to imagine that the RAF would use it as their main target. In July 1943 many such rumours were born; indeed, the vicar of Michaeliskirche in the west of the city claimed after the bombings that *his* church was 'undoubtedly the main target of the enemy attack'.[16] The area around it was so badly damaged that he could not help but take the raid personally. In fact the 'Michel', as the church is affectionately known, was the only major church in Hamburg to survive the war intact.

Rumours flew round the shocked and anxious city. People claimed that Churchill had given Hitler an ultimatum: capitulate, or Hamburg will be bombed into oblivion.[17] Others said that Turkey had declared war on the Axis powers, or that Romania and Hungary were looking to make peace with the Allies.[18] In the absence of any proper newspapers it was difficult to know what was fact and what was merely speculation.[19] The real news that Mussolini had resigned was scarcely more extraordinary than the stories. With such large parts of their city in tatters it was easy for Hamburgers to believe that the entire Reich was falling apart.

Some of the most potent rumours concerned the RAF's foil-paper strips of which intact bundles had landed all over the city. Nobody had the slightest idea what they might be. Children gathered them up enthusiastically, just as they collected shrapnel splinters, but adults were more wary. When Martha Bührick was waiting for a tram on Monday afternoon she saw that 'The ground was covered with silver strips which the aeroplanes had dropped. A woman from the bank explained that a professor had said we should not touch them, as they had been covered with typhoid bacillus. I told her that I had picked up countless strips on Sunday morning, and that she should not spread such rubbish.'[20] Fredy Borck, who was eleven at the time, remembers being told not to play with them because they were poisonous.[21] In the end the *Hamburger Zeitung* used precious space on its single sheet for an article entitled 'The Paper Strips are Harmless'.[22] The following day it was entreating people not to believe those who claimed that the RAF had dropped threatening leaflets, or that the water supply had been poisoned.[23] That the city's only functioning newspaper had been driven to print such articles is a measure of how panic-stricken the people of Hamburg had become.

★   ★   ★

To prevent things getting further out of hand, the city's gauleiter, Karl Kaufmann, declared a 'State of Major Catastrophe' early on Sunday morning, and a previously prepared disaster plan came into effect. Police battalions were called in from surrounding areas to prevent civil unrest, and signs across Hamburg stated that looting would be punishable with death. The worst-affected areas were cordoned off to stop people getting too close to the fires that were still alight and to prevent looters helping themselves to the piles of personal belongings that now lined the streets. While the appearance of the SS on the streets caused widespread resentment among Hamburg's distraught civilians, there is no doubt that it did much to ensure the smooth running of the disaster plan.[24]

Next came the clearance of the hospitals to make way for the casualties. At first, everyone with a non-serious condition was told to go home – although when the night-raids began again even the serious cases were evacuated in ambulance trains. In the meantime, most people were treated at one of the seventy-two air-raid-shelter clinics that dotted the city. Dr Wilhelm Küper worked at one of these first-aid posts, and was surprised that, in general, people looked after themselves remarkably well: 'The vast majority of the dressings were so professionally applied – evidently the fruit of many training courses – that one could leave them as they were, if their usage was not for some of the more serious wounds.[25]

With the bursting of the water mains, and the requisition of all emergency supplies by the fire service, the supply of drinking water became an immediate problem. People who had been hidden in shelters for long periods needed water urgently, yet they were frightened to take it from the reservoirs in case they were arrested.[26] Emergency pumps and hydrants were made available around Hamburg, the city's many private wells were brought into use, and specially commissioned lorries brought clean water to various locations.[27]

Emergency rations of food and cigarettes had been issued, and were handed out across the city. For those who had lost houses and apartments financial help was available, and a special ration of clothes and shoes to tide them over until more permanent replacements could be arranged.[28] In the meantime, arrangements were made to evacuate those who had lost everything. By the evening of Tuesday, 27 July, 47,000 homeless people had been sent out to Schleswig-Holstein by train.[29]

Despite the seemingly gloomy picture that the city presented, Hamburg's disaster plan was working well. In some of the lightly affected areas a measure of normality had already been restored, and work on returning the gas and water mains to service was well under way. Had they been able to continue, the city authorities would probably have been able to put Hamburg back in order within a matter of weeks.

They were not allowed that luxury. Even as they were working, RAF Bomber Command was preparing to make another, even bigger strike on the city.

15. Concentrated Bombing

The guiding principle of bombing actions should be this: the objective must
be destroyed completely in one attack, making further attack on the same
target unnecessary.
Douhet[1]

The British had sent maximum-effort attacks to Hamburg on
Saturday night, and to Essen on Sunday night. To mount a third
that Monday would have been too much to ask of the exhausted
crews, so the follow-up raid on Hamburg was postponed for
twenty-four hours. With Monday evening to themselves, the airmen were free to do whatever they pleased, but there was little
enthusiasm for carousing. Most took the opportunity to rest, and
went to bed early to catch up on sleep.

The people of Hamburg were not so lucky. After three raids in
as many days they were understandably jumpy, and most people
had abandoned their apartments for an uncomfortable night in
one of the city's many shelters. For those who had dared to stay at
home the slightest warning would have them out of their beds,
running for cover. The British knew from experience that sleep
deprivation could be almost as damaging to the economy as bombardment, so that night the RAF sent six Mosquito aircraft over
the city on a nuisance raid. The damage their few bombs caused
was minuscule compared with what had gone before, but it was
enough to keep the whole city awake.[2] It had the added effect of
distracting the rescue workers and fire-fighters from their efforts.
Much of Altona was still on fire from the raid two nights ago, and
the approaching Mosquito pilots could see the glow from twenty
miles away.[3]

The next day, Tuesday, 27 July, it was the Americans' turn for a rest. Officially, they cited uncertainty over the weather as the reason for taking the day off, but the battered and harassed crews were in desperate need of a little respite. While they recuperated, Butch Harris was eager to resume his battle on Hamburg. Whatever the Americans might have said about the weather, as far as he was concerned the forecast for that night looked promising. A Mosquito reconnaissance plane was sent out over Hamburg later that morning to confirm conditions: its pilot reported back that, other than a light smoke haze from the fires that were still burning, the skies were perfectly clear. So, without further hesitation, Harris ordered his second maximum effort on Hamburg to go ahead.

The plan for tonight was similar to the one used on the night of 24 July.[4] Once again the bombers would be using Window, and flying in a tight stream through the German defences. Zero Hour was again 1.00 a.m. and the aiming point was exactly the same as last time. The only real differences from the previous plan of attack were a slight change to the route and an alteration to the type of bombs they would be using.

Tonight, instead of flying to Hamburg from the north-west, the bomber stream would take a route right across the Schleswig peninsula, then come back to approach Hamburg from the north-east. The idea was to make it look as if they were attacking Kiel or Lübeck – indeed, some historians have stated, wrongly, that the bomber stream passed directly over Lübeck as part of the ruse.[5] Whatever the case, it was an ineffective feint: everyone in Hamburg was expecting another attack, and the defences were still on high alert. However, it did mean that the run-in to the aiming point would be coming from a different direction, so any creepback in the bombing would land on a new part of the city. In the next few weeks the people of Hamburg would come to believe that the RAF had bombed the city with a methodical precision – ending their carpet of bombing at a particular street one night, and starting again with the next street along on the following night. Of course such accuracy was impossible, but there was an element of truth in the rumour. By coming at the city from different directions, the bombers could ensure that every suburb was hit during the series

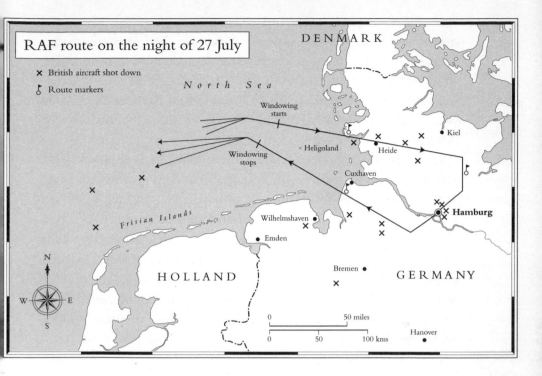

RAF route on the night of 27 July

× British aircraft shot down

ɤ Route markers

North Sea

DENMARK

Windowing starts

Heligoland

Heide

Kiel

Windowing stops

Cuxhaven

Hamburg

Frisian Islands

Wilhelmshaven

Emden

HOLLAND

Bremen

GERMANY

N

W — E

S

0   50 miles

0   50   100 kms

Hanover

of raids. Over the course of their four raids on the city the RAF attacked in turn from the north-west, the north-east, the north and the south. Effectively they were destroying the city a segment at a time.

The other main change to the plan was just as significant. Tonight the planes would be carrying far more incendiary bombs than they had on the previous attack – 240 tons more.[6] Some historians have claimed that this change was made for purely operational reasons: the aircraft had further to fly, so the Halifaxes and Stirlings had reduced the weight of their loads by replacing their high-explosive bombs with lighter incendiaries.[7] But that is not the whole story. Bomber Command planners were constantly revising the proportions of bomb loads, and it was becoming increasingly obvious that incendiaries did far more damage than explosives. Hamburg was not considered a particularly flammable city – most of the old wooden buildings in the city centre had already been burned down in the great fire of 1842 and replaced with more modern brick and stone buildings – but when the operation's planners saw how well the city had burned on the previous attack it seemed worthwhile to increase the proportion of incendiaries. The Lancasters had already been ordered to carry 'maximum economic incendiary loads' when the Hamburg raids were first conceived.[8] Tonight this order was extended to the Stirlings and Halifaxes.

As evening approached, morale was riding high at all levels of the RAF. Harris and his staff believed that they were at the start of a new era in the bombing war: now that German defences had been blinded by Window, Bomber Command effectively had command of the air, and Harris was convinced, more than ever before, that it would be only a matter of time before Germany was forced to surrender. The airmen were similarly enamoured of their new radar-jamming device. The casualty rate had plummeted since they had started using it, and the draughty job of shoving bundles of silver strips through the flare chute had become a labour of love. A new spirit of optimism was spreading through airfields up and down the country. During their briefing for that night's operation the crews were read a message from Harris congratulating them on the success of their previous attacks on Hamburg and Essen. It was greeted with great enthusiasm by the men, who were at last beginning to feel that they were making a difference. Perhaps their commander-in-chief had been right all along – perhaps they *would* be able to win the war by bombing alone.

Confidence was so high that officers of increasingly senior ranks decided to join the crews on their trip that night. Station commanders were not normally allowed to go out on more than one operation each month, but that evening no fewer than five decided that it was time to see the effects of Window for themselves.[9] Two air commodores also decided to fly – Air Commodore W. A. Brooke of 4 Group, and Air Commodore A. M. Wray of 1 Group. However, the highest-ranking officer to accompany the bomber crews was an American. Brigadier-General Fred Anderson, in charge of the Eighth Air Force's bombers, was so eager to learn how his allies operated that he joined a Pathfinder crew. He had been extremely impressed on the previous raid to Essen, but flying as second pilot to Flight Lieutenant Garvey in a Lancaster from 83 Squadron, he would witness destruction on a scale few people had ever believed possible.[10]

⋆   ⋆   ⋆

It had been a glorious summer's day, and when the bombers took off at around ten o'clock the dying sun had painted the sky blood-red. All along the eastern edge of England the air was soon filled with the drone of 787 aeroplanes heading off across the North Sea. To most of those who lived along the coast it was a comforting sound. At this stage of the war, bomber crews were still treated as celebrities by newspapers and newsreels, and as heroes by the general population: apart from the army in North Africa and Sicily, they were the only force capable of taking the war to Germany. People who lived near airfields would often come out to watch them take off, particularly on a fine, warm night. Children always waved, blissfully unaware of the realities of warfare.

Apart from a few minor mishaps, the whole bomber force took off safely. A small proportion turned back because of mechanical problems (only forty-two aircraft), but the vast majority congregated into three streams and made for their rendezvous point eighty miles off the German coast.[11] As on the previous raid, they began Windowing a few minutes later. Also as on the previous raid, the Pathfinders dropped yellow markers as they crossed the coast in order to concentrate the stream of planes more tightly. (A second set of route markers would be dropped later, further to concentrate it.)

The route markers were all that the defending Luftwaffe fighters had to guide them to the bomber stream, once their radar systems had been blinded by Window. A Pathfinder in the vanguard of the stream had been shot down before Window had taken effect, but now that the German pilots' radar screens had fuzzed over there was little they could do but head for the lights in the hope that they might stumble across some British bombers in the dark.

They were rewarded with just a single victory over a Lancaster from 467 Squadron. In return, one of their own Ju88s was shot down over Heide. In total, only five British bombers were lost on their way to the target, at a cost of two German night fighters. So far, Window had proved every bit as effective as it had been on the first raid, three nights before.

However, the German defences had not been idle over the past three days. Given how unprepared they were for Window, it is remarkable how quickly they responded to the crisis, and while their initial response was not enormously effective, it marked the beginning of a long fight back against the RAF.

The first thing the German radar controllers did was to rely much more on their long-range Freya radar, the only system not affected by the clouds of foil strips. While this was not nearly as accurate as the shorter-range Würzburg radar, and could not ascertain the altitude of the oncoming bombers, it could at least direct night fighters to the correct vicinity. Second, after two previous Window raids, the most skilled Würzburg radar operators were noticing differences between the images given off by Window and those by real aeroplanes. At high altitudes, for example, when the bundles of Window had not yet dispersed, the blips on their screens that moved slowly were likely to be puffs of undispersed Window, while those that moved faster were probably bombers. Sometimes aeroplanes on the fringes of the bomber stream could be distinguished from the fuzzy cloud of Window.

Changes were also taking place in German fighter tactics. While many pilots were still held back in their boxes in the vain hope that some means could be found to direct them towards the bombers in the old way, many others were allowed to go freelancing. This was a return to night-fighting as it had been before the advent of radar, when pilots had to rely on their eyes and intuition to find their prey. To help them, night-fighter headquarters broadcast a running commentary with information on the movements and possible intentions of the bomber stream.

The single most important change that took place that night, however, was the adoption of a brand new system of fighting:

Major Hajo Herrmann's *Wilde Sau* (literally 'Wild Boar', but the phrase is also an idiom meaning 'crazy' or 'reckless').[12] Herrmann was convinced that British bombers were much more vulnerable to fighters than they were to flak, so he devised a system whereby German day fighters could be used to reinforce the beleaguered night fighters. His idea was to fly his single-engined day fighters at high altitudes above the target, so that they could see the outlines of the bombers silhouetted below them by the fires, searchlights, marker flares and any other illumination on the ground. The German flak batteries would be ordered not to fire above a certain height, so that the fighters could swoop down on the bombers safely from above.

After a great deal of opposition, Major Herrmann had finally been given the go-ahead to try out his idea on the night of 3 July 1943, over Cologne.[13] After limited success, he was granted permission to raise a *Geschwader* of new 'Wild Boars' (i.e. three *Gruppen* of about twenty-five planes each – see Appendix D). He immediately established a *Gruppe* of modified Me109s at Hangelar airfield near Bonn, and two more at Rheine and Oldenburg. Together they would make up the famous Jagdgeschwader 300 (JG 300).

Major Herrmann's new fighter force was still in training when the attacks on Hamburg began. On the first night of the battle, only a few planes from JG 300 at Oldenburg had been sent over the city. On that night, many British crews had reported seeing strange new flak shells bursting over the city that looked 'like large Catherine wheels'. The official report remarks casually that they were not particularly lethal, and it now seems likely that they were employed as aerial signposting for the *Wilde Sau* fighters.

On 27 July, Major Herrmann received a telephone call from Goering instructing him to take his fighters out of training and employ them in full force tonight. When Herrmann protested that they were not yet ready for such a task, he was overruled: without proper radar cover, Herrmann's *Wilde Sau* were suddenly the Reich's most important form of defence.[14]

So it was that this fledgling force was employed in full for the first time over Hamburg on the night of 27/28 July. One day they would be an effective force, but now they did not have enough planes or trained pilots for the huge task that faced them.

★   ★   ★

At 12.55 a.m., two minutes ahead of schedule, the first Pathfinder dropped its load of yellow target indicators a couple of miles east of the city centre. Over the next five minutes, salvo after salvo of yellow TIs poured down on the same spot, over the suburb of Hammerbrook. When the 'backers-up' arrived with their green TIs, they dropped them on to the same area. Unlike the first raid, when the TIs had been spread out in four or five different areas, they were unusually concentrated. The German defenders tried to put off the bombers by sending up decoy flares about ten miles to the west of the city, but nobody was fooled: they had used red flares, the only colour *not* used by the British that night.[15] They were not fooled by decoy fires either – compared to the real ones, these were minuscule.

If the Pathfinders arrived early at the target, so did the main force. Unable to contain their eagerness to get in and out of the target quickly, many aircraft had cut corners along the way, guided by the route marker flares. By 1.02 a.m., when the main force was supposed to start bombing, eighty-seven planes had already dropped their loads – almost all on the single concentrated spot over Hammerbrook. The fire they caused there became a beacon for those who followed. Wave after wave of bombers came in across the north-east of Hamburg to stoke the fires, and with such a concentrated group of TIs to aim at there was at first very little creepback. As the later waves came in at around half past one, the fires were spreading north- and eastwards into the district of Hamm.

More than 2,313 tons of bombs were dropped within just fifty minutes – another new world record. Unlike the last raid, however, when a similar amount had been dispatched, most of these bombs were squeezed into a few square miles. The mass of individual fires started by the opening wave now began to join up into a single conflagration. The firestorm had begun.

In all, 722 aircraft bombed the city that night – most in the same small group of districts to the east of the city centre.[16] The scene below was unlike anything any of the crews had seen before. According to Colin Harrison, who was flying a 467 Squadron Lancaster in the last wave of the attack, the flames were already visible from miles away: 'We didn't need any navigation. We could see Hamburg from over the North Sea. We just flew where all the lights and the flares were. It looked hellish from on top. I mean, targets don't look very nice from on top, with all the coloured fires and flames . . . but this was particularly awful.'[17]

Above the fires, a pall of smoke rose so high that even the high-flying Lancasters found themselves plunged into the fumes. 'That was something frightful,' remembers Bill McCrea of 57 Squadron:

I remember the clouds that were coming up about 30,000 feet. It was just one great volcano underneath. All I was thinking about was dropping my bombs and getting home – the same as everybody . . . It was an appalling sight. Every so often it was just burbling up, like a volcano. Every so often there was another explosion, another bomb went in, and there was another flash. And you could see the photo flashes going off too – they were brighter and more sudden. They took the photographs that theoretically marked your aiming point. But of course that night you couldn't get anything, because there was no detail on the ground at all . . . there was just a whole sea, a mass of flame.[18]

Trevor Timperley of 156 Squadron also remembers the sights he saw that night:

The firestorm still grips me most out of my whole tour – both tours. The very size of it on the ground: it was just a sea of flames . . . I remember I had a navigator who would never look out at all. He used to be head down in his little office, working out one thing and another,

RAF bombs dropped on Hamburg
on the night of 27 July

but he would never come and look up. I remember saying, 'For Christ's
sake, Smithy, look at this! You'll never see the like of it again!'[19]

To some airmen the thought of what was happening on the
ground was harrowing. Leonard Cooper, for example, was a flight
engineer in a 7 Squadron Lancaster flying at an altitude of around
17,000 feet that night. He estimated that the cloud of smoke was
rising to about 20,000 feet – and they were flying directly through
it. 'We could definitely smell . . . well, it was like burning flesh,'
he says. 'It's not a thing I'd like to talk about.'[20]

★   ★   ★

With German defences in disarray, most of the bombers managed
to make their bombing runs without difficulty. Some, however,
were not so lucky. After the raid on 24/25 July, the mobile railway
flak batteries that Hamburg had sent to the Ruhr were rushed back
to defend the city. There seemed to be more searchlights than
ever, especially above the suburbs to the west and north-west that
had been hit by the previous raid. Without radar to guide them,
the vast numbers of guns and searchlights were unable to pose
anything like the threat they once had – but, even so, twenty-eight
aircraft returned to Britain with serious flak damage.

On the rare occasions when an aircraft was caught by the searchlights, the speed with which the other lights and guns locked on
to it was terrifying. When the master-beam caught a Lancaster
piloted by Sergeant C. G. Hopton, the other lights zoned in almost
immediately. Within moments the full force of all the flak batteries
in the area was focused on this one aircraft as it turned and dived
in an attempt to break free of the danger. With nothing else to
aim at, though, the flak gunners were glad of any opportunity to
bring down one of their attackers. As the Lancaster finally escaped
the lights, a shell hit the port wing and set the inner engine on
fire. Immediately the flight engineer set about feathering the engine
and extinguishing the blaze, but before he could do so they were
under attack a second time, this time from a German fighter who
had been attracted by the lights. Blinded by the searchlights, the

crew didn't spot him until he was closing in from above. He sighted his cannon on the burning engine, and raked the port wing, before he was forced away by the Lancaster's two gunners. Miraculously no one was hurt, and Hopton made it back to England on the three remaining engines.[21]

The plane that attacked Hopton's was an Me109, probably one of Major Hajo Herrmann's *Wilde Sau* fighters. These were unquestionably more effective at shooting down RAF bombers than the flak was. As they roamed the sky high above the city they could see the bombers below, clearly silhouetted against the glow of the raging fires on the ground. It is ironic that until this point the British had suffered even fewer casualties than they had on their first raid; now, with the fires illuminating them, a handful of bombers became victims of their own success.

At 1.21 a.m. the German flak batteries were ordered to limit their fire to 5,500 metres (about 18,000 feet).[22] At a stroke the defence of the city, at least in the higher altitudes, was now entirely down to the *Wilde Sau*, who swooped to attack the bomber stream from above.

Appropriately, Major Herrmann claimed the first victims:

The clouds of smoke over Hamburg were so dense that it made you shudder. I saw this great column of smoke: I even smelt it. I flew over the target several times and, then, I saw this bomber in the searchlights . . . It was like daylight in those searchlights. I could see the rear gunner; he was only looking downwards, probably at the inferno below. There was no movement of his guns. You must remember that, at this time, the British were not generally warned to watch out for us over the target. I had seen other bombers over targets with the gunners looking down. I fired and he burned . . . As he fell, he turned and dropped away from the smoke cloud. I followed him a little but, as he got lower and lower, I left him. I watched him burst on the ground.[23]

That night three more RAF planes were shot down over Hamburg. For those few doomed airmen, it was every bit as dangerous in the skies over Hamburg as it was on the ground. The flames that engulfed the planes as they fell to earth were a savage echo of the inferno below.

The narrow margin between life and death was made brutally stark to one Lancaster crew from 460 Squadron. They were as inexperienced as a crew could possibly be: their pilot, Reg Whelan, had been on the previous trip to Hamburg as a 'second dickie' pilot, but for the rest this was their first operation. Apart from the Australian navigator, Noel Knight, they were all in their early twenties.

They had reached the target without mishap, but just after they had dropped their load and were about to turn for home the plane was rocked by a massive explosion. The force turned it on to its back, and soon they were dropping out of the sky like a stone.

Ted Groom, the flight engineer, remembers the event vividly. He was at the back of the aircraft, dropping bundles of Window down the flare chute, when he found himself floating in the air, surrounded by foil strips from burst Window packets:

It all happened so quickly, in a matter of seconds. I didn't know where I was – I was just rolling around amongst all these bundles. My first thought was to get a plug in somewhere. I knew where all the intercom plugs were, right through the aircraft. I stumbled around in the pitch black, got hold of the lead and plugged myself back into the intercom. Reg the skipper was shouting out for me to get up to the front as quick as possible. By that time we were right way up. I went past the wireless operator. I went past the navigator who'd lost everything off his desk and was trying to find all his stuff in the semi-darkness. Everyone was crying out, 'What the hell's happening?' I eventually got up to the front and Reg said, 'Get this sorted out!' So I synchronized the engines at a normal climbing rate of about 2,850 revs a minute, plus seven or eight boost. I checked all the temperature gauges, and the fuel, even the oxygen to see if that was all right. I looked at the altimeter – you do this automatically when something goes wrong – and I saw that we were at 10,000 feet. I looked at the pilot, signalled to him that I didn't want him to speak, and I pointed at the altimeter.[24]

What Ted Groom was pointing out to his skipper, and what he didn't want broadcast to the others over the intercom, was that the aircraft had dropped 9,000 feet in a matter of seconds. Just twenty seconds more and they would all have died as they crashed into the fires on the ground below.

When they arrived back at Binbrook airfield just before five o'clock that morning, the ground crew checked the plane for damage. The fuel pipes were hanging out of the bottom of the aircraft, and there were loose panels where the rivets had burst, but there was nothing to indicate that they had been hit either by flak or by fighters. After an officer from the Air Ministry had checked the details, the unofficial explanation was that Reg Whelan and his crew had been directly above another British bomber when it was attacked by a German fighter. The other bomber had not yet dropped its bombs, so when it exploded the force was great enough to blow Reg Whelan's Lancaster on to its back. If this was indeed what had happened, that German fighter had almost got two bombers with a single shot.

★   ★   ★

That was by no means the last such incident of the night. Dozens of crews returned with stories of combat and near misses: ten over Hamburg, and at least a dozen on the way home. Eight planes were shot down on the return journey: six by German fighters, and two more by flak when they strayed off course over Wilhelmshaven and Bremerhaven. Excluding four aircraft that were written off when returning crews crash-landed them, seventeen British planes were lost that night: five more than on the first Hamburg raid. But that was still only half of the number that Bomber Command had become used to losing over the preceding months. Despite the rapid change in German tactics, Window was still working wonders for the British.

At 1.47 a.m. the last of the attacking aircraft dropped its mix of high explosives and incendiaries, and the tail end of the bomber stream made its way back towards the coast and over the North Sea to England. Behind them they left one of the biggest man-made fires the world has ever seen, still growing in intensity. As a young rear gunner wrote in his diary that night: 'If it had been a really clear night the fires would have been visible nearly back to our coast. As it was we could see it nearly half-way back, about 200 miles, and a column of smoke about 20,000 feet, so Hamburg must have had it.'[25]

16. Firestorm

What if the breath that kindled those grim fires
Awaked should blow them into sevenfold rage
And plunge us in the flames? . . . what if all
Her stores were opened and this firmament
Of hell should spout her cataracts of fire
John Milton, *Paradise Lost*[1]

To understand what happened on the night of Tuesday, 27 July 1943, one needs to know a little about how major fires work. Few people have any direct experience of conditions inside a major conflagration, and even those unlucky enough to have lived through a house fire cannot possibly understand what it is like to be caught in a firestorm.

Large conflagrations are different from house fires in two important respects. First, because of their sheer size they produce such vast quantities of smoke that even those far away from the flames may suffocate. This is particularly dangerous in city fires – anyone sheltering in the confined space of a basement or cellar risks death from smoke inhalation or carbon monoxide poisoning, as all the oxygen is sucked out of the air and replaced with poisonous fumes.

Second, and more importantly, the incredible temperatures such fires reach – sometimes as high as 800°C – superheat the air above and around the fire, causing it to rise rapidly. In some cases this sets off a chain reaction. As air rushes skywards it leaves a vacuum, which sucks new air from the surrounding areas to fill it. The new air brings oxygen, which feeds the fire. The process accelerates: the fire gets hotter, and the winds get faster, often reaching speeds of 60 or 70 m.p.h. This is what gives the 'firestorm' phenomenon its name: the combination of huge fires and storm-force winds. As long as there is enough fuel to keep the fire burning the winds will continue to blow, first rushing into the fire horizontally along the ground, then shooting skywards with the heat.

As I mentioned in Chapter 10, Hamburg had already had a firestorm on Saturday night, where witnesses claimed to have seen 'a frightful storm, caused by the heat', and winds so strong that it was impossible to fight one's way through them.[2] On that night British air crew reported seeing clouds of smoke billowing up to 20,000 feet and beyond, forced rapidly into the sky by the heat. This was comparable to the devastating firestorm that had enveloped Wuppertal two months before the Hamburg bombings, and that would consume Dresden eighteen months later.[3]

What happened on the night of 27 July, however, was in a different league. The winds reached speeds of at least 120 m.p.h., and in places perhaps as high as 170 m.p.h.[4] To make things worse, they were not steady in their force: they swirled and changed direction from one moment to the next. In a forest firestorm the wind is generally free to take the most direct route to the centre of the conflagration, spiralling inwards in an anti-clockwise direction, like a cyclone. By contrast, in a city like Hamburg, the winds are forced away from their natural course by all the buildings that stand in the way. That night they were channelled along streets, sometimes meeting head-on at junctions, causing eddies and swirls that knocked people off their feet. There are many reports of 'fire-whirls' at such junctions – miniature tornadoes – which added to the misery of the fugitives trying to reach safety.[5]

Some of the hottest temperatures ever experienced in a city fire accompanied the hurricane-force winds. The sheer amount of flammable material, stacked up in six-storey buildings, like huge charcoal ricks, produced enough heat to melt the glass in the windows of cars and trams on the streets – which means the temperature must have approached glass-furnace level, about 1,400°C.[6] Inside the buildings it was even hotter – cutlery and glass bottles melted, and bricks burned to ash.

In the years that followed the catastrophe, the Hamburg firestorm came under intense scientific scrutiny, and it was concluded that no other large fire in recorded history has ever equalled its intensity. It was far worse than any of the great forest fires that have engulfed large parts of America and Canada; greater even than the fires that have consumed London, Chicago or any other city bombed by the Allies across Germany.

The reason Hamburg's firestorm was so bad is as simple as the result was tragic: weather conditions – a set of circumstances so unusual for the area that they have only rarely been repeated since. Because of all the hot, sultry weather Hamburg had been experiencing, an unstable pocket of warm air was sitting directly over the city. It had been warmed by all the fires that had been burning since Sunday, and was saturated with smoke particles, which retained the heat even more effectively. All around Hamburg, however, and high above it, the air was much cooler. Surrounded on all sides by this colder air, the pocket of warm air was like a huge, pressurized balloon, sticking up some 10,000 feet. All it would take to burst the top off this balloon was a sharp rise in temperature. Once it *had* burst, the warm air over the city would rise unrestricted for thousands of feet, rapidly drawing newer air behind it, and setting off the greatest firestorm the world has ever seen.[7]

The final factor was the humidity – or, rather, the lack of it. Because the city is close to the sea, the air in Hamburg normally has a very high humidity – a seasonal average of about 78 per cent. On 27 July 1943 the humidity was a mere 30 per cent. After the long, dry summer most of the buildings in Hamburg were like tinder, but with such low humidity there was nothing to stop the rapid spread of fire. Other historians have used the analogy of a furnace with a very tall chimney, just waiting for someone to light a match.[8] That match was lit shortly before 1.00 a.m. when the RAF dropped the first of 1,174 tons of incendiaries into the eastern quarter of the city.

★   ★   ★

Part of the tragedy for Hamburg was the sheer bad luck of it all. The Allies had not planned specifically to take advantage of the prevailing weather conditions; indeed, they did not even realize that such conditions *could* lead to a firestorm.[9] Their understanding was far more basic: the weather was good because it was clear, which made navigation to the city much easier, and because it was dry, which would make it easier to start effective fires. They had no idea quite how perfect the conditions were for their purpose.

They did, however, have a good idea of how to start fires, and how to keep them going. After years of practice, they had created a highly effective system. To start with, they knew that the most important factor was concentration. If an attacking force dropped its incendiaries in a single area it would be impossible for the defenders to put out all of the fires. If enough were allowed to take hold, they would soon join up into huge conflagrations. The fire services would be unable to cope: they would be forced further and further away from each fire's centre, and would struggle to prevent them spreading to other districts.

The second most important thing was the use of high-explosive bombs. Most people assume, instinctively, that the purpose of explosives is to destroy buildings. Our perception is coloured by our modern experience: the bombs used by terrorists, or even by conventional military forces, are almost always designed to cause maximum damage to buildings by razing them to the ground. But bombing during the Second World War was carried out on such a huge scale that different tactics were required. Fire is far more efficient than high-explosive bombs at destroying large areas, so Allied tactics were aimed at getting the fires to spread as far and as quickly as possible. Military planners had learned early in the war that if they wanted their fires to spread it was counter-productive to blast buildings down because this created fire breaks. The purpose of high explosives, therefore, was not to *destroy* buildings but merely to blow in as many doors and windows as possible, to allow the air to get inside and feed the flames. Buildings that were not yet burning would catch fire as the sparks and embers from neighbouring buildings floated in, setting curtains and furniture alight. By blowing off roofs, high-explosive bombs would also allow the incendiaries to pierce the lower floors of a building, where they could do most damage. The explosions would have the added effect of keeping most fire-fighters inside their shelters long enough for the fires to take hold, and putting craters in the roads that prevented fire engines getting to affected areas. So while the incendiaries would do most damage, high explosives had an essential role, and it was important that the exact mix of the two different types of bombs was right.[10]

One might be tempted to ask what kind of mind comes up with such theories, but to be fair to the Allies a great deal of the research had been done for them – or, rather, *to* them. During the Blitz in 1940–41, the Luftwaffe had rained incendiaries on London and other cities, causing huge damage. The British, who had only really used high-explosive bombs until then, soon learned that the fires did far more damage than the explosions, and began to experiment accordingly.[11] Repugnant as it might seem now, the cruel logic of war requires such efficiency. By the summer of 1943, RAF planners had brought large-scale bombing to a fine art.

*   *   *

The concentration of bombs on Hamburg that Tuesday night was so great that the civil-defence organizations in the eastern quarter of the city had little chance of saving anything. 'After only a quarter of an hour, conditions in these districts were terrible,' claimed the official German report shortly afterwards. 'A carpet of bombs of unimaginable density caused almost complete destruction of these districts in a very short time. Extensive portions were transformed in barely half an hour into one sea of flame.'[12] The bombs came down so thick and fast it was impossible to stop the spread of fire: tens of thousands of individual fires quickly became one vast conflagration.

The people of Hamburg had been expecting another attack, but nothing could have prepared them for the hammering they were now experiencing, especially in the eastern quarter of the city. Even those who had lived through the first night of attacks must have been shocked at the intensity of tonight's bombardment. For

Fredy Borck, the eleven-year-old who lived in the riverside district of Rothenburgsort, it was the most terrifying night of his life:

Suddenly it started to happen outside. It was a bombardment that is still indescribable, even today . . . All around us were the crashes of bombs striking with appalling explosions – ear-shattering explosions that seemed to be right next to us, over us. You could even hear the howl of the nearer bombs before they hit, then the crash as they burst. It must have been hell outside! It got worse and worse. The walls of the cellar rose and sank . . . An inhuman screeching and groaning came from the walls. We screamed along with it, screaming out our terror! We lost all self-control, crouched on the benches, cowering together with our heads between our knees to cover our ears.[13]

Fifteen-year-old Herbert Wulff was sheltering in a basement in Süderstrasse, right at the centre of the main attack. He was huddling with his mother and sister when the sound of the bombs became unbearable: unlike Fredy Borck, his instinct was to leave the shelter and take his chances outside. His sister was still recovering from a gall-bladder operation – she had been discharged from Barmbek hospital early because the room where she had been recuperating was destroyed in the first night of attacks. Even so, Wulff recalled, she too was determined to get out of the basement shelter:

Shortly after everyone in the building had filled the cellar, the whole building shook, right down to the foundations, from the explosion of a huge bomb. I can still see it, how the foundation walls moved between the buttresses and swayed dangerously. Then the lighting went out abruptly, and a cry rang out through the cellar room, and I thought for a moment that my final hour had come. After that first terrifying second we had only one thought: to get out of there. Instinctively my mother, my sister and I grabbed each other's hands and pushed our way through to the cellar stairs.[14]

Some people – the foolish and the brave – were already outside their cellars watching events unfold. Most houses and factories had a fire warden who would make regular patrols for incendiaries, and call for help from the shelters when a new fire needed to be put out.[15] Many of those brave men and women died before they had a chance to do anything useful. The survivors found themselves quickly overwhelmed by the sheer numbers of incendiary bombs falling around them. The German authorities estimated that 96,429 stick incendiaries fell on every square kilometre of ground, plus a further 2,733 larger incendiary bombs. This was over five times as concentrated as the previous large-scale attack.[16] To give some idea of what this meant on a human scale, imagine a large attic room, about ten metres long and ten metres wide. On average, in this attic room alone, ten incendiary bombs would fall, each crashing through the ceiling to set the roof timbers alight.

The incendiary bombs were of two main types. The most common were the four-pound thermite stick incendiaries. They fell nose down, to strike roofs so hard that they would either lodge in the roof cavity or pierce through to the rooms below where they would burst into flame. Some were also fitted with an explosive charge, so that if a fire warden came across it in time to shovel it out of a window it would explode, killing or maiming him or her. The second type of incendiary was bigger, weighing thirty pounds, and was heavy enough to crash through the roof space into the lower storeys. They were filled with a liquid mixture of Benzol and rubber, designed to splash across whatever the bomb hit, setting fire to everything within ten metres. German civilians tended to call them, and all incendiaries, 'phosphor bombs', which gave rise to a number of gruesome myths. Phosphorus is a particularly evil substance: it sticks to the skin and is impossible to put out as long as it is in contact with the air. In fact, while a small number of bombs contained phosphorus, the vast majority were made from other substances, less immediately terrifying, but much more effective at starting fires.[17]

With dozens of apartments catching fire simultaneously, whole blocks were soon ablaze. Henni Klank, a young mother, was one of those who ventured out of her shelter.

I don't know why, but suddenly the Devil possessed me; I wanted to go into our house one more time. Perhaps I thought I could still get some things out, like papers, photographs, and such things. But as I stood in the corridor the ceiling was already crackling, and I wanted to go to my father's desk in the living-room, but there I saw only fire. The blazing and burning curtains flew in the room, the window panes burst and there was a hissing and crashing all around me. I couldn't manage the few steps to the desk, which stood at the window, my legs felt paralysed. While dashing out of the apartment I hadn't grabbed even a single article out of the wardrobe. I was in such a panic that I rushed back to the shelter as quickly as possible. The streets were already burning, the firestorm was now raging through all the streets![18]

Downstairs she found her friends and neighbours close to despair. They all knew that they must leave the building, but when one had tried to go out by the front entrance he had been blown by the wind into the fire. The front of the building was ablaze, and a timber business opposite was burning so fiercely that they would not be able to get through to the relative safety of the canal beyond it. Eventually somebody came up with the idea of breaking through the back wall of the building – Frau Klank's husband had remembered a pickaxe that stood in the corner of the basement. They smashed a hole through the wall big enough to push through the pram that contained their newborn baby.

The vision that greeted them on the other side of that wall was worthy of Hieronymus Bosch: 'We came out at the Stadtdeich but into a thundering, blazing hell. The streets were burning, the trees were burning and the tops of them were bent right down to the street, burning horses out of the Hertz hauling business ran past us, the air was burning, simply everything was burning!'[19]

The bombardment had been so fierce that many people found themselves in similar situations: their houses were on fire, yet their escape routes were blocked by rubble or flames. That was what happened to Erich Titschak, a professor of entomology, who lived on Dimpfelsweg in the centre of Hamm. At 1.15 a.m., in the middle of the attack, an incendiary set the cellar stairs alight making escape from the shelter virtually impossible. He and some others broke through to their neighbouring cellar, only to find that the way out there was also blocked by flames. In desperation they got through to the basement on the opposite side. That house and the one beyond it had been burned down in a previous raid, so they thought it would be easy to find a way through to the street. In a letter to his children shortly afterwards, he described what he found:

A labyrinth of cellars, hallways, corners and sheds opens before us . . . All kinds of useless junk block our way. We break through eleven doors, one by one, hoping to finally find the exit on to the Hammer Landstraße . . . there must be a safe way out of here, the corner house, for our wives and children. Some cellar doors fly open at the first hit, but now we are faced with two heavy doors, which resist all our efforts. We take it in turns, sweat running in streams from our foreheads, but without success. The doors are probably lined with iron on the other side. The bolts are strong, our axe glances off the concrete without leaving a trace.[20]

Disappointed, Titschak and his companion, Herr Bläß, returned to their own cellar, knowing that the only way out was up the burning stairs. On the way back they caught a view of what they were up against.

In one of the adjoining rooms, I knock out the cellar window and catch my first glimpse of Dimpfelsweg and the gardens. What I see takes my breath away. Not just our building and the neighbouring building: no, the entire Dimpfelsweg, the buildings opposite, the Wagnerische Villa, the big building by the cinema, the cinema itself, the Claudiastraße – it all is one enormous sea of fire. A tornado-strength storm sweeps through the streets, pushing a rain of embers before it as thick as a snowstorm in winter. We were supposed to go through there? We'd never make it! Our clothes would instantly catch fire. The Hammer Landstraße, which was supposed to save us – the same picture. As far as I could see through the iron bars of a small cellar window, all the big beautiful buildings were burning from top to bottom.[21]

Back in their cellar they instructed everyone to wrap wet towels round themselves and do their best to escape up the burning stairs. At that point, while they could see the immediate danger, they had no real idea of the hell that lay outside. Each person in the cellar made the short run through the flames, Titschak leading. As they stumbled out on to the street, they were confronted by the sight of their entire neighbourhood on fire.

Another survivor in similar circumstances, Hans Jedlicka, claims that the shock of this sight numbed him:

I was still convinced that the fire bombs had only hit our doorway, that once we'd run through we'd be safe. As we came through, the sight that met us was like a blow. All I could see was flames. The whole of Hammerbrook was burning! A powerful storm took hold of us and drove us in the direction of Hammerbrookstraße. That was wrong. We had to go towards Heidenkampsweg – there was water there, and the Stoltenpark. We stumbled over the first charred corpses. From there on it was like a switch turned in my head. It was like being in a dream. I saw and heard everything, crystal-clear, but in spite of the great heat felt no pain. We had to fight our way through the firestorm metre by metre. My mother's clothes caught fire. I put the flames out with my hands.[22]

It is little wonder that many people chose to stay in their cellars in the unrealistic hope that the reinforced ceilings would afford them some protection from the flames in the buildings above them. Some people must have believed they would be safer in their makeshift bunkers than they would be outside – as the public-information documents and broadcasts had told them. Others gave up in despair. When everything outside was burning, what difference did it make whether one stayed or left? Some air-raid wardens reported having to bully people into seeking safety elsewhere with blows and kicks, even though it had become obvious that to stay put meant certain death.[23]

In any normal raid, when the upper floors of a house were on fire it was still fairly safe in the cellar, and certainly better than risking the explosions outside – occupants of a burning building were encouraged to stay where they were at least until the all-clear had sounded. But, this was no normal raid. Once the firestorm had taken hold, the wind and all the flaming debris it carried made it almost impossible to escape through the streets. Many of those who survived did so because they left their cellars early – perversely, those who initially appeared to be in the most danger were the most likely to survive. Those whose buildings caught fire later in the raid found themselves trapped between their own fire and the 'hell' of the firestorm outside.

In an interview with *Der Spiegel* magazine in 2003, the poet and song-writer Wolf Biermann described how agonizing the decision was to stay or go. He was six at the time, but remembers the events of that night as clearly as if they were burned into his memory:

I sat there alone with my mother . . . She was sitting there as if she was paralysed or maybe because she was smart – because in such a panic everything you do is a mistake. It's a mistake to leave: you run to your own death. It's a mistake to stay: death will come to you. Nobody is rational in such a situation. In a sense I was rational: I pressed my little head into my mother's coat, into her lap, and thus I could breathe; the air was impossible to breathe elsewhere.

Then my mother realised we'd burn there. She took a little leather suitcase with our papers and a few photos of my dad who, just a few months ago, had gone through the fiery oven in Auschwitz, as a Jew, as a Communist. And she handed me a little bucket – a little aluminium bucket with a cover. There was mirabelle jam inside, my mother had made it. And I took my little bucket and then we got out. We crawled through the basement.[24]

As he stepped outside it was not so much the sight of all the flames that terrified him as the noise. The crash of the bombs exploding around him, the roar of the fires, the drone of the planes and, above it all, the terrifying whine of the wind: 'What a sound it was! It was hell, it was hell's fires. In hell it is not only hot but loud. The firestorm was screaming!'[25]

The odyssey that lay before people like the young Wolf

Biermann and his mother defies imagination. In a conflagration so huge it was impossible to escape the fire – the distance to the edge was too great. The best anyone could hope for was to get to some open space that would act as an island in the terrible flaming sea – a park or playing fields where the fire could not properly take hold. In Hammerbrook people made for the Stoltenpark, or the banks of the many canals that criss-crossed the area. In Hamm, those who could made their way to the Hammer Park, and in Eilbek it was the Jakobipark, just north of Hasselbrook station. Even there the heat was so great that people were overcome. Without shelter from the storm of sparks their clothes and hair were still in danger of catching fire, and many sustained such bad burns as they escaped that they perished shortly after reaching relative safety. In the smaller parks and open spaces hundreds died because they could not get far enough away from the incredible heat. In one green about 120 metres square, more than a hundred people who had sought safety in the centre were burned to death.[26]

The following account is by a man who was in his mid-forties. When the exit from his cellar was blocked by rubble he was forced to break through into his brother-in-law's pastry shop on the ground floor of the building. From that point on it became almost impossible to keep the family together as they ran through the burning streets in a desperate search for shelter:

There were only two places that might be safe; either the sports field on Grevenweg or the Ankelmannplatz in the opposite direction. The escape route to the sports field was shorter, but was more likely to be in the middle of a sea of fire. I personally, with my family, chose the somewhat longer route, racing along the middle of the street which was alight with flying sparks, in order to avoid some of the heat from the burning house façades.

Even on the short distance to the next corner, we saw the first people burning, desperately running figures, who suddenly fell, and as we approached, were already dead. We had reached the first crossroads. Here we saw a building whose roof had, exceptionally, only just caught fire. In the entrance to this building we took shelter for a few moments from the storm, the heat, the whipping whirl of sparks and the glowing mounds of phosphor. We were in desperate need of this break. Although we had only travelled a short distance, our lips were already badly swollen. Our throats were incredibly dry. Our legs felt weak . . .

All around people fled from burning buildings. Some came out with their clothes already alight, others caught fire outside, from the sparks, the blazing heat or the phosphor. Again and again we saw burning people suddenly start to run, and soon after, to fall.

After this terrible cries were to be heard, but they too grew rarer. I saw many burning people who ran and collapsed in silence. There were also people travelling in the opposite direction to us. Because of this we had only gone a few steps when I heard my sister call. We could not see her, because despite the bright fires close by, thick smoke and dust darkened everything. We followed my sister's voice, calling [to her] ourselves, but received no answer. For a short while it became lighter. Around twenty metres in front of me, I saw my brother-in-law appear from the darkness of a building's wall, and run into the middle of the street. I called to him. He turned to me. I saw from his badly swollen face that he had already suffered heavy burns. Whether or not he recognized me, I do not know. My brother-in-law suddenly turned away again and began to run. I then saw that all his clothes were burning brightly. He fell into a mass of three or four corpses which were already completely burned. When my wife and I reached there, our brother-in-law was already dead, burned. There was no way to save the people who were falling. He who fell over during his escape was lost . . .

My wife's head began to burn. Her hair had caught fire. With a small amount of water that I had in a bucket with me I was able to put out her burning hair. At the same time I cooled my hands and face . . . My wife complained, 'I can't go on! My feet are burned! My hands!' . . . I also felt great pain in my right hand, caused by a severe burn. My left hand was beginning to hurt similarly as well. My head burned as if on fire, especially my face. I also noticed that my sight began to fade.

The stretch of road upon which we now travelled brought ever worsening scenes of horror. I saw many women with their children held in their arms running, burning and then falling and not getting back up. We passed masses of people made up of four or five corpses, each probably a family, visible only as a pile of burned substance no larger than a small child. Many men and women fell over suddenly without having caught fire. Around us were hundreds of people. Some of them ran, some moved slowly, with a peculiar shuffling walk. All this happened in silence. The terrible heat had dried throats so much that no one could scream. Silently and with the last of their force, women tried to save their children. They carried them pressed close. Many of these children were already dead, without their mothers knowing.[27]

A tornado, a whirl of sparks, the tops of trees bent to the street by the force of the burning wind – what these people were witnessing was the beginning of a unique phenomenon. The word *Flammen-meer*, 'sea of flames', comes up again and again in accounts of the firestorm. It is a literal description of what those people saw: a vast sea of fire in the grip of a hurricane. When a local priest saw what had overcome his neighbourhood in Eilbek he was reminded of the apocalyptic vision of St Matthew.[28] For most people, however, they were witnessing, quite simply, a picture of hell. The fires spread for miles in each direction and there was literally no end to the flames – their entire world had been transformed into a blazing inferno.

The city authorities struggled vainly to keep the fires under control, but from the outset they were fighting a losing battle. With most of the fire service still in the west of the city there were few teams to combat the flames. Those who did appear soon gave up trying to put out the fires and concentrated instead on rescuing people from burning buildings. In Rothenburgsort, for example, the fire-service leader ordered his men to create an umbrella of water for the fugitives to escape beneath, and in this way brought up to five thousand people to safety.[29] Such rescue attempts were still possible on the outer edges of the main firestorm area – but once the fire brigade ventured into Hammerbrook, Borgfelde and Hamm they were forced to abandon all hope of saving anyone. The head of one fire-fighting unit discovered that, not only was he unable to help the fugitives, he was lucky to escape with his own life:

In Hammer Weg there were people lying on the street. We climbed out of the car to rescue them. Then suddenly, along the Landstraße, there came a colossal sheet of flame, which I tried to escape by running ahead of it. The driver got away by turning the car down Horst-Wessel-Straße. The firestorm was a hurricane. No smoke on the streets, only flames and flying sparks as thick as a snowstorm . . . I ran until I was exhausted.[30]

Ludwig Faupel was another fireman who had rushed to Hamm only to find himself embroiled in the full force of the firestorm. After driving through a 'roaring, boiling hell', he and his crew were forced to abandon their vehicle in the middle of the road and take whatever shelter they could find.[31]

Closely pressed against the ground behind a heap of stones, the heat was unbearable. Again and again I had to put out my smouldering clothes. I put my gas mask on for lack of air. Bits of fire, dust and ash flew all around. In the howling and crashing of the wind people were blown over, stumbled and lay there exhausted, doomed to die. Above it all the growling drone of hundreds of aircraft. Bombs exploding.

Our fire engine was burning. My comrades had disappeared in the storm and heat. In order to stop myself being pulled into the fire I struggled against the storm and landed up in a huge bomb crater, full of water from a broken pipe. Trapped, I ripped the gas mask from my face and clung to the edge of the crater for fear of drowning. The rim broke off, my helmet was gone, dread began to take hold of me. I ducked under the water in order to escape the glowing heat. There was an insane noise in the air.[32]

In this atmosphere, surrounded by incessant noise and unbearable heat, the terrifying scenes took on a surreal quality.

With a glance over the edge of the crater I saw a man kneeling right in front of me. With big, frightened eyes he fell forwards. I pulled the dead man into the crater. Only those who had left the cellars by this time would now survive. They rushed over glowing mountains of rubble.

Many were killed by the ruins collapsing, or torn to pieces by bombs, suffocated or burned. I could not believe what I was seeing. In the thunderous din none of them could hear the screams of the others. Each struggled for survival. Parts of a collapsing house façade poured down on the other side of the crater and into the water. The brown sludge splashed around the edge and meant the end for some of those seeking shelter.[33]

As he clung to the edge of the crater, Faupel lost all sense of time. He had no idea how long he stayed there, whether it was hours or merely minutes. Eventually, however, instinct told him to move on:

At some point in the night I ran on once more with the dripping wet jacket of the dead man over my head. In this whirling fire I had lost all sense of direction. On my way out of the chaos I came across a burnt-out tram. The windows had melted in the heat. Dead bodies lay naked on top of one another in the carriage. Their clothes had disintegrated into embers. The people had tried to shelter there from the firestorm. In Eiffestrasse they struggled for survival. Sinking into the hot Tarmac, they had tried to support themselves with their hands, and lay now on their knees. They ended their lives screaming with fear and pain. I could not help them.[34]

Although he was only a child, Wolf Biermann remembers equally chilling scenes:

The firestorm was so strong that it converted streets into jets. Schwaben-strasse, where we lived, was in a good position, aslant to the suction of the fire. But once you got into a street which was part of the suction, people started to burn like tinder and they had no chance. So we ran close to the walls to escape the storm. I saw how roofs were flying through the air; it was like in the movies, like science fiction, but real. The asphalt was burning and boiling. I saw two women running, a young one and an older one, whose shoes got stuck in the boiling asphalt. They pulled their feet out of the shoes but that wasn't a good idea because they had to step into the boiling asphalt. They fell and didn't get up again. Like flies in the hot wax of a candle.[35]

Ernst-Günther Haberland was another schoolchild who witnessed this uniquely awful vision, after leaving the safety of the main bunker at about five o'clock the next morning:

We looked around us at the area where we had once lived. All the buildings burned brightly, it was a single wall of fire. One could hear the terrible cries of people seeking help for their wounds. One saw people on Heidenkampsweg trying to cross from one side of the street to the other, where there was a canal. The asphalt of the road had become almost liquid with the immense heat. They reached the middle, where their feet got stuck in the asphalt. Their legs began to burn because of the heat, the flames ate their way up and met again above their heads. At first they screamed, then became quieter, and finally, they gave a last rattling breath and were dead.[36]

*   *   *

Survival in the open streets of Hamburg was now virtually impossible. The hurricane was full of burning debris – roofs, branches, pieces of masonry and timber – and there are many accounts of people being bowled over by items that hit them.[37] The air was so hot and so choked with smoke and poisonous gases as to be all but unbreathable. Sparks and embers caught on people's hair, setting it on fire. To make things worse, the fugitives could not allow themselves to be carried along by the wind: since the hurricane was caused by the fire sucking air inwards to feed itself, that would have been suicide. Instead they had to battle *against* it, and all the flaming debris it carried, to reach anything resembling safety. Neither were they able to seek shelter in doorways – often the heat from burning houses was so intense that they were obliged to stick to the middle of the road, where the force of the wind was strongest.

When the safety of an open space was too far for the fugitives immediately to reach, they had to try to get there in stages, taking what shelter they could along the way. One woman tells how she, her husband and daughter travelled from one burning cellar to the next, sheltering for as long as the flames were not immediately threatening, before moving on again. They did this no fewer than seven times, before finally succumbing to despair:

So we had finished with our lives. There was too little hope of escaping this hellish cauldron. No way to break through this ring. We no longer said a word to one another, we did not cry either, nor did we whine or complain, we only stared silently in front of ourselves. Suddenly we were told there was an escape route by the railroad embankment, that we should get onto the rails, since no trains could come because the station had been destroyed. We then slid down a long rope on to the platform. Today I can't imagine how we managed to get down there – but anyway, we got down. Exhausted, we threw ourselves on to the embankment. However, the grassy knolls were so hot that one could not stay on them. The opposite embankment had already caught fire. Hannelore climbed to the top of the embankment with the last of her energy in order to see how thick the smoke above was . . . She called to us, and we climbed with what little strength we still had to the top, our cramped hands in the hot grass. When we arrived at the top, we fled into a small corrugated metal toilet. Here people sat on top of each other in the disgusting air, safe only from the sparks, and in no way from the smoke.[38]

On such a hellish night, a public toilet was a welcome haven, particularly if the cisterns still had water in them. Erika Wilken and her husband Willi found shelter in a toilet under the street on Grevenweg, at the centre of the firestorm area in Hammerbrook. For a while they huddled with at least eighty others, wetting a blanket in the water from the cisterns to drape over their heads. When it ran out they used the water from the toilet bowls. There was little they could do beyond staying put, and hoping not to suffocate as all the oxygen was sucked out of the air by the fires. But worse was to come:

To our misfortune, a large phosphorus bomb fell directly outside the entrance (whose door had been blown off on Saturday evening). The people nearest the door now gave way to an indescribable panic. The inner lavatory doors were torn off and used as shields in front of the bomb. After a few minutes, they too were burning brightly.

Terrible scenes took place, since all of us saw certain death in front of us, with the only way out a sea of flames. We were caught like rats in a trap. The doors were thrown on to the canister by screaming people and more smoke and heat poured in. In the meantime, the water in the tank had been used up . . . My husband was completely worn out and we crouched next to the bowl. The other people here sat down too; some collapsed and never woke up again. Three soldiers committed suicide. I begged my husband to beat back the flames with our blanket – the one object we had brought with us apart from our papers – but he was no longer able to do so. So with my last strength I did it. My hair began to singe and my husband extinguished it . . .

What now? Our hearts were racing, our faces began to puff up and we were close to fainting. Perhaps another five or eight minutes and we would be finished too. On my question 'Willi, is this the end?', my husband decided to risk everything and try to reach the outside . . . I took the blanket and he the little suitcase. Quickly but carefully, so that we would not slip on the corpses, we reached the outside, me first and my husband behind me. One! Two! Three! We were through the wall of fire. We made it. Both without burns; only our shoes were singed. But our last strength and courage had gone. We lay down on the ground at the side of the canal . . . People swimming in it kept wetting our blanket for us.[39]

Erika and Willy Wilken had stumbled by accident upon probably the last safe haven in Hammerbrook. Away from the relative security of the parks and open spaces, the canals that criss-crossed the area proved the only salvation for thousands of people. Beside the water they were a fraction cooler, and the air near the water's surface was breathable. Most of the fugitives did not stop on the canals' banks but hurried to submerge themselves, cooling their burns in the life-saving water.

Yet even here it was not completely safe. There are many tales of people becoming drenched in liquid phosphorus and being unable to extinguish the flames, even by throwing themselves into the canals because phosphorus burns as soon as it comes back into contact with oxygen. Most of these stories can be dismissed as repetition of a particularly gruesome urban myth,[40] but the British used liquid phosphorus in some of their incendiaries, and there are enough first-hand eyewitnesses to make one or two instances of this terrible story possible.

Just as dangerous, however, was the thin layer of oil on the water's surface. Ben Witter, who witnessed the firestorm as a local journalist, describes the circumstances in which some people found themselves as they sought shelter in the canals:

It is difficult to explain how water can burn. It was burning because very many ships, small ships, had exploded and oil had been released into the water and the people who were themselves on fire jumped into it and . . . I don't know, some kind of chemical must have been in it . . . and they burned, swam, burned, and went under.[41]

The official report of the Hamburg police chief confirms that while the canals were often the only safe place to go they were still by no means comfortable. Even those who stayed in the water throughout the firestorm suffered burns on their heads; they were obliged to keep wetting their faces to avoid perishing in the heat. 'The firestorm swept over the water with its heat and its showers of sparks so that even thick wooden posts and bollards burned down to the level of the water.'[42] Many people were obliged to stand in the water or swim for hours; some became exhausted and drowned. Others died from injuries caused by falling masonry and other debris that fell on to the water's surface.

Twenty-one-year-old Heinz Masuch was driven to the Süd Kanal after being forced to abandon every other place of refuge he'd come across. Having left his shelter in Robinsonstrasse (a street so badly burned that it has since been erased from the map), he tried the docks, the Sorbenpark and a space behind the pillars of a bridge – but in each case the temperature became so unbearable that he and his companions feared that their clothes would ignite.

So we sat in the canal up to our necks in water and our wet jackets and coats over our heads. If we thought we had escaped the flames there, we were gravely mistaken, as there were glowing coal barges floating along, from which we had to protect ourselves. We must have spent two hours, maybe more, in the water, until the fires had died down.[43]

   Wolf Biermann's mother was likewise trying desperately to find a safe place for them to weather the storm. Having taken shelter in a factory for a short time, she was now steering her son towards one of Hammerbrook's canals, rightly assuming that it was the only place left that might offer them safety. As he recalls, he was still clutching a little bucket of jam she had entrusted to him in the cellar:

Back into the streets? To try that was to put yourself straight back into the blaze. That was suicide. Impossible. But we had to go. We turned left round the corner, there was a canal, a bridge. My mother tried to reach the water with me near the bridge. We crawled through the handrail, down the canal's bank . . . We reached the water, found a spot in the group of people and stood in the water. I was standing next to an old lady who on every finger was holding a little suitcase or handbag, everything she could grab. And now that was all floating on the water. I saw, from my low point of view, that my head was at the same level as her hand. And suddenly I could see right in front of me how the woman's fingers were losing their grip, how the suitcases were floating away, how the woman was sinking. Then she was gone.
   More and more pieces of debris were falling around us from above, and it became obvious we couldn't stay there. Some stayed because they could think of nothing better to do, but my mother had a feeling we should leave. So she grabbed me by my shoulders and swam with me across the canal. And on the other side it was idyllic! There was grass, there were shallow banks and there were a dozen other people who had escaped there. They were sitting there like in a theatre box: nothing

could fall down from above, and around them there was the panorama of a burning city which they could watch from a safe position. How wonderful! Believe it or not, it's true, I still had my little bucket in my hand. And as there was a good lid on it nothing bad had happened to it even when I fell into the water . . . We opened the lid and it was the most wonderful mirabelle jam of my life – little wonder when your throat is sore, from the smoke, from the fire, from all the dirt, from all the anxiety! We passed the bucket around, so that everybody could take a taste of its syrupy sweetness. It was paradise on earth, in the middle of hell![44]

From their position on the bank they had a grandstand view of the blazing buildings that stretched on all sides as far as the eye could see. Directly before them lay Hammerbrook, the centre of the firestorm, and the glow of Hamm beyond. To their right the docks were in flames, all the way down to the riverside suburb of Rothenburgsort. To their left, Borgfelde, Hohenfelde, Eilbek and Wandsbek were all burning.

* * *

It is impossible to tell precisely when the firestorm started, but certainly it was before the bombing finished. The word 'firestorm' was not written in the chronological record at Fire Service Head-quarters until 2.40 a.m., but Hans Brunswig, the chief engineer on duty that night, remembers that by two o'clock the winds were so strong that it was impossible to walk through the fire-station courtyard: the men had to crawl on their hands and knees.[45] From the study he made both at the time and after the war, Brunswig estimates that the firestorm probably began as early as twenty or thirty minutes after the first bombs fell.[46] His suggestion is backed up by the accounts of eyewitnesses.

By 1.30 a.m., the fires already extended from the Berliner Tor on the edge of the city centre to the Hammer Park in the east, and from the banks of the river as far north as the Wandsbeker Chaussee. In half an hour the RAF had created a single fire that had engulfed several square miles of the city. Had it been left to itself it would

TERDORF

WINTERHUDE

BARMBEK

WANDSBEK

UHLENHORST

EILBEK

*Alster
Lake*

HOHENFELDE

ST GEORG

BORGFELDE HAMM

HORN

Hamburg Central
Station

Fire Brigade
Headquarters

STADT

HAMMERBROOK

KLEINER
RASBROOK

ROTHENBURGSORT

BILLBROOK

VEDDEL

Buildings destroyed by earlier British and
American attacks

Buildings destroyed by RAF raid 27/28 July

probably not have spread further. A feature of firestorms is that, because all the winds blow *inwards* to feed the flames, there is little spread from the main centre. But the fire was not left to itself. The RAF continued bombing for almost half an hour after the firestorm had taken hold, dropping incendiaries across the entire eastern quarter of the city. Large parts of Eilbek, Barmbek and Wandsbek were badly hit, and soon the fire service was receiving reports that the flames had spread as far as the main railway station to the west, and the suburb of Horn to the east.[47]

The centre of this burning hell was in Borgfelde, around the point where Ausschläger Weg crosses the Mittel Kanal.[48] This was where the Lotze Engineering Works was situated, which the British War Office suspected of producing underwater mines for the Wehrmacht. However, the Nienstadt timber yard lay on the other side of the canal, and it is possible that the intense heat given off by huge stacks of burning wood acted as the first catalyst to the firestorm.[49]

For four and a half hours this unassuming corner of the city was the eye of the hurricane – the centre of a city-wide furnace that was burning at temperatures of over 1000°C. By dawn there was little left to burn. In many areas the house façades were all that was left standing, like blackened empty shells above the glowing rubble. Everything else – floors, ceilings, furniture, the stuff of people's everyday lives – had been consumed. In some buildings the fires would continue to burn for a long time, particularly those in which the occupants had stocked up early on coke and coal for the winter, but in most cases it was gradually burning itself out. As it ran out of fuel, the raging heat diminished, and the wind died down.

Morning broke darkly over the city, just as Sunday had, the sun blotted out by smoke, and no light beyond that which came from the fires. In the gloom it was impossible for the survivors to see the extent of the city's devastation. The damage immediately around them, though, was plain: buildings reduced to shells, cratered roads, burned-out cars and trams. And, most distressingly, there were corpses everywhere. Almost all eyewitness accounts of this terrible morning have in common a deep sense of shock at the gruesome and ubiquitous presence of death.

Max Kipke remembers the sight that greeted him when he came to one of the underground shelters in Hammerbrook:

I went to the shelter and wanted to see if people had already come back out. But I saw only corpses, corpses, corpses. They must have wanted to reach the shelter, but did not make it. Even today, I do not understand why they were already dead. I was still in pretty good shape. The staircase that led down to the entrance of the shelter had a bend in it, and shortly after, another: the shelter was built practically two storeys underground. The staircase was covered with bodies. The door to the shelter opened outwards, and because it was blocked by the corpses, the people could not open it. After a while the next living being arrived, a marine. I asked him if he could help me. The shelter was full of people and they probably could not open the door. A third man joined us, and together we managed to clear the entrance enough, so that we were able to open the door a short way. The first people came out; they felt their way up, because there was no light – all the power lines were destroyed. Maybe it was better that they did not see anything.[50]

The sensitivities of those leaving the bunkers would not be spared for long. Once they found themselves at street level they were greeted with the most gruesome sights, as Ruth Schramm remembers:

When we had clambered up the stairs, our first glance fell on the stacked corpses to the left of the shelter entrance. It was a double row, around ten metres long. I can still clearly see these completely blackened bodies before me. There was no time to waste thoughts on them; we were forced to protect our hair . . .[51]

Parents did what they could to shield their children from the horror. Else Lohse was a young mother who had literally thrown her children out of a ground-floor window on to the Hammer

Landstrasse to save them from the flames. Now she was doing all she could to keep them safe, both physically and emotionally:

The little ones kept asking, as we stepped over the dead: 'What is that, mama?' I said to them, 'Don't step on that or you will fall. It is a branch, fallen from a tree.' 'Mama, here is another one,' and so it went on from Meuthien to Biederbeck, one after another. Some hugged themselves, others folded together or their limbs spread . . . You cannot imagine the scene, how the Hammer Landstrasse looked. Burned-out cars stood at angles in the road, dead upon dead.[52]

Traute Koch also remembers the corpses on Hammer Landstrasse. She had spent the night in a house that was relatively safe because it had been burned out in a previous raid. Now her mother was trying to lead her away from the fires to safety:

We came to the junction of the Hammer Landstrasse and Louisenweg. I carried my little sister and also helped my mother climb over the ruins. Suddenly, I saw tailors' dummies lying around. I said, 'Mummy, no tailors lived here and, yet, so many dummies lying around.' My mother grabbed me by my arm and said, 'Go on. Don't look too closely. On. On.'[53]

It is impossible to imagine the trauma that such sights inflicted on the exhausted people, who were already in shock from their experiences of the night. Many were driven to the brink of madness. Erich Titschak, who had spent the night out in the streets remembers seeing a woman screaming, 'They're coming to kill us!' repeatedly, although the bombers and the firestorm had long gone.[54]

With so many people struggling to reach the open spaces, the parks were soon filled with the screams of the injured and the weeping of those who had been forced to leave behind loved ones. One woman describes sitting in what was left of the rose garden in the Stoltenpark, listening to all the terrifying sounds around her:

In front of me was the front of Heidenkampsweg, and I saw building after building collapse. Behind me was the animal sanctuary where the animals slowly burned. On top of the cries from the surrounding burned and wounded, the last calls of the dying, and the cries for help from the collapsing buildings, came the barking and screeching of the cats and dogs. It was enough to drive you to despair.[55]

Hans Jedlicka, who was also sheltering in this park, witnessed similar things:

How long we stayed in the Stoltenpark I no longer know. We watched the flaming hell of Hammerbrook. It still surprises me that anyone at all was able to make it through there alive. Again and again people came running over the bridge into the park. Screaming people with dreadful burns. One young woman especially stays in my memory. I still have the picture before my eyes. She came screaming out of the smoke over the bridge. She was completely naked and barefoot. As she came closer I saw that her feet were nothing but charred stumps. As soon as she found safety she fell down and died.[56]

Herbert Wulff, who had spent the night huddling between an advertising pillar and the wall of a bridge, remembers the scene the next morning, after the fires had died down. Buildings were still burning, his city was utterly ruined and horribly disfigured corpses were scattered across the Heidenkampsweg:

The most gruesome sight we must have seen was the people, lying on the ground completely naked, no longer recognizable as man or woman, with a centimetre-thick burned crust covering them, seemingly dead, but still giving their last signs of life through guttural sounds and small movements of their arms. This appalling sight will stay with me all my life.[57]

★   ★   ★

It is impossible to say with any accuracy how many people died that night. At the time rumours put the death-toll at a hundred thousand, and for once the figure was not entirely far-fetched.

Because of the chaos that reigned in the aftermath of the catastrophe, German officials were never able to say for certain which
deaths had occurred during which air raid, but the official number
for the series of attacks that week was eventually calculated at
42,600,[58] of whom the vast majority died during the firestorm of
27/28 July.

Terrifying as that total is, it is a miracle that the final figure was
not higher. A quarter of the population of Hamburg lived within
the bombed area – 427,637 people, according to official figures –
and their numbers had been swelled by the influx of people made
homeless by the first heavy attack.[59] Yet more than 90 per cent of
the population escaped with their lives. Many of these people lived
beyond the edges of the firestorm, but even in Hammerbrook and
Hamm the number who survived still outweighed the number
who died.[60]

To survive the terrible conditions caused by the firestorm
required not only incredible physical stamina, but huge courage
and an unwavering determination to survive. Fugitives had to
face the combined dangers of fire, high-explosive bombs (many of
which were on time-delay fuses), falling masonry and hurricane-
force winds. In addition, they had to maintain the presence of
mind to battle against the wind rather than let themselves be carried
along by it, and seek out shelter in the most unpromising places.
Many people refused to give up despite terrible injuries: more than
thirty-seven thousand people were hurt during this series of attacks
– again, the vast majority on the night of the firestorm.[61]

There was a strong element of chance involved in who survived
and who did not: sometimes a family would make a sensible
decision over which way to run only to find their hopes crushed
by the collapse of a building or a sudden change in wind direction.
Even so, certain groups were more vulnerable than others. The
very old or the very young were often the first to succumb.
According to the Hamburg police chief's report the winds were
so strong that 'Children were torn away from their parents' hands
by the force of the hurricane and whirled into the fire.'[62] Another
eyewitness, who described the 'tornado-like storm', claimed it was

so strong that it was almost impossible to fight it: 'Elderly people, who were unable to walk well, were obliged to give up this impossible fight, and the flames greedily made their way over this prey.'[63] A man in front of her was set alight like that, and 'in less than ten seconds he too became a living pillar of fire'.

Their bodies, with hundreds of others, were found where they had fallen. They were nearly always face downwards, arms thrown round their heads as if they were trying to shelter their faces from the heat as they died.[64] Most of the bodies were charred and shrivelled to half their normal size. Some were so badly burned that the fat had seeped out to form pools round them. By contrast, others were not burned. Many were naked except for their shoes – the city coroner concluded later that they had probably tried to flee in their nightwear, only to have it torn or burned off in an instant by the heat of the firestorm.

Far more died in the shelters. In the east of Hamburg, there were relatively few purpose-built public bunkers and most people were forced to make do with the basements of their apartment buildings. When some were opened the next day, nobody was alive inside: they had all succumbed to the fierce temperatures generated by the fires. In some basements the heat had been so great that everything inside was charred beyond recognition, including the bodies of the occupants. But the worst killers were smoke and carbon monoxide. One woman remembered afterwards how the lack of oxygen had affected those in her shelter:

The very small children fell asleep first, then the four to six-year-olds, then the slightly older, then the adolescents and finally the old. I knew what this sleep meant. Many never woke up, because our rescue came very late – we could not be saved sooner because of the terrible heat that raged on the street . . . We owe our lives to an armaments-factory worker who was looking for his flat and his wife, and looked in the Gothenkeller and found us all unconscious. This man then informed the police station on Nagelsweg. Consequently fifty soldiers were sent to carry us out and lay us in the open, first in front of Gothenhaus so we could breathe some oxygen . . . I regained consciousness as three soldiers lifted me, and a fourth, who stood nearby, said: 'That is number 238'.[65]

It is probable that as many as 70 per cent of those who died were killed by smoke inhalation or carbon monoxide poisoning.[66] Their bodies were sometimes found piled up around the exits to the shelters, as if they knew they were in danger but were unable to escape. More often, though, they were found seated at tables, or leaning peacefully against walls, as if they had simply fallen asleep.[67] Those men, women and children paid the price for having followed official advice to remain in their cellars until the all-clear sounded. Had they taken their chances in the inferno of the firestorm, many more might have been saved.

★   ★   ★

As the storm died down, those who had survived the night began to move. Often their first instinct was to leave the city, but many had become separated from their families during the frantic escape from their basement shelters, and to leave without them was too painful to consider. People milled about, some venturing back towards the fires in the hope of finding friends and loved ones still alive.

Sixteen-year-old Herbert Wulff was one of the lucky ones. He had seen his sister run off several hours before, and had lost his mother in the smoke and chaos of the night. Now, in the gloom of morning, he was trying desperately to find them:

It was a terrible twilight, as I first began to make out the many corpses and the devastation all around. But of course my first worries were now for my family. Had they managed to survive? Luckily I found my mother again nearby, where I'd left her. She herself was unhurt, but beside her lay two dead bodies. Our joy at seeing one another again was huge. I took my mother with me to the other side of the street and started the search for my sister and father. And I was lucky. I found my sister nearby where we had last seen her during the night. She too had survived, albeit with bad burns on her legs caused by the devilish phosphorus. I myself had picked up some small burns, but nothing too bad. And then, like a wonder, my father turned up, relatively unscathed. He had had an unbelievable odyssey. Our joy at seeing one another again was over-whelming, and we were simply indescribably lucky to have survived this purgatory.[68]

Others were not so lucky. Desperate stories emerged, of mothers losing their children in all the smoke and darkness, of children losing their parents when their buildings collapsed – stories that would be repeated again and again in the days to come. Countless others did not know what had become of their loved ones. They picked their way through the crowds searching and calling names. Occasionally family members were reunited in this way, but for the most part the calls echoed round the parks unanswered.

Meanwhile, those who had no one to look for remained silent, dazed by what they had experienced. Many, including some of the eyewitnesses quoted here, were too badly injured or burned to do anything but stay where they were. Herbert Wulff and his sister had fairly bad burns. The man in his forties who had watched his brother-in-law die in the fire, was himself badly burned and suffering from exhaustion. Fredy Borck's eight-year-old brother fell into the flames as they were being evacuated from their Rothenburgsort cellar, and burned his legs severely.

One of the most common injuries was burns to the eyes. After spending the night in the open Erich Titschak complained that his eyes hurt so much he could no longer keep them open. Hans Jedlicka's were scorched, as were those of Else Lohse and her son Peter, who soon began to lose their sight.[69] Erika Wilken's eyes were so badly damaged during her ordeal in the Grevenweg public lavatory that by the time she and her husband were evacuated she could no longer see. 'From Horn onwards our eyesight became worse and worse, and once we reached the compound we were already blind.'[70] Perhaps it was a blessing in disguise. In most cases people's eyesight would return, but for now at least they were spared some of the gruesome sights others had to endure.

Most of the injuries that occurred were caused by the great heat

– inflamed lungs, scorched eyes, severe burns – but many people had broken bones from the blasts of high-explosive bombs and falling masonry. When the authorities arrived *en masse* to oversee the evacuation, these people were taken away first, carried off in whatever vehicles could be commandeered: boats, lorries and even horse-drawn carriages. Most people, however, had to walk to the edge of the city to find transport. All the normal methods of escape – trams, subways and the railway – had been destroyed. Most roads were impassable. The only transport conduit relatively unaffected was the river, and even that was strewn with debris.

As tens of thousands of people streamed out of Hamburg, they left behind a broken city, shrouded in smoke, in many places still burning. Despite the terror they had all experienced, it was impossible to leave without a last glance at the place that had been their home. For many it seemed like their final farewell and, in a sense, it was: although most would return to Hamburg in future months and years, it would never be the same city again. In the course of a single night almost a quarter of it had been erased from the map.

Henni Klank, who had escaped to the river with her newborn baby, left the city by boat. She remembers her departure as a final moment of supreme sadness:

The boat was supposed to go to Lauenburg, and what took place aboard it on the journey is almost beyond description. There was no wound-dressing material, only paper bandages. I helped a young mother dress her half-burned baby with my makeshift gauze-nappy. We couldn't do more . . . The woman and the others were all in a state of shock. We glanced back once more at our broken and beloved Hamburg, across which a giant mushroom-cloud was spreading. It was as if it wanted to say: I'll cover up all of this horror that descended on Hamburg tonight, for ever![71]

17. The 'Terror of Hamburg'

A stream of haggard, terrified refugees flowed into the neighbouring provinces.
In every large town people said: 'What happened to Hamburg yesterday
can happen to us tomorrow.'
Luftwaffe General Adolf Galland[1]

The events of 27/28 July 1943 shook the Nazi hierarchy to its core. Writing in his diary a few days later, Josef Goebbels called the disaster 'the greatest crisis of the war'.[2] For once, the normally resourceful propaganda minister seemed at a loss for what to do.

A city of a million inhabitants has been destroyed in a manner unparalleled in history. We are faced with problems that are almost impossible of solution. Food must be found for this population of a million. Shelter must be secured. The people must be evacuated as fast as possible. They must be given clothing. In short, we are facing problems there of which we had no conception even a few weeks ago.[3]

Many other key figures in the Nazi establishment were just as shaken. Albert Speer, the Minister of Armaments and War Production, told Hitler that if the British managed to attack another six German towns on the same scale then armaments production would be brought to a halt.[4] Erhard Milch, the State Secretary for Air, went further: 'It's much blacker than Speer paints it,' he told the members of his ministry. 'If we get just five or six more attacks like these on Hamburg, the German people will just lay down their tools, however great their willpower.'[5]

The crisis of confidence became so bad that Hitler was forced to take action to avert a collapse of morale in the Party. A few days after the catastrophe, he instructed Goebbels to speak to an assembly of ministers and gauleiters to 'inject some concrete into them'. Ever faithful to his master, Goebbels did as he was told. It was a tense meeting. During the discussion, Milch repeatedly interrupted Goebbels with the almost treasonable outcry, 'We have lost the war! Finally lost the war!' The propaganda minister had to appeal to his honour as an officer to quieten him.[6]

While those around him were in deep shock at the scale of the disaster, Hitler appeared to react in much the same way as he did to all such catastrophes: by remaining in denial. To Speer's announcement that further British attacks might halt German arms production, he simply said, 'You'll straighten all that out again.' Neither was he sympathetic to the victims of the firestorm. When Hamburg's gauleiter, Karl Kaufmann, repeatedly telegraphed him, begging him to visit the stricken city, Hitler steadfastly refused. When Kaufmann asked him at least to receive a delegation of the heroic rescue crews, Hitler refused that too. He was simply not interested in Hamburg, or the fate of its people.[7]

⋆   ⋆   ⋆

On the other side of the North Sea, the mood was precisely the opposite of that in Germany. While the Nazis imposed a virtual news freeze on all but the most general reports of the firestorm, the British and American authorities were quick to announce their success to the international press. In London, *The Times* printed a large photograph of American bombs falling on the Howaldt-swerke shipyards under the headline 'Hamburg Battered': 'Air bombing reached a new intensity on Tuesday night,' it said, causing damage that would 'far exceed that caused in any previous attack'.[8] The *Daily Express* was more graphic. 'RAF blitz to wipe Hamburg off the war map' was the front-page headline on 31 July:

It now seems plain that Air Chief Marshal Sir Arthur Harris, our bomber chief, has set himself the task of wiping out completely the town of Hamburg from the enemy's war effort . . . Bombs went down at the rate of about 50 tons a minute for 45 minutes, and nothing the guns and night fighters could do could stop them.[9]

19 A typical formation of B-17 Flying Fortresses, with German fighter aircraft above.

20 The lead crew of the USAAF's 303rd Bomb Group before their mission to Hamburg on 25 July. The pilot, Major K. R. Mitchell, is second from left at the back.

21 American bombs fall on Howaldtswerke shipyards, 26 July.

22 Hamburg women and children run for cover during an air-raid warning.

23 German propaganda poster, 1943: 'The enemy sees your light. Black out!'

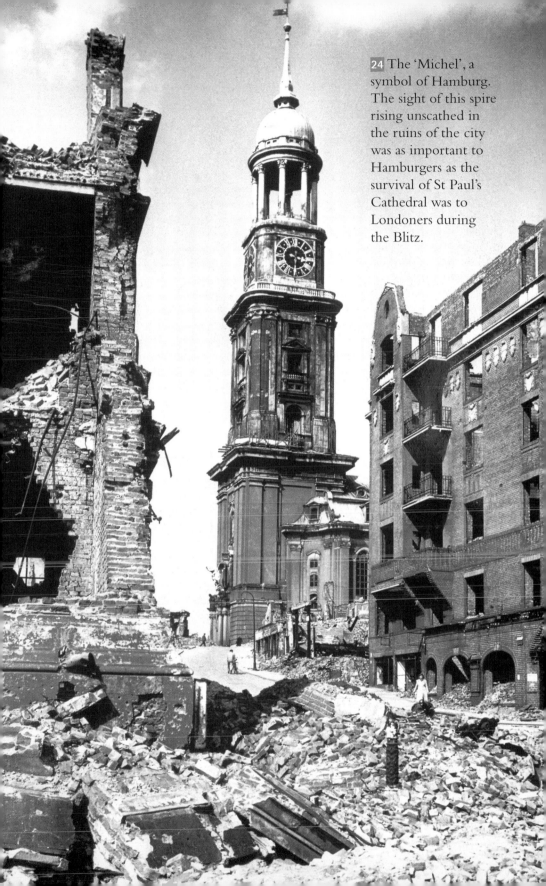

24 The 'Michel', a symbol of Hamburg. The sight of this spire rising unscathed in the ruins of the city was as important to Hamburgers as the survival of St Paul's Cathedral was to Londoners during the Blitz.

25 A group of men clears the rubble on
Grosse Bergstrasse in Altona, shortly after
the opening raids.

26 Elbstrasse (now Neanderstrasse) before the raids.

27 Elbstrasse after the raids.

28 and **29** Even before the evacuation order was given, the *Ausgebombten* began to flee the city. *Above*: A family rescues a few of its possessions. *Below*: Refugees being evacuated on open lorries.

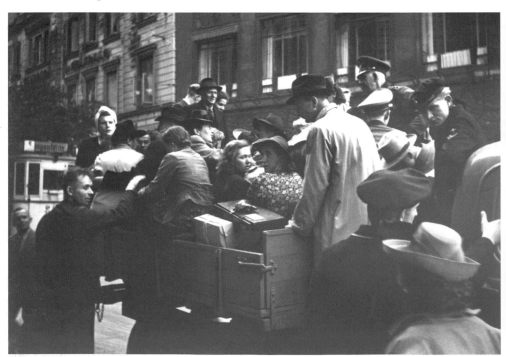

In America, the headlines were equally triumphant: 'Hamburg Pictured in Ruin and Death,' wrote the *New York Times*; 'Swedes Report Hamburg Has "Ceased to Exist"' claimed the *New York Herald Tribune*; while the *Washington Post* went with 'Heaviest Raid Dumps Death on Hamburg'.[10] To add weight to their reports, they quoted statistics and eyewitness statements from the neutral press in Sweden and Switzerland. Lest the German people missed out on the news, propaganda leaflets were printed, showing photographs of the devastation, to be dropped across Germany over the next few weeks. The photographs' caption read, 'Das war Hamburg' ('This was Hamburg'), the verb deliberately in the past tense.[11]

The Soviets also appreciated the propaganda value of the catastrophe. In the days after the firestorm Russian soldiers erected loudspeakers along the front to broadcast the news across no man's land to the German troops. The announcements came with the suggestion that, since the Germans were suffering as badly at home as they were at the front, they should surrender. Most German troops did not believe what they heard, of course; they were used to enemy propaganda. It was not until they were able to return to Hamburg on leave that they discovered the truth for themselves. As one veteran from the Russian Front remembers, their first view of the city left them in a state of shock, despite the warnings. 'When we saw it [Hamburg] we just stood there in the train and thought, This cannot be. It was not only me, but all of us were completely shattered by it. We thought, that's it, the war's over.'[12]

Soldiers caught up in the bombing said that it was far worse than being at the front.[13] Some claimed that it was worse even than the military disaster at Stalingrad. Martha Bührich remembers meeting a soldier in the street who said that 'he had witnessed the hell of Stalingrad, but that it was nothing compared to this terrible night'. After the war, many others said exactly the same thing.[14]

Looking back, the implication of such statements is clear. If Stalingrad was the great turning point of the war for the German Army, then Hamburg was the equivalent for German civilians.

Before the firestorm most people believed that their towns were largely safe from Allied bombers; afterwards they realized that they would be lucky to escape erasure from the map. Hamburg made it clear that the Allies, and the British in particular, were intent on annihilating one city after another until Germany capitulated. It was beginning to look as though the terrible predictions that Douhet had made in the 1920s were at last coming true: the home cities had become more dangerous than the battlefields.[15]

*   *   *

While government ministers were panicking over how to handle the disaster, the city authorities in Hamburg could not allow themselves such a luxury. With vast swathes of the city still on fire, and tens of thousands abandoning it in panic, something had to be done immediately. Early on the morning of Wednesday, 28 July, Gauleiter Karl Kaufmann officially announced the evacuation of Hamburg. Women and children were told, not asked, to leave the city within the next few hours.

As Goebbels had suspected, the evacuation of Hamburg was a logistical nightmare. According to the city's disaster plan, displaced people were supposed to be evacuated by rail – but since all the train lines in the centre of Hamburg and most of the city's stations had been destroyed, this was impossible. The roads were not much better. Throughout the main disaster area the streets were full of craters, and rubble from collapsing buildings had made many impassable. To make things worse, whole districts were still on fire. In such circumstances the only course of action was for refugees to make their way to the edge of the firestorm area on foot. They would be guided by the emergency services, and evacuation would take place from there.[16]

In an attempt to bring order to the chaos, the city authorities were forced to improvise wildly. Almost all of the collection centres for the homeless had been destroyed or damaged, so the authorities designated four huge refugee camps: at the Moorweide Park, at the horse-racing courses in Horn and Farmsen, and at a large open space in Billstedt. Since nobody knew about them, loudspeaker vans were sent to roam the outer edges of the firestorm area telling people where to go. At the same time dressing stations were set up on all the major exit roads to cope with the huge numbers of injured staggering out of the destroyed city. Enormous amounts of food and drink were brought in to feed everyone. On the first day alone half a million loaves were given out, along with sixteen thousand litres of milk, beer, tea and coffee.[17]

Meanwhile, the authorities commandeered lorries, buses and horse-drawn carriages from every possible source to get people out of the city. Ten thousand men from the armed forces were brought in to help with the operation, along with all the police and SS forces that neighbouring areas could spare. They shuttled people from the refugee camps to the nearest major stations – more than three-quarters of a million people in total – then sent them to cities throughout the Reich. A further fifty thousand were evacuated on the river, and thousands more were flown out from Fuhlsbüttel airfield. Within a few days more than a million people had been evacuated from the city, the largest such transfer ever carried out in Germany at such short notice.

*   *   *

The figures are undeniably impressive. On a grand scale it seems that the evacuation worked smoothly and efficiently – incredibly so, given the extent to which the authorities had to improvise. But this was not how most people experienced it. As they stumbled out of the burning suburbs, the streets strewn with corpses and rubble, many refugees were too exhausted to walk as far as the collection centres. Occasionally lorries arrived at seemingly random locations to help them on their way, but there were too few to make much difference. Many mothers were forced to stand with their children on street corners hoping to catch a ride on an army truck or in a private car.[18]

Huge numbers of people did not wait to be processed through the official collection centres, but made their way to nearby towns and villages in the hope of finding shelter there. It is important to remember that not everyone was supposed to go: officially, it was only the city's women and children who were evacuated, while the men were meant to stay behind to continue working. In reality, many men left to take their families to safety. Nobody considered stopping them.

Within hours, all the satellite towns of Hamburg were swamped with refugees. Even those further away were unable to cope with the numbers: it was one thing to take people away from Hamburg, but another to find them places to stay. For example, when Heino Merck fled to his sister's house in Kellinghusen he found it already full of refugees.[19] Ilse Grassmann and her children were unable to stay with her sister-in-law in Wittenburg because the house was jam-packed with other relatives in the same plight.[20] Erwin Krohn described the scene when he arrived in Neumünster as 'unparalleled chaos. Forty thousand inhabitants and 160,000 Hamburgers. Nobody knew where to go.'[21]

With so many people on the move, the city authorities were terrified of a breakdown in law and order. To prevent possible riots they stationed extra police and even SS units in the refugee-collection points. Helmuth Saß describes the scene he witnessed when he arrived in the Stadtpark on Friday morning:

On one side of the grass, I saw a detachment of the SS marching. They set up heavy machine-guns every two metres. As I approached this row, I was curtly sent away. I asked Mr Lukas what the SS were doing here. He answered: 'They are supposed to guard us.' And so it was that we, the *Ausgebombten*, were not to make a stand against the Nazi Party, otherwise we would be shot.[22]

However, the police could not be everywhere at once, and there are countless examples of ordinary people expressing hostility openly towards the Nazi authorities away from the main collection points. Hans J. Massaquoi describes an incident at a station where 'a man in a brown Nazi uniform came into sight, and a woman screamed at him from the train, "You pigs, it's all your fault!"' She continued shouting similar accusations until someone from her company 'literally gagged her by holding a towel over her mouth'.[23] He also tells of a soldier friend who was determined to desert the army, on the grounds that in the wake of this catastrophe 'the war can't last longer than a couple of weeks, perhaps only a couple of days'.[24] Another refugee, Lore Bünger, remembers hearing a man proclaiming loudly, 'That Hitler! The pig should be hung!' before his wife warned him to be quiet.[25]

There was little the authorities could do about such outbursts. They certainly could not have arrested everyone who voiced their anger – in the desperate atmosphere that prevailed in the wake of the firestorm, to do so would have risked causing riots. People no longer felt they had anything more to lose; consequently, for the first time in ten years, they were defying the Nazis without fear of reprisal. Hans Erich Nossack recounts a scene that speaks volumes: 'In the Harburg railway station I heard a woman who had broken some rule or other screaming, "Go ahead, put me in prison, then at least I'll have a roof over my head!" and three railway policemen didn't know what else to do but turn away, embarrassed, leaving the crowd to calm the woman.'[26]

Had they known how common such outbursts were, the Allies would have been delighted. This was exactly what was supposed to happen in the wake of a huge bombing raid: anger at the authorities leading to open defiance and, finally, revolution. But the final link in the chain never materialized. The speed and relative efficiency of the evacuation was certainly a factor in avoiding serious civil unrest: by carrying people away from the city the authorities dispersed potential trouble. Besides, the disaster had left most people too exhausted and apathetic to cause much more than a token fuss. It was simply too big an event to blame wholly on the Nazis. It seems that most people regarded the firestorm almost as an act of God: in such circumstances the state was 'something completely irrelevant that could neither be blamed for a fate such as Hamburg had suffered nor be expected to do anything about it'.[27]

*   *   *

The evacuation of Hamburg was a huge event for Germany, arguably more important to the course of the war than even the firestorm. Terrifying as it had been, the firestorm had affected only a single city. The evacuation, on the other hand, affected the entire Reich – indeed, until the Allied invasion in 1945, the mass migration of refugees from Hamburg was probably the biggest single event on the home front of the war. Until now, many ordinary Germans in the smaller towns and cities knew of the scale of Allied bombing only through what they read in the newspapers or heard on radio broadcasts. But as a deluge of refugees poured over the country, even those in rural areas came face to face with people who had suffered the most unimaginable horror. The stories they brought with them could not be dismissed as rumour, and the message was clear: nobody was safe. What had happened in Hamburg would soon happen, in some degree, to every city in Germany.

The psychological effect this had on the country is incalculable. Years later, many would remember it as a defining moment of the war. For example, Adolf Galland, the Luftwaffe's most senior fighter general, claimed in his memoirs that the constant stream of shattered, frightened refugees spread what he called the 'Terror of Hamburg' to even the remotest villages of the Reich: 'A wave of terror radiated from the suffering city and spread throughout Germany . . . Psychologically the war at that moment had perhaps reached its most critical point.'[28]

Accounts from ordinary civilians back up his claim. 'I'll never forget the scene,' says Margret Klauß, who was sixteen at the time. She had turned out at Lübeck station with the League of German Girls to hand out food and drinks to the refugees. 'Most of them just sat there full of apathy, the horror still in their faces. Others hurried from wagon to wagon, calling the names of missing relatives in the desperate hope of finding their spouses, parents or siblings again. It was heart-breaking.'[29]

Hiltgunt Zassenhaus saw the beginning of the exodus after the first night of attacks, as lines of bizarrely dressed people traipsed past her window:

There were women who dragged along in their winter clothes, who had draped themselves in fur coats. They panted in the heat. There were women in flimsy summer dresses with stockings of differing colours. The bombs had torn them out of their sleep. In their mad haste they had pulled on whatever they found as they fell out of their burning houses. They pulled their children along with them; little feet that couldn't keep in step with their big ones. The men dragged suitcases and boxes tied up with string. They lay down on the paving stones. They pulled their shoes off. Or they lay down on the surface of the road and stared up into the darkened sky. Hardly anyone cried or complained. In their faces all life had been extinguished.[30]

Hannah Voss saw a later stage of the evacuation, on Wednesday afternoon, as trains full of refugees arrived in her home town, ninety kilometres south of Hamburg. She and a friend went to the station to meet the hordes who were piling out of the trains; it was their job to lead the refugees to the school, where straw pallets had been laid out for them to sleep on. The sight that greeted her when she arrived at the station was pathetic:

They were just standing there with nothing except their bags and the clothes they were in . . . One female came out of the train on to the platform, and all she had . . . was a budgerigar in a cage. I don't know how the budgerigar survived the blast or whatever. But that was all this woman had in the world: a flimsy nightgown, no cardigan, no wrap, nothing except the cage and the budgie.[31]

Such images are poignant, but they are nothing compared to the distressing scenes that occurred when some refugees had their luggage searched. One twelve-year-old boy fleeing Hamburg was stopped at the Danish border. He was travelling alone, carrying two sacks. When customs officers made him open them they found that one contained the corpse of his two-year-old brother, killed in the raid, the other the bodies of his pet rabbits.[32]

Since this is a third-hand report its veracity is perhaps questionable, but many refugees did bring the bodies of their loved ones when they fled Hamburg. Friedrich Reck described seeing one woman drop her suitcase as she tried to board a train in Bavaria. As its contents spilled across the platform, among the toys, manicure case and singed underwear was 'the roasted corpse of a child, shrunk like a mummy, which its half-deranged mother has been carrying about with her, the relic of a past that was still intact a few days ago'.[33]

Ernst-Günter Haberland described a similar event, when he met a man from his neighbourhood shortly after the catastrophe:

He had a small and a large case in his hand, and did not know where he should go. He opened the cases; in the larger one was something which looked like a burned tree stump, in the other, two objects, smaller but otherwise similar. They were his wife and children, their bodies melted by the phosphor; he could not leave them behind.[34]

Many others brought the bodies of children who had suffocated as their families were in the very act of escaping.[35] In the hurry to flee Hamburg there was no time to bury them, and to abandon them was unthinkable. As a consequence, many ordinary people across Germany did not merely hear about the deaths in Hamburg, they saw the corpses for themselves.

*   *   *

Despite the official suppression of detailed news about the disaster, those who witnessed scenes like this could only conclude that what had happened in Hamburg must have been truly extraordinary in its horror. To their infinite credit, most people extended whatever help they could offer to the refugees. Families all over Germany opened their doors, and shared what they had with those who had lost everything. The state provided free food in all the major towns, but it could not have been distributed properly without the help of thousands of volunteers from the Hitler Youth, the League of German Girls and many other community groups.

The outpouring of goodwill towards the Hamburg refugees was as spontaneous as it was phenomenal. Hans Erich Nossack wrote shortly afterwards about the 'heartening experience of seeing those who had been most distant, sometimes the most fleeting acquaintances or business associates, voluntarily step into the breach with such kindness that one is shamed into asking oneself whether one would have done the same if the situation were reversed'.[36] Inevitably there were some exceptions, but in general refugees were accepted with open arms, and the welcome did not wear thin for several weeks.[37]

Those who came into contact with the refugees could not help but be affected by them. Their stories were horrific. One woman told how a succession of badly injured people had clutched at her feet and clothes as she scrambled through the fiery ruins, begging her to take them with her. She had been forced to kick them off, because only by doing so could she escape death herself.[38] Another told of how she had wrapped her children in pillows and thrown them out of the window to save them from the fire. Her baby slipped out of the padding and died when it hit the pavement. The mother who told this story 'did not cry or complain; with the general fear, the thousands in agony, her pain was nothing special'.[39] Tales like these were repeated *ad infinitum* all over Germany in the weeks to come.

Inevitably, gloom descended wherever the refugees gathered. Writing in the months shortly after the firestorm, Hans Erich Nossack claimed that the sense of total defeat was universal among the people of his city.

I have spoken with several thousand people . . . We were without exception firmly convinced that the war would be over very shortly; there was no debating this point at all; for us, after all, the decision had already been reached. There remained only the question of how and in what place of refuge we would be able to survive this brief interval.[40]

This sense of foreboding quickly spread throughout the nation. The general depression was directly comparable to the mood of the country after the defeat at Stalingrad – the difference was that, while the Stalingrad disaster had taken place more than two

thousand kilometres away, Hamburg was at the heart of northern
Germany. The conclusion that everyone came to was that if Hamburg could not defend itself, even though it had been one of the
most heavily protected cities in the Reich, the same fate would
come soon to other cities.

*   *   *

As far as the Allies were concerned, this gloomy atmosphere was
the greatest success of all. The intention had been to undermine
the morale of the German people to such a degree that they would
either abandon their workplaces or rise up against their government
and demand an end to the war. Until now the Allies had been
unable to deliver a blow hard enough to cause such a drop in
morale.

However, to produce the 'knock-out blow' that would win the
war, the RAF would have to do as Albert Speer had warned
Hitler, and follow up with the devastation of another major city.
The most obvious target was Berlin, and everybody, including the
Germans, expected the Allies to strike there next. The only thing
that stopped them was that the nights were not yet long enough
for RAF bombers to get there and back under cover of darkness
– but they were lengthening, and by the end of August the Reich
capital would be within range. Soon observers in Washington were
giving Berlin just 'three weeks to live', and RAF officials in
London were hinting that the city was about to get 'the Hamburg
bombing treatment'.[41]

Germany was rife with similar speculation. In Berlin the people
were so worried about what was coming to them that even the
neutral press remarked on the change of atmosphere in the city.
'Fear approaching panic prevails in Berlin, and the people expect
the city to be laid in ruins at any moment,' claimed one correspondent from the Swedish *Aftonbladet*.[42] He described how trenches
were being dug in the parks to protect people from the effects of
a possible firestorm, and how frightened civilians were fleeing the
city. While the German authorities must have been dismayed at
such gifts to Allied propaganda, there was nothing they could do

to deny the reports. Indeed, a partial evacuation of the city had already been ordered by Goebbels himself, in his capacity as Berlin's gauleiter: to prevent an unauthorized exodus, he had instructed women, children and non-essential civilians to leave the city at the beginning of August. When this was confirmed in an official release to the Nazi *Völkischer Beobachter* a few days later, the British and American press could barely contain their glee.[43]

With the benefit of hindsight, however, all the speculation about Berlin's fate was hopelessly premature. The RAF could not possibly live up to what was now expected of them: the firestorm they had created in Hamburg had been a matter of chance, and would be virtually impossible to replicate in other cities. Nor were the Allies about to produce the knock-out blow that would end the war. To do so they would have had to demonstrate the power to obliterate any city they wanted at will, which meant destroying Berlin within days, not weeks, then following it up with two or three other cities for good measure. Then, perhaps, Speer's fears might have been realized. But the RAF had no intention of even trying to accomplish such a feat. While Sir Arthur Harris cherished hopes of teaming up with the USAAF to 'wreck Berlin from end to end', he would not make the attempt until the winter of 1943–4.[44] In the meantime, there were few suitable alternatives for a second strike: to find new targets of even half Hamburg's size they would have had to fly as far as Breslau or Dresden – but during the short summer nights that would have posed too great a risk for RAF crews.[45] In the end, therefore, the concept of a knock-out blow was nothing more than a mirage.

In the absence of other targets, the RAF contented themselves with bombing those cities in western Germany that were within easy reach. There was nothing new about attacking Essen, Remscheid or Mannheim – they had all been hit during the battle of the Ruhr earlier in the year – but Bomber Command Headquarters felt it better to attack something than nothing. While important cities like Berlin were still out of range, the RAF might at least destroy the industrial plants in familiar targets that had been missed on earlier visits.

With this in mind, Harris decided that he would finish the job he had started on Saturday night. On the morning of Thursday, 29 July, he ordered a third massive strike against Hamburg. If he could not finish the war by bombing, for now he would content himself with finishing off, once and for all, what was left of the city on the Elbe.

18. Coup de Grâce

I am in blood
Stepp'd in so far that, should I wade no more,
Returning were as tedious as go o'er
William Shakespeare, *Macbeth*[1]

Everybody in Hamburg knew that another raid was coming. In the areas that had not yet been hit, people stowed their most prized possessions in basements and cellars, in the vain hope that they might be spared when the bombs fell. Anything portable was piled into cars, wagons or even prams, and the roads were soon jammed with people carting their belongings out of the city. Many travelled on foot, content to get themselves and their families away with little more than a suitcase between them. The single thought that occupied their minds was to get as far away from the city as possible.

While the exodus of civilians accelerated, there was also significant movement in the opposite direction. Not only were the emergency services pouring men and equipment into Hamburg, but the Luftwaffe was doing all it could to bolster the city's defences. Mobile flak units were brought to the outskirts of Hamburg by train from all around, and huge numbers of searchlights arrived. Fire-fighters worked ceaselessly to control the flames before the Allies could return to stoke them, certain that the bombers would indeed be back. It was now merely a matter of time.

Whenever the air-raid alarm sounded, everyone made directly for their shelters. The relaxed atmosphere that had prevailed a week ago was now a thing of the past, and there was a new, frightened urgency to everyone's actions. On Wednesday night, not even twenty-four hours after the firestorm, the sirens sounded and there was an immediate rush for the bunkers. It was a false alarm – the RAF were resting their crews, and had merely sent four Mosquitos over the city on a nuisance raid – but it meant that the remnants of Hamburg's exhausted population were deprived of sleep for a fifth night in a row. The next day there were no fewer than five major alarms, which repeatedly threw the rescue and evacuation effort into chaos. Some were caused by British reconnaissance planes, but the most serious one was brought about by a large force of American B-17s heading for the area. It turned out that the USAAF were flying on to Kiel, so Hamburg was spared for another few hours, but its people remained in a state of high anxiety for the rest of the day.

Although it was aimed at a different city, this last American raid had an unforeseen effect on Hamburg. Afraid that disaster was about to overtake Kiel, the authorities suddenly withdrew all the motorized Air Protection battalions that had been drafted into Hamburg and sent them northwards. In their absence, fires that had been half extinguished flared up, and the Hamburg fire service was hopelessly stretched again. The authorities had allowed panic to get the better of them, and for several hours in the middle of the day confusion reigned before the units were sent back to where they were most needed.[2]

That the Nazi authorities were so worried about this daytime raid on Kiel is a measure of how seriously they were beginning to take the new American threat. However, for the moment at least, the USAAF was a spent force. General Eaker had been fighting a desperate battle over the past few days. On Wednesday he had lost twenty-two planes in two ill-fated missions over Kassel and Oschersleben. On Thursday he lost a further ten planes over Kiel and Warnemünde. By the end of that week alone the total loss would be a hundred planes, with the equivalent of ninety crews killed, wounded or missing; he was forced to ground his shaken and exhausted crews for the next two weeks to give them time to rebuild their strength.[3]

As dusk approached on Thursday, 29 July, the few people who

remained in Hamburg headed straight for the bunkers – or at least made certain they were within immediate running distance of somewhere safe, should the alarm sound. Most no longer cared whether the shelters were comfortable or convenient: the only criterion now was how safe they were. The huge *Hochbunkers*, like those at Dammtor and the Heiligengeistfeld, had become popular because of the way they had withstood the previous attacks. Few people trusted their cellars now – there was no longer any sense in taking risks.

As darkness fell, the streets were quickly deserted. A stillness descended on Hamburg unlike anything it had experienced in all its 750-year history. Almost a million people had fled, leaving whole districts empty, and soon there was nothing to disturb the silence but the wind that whistled through the glowing ruins. The city on the Elbe was little more than a ghost town.

* * *

While the remnants of Hamburg's population was seeking refuge for the night, the British were preparing to attack. For most of the day it had seemed doubtful that another raid on Hamburg would be worthwhile: Harris was worried that smoke would obscure the target, making it impossible for the bomber force to locate it properly. But that afternoon a reconnaissance flight over the city had returned with the news that a light wind was blowing the smoke inland, leaving the skies above Hamburg relatively clear. He gave the order to proceed as planned.

For the 5,500 men who attended briefings that evening it was a case of *déjà vu*. Not only was the target the same, but the route there and back was similar too. They would be taking off at the same time (around 10.00 p.m.), bombing at approximately the same time (shortly before 1.00 a.m.), and returning to base at the same time (at around 4.00 a.m.). The first and last turning points were identical to Tuesday night's, and the final approach to Hamburg would be almost the same line they had taken on Saturday night.[4] In fact, everything was so similar to what had gone before that some crews felt they were tempting Fate. On the whole, however, most airmen seemed to think that it would be an easy ride, as the previous Hamburg raids had been.

The RAF planners at High Wycombe knew that it was dangerous to cross into northern Germany so close to the points they had chosen on the two previous nights, but such was their faith in Window that they believed it was a risk worth taking. The route they had chosen was as short as they could practically make it, so that the 777 planes could carry heavier bomb loads. In short, they believed that it was worth sacrificing a little security to deal Hamburg the hardest blow possible.

They knew exactly where the danger zones would be. As the British Pathfinders crossed the German coast they were supposed to drop red route markers to show the way for the rest of the bomber stream. But the flares would be just as useful to the German night fighters in their search for prey – as soon as they were dropped, every night fighter in the area would flock to them like moths to a flame, certain that the British planes would pass through that one point.

The only way to protect the bombers against ambush was to create a diversion. With this in mind, four Mosquitos were sent to drop bundles of Window along an alternative route, to make it look as though a second bomber stream was approaching Hamburg from the direction of Bremen. To add to the deception they would also drop decoy route markers about sixty miles south-west of the bombers' real landfall.[5] The idea was that the Germans would have to split their defences in two, making it twice as likely that the real bomber stream would slip through unmolested.

This, then, was the plan of attack for the night of Thursday, 29 July 1943, and, with Window still working wonders, nobody had any reason to suspect that it would be anything but a milk run.

There were a few mishaps on take-off, and a small percentage of early returns due to technical problems. By and large this was nothing to be concerned about, although a 100 Squadron Lancaster collapsed on the runway at Grimsby, blocking it so badly that the twelve aircraft behind it could not take off.[6] While ground staff tried to sort out the mess, the rest of the bomber stream was gathering over the North Sea and heading towards Germany. They flew largely undisturbed until they reached their first turning point, about sixty miles north-west of Heligoland.

The problems started shortly after the Pathfinders began to drop the first route markers. As predicted, all the German fighters in the area headed straight for them, knowing that this was the one place they were guaranteed to find their prey. What the British had *not* anticipated was how strong the German response would be. Over the past five days there had been a radical change in German tactics of which the introduction of *Wilde Sau* fighters was only a part. Now that the Luftwaffe could no longer rely on radar they had been forced to give their individual fighters a much freer rein. No longer were they expected to stick to their allocated boxes along the coast, they were now allowed to amass wherever they were most likely to find the British. German fighter controllers still gave a running commentary over the radio about the height and general position of the bomber stream, but it was up to individual fighters to find and kill their prey, using nothing more technical than their eyes.[7]

That the British took such a predictable route into Germany can only have helped the Luftwaffe. They were expecting the RAF to arrive at a similar point to last time, and had deployed their forces accordingly; the British decoy further south did not do much to divert their attention. With hindsight this is hardly surprising: no matter how many bundles of Window the four decoy Mosquitos dropped, the image on German radar screens could never have been as strong as that produced by the bomber stream. While there is some evidence that the Germans thought a second bomber stream was approaching from the south-west, it must have been obvious that it was simply a diversion.[8] So, most of the coastal night fighters seem to have remained in the areas where they expected the British to arrive. And as soon as the route markers went down, they pounced.

The first British bomber to be shot down was probably a Halifax from 78 Squadron piloted by Sergeant R. Snape, which crashed into the sea. Six other British planes soon suffered the same fate, all but one within a few miles of the first route markers.[9] The area around the Pathfinder flares had suddenly become the most dangerous part of the sky. Six other bomber crews were attacked there too, but were lucky enough to come back and tell the tale.[10] Out of the forty-nine crewmen shot down, only one survived – Flight Officer A. H. Boyle parachuted out of his 158 Squadron Halifax shortly before it crashed into German countryside between Heide and Tellingstedt.

Veterans of the bomber war all agree on this fact: an attack from a night fighter came so quickly that there was little time to react, and certainly no time to feel fear. Within moments it was all over, one way or the other. An attack on one Lancaster about this time showed what might happen. Flight Sergeant E. L. Pickles of 100 Squadron was approaching the German coast when a burst of fire came from nowhere, blowing away the whole of the mid-upper turret and killing the gunner. The flight engineer, who had been dispensing Window, was also killed, and the rear gunner wounded in the face. Pickles took immediate action, and dived away fast, but without his gunners to protect him it was plain that he would have to turn back. After instructing the bomb-aimer to jettison his bombs, he turned and headed home. At no point during the attack had he seen the enemy aircraft that was attacking him; and since none of the crew warned him it seems they had been equally surprised.[11] The mid-upper gunner in particular had probably died without knowing he was even in danger.

Once the bomber stream had crossed the coast they headed inland and turned towards Hamburg. Three more Halifaxes were shot down over Schleswig-Holstein, two by fighters and one by flak.[12] They were all on the fringes of the bomber stream and therefore more easily identified by the radar operators – but in any case it seems that Window was not having quite the same effect tonight as it had had on its previous outings. As I have already mentioned, some of the more experienced German radar operators were already learning to tell the difference between the traces left by bombers and those produced by the foil strips. Window, which

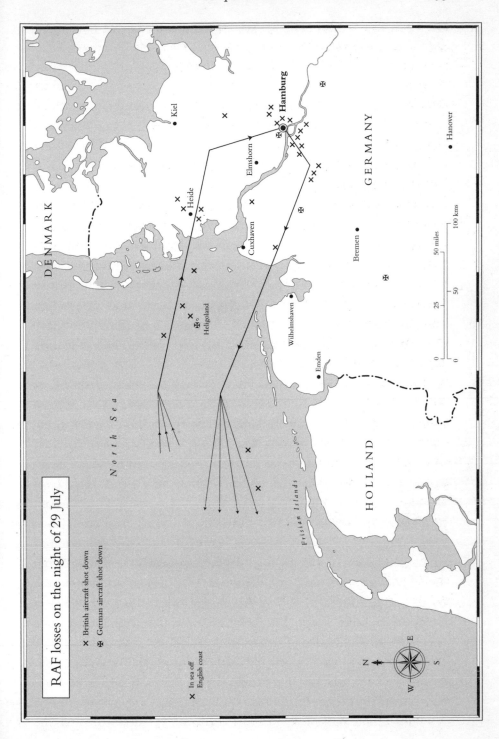

RAF losses on the night of 29 July

× British aircraft shot down
✠ German aircraft shot down

× In sea off
  English coast

Kiel

Hamburg

Hanover

GERMANY

Elmshorn

Heide

Cuxhaven

Bremen

Wilhelmshaven

Emden

North Sea

Heligoland

Frisian Islands

HOLLAND

DENMARK

0   25   50 miles
0   50   100 kms

N
W   E
S

had been so effective when it was first introduced just five nights ago, was already losing its potency.

★   ★   ★

The Luftwaffe's next victims were shot down over the target, and it was only here that some British airmen realized they were not going to have the easy ride they had been expecting. There were searchlights everywhere. And not only had the number of lights increased, the way they were being used had also vastly improved. On previous visits to the city, Window had confused the search-lights so badly that they had waved randomly across the sky, or stood perfectly still as though their operators had given up try-ing to find anything. Tonight, however, they swept the sky with renewed purpose, occasionally grouping together to trap British bombers within vast cones of light until they either escaped or were blasted down by the city's defences. The flak was more accurate tonight too, claiming three British bombers in and around the target area.[13]

But it was the fighters that posed by far the greatest risk. Freed from the constraints of the old radar-based *Himmelbett* system (whereby night fighters were kept rigidly in separate 'boxes' along the coast), Luftwaffe pilots were taking enthusiastically to their new, freelance role – but the greatest successes fell to Major Hajo Herrmann and his *Wilde Sau* fighters. They were out in force over the city, and that night they came into their own, lying in wait until they spotted a bomber silhouetted against the fires, then swooping down, sometimes even venturing into the flak zone to make good their attack. Of the nine bombers that were shot down above and around Hamburg, three were hit almost simultaneously by flak and fighters, which shows how fearless this new breed of freelance fighters was.[14] There was a new determination in the way the Luftwaffe were prepared to defend their city, and it looked as though it was paying off: half-way through the operation, the British had already lost far more planes than on either of their previous trips to Hamburg.

Flight Lieutenant H. C. 'Ben' Pexton of 35 Squadron was one

of the unlucky ones. As he was beginning the bombing run his Halifax was caught by one searchlight, then several more, until the cockpit was lit up like day. He released his bombs on target, but almost immediately afterwards the plane was hit by flak and the navigator mortally wounded. Despite throwing the aeroplane around the sky Pexton could not shake off the searchlights, which simply passed him from one to another as he flew, and it was not long before a fighter came in to attack, attracted by the lights. A series of cannon shells blasted into the back of the plane, and both the rear gunner and the flight engineer were killed. As the fighter turned and came in for a second attack, Pexton's plane was virtually defenceless. Joe Weldon, the wireless operator, tells what happened next:

It didn't seem long before we were being hit again and, this time, he got the starboard outer engine, which was set on fire. Ben pressed the fire extinguisher but nothing happened. Then the fighter made another run and the pilot told us to bale out. 'Better go, lads.' Then, almost immediately, I think, he was hit because he flopped forwards.

All hell broke loose after that. The aircraft went over and must have gone into a spin. I was thrown into a heap and, when I was able to get to my feet, I found the open escape hatch above my head; it was normally in the floor. I can remember what I thought then. Bloody hell! The wife's going to get a telegram in the morning, saying I was missing. But I didn't think I was going to be killed; that was the last thought in my mind. There was someone else in there but I don't know whether it was the bomb-aimer or the navigator. I went for that hatch; I didn't hang about, I can assure you.[15]

The crew member behind him was in fact the bomb-aimer, Frank Fenton, who gave him a push, then followed him out. The two were the only survivors of the attack. Their Halifax crashed a few miles outside the city they had bombed.

By now it should be obvious just how dangerous the skies over Hamburg had become. However, for one small group of bombers the situation was even worse than it was for the others. Due to a mix-up at Scampton airfield, nine Lancasters of 57 Squadron had been sent out with the wrong 'time on target' – while everyone else was due to have finished bombing by 0130 hours, this small group did not arrive at the target until twenty minutes later. Deprived of collective security, and brightly lit by fires so huge they could be seen for almost two hundred miles,[16] this small group of planes was more vulnerable than it had ever been. The entire strength of the city's defences was now aimed at them, and them alone.

One of the pilots, Bill McCrea, still remembers the terror that gripped him when he grasped that he and his comrades had arrived late:

The journey across and above a blazing Hamburg was one of the strangest I have ever undertaken. No one fired at us, no fighter attacked us, no searchlight was pointed in our direction. But as I turned away after dropping our bombs, I have never felt so exposed and so vulnerable. All I could do was to fix my eyes on the darkness beyond the fires and pray that we could reach that darkness before we were spotted by a fighter. Although we managed to fly clear without incident, one of our colleagues was not so lucky. I watched as a bomber just ahead and slightly below was subjected to a series of attacks from a fighter. It burst into flames and soon commenced its final fiery spiral into the earth below.[17]

The bomber that went down was piloted by Flight Sergeant E. F. Allwright, one of two planes in this small group that were shot down over Hamburg. The other belonged to Pilot Officer G. A. N. Parker; it was hit by flak and crashed in the north of the city. Of the fourteen men in the two planes, only one escaped with his parachute on. The rest were casualties of an administrative bungle that had sent them out virtually unprotected.

The Luftwaffe fought the British all the way back to the coast, then followed them far out to sea, giving up only when they reached the limit of their range. On the return journey a further four RAF planes were shot down, bringing the grand total to twenty-eight – almost the same number of planes that had been lost on both previous raids put together. In return, British gunners claimed to have destroyed four fighters, with another two probably destroyed and three more damaged.[18]

It had been a busy night in the skies over northern Europe, and one of which the Luftwaffe could feel justifiably proud. The German defenders, temporarily shocked into submission by the advent of Window, had not only reorganized, but had also learned an entirely new set of tactics to fight back. The general in charge of air defence, Generaloberst Weise, was so impressed with them that two days later he ordered that they be adopted across the Reich.[19] The lessons the Luftwaffe learned from Hamburg had a huge effect on the way it waged war, and would gradually win it the upper hand once more in the months to come.

* * *

Despite the Luftwaffe's relative success in the skies, there was little cause for celebration in Germany. The RAF's bombing had been more scattered that night, but even so it had been devastating. The chief of police claimed later that, in terms of physical damage, the raid had been every bit as bad as that of Tuesday night. In Barmbek alone a single huge fire covered six square kilometres, where a combined street frontage of 167 kilometres was burning. Other parts of the city had also been badly hit, especially the old town, the port, and some western suburbs like Eppendorf. In effect, 'The whole of Hamburg had become one area fire.'[20]

All of this had happened even though the RAF had wandered off course, and marked the target fairly badly. The British plan had always been to concentrate the bombing in the north-west of Hamburg, to destroy the suburbs of Harvestehude, Rotherbaum and Eppendorf. However, a cross-wind had blown the Pathfinders off course, and they had dropped most of their target indicators in the east of the city, directly over the part of Hamburg that had been bombed on Tuesday night. Indeed, many of the early bombs dropped on the suburb of Hamm, which was already so completely destroyed that a few more incendiaries could hardly have made much difference. But the bombing soon crept back over Eilbek

Crosswind blows bombers
3 miles off course

Direction of approach

RAF bombs dropped on Hamburg
on the night of 29 July

N
W   E
S

Alster
Lake

Norder Elbe

1 mile limit

2 mile limit

3 mile limit

☆   Target indicators dropped
•   Bomb load
△   Aiming point
    Industrial areas
    Residential areas

0   1   2 miles
0   1   2   3 kms

and Barmbek, causing huge destruction in the north-east of the city. The original target to the west of the Alster was also badly hit, but only because the target markers were so scattered.

After two whole days of desperate evacuation, there was hardly anyone left in the city to be killed. For those few who had stayed behind, though, it was every bit as horrific as the night of the firestorm. Helmuth Saß was sheltering in a bunker beneath the Baptist church on Weidestrasse, but was forced to leave when a collapsing building blocked the entrance. He climbed out through the shutter openings only to find himself confronted with a mountain of burning rubble, a blizzard of sparks, and four-storey houses burning all around him. As he made his escape down Vogteiweg with his mother and younger brother he suddenly became aware of the sheer absurdity of the situation:

I thought that I was experiencing some sort of macabre play. Above in the aeroplanes sat the English, who were under orders to bomb us, while we ran through this burning hell for our lives. We did not know or hate each other. Suddenly my brother's hair was burning. Shocked, we smothered the flames, but a welt remained. Shortly afterwards, my mother screamed. A falling burning piece of wood had hit her calf, causing her to limp. We took shelter in the entrance to a shop, until a man who was hurrying past noticed that in the shop window firelighters, of all things, were on display. We had to get away from there.[21]

They struggled onwards to an abandoned apartment building, where they found a barrel of water with which to douse themselves. Then they were off through the streets once more until they reached relative safety under a railway bridge on Barmbeker Markt. The absurdity of this kind of warfare manifested itself once more when they saw a group of men deliberately setting fire to a uniform shop at the start of the Dehnhaide. To perform an act of arson in the midst of a city that was already ablaze seems like madness, but the men justified their actions: 'When everything is burning, the Party uniforms should burn too.' Nobody bothered to contradict them.[22]

It was not only Helmuth Saß's shelter that was hit in this attack. Several of the larger 'indestructible' public shelters were also struck. In Eilbek a high-explosive bomb hit the *Hochbunker* on the corner of Wielandstrasse and Schellingstrasse, blowing a hole through two and a half metres of reinforced concrete on the seventh floor. Two women were killed, and the other two thousand shelterers were left in shock that such a thing was even possible.[23] By far the worst calamity of the night was the collapse of the Karstadt department store on Hamburgerstrasse, blocking the entrances to the store's two large air-raid bunkers. Rescue workers managed to open one of the shelters the next day, releasing 1,200 employees from the debris. It took longer to reach the second bunker, and 370 people died inside from carbon-monoxide poisoning.[24]

When such disasters were possible it is not surprising that even in the biggest shelters people were afraid. Adolf Pauly took refuge in a bunker on the corner of Maxstrasse in Eilbek:

Hardly had we got there when all hell broke loose. In the bunker absolute darkness reigned, so we sat in our places, motionless, for hour upon hour upon hour. In the sweltering heat the air was suffocating. No matches, let alone a lamp, would light, so scarce was the oxygen. No ventilation flaps were allowed to be opened, otherwise the embers would have found their way in and 3,000 people would have suffocated in the bunker. Again and again the bunker shook under the resounding blows. Whether it was the collapsing walls of the neighbouring houses, or (as was claimed) actual bombs falling on the bunker, I don't know. In the darkness we could hear general noise and cries in the floors below. There were burning people saved from the streets. Also that night two children were born in the bunker. Now and then the names of the missing would be called out . . . For twelve hours I sat there with my wife in absolute darkness, fastened motionless to my place.[25]

When he came out the following day the whole of his neighbourhood was on fire once again. His apartment, which had survived the previous two raids, was now ablaze, and there was no longer any choice but to follow the refugees who had gone before him. He was stunned by the event. The very reason he had not left the city earlier was because he did not think the British would bother to bomb his neighbourhood a third time: 'Yet another bomb attack on this field of ruins seemed senseless.'[26]

Hans J. Massaquoi was just as shocked by the sight that greeted him when he left a public shelter in Barmbek:

What awaited us was one of the saddest and most dreadful sights of our lives. The whole of Stückenstraße – no, the whole of Barmbek, our beloved neighbourhood – was practically razed to the ground. As far as the eye could see there was nothing but total devastation. In contrast to the ear-splitting noise of last night there was now a muted silence over the gruesome scenery. Here and there could be seen mummified, charred corpses. Obviously these people had decided to leave their apartments too late in order to get to a shelter. Most houses had been burnt right down to their foundations. Others were still in flames, and more still were nothing but burned out ruins. One of these smoking heaps of rubble had been my home since childhood.[27]

★   ★   ★

Tonight's bombing had not caused anything like the human toll of the last attack. The official report did not attempt to put a figure on the number of dead – the city was in such chaos that it was impossible to separate the victims of one raid from another – but after the war a senior figure in the United States Strategic Bombing Survey made an estimate of about eight hundred, and later estimates range between a thousand and five thousand.[28] The material damage, however, was appalling. Only a few outlying suburbs now remained relatively untouched by the bombing – the rest was fire and ruins. There was seemingly nothing left to bomb.

And yet the RAF had still not finished with the city. In four nights' time they would direct a fourth and final massive raid against Hamburg, this time attacking from the south. That they should want to do so no longer surprised anyone in Hamburg. As the final survivors straggled out of Eilbek towards the fringes of the city they came across a scene that seemed to symbolize the

Damage caused on the night of 29 July

STERDORF

WINTERHUDE

BARMBEK

WANDSBEK

UHLENHORST

EILBEK

Alster
Lake

HOHENFELDE

ST GEORG

Hamburg Central
Station
LTSTADT

BORGFELDE

Fire Brigade
Headquarters

HAMM

HORN

HAMMERBROOK

KLEINER
GRASBROOK

ROTHENBURGSORT

BILLBROOK

VEDDEL

Buildings destroyed by earlier British and
American attacks

Buildings destroyed by RAF raid 29/30 July

sheer insanity of the war that had overtaken them: the Jakobi Friedhof, a huge graveyard on the Wandsbeker Chaussee, was on fire. It was a sight that imprinted itself on Adolf Pauly's memory: 'The cemetery had been laid waste, covered with incendiary bombs, the gravestones overturned, and there was thick smoke pouring out of a family vault.'[29]

Now, it seemed, the British were even bombing their dead.

19. The Tempest

For my part, I have walk'd about the streets,
Submitting me unto the perilous night . . .
And when the cross blue lightning seem'd to open
The very breast of heaven, I did present myself
Even in the aim and very flash of it.
      William Shakespeare, *Julius Caesar*[1]

In a matter of days Hamburg, a proud Hanseatic city that had existed for over seven centuries, had been reduced to an endless field of smoking ruins. Neighbourhoods that had once been filled with bustling activity were now deserted, their streets filled with rubble, their houses reduced to empty, roofless shells. In many areas the only things left standing were the chimneys: 'solitary chimneys,' Hans Erich Nossack recalled, 'that grew from the ground like cenotaphs'.[2]

This ghost town was populated only by small groups of soldiers, firemen and rescue workers, with occasional gangs of concentration-camp prisoners brought in to help recover the dead. Almost everyone else had gone. Thousands of wounded had been taken to hospitals in other cities, some in specially commissioned hospital trains. Orphans had been gathered together and sent to join other evacuated children in countryside schools away from the bombing. Even the inmates of the city's prisons had either been released, shipped away or drafted in to help with the clean-up effort.[3]

One group of people, however, were initially forgotten by the authorities. Many of the city's forced labourers were abandoned, while their guards fled Hamburg with their families. Some made their way to the refugee camps, following the general exodus, but many simply stayed where they were, afraid to move without written authorization.

Wanda Chantler, a twenty-year-old woman from Poland, was one of those left behind. As mentioned previously, her barracks in Lokstedt had received a direct hit on the night of 24 July, killing most of the women with whom she lived and worked. With nowhere to sleep, she had initially spent the nights outside on the grass of the factory compound, but eventually she and the few other survivors moved into the communal dining hall. All were in a chronic state of shock, and weak from lack of food and water. There was nobody left to provide for them; apart from the other forced labourers in other blocks, the entire city seemed deserted. Wanda remembers that her perception of the world took on an apocalyptic quality:

All these dead bodies were lying about, and nobody knew what to do with them. And the weather was terrible. It was hot, and it was windy. It was as if all the walls had been taken away from the world, and all the clouds and the winds concentrated on Hamburg. It was terrible. It was light from the fires, but the smoke made it dark. I've never seen anything like it, and I don't think I ever will again. It was light, and yet it was dark. And you had no direction, you could not see. The smoke was choking.[4]

After three huge bombardments their whole world had been reduced to nothing but fire and smoke. On 2 August, the elements conspired to complete the apocalyptic picture. A violent electrical storm descended on the ruined city, the thunder and lightning a celestial echo of the bombs that had been falling all week. By this point the abandoned girl had been living among the ruins of her barracks for over a week. As she and her few companions huddled together in the darkness of the factory dining hall, they watched the torrential rain outside with growing awe. 'The elements seemed to have clubbed together to hit the earth at the particular point that was Hamburg,' Wanda Chantler remembers. Tonight, after everything they had already been through, it was easy to imagine that the stormclouds had come from 'all around the globe', that the world war had given way to something even greater, that they were witnessing not merely the destruction of a city but the end of the world.

Astonishingly, that was the night on which the British launched their fourth and final major bombardment. Through the thunder and lightning, the frightened girls soon made out the distant sound of sirens and the drone of planes, although it was sometimes difficult to tell the difference between the storm and the bombs exploding. As the police report later made clear, this raid was the climax to ten days of terror, 'in which the detonation of exploding bombs, the peals of thunder and the crackling of the flames and ceaseless downpour of the rain combined to form a hellish inferno'.[5]

Other witnesses expressed similar dismay that the RAF should be willing to brave such infernal conditions to pound the city all over again. Franz Termer had fled with his family to Pinneberg, ten or twelve miles outside Hamburg to the north-west, where he took shelter in a farmhouse. The storm was so violent that it had woken him, but as he and his wife were checking on their children their attention was soon caught by a more disturbing noise:

We had hardly finished when we heard the sirens sounding from Pinne-berg between breaks in the thunder. We couldn't believe our ears, thought it must be a mistake. Surely the planes couldn't be coming now, in such a heavy storm. But soon afterwards a heavy flak barrage started up a short distance away, and we could already hear the terrible buzz and drone of heavy, four-engined bombers directly over our roof. Uninterrupted, one formation after another. The lightning flashed brightly, the British flares shone yellow and red, and the muzzles of the flak guns flashed like lightning in the dark night.[6]

Despite the electrical storm, the RAF had indeed arrived, yet again, in the skies over Hamburg.

★　　★　　★

It should go without saying that Bomber Command Headquarters had never intended to send their force into the face of this storm. No matter how frightening the effect of the thunder and lightning on the shattered nerves of Hamburg's civil population, the effect on the bomber crews, both physically and psychologically, was exponentially worse. Flying over German territory was bad enough without having to contend with such weather. And the likelihood of achieving a concentrated strike on the city was virtually nil. So why were they there? What miscalculation or error of judgement could have sent them into such danger?

Part of the blame at least must lie with Sir Arthur Harris. Ever since the previous attack on Hamburg, on 29 July, he had been itching to finish the job, and it seems he had intended originally to do so on the following night. However, he was prevented by political considerations – in the wake of Mussolini's downfall, Churchill had been keen to increase pressure on the Italians, and an urgent directive required him to plan immediate attacks on Milan, Turin and Genoa.[7] On the night of 1 August Hamburg was back on the cards, but the raid had to be cancelled because of bad weather. (Ironically it was this storm that prevented the crews taking off: it passed through England on 1 August on its way to northern Germany, where bomber crews caught up with it twenty-four hours later.) By 2 August Harris's frustration was getting the better of him. Tonight, if there was the slightest chance of destroying what was left of Hamburg, he was determined to take it.

The British held high expectations of this last raid. Their plan of attack was significantly different from previous operations, and reflected their growing confidence in their destructive abilities. Tonight, for the first time, they would approach Hamburg from the south, and they would have not one but two aiming points. The first waves were to drop their bombs on to a point towards the north end of the Alster lake, with the idea that the creepback would sweep a curtain of destruction over Harvesthude and Rotherbaum – two districts that had suffered only lightly in the previous attacks. Then, half-way through the raid, the aiming point would be switched to the town of Harburg on the southern edge of the vast harbour complex.[8] It was an ambitious but well-thought-out scheme that would spell the end of those areas of the city that had so far escaped the bombs – provided everything went to plan.

After all the postponements, Harris was keen to get started, weather allowing. As evening approached, a Mosquito was sent to check conditions over northern Germany: if the storms had cleared the area the RAF could head for Hamburg a fourth time, otherwise they would have to scrap the operation again. To make sure they had the most up-to-date weather report, and to give themselves the greatest chance of sticking to their plan, Bomber Command delayed the weather reconnaissance flight until the last possible moment: the Mosquito did not leave Wyton airfield until 6.45 p.m. When it returned three hours later, the two-man crew told the Meteorological Office what they had seen: the skies over Hamburg looked relatively clear, but a huge cumulo-nimbus to the south-west of Oldenburg was moving briskly in the direction of tonight's target.[9] There was a chance that it would have moved on by the time the bombers reached Hamburg, but it would be a risk.

Bomber Command was fast running out of time to make a decision one way or the other: if the squadrons were to get to Hamburg and back under cover of darkness they had to leave before midnight. After a hurried assessment, the Meteorological Office sent its weather report to Bomber Command at 10 p.m. Crucially, they had watered down any worries about the storm: they claimed that there was only a 'slight risk' that the bombers would encounter this dangerous weather.

When it came to the lives of his men Harris was normally fairly cautious, and on any other night he might have chosen an alternative target, or scrapped his plans. That night, however, impatience got the better of him: for such an important target a 'slight risk' was worth taking. The only concession to the weather was a modest alteration to the plan: instead of attacking two separate aiming points in the city, the bomber force would concentrate on one, on the north-west shoulder of the Alster lake. Otherwise the raid would go ahead as briefed.[10]

Thus it was that 740 crews who had been on stand-by for the past couple of hours now made their way to dispersal. Many were astonished that the raid was going ahead. Some had already been told to expect violent weather, but others were left to guess at the strength of the conditions from the vague warnings they had received at briefing. But all were about to experience a night they would never forget.

★   ★   ★

It was a blustery, overcast night when the bomber force took off. By midnight most of the planes were airborne and beginning to break through the cloud that covered the North Sea. For some crews the problems began almost as soon as they took off. At Scampton a Lancaster from 57 Squadron crashed on the runway and promptly caught fire, preventing six others behind it from taking off.[11] Several planes from other squadrons did not even reach the English coast before they were forced to turn back with engine trouble – two of those landed so badly that they were written off, with injuries to seven crewmen.[12] A further shock came over the sea when a startled Royal Navy convoy mistook the bomber stream for a German force and opened fire on them. While it seems they did not do any damage, it was hardly a good omen.

Whatever happened on the journey across the North Sea, the real trouble did not begin until the bombers reached the German coast. Of all the operations those airmen flew on, this was the one they universally remembered, even to this day; and for those who completed their tour, nothing came close to the fear and confusion they experienced that night. It began with a sinister, almost surreal vision. Up ahead they saw a cloud unlike any they had seen before: a huge, dark mountain of cloud, its sides cracked with deep fissures and chasms, and lit by the continual flashes of light that glinted from its depths. Some of the crews thought it was smoke, still rising from the burning ruins of Hamburg; many believed that the heavy flashes that lit it were from some terrific new weapon among the German flak. It was not until they got closer that they realized the truth: that it was the biggest and most violent electrical storm any of them had ever seen.

No pilot likes to fly through conditions so bad, but that night there was nothing they could do to avoid it. To fly over the storm was impossible – the summit of the cloud rose to 30,000 feet, perhaps even higher, and apart from the handful of Mosquitos from 139 Squadron there was not an aircraft among them capable of flying so high while laden with bombs. There was no point in trying to fly round it either – to do that would have isolated anyone who tried it and taken him so far out of his way that he would never have had enough fuel to return home. One or two crews tried to fly under it, but gave up after sinking below 7,000 feet without managing to break free of the cloud. If they were to complete the raid they had to head directly into the storm.

As they approached the lower peaks of the massive cumulo-nimbus the temperature plummeted. Many crews chose this moment to turn round and head for home, sensing the danger that lay ahead. Of those that continued, most tried to delay flying through the cloud for as long as they could, choosing instead to follow the sinister rifts and valleys along its fringes. High walls of cloud loomed over them on both flanks, their dark bulk lit intermittently by sheets of lightning. Eventually the ravines ended. Then there was no alternative but to head straight for the seemingly impenetrable wall before them and break through into the heart of the storm.

Bill McCrea, the pilot who had found himself isolated on the previous raid when his squadron had sent him out twenty minutes late, remembers those moments as among the most terrifying of his life:

The stormclouds that had been over England some twenty-four hours earlier were now dead ahead, dark and forbidding, and towering above the bombers by several thousand feet. I realized that what I first took to be flak were in reality lightning flashes emanating from the stormclouds that we were rapidly approaching. As we flew into the lightning-charged clouds the effect was immediate and terrifying. The air currents came first, throwing the aircraft from side to side as well as up and down. One could almost hear the airframe protest as it was subjected to these external forces. The lightning was continuous; as it flashed one could see that the clouds were sometimes broken up by eerie canyons and ravines.[13]

J. K. Christie, who flew a Lancaster with 35 Squadron, approached the storm with mounting anxiety. Afterwards he recorded the impressions in his diary:

Everything went smooth and according to plan until we approached Heligoland, where we started to run into clouds up to more than 20,000 feet. I carried on trying to keep above it and for some time just managed to keep popping in and out of the tops. By this time we were just about crossing the German coast. I saw numerous and colossal flashes all over the sky and for a long time I believed that the Germans had brought into action a new and terrific anti-aircraft weapon. After a certain while, we did not manage to keep on the top of the clouds and had to continue flying blind, shaken every ten seconds by terrific flashes which totally blinded me for many seconds afterwards. We got fairly heavy icing and very heavy statics.

In addition to this I had a new and very spectacular experience as the whole aircraft seemed to be completely electrified. There were huge luminous rings around the propellers, blue flames out of the wing-tips, gun muzzles and also everywhere else on the aircraft where its surface is pointed. For instance, the de-icing tube in front of my window had a blue flame around it. Electrical flowers were dancing on the windows all the time until they got iced up, when the flowers disappeared. The wireless operator told me afterwards that sparks were shooting across his equipment all the time and that his aerials were luminous throughout their lengths. I didn't feel a bit happy and tried to go down below the clouds.[14]

The mysterious blue flames were St Elmo's fire, the phenomenon that had mystified seafarers during the golden age of sailing ships. The stormcloud through which they were flying had been so highly charged with electricity that it had begun to materialize in the form of a ghostly blue light around the aircraft.

Christie was not alone in seeing this unearthly sight; almost everyone who flew through the storm experienced the phenomenon. 'Blue electrical discharges flashed between the muzzles of the guns,' says Bill McCrea, 'and our propellers looked like catherine wheels, as if a torch had been fastened to the end of each blade. From time to time the whole aircraft became shrouded in a blue shimmering light.'[15] Colin Harrison of 467 Squadron still remembers the sight with awe: 'We were lit up in blue lights . . . sparks in all directions, jumping from one thing to another. And the props – there was a beautiful blue arc where the props were turning.' James Sullivan, a wireless operator with 156 Squadron, remembers: 'The lightning was sparking all along the fuselage and along the guns. It looked like an electrical aircraft!'[16]

When all around them was pitch dark, the effect of the luminous blue light could be unnerving – but it was virtually harmless. Much more dangerous was the ice that built on all the leading edges of the aircraft: if enough was allowed to accumulate it could make the plane too heavy to fly so that it would literally fall out of the sky.

That happened to a Stirling of 620 Squadron, as one of its crew members recalls:

I have never been as scared in my life and never will be again. I sat there, petrified, then called to the skipper, 'For Christ's sake, get out of this.' He started to climb more steeply but, as the Stirling's ceiling was only about 15,000 feet loaded, we reached our maximum height and we were still in cloud. Suddenly, we started icing up. The wings of the kite were a white sheet. Great chunks of ice were flying from the propellers and hitting the fuselage like machine-gun fire. Then the port wing went down and we started dropping like a stone. After what seemed a lifetime, I heard a distant voice whisper, 'Jettison. Jettison.' I have prayed very few times in my life but this occasion was one of them and, thank heaven, someone was listening.'[17]

Ted Groom, a flight engineer with 460 Squadron, remembers a similar thing happening to his Lancaster:

The propellers appeared like huge catherine wheels, with ice forming and static electricity. Chunks of ice were hitting the aircraft, and the props and the control surfaces were being covered with ice . . . All this time we were losing height. This happened frighteningly quickly, and the pilot and myself were overwhelmed with these conditions. The rest of the crew wanted to know what was happening. Eventually, after losing several thousand feet, we were back in control again. But the aircraft was still in thick cloud. As we could not see any sky markers the decision was made to drop the bombs and return to base.[18]

The only way to regain control of the plane was to lose as much weight as possible, as quickly as possible, to stop the rate of fall, so both planes jettisoned their bombs. It was also important to get rid of the ice since it could jam up the ailerons and elevators, making it virtually impossible for the pilot to control the plane. Ted Groom did this by desynchronizing the engines, which caused such vibration in the aircraft that it shook off much of the ice. It was a dangerous thing to do for any length of time, but in his case, fortunately, it worked.

In such conditions it was a battle just to keep the aircraft controls working. The flight engineers found themselves dealing simultaneously with several dangerous problems, as Sergeant Dennis Brookes recalled shortly afterwards:

The lightning was terrifying, flashing from one end of the kite to the other. Both gun turrets went u/s owing to ice and the lightning. We were thrown about by thunder, and the outer hatch was struck and wrenched open. Ice formed everywhere, and I was sweating to help keep the controls free . . . Great quantities of flak were bursting all around but could not be distinguished owing to the lightning. Both the compasses went u/s and very little control of the aircraft could be kept. It was impossible to keep the engine tempo up and the boost suddenly dropped off as the intake became clammed up with ice. Skipp, whom

I was standing by, told us the controls were getting very stiff to handle and was far beyond the control of George [the auto-pilot]. We were all expecting the worst and were ready to abandon aircraft, when suddenly at 7,000 feet Skipp managed to pull her out of the dive and began to climb again, having lost 10,000 feet in a few seconds.[19]

Tales of falling like a stone in such conditions were common. Sergeant J. Benny of 15 Squadron only managed to pull out of his dive at 4,000 feet. His squadron colleague, Flight Lieutenant G. Bould, was a mere 500 feet above the ground when he re-gained control of his plane; finding himself over Bremerhaven he immediately dropped his bombs and hedge-hopped back to the German coast.[20]

One Halifax of 35 Squadron paid the ultimate price for the horrendous conditions. Sergeant A. Stephen, the mid-upper gun-ner, had to watch helplessly as, within seconds, the aircraft's wings and propellers had become coated with thick ice, then his turret.

I got out of the turret quickly to get my 'chute, for I felt we were not going to get out of this, and I was no sooner inside the fuselage than we went into a spin. The G force was very strong; I could not even lift my arm. I was in the centre section at this time and I felt someone kicking to get to the exit but he was pinned down like me. The spin seemed to go on for hours but, then, there was a crash and everything was thrown about.

After dropping through three miles of sky, Sergeant Stephen's Halifax had crashed into German countryside. Miraculously, he and the flight engineer were still alive.

When I came round . . . it was daylight and I saw that I was sitting in a heap of wreckage and Bert, the engineer, was lying beside me. I could not move but I heard someone talking outside and gave a shout. They were German soldiers and they came and lifted Bert and me out of the remains of the Halifax. I remember cursing them for lifting me by the legs because they were fractured. The soldiers put us down in a field about a hundred yards from the wreckage and I saw that the part I had been in was just the two wings and the centre section. The target indicators were hanging out and the petrol tanks were right above them. How the lot did not blow up, I'll never know.[21]

Sergeant Stephen was the only one to survive the crash: his friend Bert died in his arms a short time later. The rest of the crew had been killed instantly.

That night at least four British planes were lost because of the ice: they crashed into the sea, or into the German countryside, their pilots unable to save them.[22] Another bomber was struck by lightning so badly that the pilot lost control. It crashed without reaching the target, killing everyone on board.[23]

*   *   *

The only consolation for the British was that the terrible conditions were as bad for the German fighters as they were for the RAF. Wilhelm Johnen, a fighter pilot with III/NJG1,[24] later recorded his thoughts on the sort of conditions he and his fellows had to endure on that terrible night:

When gusts of wind at gale force flung the machine about the sky; when in a fraction of a second the propellers, wings and engines were swathed in thick, heavy ice . . . When devilish St Elmo's fire began to dance on the aerials, cockpit panes and propellers, blinding the pilot . . . In these moments is born the airman . . . Pilots trust in God far more than people would believe.[25]

Without their radar, German night fighters were relying on their eyes to find their victims, but this was almost impossible in the midst of the stormclouds that filled the sky. Every now and then one would find a British bomber, and an extraordinary game of cat-and-mouse would develop as each aircraft wove in and out of the clouds to escape the shots of the other.[26] Visibility was so bad that one Dorner 217 of II/NJG3 actually collided with the bomber it was trying to attack: the pilot, Feldwebel Krauter, could

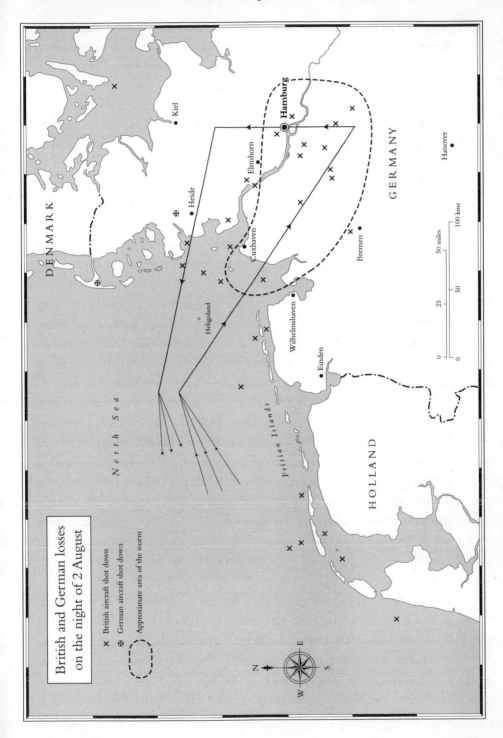

British and German losses on the night of 2 August

× British aircraft shot down

✠ German aircraft shot down

⌇ Approximate area of the storm

DENMARK

GERMANY

HOLLAND

North Sea

Frisian Islands

Heligoland

Kiel

Heide

Elmshorn

Cuxhaven

Hamburg

Hanover

Bremen

Wilhelmshaven

Emden

50 miles

100 kms

N E S W

not see to pull out of his attacking run and crashed into Flight Sergeant J. A. Couper's 75 Squadron Stirling. Both planes crashed to the ground. Krauter escaped alive, but the crew of the British plane died in the crash.[27]

As the British bomber force approached their target they became steadily more ragged: what had begun as a tight stream was now degenerating into a dispersed scattering of individual aeroplanes. This was the final, and perhaps most deadly, effect of the storm. As the British planes were blown about the sky, their navigational instruments rendered useless by the effects of static electricity, many were separated from the bunch. Since Window only worked when the bomber stream was fairly concentrated, the isolated planes showed up on German radar screens. Consequently they were now in more danger than ever.

The German defences wasted no time in picking them up. The fighters were also beginning to pick up lone bombers on their Lichtenstein airborne radar sets. Flak batteries won back some of their old accuracy: it seems that at least four British planes were brought down by flak alone, and many more seriously damaged.[28]

Barely half of the bombers that set off that night reached Hamburg, and by the time they arrived they were in serious trouble. Hamburg's flak batteries had been heavily reinforced since the night of the firestorm, and now let loose a barrage that rivalled the storm itself. According to Rudolf Schurig, the commander of a flak battery in the north-east of the city, 'the storm paled in the diabolic noise' given off by the German artillery. Their battery alone fired 776 rounds into the sky (compared with only 547 rounds on the night of the first attack – more than 40 per cent more).[29]

Not only was there more flak for the British to contend with, it was now far more concentrated than before. Two days earlier Generaloberst Weise had decreed that all flak above a target city should be limited to 4,500 metres (14,700 feet), to give the German fighters space to attack the bombers from above. The skies over Hamburg had therefore become doubly dangerous. Above the flak level the bombers faced the combined perils of ice, lightning and the gun-power of every fighter aircraft for miles, yet if they tried to venture out of the bottom of the stormcloud they faced an alternative storm of shells from Hamburg's greatly reinforced flak batteries.

As the raid progressed, the British situation became yet more miserable. When a greatly depleted force at last turned for home it was so broken up that any protection it might have gained from Window was long gone. Many of the crews were lost, scattered across the sky from Holland to Denmark. One 405 Squadron Halifax was so badly damaged by flak that its pilot decided to fly to Sweden: he and his crew eventually bailed out over Malmö and were interned by the Swedish authorities for the rest of the war. At the opposite extreme, six bombers were shot down just off the coast of Holland, some more than fifty miles off course. Alone, damaged by flak and forced to lose height by the power of the storm, they were no match for the fighter aces of the Luftwaffe's coastal squadrons.

Of these six crews there was just one survivor. Peter Swan, a bomb-aimer with 44 Squadron, was the only member of his crew who bailed out before his Lancaster crashed into the sea: he hit his head on the escape hatch and passed out in mid-air, but regained consciousness just in time to pull the ripcord of his parachute. After four hours in the cold waters of the North Sea, he was eventually picked up by a German E-boat. He spent the rest of the war in a prisoner-of-war camp.[30]

*　　*　　*

It was not until almost six o'clock the next morning that the last of the battered British force returned to the ground in England. As the tired, shaken crews climbed down from their aircraft, they were immediately taken to the debriefing rooms, where a fairly depressing picture of the night's operations emerged. Some described being attacked by night fighters, many more described the increased intensity of the flak, but all spoke in awe about the violence of the storm.

It soon became apparent that many crews had not even

attempted to bomb Hamburg, prevented by the conditions. To make things worse, even those who had reached the target had been unable to bomb it properly: they had been instructed to drop their loads on the green TIs, but often there were none to be seen.

Trevor Timperley, who flew one of the Pathfinder aircraft that night, explains what went wrong. It was his job to mark the target using the Wanganui method: rather than illuminating the target on the ground he had to drop indicators into the air above the aiming point, which would float down for all the other bombers to see. This was the method the Pathfinder Force used when clouds obscured the target. The problem was that even in relatively still conditions the TIs tended to drift away from where they were supposed to go. In a storm they were blown all over the sky. Even so, that was the least of Trevor Timperley's worries:

They had forecast some cumulo-nimbus cloud, but nothing like the scale that was encountered. I was supposed to be towards the end of the raid, illuminating with this Wanganui air marker. There was no point unless it was *outside* the cloud: if you drop it in a cloud, nobody will be able to see it. As we got closer, and we were climbing up to get over the top of it, I realized that I was still going to go in the cloud . . . I decided that if I kept my markers only, which was the important thing, and jettisoned the bombs, I would get the height [to break out of the clouds]. This turned out in the end to be 29,000 feet, which is pretty good in a Lancaster. Anyway, I just managed it . . . There were big gaps between the cloud, and I dropped my markers into one of them. But whether my markers slowly drifted into cloud as they went lower, I don't know. It was the best I could do.[31]

With the impossible conditions, their instruments failing, and TIs that drifted into the clouds, it is no wonder that many of those who battled their way through the storm failed to find Hamburg. Pilot Colin Harrison was completely disillusioned with the attack:

I never saw the target. I was weighted down – the aircraft was badly iced up – and battered from all the thunder and turbulence and the like.

I got knocked down from the 20,000 feet where we used to fly most of the time, to about 10,000 feet, and I came into a sort of a clear area. We were below cloud – it was practically a hole in the cloud – and there was no sign of the target. And I thought, well, this is a waste of time.[32]

Other pilots are even more outspoken about the seemingly pointless nature of their ordeal. Bill McCrea, still upset at having been sent to Hamburg twenty minutes late on the previous raid, is unforgiving about being dispatched into such danger a second time:

The fourth raid was a shambles. An absolute shambles – entirely the fault of the Met men. We should never have gone, because this electric storm came through England the previous day . . . They said it would have cleared Hamburg in twenty-four hours – well, it hadn't, it was right across the city. I think I flew in it for five minutes and I could feel the ice building up, so I turned round the other way. I got what I thought was a source of light coming from down below, so of course I dropped my bombs on that. I think it was Bremerhaven but I couldn't be sure.[33]

He and his crew didn't care what they had bombed. Shaken and silent, they were merely glad to be on their way home.

★   ★   ★

If the previous raids had been uniquely devastating in the history of bombing, tonight's operation had been an expensive RAF flop: a miserable performance conducted in miserable conditions. The RAF had lost thirty aircraft, at least a handful of which had been defeated by the sheer force of the storm;[34] 106 planes had dropped their bombs in the sea, 14 had jettisoned them over land, and 197 had given up on Hamburg and attacked targets of opportunity elsewhere.[35] Some crews had bombed Bremen, more than fifty miles to the south-west of the place they were supposed to be bombing; others had bombed Kiel, about fifty miles to the north. In fact, only 393 aircraft had made it as far as the target, barely half of the total British force, and even the planes that reached Hamburg did not attack the areas they were supposed to. In the words of

the Hamburg police chief, 'No focal point of the raid was observ-
able . . . Casualties among the population remained small.'[36] In
other words, the city had been spared the final, lethal blow that
everyone had been dreading.

It seems that many of the crews who made it to Hamburg
had dropped their loads early. In the poor visibility, with their
instruments affected by the storm, many navigators had been forced
to calculate where they were by dead reckoning: most crews
dropped their loads well south of the city, but a few hit Harburg.
This southern part of the port area had been one of the two original
targets and, ironically, had been taken off the list that afternoon;
several bombers hit it by mistake.

A large number of planes overshot the city. The small town of
Elmshorn lay about twelve miles to the north-west of Hamburg;
that night a large fire was burning in the town centre, caused either
by lightning or by some of the initial stray bombs. Drawn towards
it, as many as seventy British planes dropped their bombs on
the hapless town, destroying more than 250 houses and severely
damaging 200 more. Elmshorn was one of the evacuation points
from the previous raids, and was still packed with refugees, some
of whom could be forgiven for thinking that the British were
deliberately targeting them as they fled.[37] Fifty-seven people
were killed there.

As for Hamburg, a few fires were started in the centre of the
city and in the eastern part of the port, but they were scattered and
the city's fire-fighters were able to deal with them relatively easily.[38]
Some bombs fell into areas that had already been destroyed, and
many more fell uselessly into the surrounding countryside. For the
few people who still remained in the city, like Wanda Chantler
and her friends in the remains of their forced-labour camp, it was
a blessed relief. Far from being a threat, the awesome force of the
storm had come to their rescue.

★   ★   ★

The raid of 2/3 August brought an end to Operation Gomorrah,
and also, for the moment, the devastation of Hamburg. After nearly

ten thousand tons of bombs had been dropped on the city there seemed little point in repeating the attack. As far as the Allies were concerned, the job had been done.

PART THREE

The Aftermath

20. City of the Dead

*Who could ever, even with unbound words, tell in full of the blood and wounds
that I now saw, though he should narrate them many times?*
Dante[1]

In the days following Operation Gomorrah, the Hamburg authorities found themselves facing one of the biggest clean-up operations
in history. Hundreds of miles of streets were now buried beneath
mounds of rubble. The city centre had been transformed into a
collection of smashed monuments, broken church spires, gutted
architecture. Its famous waterways were choked with floating
detritus, charred wood, sunken boats. And the harbour – the heart
and soul of the city – was in a terrible state. The parts that were
visible across the river, such as the Blohm & Voss shipyards and
the surrounding docklands, had been reduced to a mess of burned-
out warehouses, sunken ships and the mangled remains of some
122 cranes.[2]

At the centre of the wasteland, like a huge black hole in the
landscape, lay the charred remains of what would soon become
known as the 'dead city'. It was there, in the districts of Hammerbrook, Rothenburgsort and Hamm, that the worst damage
had occurred. Streets that had once teemed with activity were
now a virtual moonscape, devoid of life. The whole area was
fundamentally unstable: unexploded bombs lurked beneath the
rubble, fires still raged in coke stores and lumber yards, and some
of the house façades that had not already collapsed swayed visibly
whenever the wind changed. Bodies were scattered across the
streets, many so badly scorched that they were indistinguishable
from the blackened tree trunks torn up by the force of the firestorm.

In the face of such devastation, not only here but in many other parts of the city, it was difficult for the authorities to know what to prioritize. The rubble had to be cleared off the roads before any major work could begin. Many damaged façades were so unstable that they had to be torn down to prevent them collapsing on rescue workers. Supplies of drinking water had to be restored to prevent outbreaks of disease, and there was pressure from Berlin to get the city's damaged war industries back up and running. There were still fears that some of the larger fires might burn out of control again. Indeed, some would not be put out until the beginning of October, a full two months after they had first been set alight.[3]

However, the authorities realized that the first priority, for everyone's sake, had to be the recovery and burial of the dead. This was easier said than done: the sheer numbers involved meant it was impossible to recover more than a fraction of the bodies within the first week. So they decided to concentrate on those that the population would find most distressing – the ones that were strewn, visibly, throughout the streets of the firestorm area. In this they were motivated by a genuine desire to spare the people of Hamburg any further anguish: they had experienced enough without having to contend with the gruesome sight of bodies lining the roads.

Of course, it was inevitable that many people were not spared this sight – especially in the early days. Annegret Hennings was one of those who ventured through the district of Hamm a few days after the firestorm. What she saw there shook her to the core:

In the Hammer Landstrasse I saw something lying there that looked like a charred tree trunk, and next to it another, smaller thing. They were a mother and child. Totally charred, so that they were unrecognizable. The dead lay everywhere. With some of them you couldn't tell if they had been burnt to death or killed by the blast. None of them had any bodyhair left. After some time these streets were closed off, walls were built across them. Prisoners had to go into the cellars and fetch the people out. I felt very sorry for them.[4]

Gretl Büttner also describes making a journey into the 'dead city'. She and her companion, Dr Maack, were investigating what had happened in these areas, and looking for the remains of some colleagues in the Air-raid Protection Service. After clambering over the rubble for a short way, they found themselves overlooking a sea of corpses:

On a little open square near Boonsweg – I shall never forget the sight – there lay hundreds of men and women, soldiers in uniform, children, old people. Many had torn the clothes from their bodies shortly before their death. They were naked, their bodies seemed unmarked, the faces showed peaceful expressions, like in deep sleep. Other bodies could hardly be recognized; they were charred, torn to pieces, and had shattered skulls . . . There an old woman lay. Her face was peaceful, soft, and tired . . . And there, a mother with a child on each hand. They were all three lying on their faces in an almost gracefully relaxed position . . . And there a soldier, with charred stumps for legs. There a woman with a torn body, on whose bulging-out intestines the flies were feeding. And there a child, clutching a birdcage in his hand. And there, detached from the body, a boy's foot with a black boot; a small, brown girl's hand with a blue ring . . . The heart almost stops beating at such sights.[5]

Scenes like that were only the tip of the iceberg. There were literally hundreds of streets and squares in the affected areas, and many were strewn with corpses. Most of the bodies, however, were out of sight, hidden in the cellars where they had succumbed to the combined effects of heat, smoke and carbon-monoxide poisoning.

Hamburg had an efficient system for collecting, identifying and burying those who died in air raids, but in the summer of 1943 it was overwhelmed by the sheer number of bodies it had to collect, and by the inaccessibility of the areas in which people had died. With rubble strewing the streets, often the only way to get to them was on foot. Corpses in the worst-affected areas had to be left for days or even weeks until the roads were clear enough for lorries to get in to take them away. Many were buried beneath piles of

stone, requiring heavy lifting equipment before they could be
recovered. Those bodies that were still underground were especially difficult to recover. Sometimes the inrush of air as cellars were
opened caused fires to break out afresh, and many cellar shelters
had to be left for up to ten days before they were cool enough for
the disposal squads to enter.[6]

In the first few days after the firestorm ten thousand corpses
were collected from the streets for burial. This was the sort of
work normally carried out by the Air-raid Protection Service, but
the sheer scale of the clean-up operation meant that hundreds of
auxiliary workers had to be drafted in to help. Most came from
the armed forces, but the SS were also called in, as were prisoners
from the concentration camp at Neuengamme. The bodies were
gathered without ceremony: there was barely time to identify them
before they were taken away. After their details had been logged,
with a description of where they had been found and any possessions they had had, they were piled on to the back of a lorry
and transported to Ohlsdorf cemetery.[7]

Ludwig Faupel was one of those who dealt with the bodies.
The company at which he was apprenticed had been destroyed,
so he and his surviving colleagues were immediately drafted by the
Rescue and Repair Service to help clear up the city.

The clean-up work went on. The streets had to be rubble-free, burned
out façades had to be levelled . . . With the rest of our group we were
obliged to join in with the clean-up work, in which the mountains of
corpses were regarded as the worst part. It was not the sight of it, but the
smell that made this activity so hard. As you walked through the ruins
every now and then the smell of burned flesh, or the sickly sweet stink
of decomposing tissue, would bring on a strong and immediate nausea.[8]

Corpses everywhere were sprinkled with chlorinated lime,
partly as a hygiene measure, but mostly in an attempt to counteract the terrible stench of advanced decomposition. Soon whole
areas of the city smelt of the powder – it was the only way to
keep nausea at bay. Clean-up crews entering the cellars had a

particularly hard job. Here the stench was so bad that some military detachments insisted on blasting the cellars with flame-throwers before entering.[9] Recovery squads were issued with gas masks, in which the filter had been replaced by a pad soaked in rum or Cognac. The mental and physical strain on those men was so great that many took to drinking the rum instead, and extra rations of alcohol and cigarettes were freely distributed throughout the Decontamination Service to keep the men working.[10]

The most unpleasant jobs were often reserved for the concentration-camp inmates. Jan Melsen had been in Neuengamme since 1942, when he had been arrested as a member of the Dutch resistance. By the summer of 1943 he was a virtual wraith. Perversely, his work clearing up corpses probably saved his life since it allowed him access to extra food – often stolen from kitchens and factories among the ruins. However, as he explained after the war, the extra food came at a high price:

Later a lorry came. Then we formed a chain and passed the corpses along until they were laid on the back of the truck . . . After we had carried the corpses out of the cellars we had to start afresh with searching through the rubble for body parts, because they wanted to know approximately how many dead there were. We fetched ourselves bowls and buckets – there were enough lying around – then dug through the rubble and put whatever body parts we found in the buckets. In the evenings an SS doctor came with his assistants, and then we had to spread the body parts across the ground. From this he would estimate the number of men and women.[11]

As Melsen goes on to explain, it was not always easy to guess at the number of people who had died, simply because of the extreme circumstances of their deaths:

I had just cleaned up a cellar when a civilian came up with the unit leader and said, 'My wife and daughter were here – they must be in this cellar.' But we had found nothing. The man cried out, 'They must be here inside.' It was nothing to do with me, but I had a pickaxe beside me, so we went back and forth, scraping around the entrance with the pickaxe. As I dug at the ground a bracelet sprang up. The people had been burnt right down to their hair and skin – there was nothing left but this piece of gold.[12]

With some shelters they could make only vague estimates of between 250 and 300 dead; greater accuracy was impossible.[13]

In such circumstances, identification was a real problem. In a rather harrowing account, Ben Witter describes pulling body parts from the rubble, with wallets, ID cards, wedding rings and other material that might be used to identify the bodies. (In the end he was taken off this duty, because his hands were covered in staphylococcic blisters, brought on by continual contact with the cadavers he was handling.)[14] Gruesome though the work was, it took on a much more personal dimension when he discovered his own grandparents among the dead:

My grandmother was a really stately lady, rather fat. A fat dead lady without a head was lying there: I wondered if it could be her and came to the conclusion it was. My grandfather I found later in the harbour hospital. A lot of unknown bodies had been brought there – parts of bodies too . . . I examined all of them, and in a basin there was a belly with a watch sticking out from it. That was my grandfather's watch. There was only so much left of him . . . The rest was God's.[15]

Originally the plan was to burn all of the corpses and body parts in the open. But when it was discovered that they did not pose much of a health risk after all, the authorities decided to bury them, and four mass graves were prepared in a corner of Ohlsdorf cemetery in the north of the city. Jan Melsen was one of the concentration-camp inmates who was sent to dig them.

I thought that all the corpses had been put in graves already, but that was not so – they had simply been laid out in a huge heap and doused with lime and chlorine, nothing more. The same people who had fetched the corpses out of the cellars now had to dig mass graves for them. So we dug mass graves in the form of a cross. They are still there, in exactly that form, just as we laid them.[16]

Ben Witter witnessed how the graves were filled. From the back of one of the lorries he saw concentration-camp inmates standing inside the graves among the dead, stacking literally thousands of bodies on top of each other. Round the top of the grave a circle of SS men was standing, for obvious reasons, with their backs to the corpses. They were all drinking, and two became overpowered by the combined effects of alcohol, heat and the stench. While they were thus distracted, a few of their prisoners took some clothes from the corpses, climbed over the edge of the grave and disappeared into the trees. 'I don't know how many escaped but I believe half a dozen managed it.'[17]

★   ★   ★

During the first two weeks of August, the authorities became increasingly anxious about the possibility of epidemics breaking out. It was not only the vast number of corpses in the city that fuelled their fears, but several other factors. With the city in ruins, those who remained found themselves living in extremely close quarters, and eating from communal kitchens. The conditions were ideal for the spread of disease, and in an attempt to stop typhus breaking out free vaccinations were offered to anyone who wanted them.

The most worrying thing was the lack of drinking water. Instructions were issued repeatedly through the press telling every-one to boil all water before drinking it, but without any gas or electricity available this was often impossible. The city's toilets were another problem. The main sewers, remarkably, had re-mained intact, but without water for flushing, toilets everywhere were hopelessly blocked. The authorities suggested that each sur-viving community should dig latrines, with strict instructions that they should be sited at least fifty metres from any of the city's seven thousand artesian wells, which had become important in recent days for supplying water. But outdoor latrines were unpopular, especially during spells of rain, and many people poured their waste into the canals, although this was strictly prohibited. The resulting stench merely added to the catalogue of repugnant odours that now filled the city.[18]

Since most of the city's dustcarts had been destroyed in the raids, and the streets were impassable, the garbage-collection service was virtually non-existent. Soon, huge piles of rubbish developed everywhere.[19] At the end of August, Mathilde Wolff-Mönckeberg described the streets as 'full of dirt and rubbish'. She was still complaining at the beginning of the following year:

In the streets mountains of rubbish are piling up. The big metal dustbins are never emptied and garbage is bursting out all over the place. Paper, potato peel, cabbage leaves – the muck-containers open their lids like gaping throats, vomiting out their evil contents. Then the wind takes it all and scatters it over the wet roads, leaving a stale, foul stench. We are told that every street must dig its own rubbish pit to avoid further contamination.[20]

A plague of flies and rats was soon swarming throughout Hamburg. They fed on the corpses, the rubbish and the huge amounts of rotting food that had been abandoned in the ruins. Hans Erich Nossack describes the revulsion he felt whenever he saw these pests:

Rats and flies were the lords of the city. Bold and fat, the rats frolicked in the streets. But even more disgusting were the flies, huge and iridescent green – no one had ever seen flies like this before. They swarmed in great clumps on the roads, settled, copulating, on top of the ruined walls, and basked, weary and satiated, on the splinters of windowpanes. When they could no longer fly they would crawl after us through the tiniest of cracks, soiling everything, and their buzzing and whirring was the first thing we heard in the mornings. This didn't stop until October.[21]

The increasing plague of flies began to pose a serious health risk, particularly when latrines and rubbish tips were located close to communal kitchens. People were exhorted to bury their rubbish, but this was very difficult: picks and shovels were in short supply, and the earth had been baked hard by weeks of hot sunshine.[22] So the plague worsened. Supplies of chemicals for killing flies did not appear until the end of September, but it was the onset of colder autumn weather that brought an end to them. The rats, however, remained. With piles of rubbish lining the streets there was little anyone could do to get rid of them.

★   ★   ★

Once again, the centre of all this devastation and squalor was the 'dead city', where the highest proportion of buildings had been destroyed and the remaining buildings were most unstable. People were warned to walk in the middle of streets throughout the city, in case of collapsing house façades, but they were told not to come into this area at all.

The sheer scale of the damage there was so great that even those eyewitnesses who did venture inside the 'dead city' often found it impossible to describe what they saw. Most contemporary descriptions do not even attempt to give an impression of the vast field of ruins. Instead they invariably focus on smaller details in a series of broken images. For example, Gretl Büttner is able to describe what she saw only in a list of images:

Ruins everywhere, as far as the eye could see. Debris on the streets, collapsed house fronts, far-flung stones on kerbs, charred trees and devastated gardens. Over it all a bright blue sky, little white clouds, and a bright sun. This made the picture of endless grief and terrible devastation even more noticeable. And always the sound of new buildings collapsing and the crackling of the ravenous fire still feeding could be heard. Poor, beautiful, beloved, raped city! One was without words.[23]

It is revealing that eyewitnesses like her, who were otherwise eloquent, found themselves so tongue-tied by what they saw. It is as if the scale of the destruction was so great that the only way to make sense of it was by seizing on a handful of tangible details.

According to Hans Erich Nossack, people did this because the bigger picture was unrecognizable. When he tried to take it in he was struck by a sense of unreality: it was as if the city he knew had not merely been destroyed but taken away and replaced with something completely alien. 'What surrounded us did not remind us in any way of what was lost,' he says. 'It had nothing to do with it. It was something else, it was strangeness itself, it was the essentially not possible.'[24] So complete was the transformation that he was unable to navigate his way through the 'dead city', even in areas he knew well:

I have gone through all these districts, by foot or by car. Only a few main streets were cleared, but mile after mile there was not a single living house. And if you tried to work your way through the ruins on either side, you immediately lost all sense of time and direction. In areas I thought I knew well, I lost my way completely. I searched for a street that I should have been able to find in my sleep. I stood where I thought it must be and didn't know which way to turn.[25]

That was why people focused on little things. It was impossible to mourn a city that had become so alien: much better to concentrate on something specific – a particular street corner or a ruined shop – as a tangible fragment of a lost past.

★   ★   ★

If mourning the city was difficult, then mourning the people who had died was often impossible. The bodies had been removed so hastily that there was often nothing left to mourn – no proof that they had died. Indeed, with almost a million refugees spread out across Germany, most Hamburgers had no way of knowing whether their friends and relatives were not in fact alive. There are countless stories of people fearing the worst, only to discover that their wife, father or daughter was living somewhere in Bavaria. Equally there are stories of those who refused to believe that their loved ones were dead, even to the point of madness.

In the days after the catastrophe, signs appeared all over the city, chalked on the walls of ruined apartment buildings: 'Where are you, Hilde?' 'We are alive', 'Aunt Anna is living in Blankenese'. Soldiers on leave travelled from town to town, searching desperately for families who had disappeared.

In an attempt to bring order to the chaos, the police authority began to catalogue the names of the missing and dead. It was hoped that the central register they created would become the first port of call for those looking for loved ones; it was also a way of re-establishing the Nazi Party's grip on the exact whereabouts of the roving population.

There were two main catalogues. The first was a card index of all the refugees who had fled Hamburg in the days after the firestorm. They were required to register themselves with the local police when they arrived at their destination, so that details of where they had moved to could be sent back to Hamburg. In the first week alone the Hamburg police received more than a million such communications; even in November they were still receiving two to three thousand each day. They used this information to produce a fairly accurate record of where everyone had gone.[26]

People returning to Hamburg could consult this index in the hope of locating their lost relatives. If a particular person was not listed on the refugees register, then the second card index listed the details of the dead, starting with where the body had been found and any belongings that might help with identification. Each time some unfortunate relative or friend recognized the details on one of the cards, a name could be matched to one of the bodies that had been buried, without ceremony, in the mass grave at Ohlsdorf. It was a painstaking process. By the end of the year the police had still not discovered the names of even half of the 31,647 corpses they had buried.[27] Indeed, many remain nameless to this day.

Some of the missing proved as difficult to track down. By the end of the war two thousand people were still unaccounted for.[28] Some, presumably, were happy to slip off the Nazi registers, perhaps disappearing under pseudonyms in other areas of the Reich.

But it is likely that the vast majority were – and perhaps some still are – buried, undiscovered, beneath the ashes of Hamburg.

⋆   ⋆   ⋆

At the beginning of August the 'dead city' was cordoned off with barbed wire, and walls built with blocks of rubble from the collapsed buildings. Signs appeared round the perimeter: 'Forbidden zone. Entry allowed only with written police permission.'[29] The few roads into it that remained open were guarded day and night to prevent people coming in. The initial reason for the perimeter fence was to prevent the possible spread of disease from corpses, and to stop looters disturbing the few remaining belongings of the dead. But it was also done for moral reasons: it was considered indecent that the recovery of cadavers should be carried out in public.

Needless to say, the forbidden area soon gained almost mythical status among the surviving population, and terrifying rumours circulated. Some said the voices of the dead could still be heard, screaming as they had when they perished in the flames. There were stories of children who had sneaked into the ruins coming home with sores all over their arms and legs. Although this was probably brought on by chemical residues in the rubble left by the incendiaries, some children believed it was a kind of curse put on them by the malevolent spirit of this 'forbidden city'.[30] Worse, it was said that decontamination squads had to use flame-throwers not only to cremate the decomposing bodies where they were but because 'The flies were so thick that the men couldn't get into the cellars: they kept slipping on maggots the size of fingers, and the flames had to clear the way for them to reach those who had perished in flames.'[31]

For the rest of the war, the forbidden zone sat in the centre of the eastern quarter like a dark reminder of the catastrophe, emanating a sense of horror and a stench of death to the rest of Hamburg. For years afterwards, the reality of what had happened there, hideous enough in itself, was routinely exaggerated into the grotesque. Myths grew up about the whole area having been doused in a 'rain of phosphor' during the attacks – myths that were repeated well into the 1960s.[32] Official death tolls were ignored in favour of higher figures – 60,000, 80,000, 100,000 – as if the city was afraid to admit the truth: that nobody knew how many had died because the number was simply unquantifiable. Even sixty years after the event the final count is uncertain, though the most reliable sources put it somewhere around 45,000.[33] However many had died, the one thing everyone knew for certain was that the vast majority of deaths had taken place in the shattered streets of Hammerbrook, Rothenburgsort and Hamm. It was a 'dead city' in every sense of the phrase.

21. Survival

Look not behind thee . . . lest thou be consumed
Genesis 19:17[1]

Gradually, people started to return to Hamburg. Foreign workers
and slave labourers had no choice: they were herded back and
allocated new barracks to live in among the ruins. Workers in
essential industries were also required to return and help get the
city back on its feet: if they did not, they would be denied ration
cards. But the majority drifted back because they felt they had
nowhere else to go. They were tired of being tolerated as refugees
in other parts of the country – they just wanted to come home.
Hans Erich Nossack described it as a law of inertia: 'The drops
that were hurled in all directions by the city's collapse now flooded
back to fill the crater.'[2]

The return to the shattered city was a miserable experience.
Even those who found their apartments intact were heartbroken
by the destruction in their neighbourhoods. All the places where
they had done their shopping, worshipped, socialized and relaxed
had gone. The transformation struck even the forced labourers as
tragic, as a Frenchman later described:

The damage from July's bombings was, of course, not confined to the
restaurants. There were no more music-halls or cafés with orchestras.
The clowns were gone, the pom-pom of the Teutons' music had been
silenced and the horses that circled around a ridiculous rink were
nowhere to be found. The brothels had disappeared; there was no more
wrangling on the street outside forbidding entry; the whorehouses were
diminished to piles of bricks and the women who had not managed to
escape in time had perished. Only two cinemas were still working, as a

last testimony of former happy times for Hamburg society. The public baths had also vanished.[3]

Most of those who returned found they had nowhere to live: they were forced to sleep in the bunkers every night until they found friends or relatives with space to put them up. Those whose houses were still standing often found that other families had moved in while they were away. Rather than turn them out they were often obliged to let them stay, at least until they had found somewhere else to go – but with the sheer lack of living accommodation in the city, this sometimes took months. It was common to find two or three families sharing even the smallest of apartments.[4] For those who could not find such shelter there was little choice but to return to the ruins. Gradually a shanty-town grew up, as people found cellars to live in, or stacked up debris around ruined walls to create makeshift dwellings.

Mathilde Wolff-Mönckeberg described the spirit of this grim time with a mixture of incredulity and admiration for the ordinary people of Hamburg:

It is amazing how these poor human beings manage to create something, some kind of homestead, out of the rawest of materials, charred wooden boards and broken bricks. Everybody lends a hand: the husband if he is at home, the wife and all the children. And they are so proud of their achievement, preferring to live like Robinson Crusoe in one single room on the lonely heath, rather than be billeted out amongst strangers.[5]

They lived without electricity or gas, cooked on open fires, as if they were camping, and washed in the open at water pumps or from buckets. In the absence of any kind of transport, people walked everywhere, often clambering through rubble-lined streets for three or four hours each day just to get to work and back.[6] And while the adults were at work, the children ran wild, as Mathilde Wolff-Mönckeberg continues: 'There are children everywhere, hordes of them. There is no school and they roam the streets all day long . . . they forage in the garbage, dig tunnels in the rubble and imitate the siren to perfection.'[7] Johannes Schoene, the pastor of Christuskirche in Eimsbüttel, also wrote of 'countless children' running around the ruins and 'getting into mischief'.[8]

Generally speaking, it was the children who adapted first to the new realities of the war. In her diary of the time, Ilse Grassmann tells a story about her son and daughter playing 'air raids' under the kitchen table. The table was their shelter, and while one hid beneath it, the other dropped building blocks round it, claiming they were bombs. The sight of her children playing like this filled her with a unique dismay. 'Is there no escape from this dreadful time?' she wrote. 'Not even for the children?'[9] But no matter how disturbing such games were, they demonstrated a fundamental truth: huge bombardments were part of everyday life. What had once been considered 'normal' no longer existed. There was a different 'normality' now: one of bombs, sirens, and ruins surrounded by barbed wire.

The younger children could not remember a time before the war – they had never known a time when the threat of British or Allied bombs had not hung over their city. Even the older ones found it difficult to imagine how things could be different. Since they were powerless to change the way things were, they had to get used to the devastation that now surrounded them.

Eventually the adults were forced to follow their children's lead: it was surprising what one could get used to, given time. The shock of the first few weeks wore off, to be replaced instead with a numb insensibility to all but the most traumatic sights. In varying degrees, everyone was slowly becoming accustomed to the terrible conditions in Hamburg: 'You get used to the sight,' wrote Maria Bartels, to her husband at the front. 'It's only when you go through Hamm that you realize once again what we've lost.'[10] Soon, people no longer noticed the rubble. They walked past ruins without seeing them. They no longer even noticed the smell, which hung over the city in a permanent fug. They learned how to cope by keeping themselves busy. Maria Bartels continued:

There is no radio (I dare not think of all the other wonderful comforts we've lost); it is too hopeless. It is best to work as much as possible, or go to the cinema for a change; that is the best medicine, so that you don't need to think. But on Sundays I will come out to see you, to recover, and gradually the year will come to an end and we'll look forward to a new spring. Hopefully that will bring something better than this year.[11]

★   ★   ★

After a while life did get better. The bombed-out population were soon issued with new ration cards, and provided with beds, warm clothes and even furniture for their new homes among the ruins. Soon there were signs that a degree of normality was being restored. By 10 August several stretches of main road had been cleared and were open to traffic. The following day the post office reopened, and a week later the city's three daily newspapers were back in circulation. New shops were trading, a few small bars appeared, and some of the destroyed cinemas were re-established. On 20 August, the Ufa-Palast cinema opened to show *Geliebter Schatz* (*Beloved Sweetheart*), a romance starring Ursula Herking and Sonja Ziemann, and people like Maria Bartels could lose themselves for a couple of hours in the harmless flickering of the big screen.[12]

The city's utilities were a major priority, and work on them was remarkably rapid. As the Americans discovered after the war, the restoration of the city's electricity 'did much to reverse the original pessimistic outlook that fell over Hamburg after the raids'.[13] It took only three and a half days to repair Tiefstack power station, and Neuhof power station was back in service after only twenty days, although it had been the main focus of 303rd Bombardment Group on the second American raid. Even Barmbek power station, all but demolished on the night of 29 July, was back in service by the end of October.[14]

Hamburg's other utilities were restored just as quickly. The air raids had hit the gas industry so hard that in the days after the catastrophe it was incapable of delivering even three per cent of pre-raid output. By the end of November, however, it was back up to 80 per cent, and gas services had been restored to all but the worst-hit areas in the east of the city. It was the same story with the water supplies. The raids had destroyed the city's main pumping station in Rothenburgsort, and put 847 breaks in the water mains throughout the city; but within four months most had been repaired, and the pumping station was up and running. By the following spring the network of water mains was working at 97 per cent of its previous capacity. The telephone system was less of a priority, but even so many phone lines, for business use at least, were working again as early as mid–August.[15]

It was not long, either, before the most important war industries were back in production. By the end of the year, the aircraft industry was operating at 91 per cent of its previous capacity. The manufacture of electrical goods, optics and precision tools was soon surpassing its previous level, and even the badly hit chemical industry was producing 71 per cent of its original total.[16]

The recovery of the all important U-boat industry was even more miraculous. The Blohm & Voss shipyards had been the original target for both US raids, and had also been hit by British bombs on the first night of attacks, yet despite the complete destruction of the administration building, workshop and store buildings, the factory was running almost to capacity within two months.[17] René Ratouis, a French labourer who had been in the shipyard when it was hit, could barely believe his eyes when he returned to work there at the end of September: 'To our great astonishment, the Blohm & Voss factory hardly seemed to have suffered from the bombardments of July at all. We were completely bewildered by the thought that the incendiaries could have missed the most important factory in Hamburg.'[18] The recovery of the U-boat yards was underlined on 28 September when the first Walter U-boat Wa 201 entered the water. Far from being knocked out of the war, the Blohm & Voss yards appeared to be flourishing once more.[19]

In the wake of all the physical recovery, the morale of the people of Hamburg also picked up. Hannah Kelson lived in the west of the city at the time, and she remembers the atmosphere becoming quite positive fairly soon after the disaster:

Slowly some form of order returned. In fact, it returned remarkably quickly. I remember reading afterwards that the intention of the air raids had been to break the spirit of the population. And I think I can say with total authority that this absolutely did not happen. People's spirit was quite tremendous. I know much is made of the spirit of the British during the Blitz, no doubt with every justification, but I think the same could be said about the civilian population, certainly as I saw it and knew it in those days, and I was right in the middle of it. There was no question of defeatism, or a sense of wanting to give up. In fact, if anything I think it strengthened people's resolve and gave them more backbone.[20]

Even in the east of the city the recovery in morale was remarkable. By the end of the year, Pastor Jürgen Wehrmann was able to look back with pride at the way his parishioners had dealt with the crisis:

The population of Eilbek was growing from day to day. One met ever more people in the street, their faces lit up with joy over the reclamation of their home town. I spoke with them and began to visit them in what they often sincerely called their apartments. It was now becoming quite apparent: Eilbek was beginning to rise up out of the ruins.[21]

The people of Hamburg were coping surprisingly well.

In an attempt to bolster this fragile new sense of resolve, a succession of party leaders came to visit the city. The first was Goering, whose visit on 6 August was the first item of news in the *Hamburger Zeitung* the following day. He was followed by Himmler, on the thirteenth, then Goebbels and Wilhelm Frick on the seventeenth. Admiral Doenitz visited the docks to survey the damage done to the Blohm & Voss shipyards. The general panic and dismay that had gripped the higher echelons of the Nazi Party in the days just after the catastrophe had now subsided – so much so that they were already trying to put a positive spin on events. On 19 August, State Secretary Georg Ahrens, who had accompanied Doenitz, was already writing to his relatives about what he called the 'Miracle of Hamburg':

The intention of the enemy to strike a blow at the very foundations of the Reich has failed, and though Hamburg and the Hamburgers have received wounds that will bleed for a long time yet, the fact they have survived this blow in relative safety means that the enemy's method of murdering women and children in the major cities will not succeed in bringing down the Reich, not even if he makes the same attempt on other major cities. Amidst all the pain and hardship there is perhaps a positive thing that has come out of this: many would have believed that such a blow would have meant a complete breakdown . . . Now we are all convinced not only that our city, our bleeding city, will live, but that the eternal German Reich will never come to an end when the people show such faith, such strength and such courage.[22]

Rhetoric like this might have provoked a sneer from most ordinary Hamburgers, but the essence of the State Secretary's words was undeniably true: the Allies' grand strategy of trying to undermine the Reich by bombing had not worked. Nor would it work in the coming years. Despite all they had been through, and all they were still suffering, the people of Hamburg had not given up.

The symbols of their determination to survive were all around them in the gradual clearance of the rubble, the restoration of electricity and water, and the stubborn pockets of life among the ruins. Throughout the city messages were written in chalk on the front of bombed-out houses, saying, 'Wir leben' ('We are alive'). They had been intended to reassure friends and neighbours in the direct aftermath of the catastrophe; now they seemed more like a statement of defiance.

Then, at the beginning of September, just a month after the firestorm, something happened that had a huge psychological effect on the people: the trees began to bloom. There are numerous accounts of this strange natural phenomenon.[23] Presumably it was some kind of defence mechanism in the tree population to ensure the survival of the species, but for the people of Hamburg, the sight of those apparently dead trees springing into glorious life became a unique symbol of hope. As autumn approached, Gretl Büttner wrote:

A miracle happened in the 'dead city'. By the end of August and the beginning of September the charred, burned trees sprouted new life; light green leaves dared to come out. So close to autumn, it was spring once again over the endless horrors. White lilacs bloomed in the destroyed gardens of the houses. Chestnut trees once more lit their white candles. And in this continuing life something mild and comforting, a change from helpless hatred to sorrow or resignation took place. One not only saw the dark, accusing debris. One saw the future again and learned to hope once more in the midst of the worst time of grief. Like a mantle . . . Nature spread her strangest spring over the thousands of still bleeding wounds of the city. Hamburg was not dead. Hamburg must not die.[24]

22. Famine

Eating no longer seemed a pleasant necessity, but rather a dark law that forced
them to swallow, to swallow at any cost, in a hunger that was never satisfied
but appeared instead to swell . . .
Heinrich Böll[1]

Hamburg held on for almost two years before the city was forced
to surrender. There were many more raids – a further sixty-eight,
to be precise, involving a combined total of more than eleven
thousand aircraft. There were many more casualties too: 5,666
men, women and children lost their lives, and a further 6,463 were
injured.[2] The numbers might have been far worse, but the people
of Hamburg were no longer prepared to take risks with air raids.
At the first sound of the siren they now headed directly for the
nearest reinforced bunker. Even when the sirens were not ringing
they did not feel safe in their ruined apartments and makeshift
homes: 'It is like lying in a coffin,' said one survivor, 'waiting for the
lid to snap shut.'[3] 'We live through a fearful symphony of horror,'
wrote another. 'There is no day, hardly a night without air-raid
warnings. . . The end is bound to be near, whichever way it comes.'[4]

The long endgame of the war began in June 1944, when the
British and American armies launched their invasion of mainland
Europe. By March 1945 they had fought their way across France
to the Rhine, and by the end of April they had reached the west
bank of the Elbe, overlooking Hamburg. Along the way they had
captured hundreds of thousands of German soldiers, they had
crushed the Luftwaffe and inflicted a devastating firestorm on the
beautiful city of Dresden. By now it was obvious even to Hitler
that the end was in sight. On 30 April he retired to the back room
of his bunker and committed suicide.

One of Hitler's last instructions was a message to all his troops 'not to give up under any circumstances, but . . . to continue the fight against the enemies of the Fatherland'. As always, they were to resist the Allied advance to the last man.[5] To his eternal credit, Hamburg's gauleiter disobeyed those instructions almost immediately. Having seen his city devastated from the air he was unwilling to stand by while the Allies finished off the job from the ground. On 3 May, Karl Kaufmann handed over the city to the British Second Army without firing a shot. In the midst of a brutal, often insane war, it was an admirable example of common sense. Five days later, the rest of Germany followed suit, and surrendered unconditionally. The Second World War in the west had ended.

*   *   *

The scenes that greeted the British troops as they marched into the city were shocking in the extreme. Even battle-hardened soldiers were appalled by what they found. Tommy Wilmott, who had fought his way across Europe with the 2nd Fife and Forfar Yeomanry sums it up succinctly: 'All I remember about Hamburg was the smell. Even where we were, standing back looking on it, the smell from Hamburg was awful. The smell of death. It was terrible.'[6]

Alongside this frightful odour was the terrifying physical devastation. Dr P. J. Horsey was used to some fairly disturbing scenes – he had been among the group of medics sent to help the victims of Belsen concentration camp in the final days of the war – but he, too, was shocked by the sight of Hamburg when he visited in mid-May:

The city itself was the scene of utter destruction. In the dock area, with one or two exceptions, there were acres and acres of rubble, which showed little evidence of having once composed houses. In many places even the streets were buried. Of the few buildings which did still stand, the majority had been gutted with fire, or were so badly damaged as to be uninhabitable. In spite of this the streets were full of Germans walking

about purposefully: what they were doing or where they lived I cannot
think . . .[7]

There is an implied guilt in Dr Horsey's account, especially when
he describes the people he came across in the street:

Some of the Germans looked away when we passed them: the children
looked at us with great curiosity, but were kept well out of our way by
their mothers, as though we might kick them. Most of the women
looked at us with hate in their faces, but the men looked more cowed
and ashamed.[8]

The truth is that men like Dr Horsey had had no idea what to
expect when they came to Hamburg. They might have read in the
newspapers about how the city had been 'wiped off the war map',
but they had no concept of what that meant, and the reality
was beyond their wildest imaginings. Another British eyewitness,
Philip Dark, remembers the Hamburg landscape with horror. Lieutenant Dark was a prisoner-of-war who had been transported
through the city in mid-April, just before the surrender. What he
saw there would stay with him for the rest of his life.

. . . we swung in towards the centre and started to enter a city devastated
beyond all comprehension. It was more than appalling. As far as the eye
could see, square mile after square mile of empty shells of buildings with
twisted girders scarecrowed in the air, radiators of a flat jutting out
from a shaft of a still-standing wall, like a crucified pterodactyl skeleton.
Horrible, hideous shapes of chimneys sprouting from the frame of a wall.
The whole pervaded by an atmosphere of ageless quiet, a monument to
man's power of self-destruction . . . Such impressions are incomprehen-
sible unless seen . . . Coventry and Bath, any bombing in England, just
can't be compared to this.[9]

The last point is perhaps the most important of all. Until they
arrived in Hamburg, most British soldiers thought they knew the
worst of bombing – they had witnessed it at home in London,

Glasgow, Southampton and countless other cities. But the German Blitz on Britain was insignificant compared with what they saw in Hamburg. The rubble, the ruins, the smell – as one British official wrote in 1946, it seemed 'impossible ever to rebuild this city . . . Another site must be developed for the traffic of the Elbe, to replace the essential heart of this historic port.'[10]

Of course, not only Hamburg was affected: by the end of the war the devastation had spread to every corner of the Reich – as the refugees of 1943 had predicted – and post-war descriptions of Germany's other cities are equally devoid of hope. Cologne was a city 'recumbent, without beauty, shapeless in the rubble and loneliness of complete physical defeat'.[11] Dresden no longer resembled 'Florence on the Elbe' but was more like 'the face of the moon', and planning directors believed that it would take 'at least seventy years' to rebuild.[12] Munich was so badly devastated that 'It truly did almost make one think that a Last Judgement was imminent.'[13] The damage in Berlin was so great that a former envoy to President Roosevelt described it as 'a second Carthage'.[14]

This, then, was the final result of the bomber dream, the fruit of decades of investment and research. The Allies had perfected the art of devastating cities. As a consequence barely a town in Germany remained untouched by destruction.

*   *   *

In the aftermath of war, the Allies set about trying to rebuild the shattered country. Under the Marshall Plan the Americans agreed to pour $29 billion into Western Europe, and by far the biggest share was to go to Germany.[15] With the British and the French, they steered the western half of the country towards recovery, and eventually to prosperity. However, while the Allies are fond of congratulating themselves on creating the foundations of the German 'economic miracle', it is important to remember that things got much, *much* worse for Germany before they improved.

When the Allies had taken over they had inherited an extremely efficient economic system. British observers were astonished to find that, despite all the bombing and disruption, Germans were still spending evenings at the theatre and the opera, hair and beauty salons were still open, and food was still relatively plentiful. The welfare system ensured that every German citizen was fairly well looked after, no matter what had happened to their homes. After Dr Horsey visited Hamburg in May 1945 he was able to write that 'All the Germans I ever saw were well dressed and looked very well fed.'[16]

Under Allied control, however, the situation changed dramatically. By the time Victor Gollancz arrived in Hamburg in the autumn of 1946, the people had been reduced to scavenging for food, malnutrition was rife, and children could only attend school on alternate days because they were obliged to share their shoes with their brothers and sisters.[17] Worse still was the threat of disease, which was much more of a danger than it had ever been in the aftermath of the firestorm. Tuberculosis was five times as prevalent as it had been before the war; penicillin was in short supply; there was only enough insulin available to treat a third of the diabetics in the city, and only enough bandages for a fifth of those who needed them.[18] One British medical officer, who mistook Gollancz for a visiting politician, came up to harangue him:

What on earth are you politicians in London up to? Do you realize what's going on here? Ignoramuses see some people in the streets looking fairly well nourished but don't realize that they are living on carbo-hydrates and have no resistance, and they forget that the most seriously undernourished people are at home. The present figure of tuberculosis is appalling, and it may be double next year. An epidemic of any kind would sweep everything before it. We are on the edge of a frightful catastrophe . . .[19]

Katherine Morris, who worked for the British administration in the city, backs up Gollancz's observations. When she arrived in 1946 the faces of many Hamburgers 'were almost yellow with malnutrition'.[20] Crowds of German children routinely gathered outside the British clubs and barracks to beg for food, while other, even more hopeless people, were forced to scavenge in the city's dustbins: 'Spectral figures, gaunt and ragged, were moving with the lifeless gait of some macabre nightmare along the pavement . . . drifting from ash-can to ash-can, poking among the contents for something to eat, their rags flapping in the wind. (It became increasingly obvious why one never saw a cat in this city.)'[21] Germans had never suffered like this while the war was on. Until now, hardship to this degree had been confined to foreigners and forced labourers – but under Allied occupation, everybody suffered.

The fault lay directly with the policies of the British and American occupying forces. One of the first things the Allies did in the direct aftermath of the war was to arrest senior members of the Nazi Party, and to remove all party members from positions of influence. It is understandable why they did this, but the immediate effect was a breakdown of order. Getting rid of all party members meant sacking virtually the entire administrative workforce practically overnight. At a stroke, all the systems that had been keeping the German economy going so miraculously throughout the war were removed. The efficient German welfare network collapsed. The ration cards issued by the Allies were worthless because there was no food in the shops – the food-distribution systems had disintegrated. The torturously slow German bureaucracy was replaced by an even slower and less well-organized Allied one. And in the administrative chaos that ensued, all those people who would once have been looked after by the state – not only the armies of orphans and homeless people, but now also concentration-camp victims and literally millions of refugees from the East – were effectively left to fend for themselves.

The next thing the occupying forces did was far more shameful. Partly to prevent the Germans rearming, but also to eliminate Germany as an economic rival, they began systematically to dismantle the country's industrial infrastructure. Factories that had survived the war were now closed, or even dynamited. The docks in Hamburg were blown up, the warehouses emptied, the cranes dismantled and used for scrap. Even fishing vessels were scuttled, in case someone might try to convert them into minelayers – and this at a time when food was becoming desperately short. It can only have looked to the people as though the Allies were trying to carry on where the bombs had left off. In the words of Rudolf Petersen, Hamburg's first *Bürgermeister* after the war, 'The sea's full of fish, but they want to starve us.'[22]

In such conditions, the black-market flourished. Just as with other cities, the population of Hamburg had no option but to go 'hamstering' – that is, taking day-trips to the countryside to find food. Consequently, prices sky-rocketed. Hamburgers would barter anything for a few extra rations of meat or eggs: watches, jewellery, even their all-important winter clothes. There was soon a rather bleak saying doing the rounds in Hamburg: 'All the farmers need now are Persian rugs for their pig-sties.'[23] But the black-market was the only thing keeping many people alive. Official rations at the beginning of the winter provided people with only 1,550 calories per day – less than 60 per cent of the recommended amount needed to keep them healthy. In reality, most were receiving between 400 and 1,000 calories per day – a comparable amount to the inmates at Belsen.[24] Without the black-market to supplement their rations, the population of Hamburg faced famine.

In desperation, the people threatened riots over food, as they had done after the First World War. Martial law was declared in many parts of the country, and in Hesse the US military governor was forced to issue warnings that the death penalty would be invoked for anyone rioting over food shortages.[25] A curfew was strictly enforced to keep the streets clear after dark. There was a growing sense of irony that such draconian methods were being used by the very people who were supposed to have liberated Germany from a totalitarian regime. Throughout the country there were serious concerns that the youth were becoming embittered, even 'renazified', out of disillusionment.

Things began to improve in 1948, but in 1946 they looked impossibly bleak. There was widespread despair about what the future might bring, and the goodwill that many in Germany had felt for their liberators had vanished. In Victor Gollancz's words –

which were frequently echoed after the occupation of Iraq nearly sixty years later – the Allies might have won the war but they had 'all but lost the peace'.[26]

★   ★   ★

As if the situation was not bad enough, the winter that followed Gollancz's visit to Germany turned out to be one of the worst on record. At the beginning of January 1947 the temperature plunged to a terrifying −28°C, and remained below −10°C for several weeks. It was so cold that the Alster lake froze solid – according to one British soldier, who was detailed to drill holes through it, the ice was three feet thick.[27] The surface of the Elbe froze too, and large ice floes appeared in the North Sea around the Elbe estuary, making it near-impossible for ships to enter. Such conditions would be dangerous at the best of times, but in the aftermath of war they were almost catastrophic. Even those people who had proper homes had no means of heating them. All domestic electricity was cut between 7 a.m. and 8 p.m. in order to conserve power, and coal was in such short supply that goods trains from the Ruhr were routinely plundered by hordes of children trying to gather fuel.[28]

The temperature did not rise above zero until mid-March, more than three months after the cold snap began. For some people who lived through both events, the terrible winter was every bit as soul-destroying as the night of the firestorm – they were as powerless against the cold as they had been against the heat. Nobody knows how many perished that winter, but the number was certainly in the hundreds, and perhaps even higher.[29]

★   ★   ★

For Hamburg, things did get better – eventually. Over the next ten years the bulk of the rubble was cleared away, and the huge holes blasted into the cityscape were gradually filled with new streets and buildings. Slowly, the city showed signs of returning prosperity. The shipbuilding industry re-established itself on the banks of the Elbe, and the port began to flourish once more. A new bridge was built across the Alster. In 1948 the Deutschmark was introduced as a stable currency, and a larger variety of goods at last appeared in the shops. By the beginning of the 1950s the city was free to concentrate once more on what it had always been good at – trade – and the only major battles it was forced to fight were those against the ever-fickle floodwaters of the Elbe.[30]

Over the coming decades, Hamburg would again become one of the richest cities in Europe. The port on the southern banks of the Elbe regained its status as one of the biggest in the world, and was soon the city's principal employer. Trade worth billions of dollars every year now passes along the river. The city's proud tradition as the media capital of Germany also re-established itself: national newspapers and magazines such as *Die Welt, Die Zeit, Stern* and *Der Spiegel* are based there, as are several television and radio stations, and literally thousands of advertising agencies, film studios, record labels and book publishers.[31] Today it is impossible not to be impressed by the wealth, zeal and sheer industry of the place.

And yet, even now, one cannot visit the city without remembering what happened here. The bombsites and rubble have disappeared, but there are obvious gaps in the landscape where buildings once stood. Air-raid shelters still dot the city like a pox. The huge bunker on the Heiligengeistfeld, with its four vast flak towers, could not be demolished – it was designed to be indestructible – and it remains on the site to this day, an embarrassing, windowless eyesore. In the city centre stands the ruin of the Nikolaikirche, its Gothic spire pointing to the sky like an admonishing finger. There are memorials to the catastrophe in every quarter. In the east, in one of Hamburg's busiest shopping areas, there is a sculpture of a terrified figure cowering in the corner of an air-raid shelter.[32] In the west, there is an 'Anti-War Memorial', deliberately placed next to the old Nazi monument that glorifies the patriotism of war.[33] And in the north, in Ohlsdorf cemetery, there is perhaps the best-known memorial to the countless victims of the firestorm: a sculpture of Charon ferrying souls across the river Styx to the underworld. It sits in the midpoint between the four mass graves where over thirty-six thousand bodies lie buried.[34]

Perhaps the most poignant legacy of the firestorm is in the attitudes of those who survived its horrors. Klaus Müller still has an irrational fear of fireworks. His sister, who suffered from black-outs in the overpacked bunkers as a child, still cannot bring herself to board a full underground train.[35] Some of the people quoted in this book admitted to experiencing flashbacks, especially on the catastrophe's anniversary, when memories roll before their eyes 'like some appalling horror film'.[36] At least two experienced nervous breakdowns later in life that put them in hospital.[37]

For those people, and for countless more like them, the firestorm is not merely something that happened over sixty years ago. It is a continual burden, like a disease without a cure, that they will carry with them for the rest of their lives.

23. The Reckoning

You can't have this kind of war. There just aren't enough bulldozers to scrape the bodies off the streets
Dwight D. Eisenhower[1]

After the war, the British and American governments spent a great deal of time and energy trying to discover exactly how effective their bombing had been in Germany. The Americans immediately set up the United States Strategic Bombing Survey, and travelled all over the country interviewing factory managers and gathering captured German documents that described the damage caused by the bombs. Not to be outdone, the British set up a Bombing Survey Unit of their own. Both groups looked very carefully at what had happened at Hamburg in particular – partly because the attacks on this city had been so dramatic, but also because the damage had been so well documented by the Hamburg authorities at the time.

This was what they discovered: over the course of the six British and American attacks, the entire eastern quarter of the city and much of the western quarter had been razed to the ground. The number of homes that were incinerated by the firestorm defies the imagination: 40,385 residential buildings were either completely obliterated or rendered so badly damaged that they were uninhabitable. They contained around 275,000 apartments, or roughly 61 per cent of Hamburg's total living accommodation. None was rebuilt until after the war. A further 109,471 homes were less badly damaged, but the city's economy had been wrecked so completely that two-thirds even of those remained unrepaired until after the war was over.[2]

Among the homes were the other buildings that make up a

city: shops, schools, offices and so on. According to the American bombing survey, 3,785 industrial plants were destroyed by this series of raids, as were 7,190 small businesses, employing 21,000 craftsmen. About five thousand of the city's seven thousand retail stores were also destroyed.[3] The Hamburg chief of police also claimed that 83 banks, 379 office buildings, 112 Nazi Party offices, seven warehouses, 13 public utility premises, 22 transport premises, 76 public offices, 80 military installations and 12 bridges were also completely destroyed. All of those buildings could be considered military targets, at least to some degree. A further 437 buildings were destroyed that had nothing to do with the war whatsoever, including 24 hospitals, 277 schools, 58 churches, 77 cultural centres (cinemas, theatres and opera houses), and one zoo.[4]

By any normal standards, Hamburg had ceased to exist. Even in those areas where the buildings were still standing many of the streets were blocked with rubble, making travel all but impossible. The trams could not run, and all of the central subway and overground railway stations were out of action. There was no running water, no electricity and no gas. There was no radio, no postal service and no telephone. But, most importantly, there were no people. In the wake of the firestorm almost the entire population had fled, leaving the ruins devoid of human life.

If the material destruction was breathtaking, the human cost was truly tragic in scale. In just one week, 45,000 people had lost their lives. A further 37,439 had been injured, while almost a million people had fled the city and were now officially homeless.[5] All that they owned – everything from clothes and furniture to ornaments, letters and photographs – had been burned or blown to pieces in the raids.

To put these numbers in context, the death toll at Hamburg was more than ten times greater than that of *any* previous raid. At Nagasaki, where the Americans dropped their second nuclear bomb, the immediate death toll was 40,000 – about five thousand fewer than at Hamburg.[6] The devastation of this Hanseatic city cannot, therefore, be compared accurately with the sort of destruction

Total damage to Hamburg in the
Gomorrah raids, 24 July–3 August

LOKSTEDT

EPPENDORF

HOHELUFT

HARVESTEHU

EIMSBÜTTEL

BAHRENFELD

ROTHERBA

ALTONA

OTTENSEN

NEUSTAD

FLOTTBEK

ST PAULI

N o r d e r   E l b e

Blohm & Voss
Shipyards

STEINWÄRDER

Köhlbrand

Howaldtswerke
shipyard

1 mile

To Neuhof Power Station

WILHELMSBURG

STERDORF

WINTERHUDE

BARMBEK

WANDSBEK

UHLENHORST

EILBEK

Alster Lake

HOHENFELDE

ST GEORG

Hamburg Central Station

BORGFELDE

HAMM

Fire Brigade Headquarters

HORN

LTSTADT

HAMMERBROOK

KLEINER GRASBROOK

ROTHENBURGSORT

BILLBROOK

VEDDEL

Buildings destroyed 24 July–3 August 1943

normally associated with conventional bombing: it was more akin to the annihilation that would soon become possible in the nuclear age.

*   *   *

The question remains as to what all the destruction achieved. Did it knock Hamburg's U-boat and aircraft industries out of the war? Did it prevent the rest of Hitler's war machine working efficiently? Did it shorten the war to any degree? Or did it merely take the lives of innocent civilians, who in any case contributed little to Germany's war effort?

It cannot be denied that the immediate effect on Hamburg's industries was huge. Almost half of the city's 81,000 commercial and industrial buildings had been completely destroyed, and the majority of its workers had fled. By the end of the year 226,000 people had still failed to come back to work – that is, 35 per cent of the city's workforce.[7] With no buildings to work in, and no people to do the work, the drop in industrial output was massive. In August 1943, Hamburg produced only half of the total output it had achieved in July. By the end of 1943 the city was still producing only 82 per cent of its normal capacity. To some degree Hamburg never truly rallied from the shock of these raids, and throughout the rest of the war industrial output never fully recovered.[8]

After the war, the Americans estimated that Hamburg lost 1.8 months of its entire industrial production as a direct result of the raids, about half of which was intended for the armed forces.[9] This meant that fewer supplies were sent to the Russian Front, fewer aircraft took to the skies, and fewer U-boats were launched to attack British shipping in the north Atlantic. To be more precise about this last point, twenty U-boats that would otherwise have taken to the seas around Britain were prevented from doing so.[10] When one considers that U-boats had been responsible for decimating the British economy before 1943, any reduction in their numbers, by whatever means, was essential to the Allies.

However, impressive though such figures are, it is important to remember that they represented only a temporary setback for the German war machine. Despite the enormous destruction in Hamburg's residential areas, the main industrial areas of the city remained relatively untouched. Much of the harbour complex had been spared, and even those parts that had suffered quite badly were soon repaired. For example, the Neuhof power station, which suffered direct hits in the US raids, was back up and running within twenty days.[11] As I have mentioned, the city's most important war industries were also coping extraordinarily well (see page 304).

According to the United States Strategic Bombing Survey, the effects of the 1943 catastrophe were nowhere near as disruptive to the war economy as the much smaller attacks later in the war, which targeted the city's transport links with the Ruhr. Even the British had to concede that, despite the huge destruction such attacks caused, they 'had only an irritant effect on German production'.[12] So does this mean that the bombing didn't work? Is it conceivable that the deaths of 45,000 people could have had little or no effect on the outcome of the war?

It is impossible to ask such a question without first considering some of the other by-products of the bombing war. First, it must never be forgotten that in 1943 the single most important member of the Allies was not Britain or America but the Soviet Union: it was they who were doing most of the fighting, and most of the dying, and as a consequence it was essential that Britain and America did all they could to show the Russians that they were not alone. By bombing cities like Hamburg they could demonstrate their solidarity with their eastern ally, and prove that they, too, were exerting huge pressure on the Germans. It is a common argument that had Britain and America refrained from bombing Germany, the Wehrmacht would have had ten thousand more 88mm guns to deploy against the advancing Russian tanks.[13] About a million people manned Germany's civil defences, and although many might have been women and schoolboys, it was still a huge drain on resources. As Albert Speer wrote in his secret diary in Spandau prison, while the actual effects of bombing on German war industries were not particularly serious, the secondary effects were pivotal:

The real importance of the air war consisted in the fact that it opened a second front long before the invasion of Europe . . . Defence against air attacks required the production of thousands of anti-aircraft guns, the stockpiling of tremendous quantities of ammunition all over the country, and holding in readiness hundreds of thousands of soldiers . . . This was the greatest lost battle on the German side.[14]

The devastation of cities like Hamburg ensured the diversion of huge quantities of manpower and matériel, and in those terms it can only be seen as part of a much larger victory for the Allies.

However, there is a certain degree of hindsight to such arguments: in 1943 these consequences were by no means the main intention behind area bombing. From the British point of view, the most important reason at the time for such area raids was the effect they had on German morale. As explained earlier, the effect of Operation Gomorrah on ordinary Germans – not only survivors of Hamburg, but people across the country – was phenomenal. For the first time since the defeat at Stalingrad, people were speaking openly about the possibility of Germany losing the war. The morale of the armed forces was similarly subdued. A new kind of war had opened up in the skies above their cities – one against which they were powerless to defend themselves – and for some the fighting now seemed pointless. Despite their best efforts to push the battlefields far away from the borders of the Fatherland, their wives and children were being killed at home in their tens of thousands.

Of all the armed services it was the Luftwaffe that suffered most from the plummet in morale. After all, it had been responsible for protecting the Reich, and it had to shoulder the blame when its efforts failed, due to a huge shortfall in resources, manpower and, most importantly, adequate leadership. It had been obvious for well over a year that the Luftwaffe was incapable of defending Germany against the enormous fleets of bombers that were beginning to fly across the North Sea. To do so they needed a huge increase in the number of fighter aircraft they could put into the sky. But the only man capable of ordering the increase – Hermann Goering – had long since retreated into a life of debauched luxury. The generals under his command seemed more concerned with political infighting than with defending the homeland, largely because they felt powerless to influence the way the air war was being run. For many, the catastrophe at Hamburg merely underlined the crisis that had existed in the Luftwaffe for years.[15]

General der Flieger Adolf Galland tells a revealing story about the atmosphere in the higher echelons of the Luftwaffe just after the devastation of Hamburg. He was at a meeting in Hitler's headquarters when all of the most important Luftwaffe commanders were present. With one voice they demanded an end to the emphasis on offensive operations, so that they could concentrate instead on a single purpose: the defence of the Reich. Most importantly, they wanted to start producing thousands of new fighter planes, fast, to stop the Allied bombers getting through.

Never before and never again did I witness such determination and agreement among the circle of those responsible for the leadership of the Luftwaffe. It was as though under the impact of the Hamburg catastrophe everyone had put aside either personal or departmental ambitions. There was no conflict between General Staff and war industry, no rivalry between bombers and fighters; only the one common will to do everything in this critical hour for the defence of the Reich and to leave nothing undone to prevent a second national misfortune of this dimension.[16]

But when Goering put their demands to Hitler, the Führer flatly rejected the idea. He merely repeated the mantra he had always followed: 'Terror can only be broken by terror.'[17] There was no point in trying to defend Germany: instead they should forge ahead with reprisal attacks against Britain. The fact that the Luftwaffe was barely equipped for any such reprisal attacks seems to have entirely escaped him. 'In this hour,' says Galland, 'the fate of the Luftwaffe was decided.'

Galland found Goering some time later in an adjoining room, his head buried in his arms on the table, moaning like a wounded animal. It seemed that the Führer had lost faith in his ability once and for all, and the dressing-down he had given him had sent the Reichsmarschall into a slough of self-pity and despair from which he never recovered. In the following days a cloud of gloom descended on the Luftwaffe command. A few weeks later, Galland asked to be relieved of his post as C-in-C of Fighter Command, and Goering angrily granted his request.[18] One other senior Luftwaffe figure was so affected by the general depression that he went even further than Galland. On 17 August, just two weeks after the catastrophe at Hamburg, Luftwaffe Chief of Staff Hans Jeschonnek put a gun to his head and shot himself.

However, the German situation was not all negative. Despite Hitler's refusal to defend the Fatherland against further attacks, others made sure that the defence of the Reich was not neglected. The organizational brilliance of Erhard Milch (the State Secretary of Aviation) and Albert Speer (Reichsminister of Armaments and War Production) ensured that German fighter production, against all odds, increased dramatically over the coming months. With more fighters, the Luftwaffe were better able to defend the Reich, and it is largely due to the efforts of those two men that Germany was able to withstand the terrible Allied onslaught as long as it did.

Second, while Hitler might have prevented a wholehearted change in *strategy*, he did nothing to stand in the way of a change in *tactics*. The Luftwaffe changed its tactics to a remarkable degree over the next few weeks, and it did so as a direct result of what it had experienced at Hamburg. General Kammhuber's constrictive system of tying night fighters to specific 'boxes' in a long thin line along the coast was abandoned, allowing them to defend individual cities in larger numbers – especially the *Wilde Sau* fighters of Major Hajo Herrmann. An even more effective tactic was for German fighters to insert themselves into the bomber streams, so that they could follow their prey to the target and out. All this became standard practice as a direct reaction to what had happened at Hamburg: the disaster had not only united the leadership in their resolve to defend the Fatherland, but provided a long-overdue catalyst for change.

★   ★   ★

It is important to remember that it was not only Germany that suffered as a result of the raids. The cost to the Allies was huge. In an extraordinary document produced a few months after the bombings, the US government calculated the financial cost of attacking Hamburg. By giving a monetary value to the number of aircraft destroyed, bombs dropped and even lives lost, the conservative figure they came up with was $46,412,700 (see Appendix K).[19] While this pales into insignificance next to the cost of rebuilding Hamburg (some 23,050 million Reich Marks, or $9,220 million), it was nevertheless a huge amount of money, equivalent to more than half a billion dollars today.[20]

When one considers that this level of activity was carried out night after night it is little wonder that Britain ended the war virtually bankrupt. According to some estimates, the pursuit of the bomber war consumed as much as a third of the entire British economy.[21] When looking at figures like this the question naturally arises, was it worth it? With hindsight it seems inconceivable that this level of expenditure could ever have been considered good value for money. Even at the time there were serious doubts over the efficacy of bombing, and earlier in the war there had been many who had pushed for an end to it purely for financial reasons.[22] But we must remember that at the time the politicians and planners had not yet seen the final result of the bombing war. They could only measure the cost against their predictions – or, more importantly, their expectations, which were great indeed.

In the summer of 1943, Sir Arthur Harris confidently believed that he could win the war by bombing alone. In destroying whole cities, so the theory went, the Allies were undermining the morale of the German people to such a degree that their 'capacity for armed resistance' would be 'fatally weakened'. What they had

achieved against Hamburg seemed only to prove that the theory
was working. In September the Joint Intelligence Committee produced a report that compared the atmosphere in Germany then to
that in 1918, when mutiny and revolution had swept the country.
'A study of the picture as a whole,' it said, 'leads us inevitably to
the conclusion that Germany is if anything in a worse position
today than she was at the same period in 1918.' The collapse of
Germany might come 'even this year'.[23]

If bombing had lived up to those expectations then the cost, in
financial terms and in terms of human life, would have seemed a
small price to pay. Had Harris been able to devastate a handful of
other German cities in quick succession his predictions of an early
end to the war might indeed have been proven right. If Berlin had
suffered the same fate within a few weeks, it is conceivable that
that alone might have tipped the balance. But neither the RAF
nor the USAAF had the ability to do such a thing, let alone do it
quickly, and the small window of opportunity created by their
new, radar-jamming techniques soon began to close. By the time
the Allies attacked Berlin in force that autumn the tactical advantage had already swung back towards the Luftwaffe.

The Allies did not achieve such air supremacy again for another
eighteen months. It was not until February 1945, when they
bombed Dresden, that they finally demonstrated the ability to
replicate what had happened at Hamburg, seemingly at will. However, by this time few believed in bombing as the ultimate weapon.
With the Allies poised to enter Germany from both sides, the
emphasis had long since changed to land operations. It is perhaps
ironic that air bombardment only ever reached its full, war-
winning potential after it was no longer required to deliver the
decisive blow.

This, then, is the final tragedy of what happened at Hamburg.
It did not herald an end to the war, as so many people in the RAF
hoped and believed that it would: instead, it was merely the
opening page of the most destructive chapter in the history of air
warfare. While it was the forerunner of the catastrophes at Dresden
and Tokyo, Hiroshima and Nagasaki, Allied air supremacy did not

come soon enough to make Hamburg truly count. Instead Germany was subjected to a death by a thousand cuts. The countless lesser destructions that took place in the following two years would spell the devastation not only of individual cities, but of an entire nation. By the time Germany capitulated in May 1945, the country was a virtual wasteland.

24. Redemption

This only is denied even to God,
The power to make what has been done undone
Agathon[1]

I am aware that this book might have made uncomfortable reading
for some. There is still a great deal of bitterness towards Germany,
despite the decades that have passed, and many people simply do
not care if the Germans suffered or not. During the course of my
research I have spoken to scores of people – Jews, Gypsies, Poles,
Danes, Dutchmen, Frenchmen, the list goes on – who have listened
to my descriptions of the Hamburg firestorm and merely shrugged
their shoulders. 'It was their own fault,' is the standard reply. 'They
started it.' I would be surprised if even the most intransigent of
these people could remain unmoved by some of the eyewitness
accounts of the firestorm and its horrific effects; however, I do not
imagine this will produce a change of heart, especially among those
who suffered directly as a result of the way the Germans conducted
the war. Indeed, some may resent being manipulated into feeling
an empathy they had never intended. I make no apology for their
unease. War is a horrific thing, and it would be unnatural to feel
comfortable in its presence.

For readers from Germany, America or the British Commonwealth there may be an added dimension to their discomfort. The
legacy of guilt that surrounds the European bombings of the
Second World War is huge, and both sides are still struggling to
come to terms with it, even today. In Germany it remains virtually
impossible to mention the bombs without the immediate acknowl-
edgement that it was they who opened Pandora's box in the first
place. A modern generation still feels duty-bound to apologize for

30 The face of the victim: the trauma of being bombed scarred an entire generation of Germans.

31 Some of the city's 45,000 dead litter a street in the suburb of Hamm.

32 According to the late W. G. Sebald, in the immediate post-war years shopkeepers would pull photographs like this from under the counter with a furtiveness usually reserved for pornography. These unfortunates were not burned but baked in the heat of their shelter.

33 The changeful nature of the firestorm produced some gruesome contrasts: this body of a pregnant woman could almost be sleeping, while the corpses behind her are charred and mumified beyond recognition.

34 The clean-up operation: Hamburg workers clear the entrance to a buried air-raid shelter.

35 A prisoner from Neuengamme concentration camp loads charred body parts into a bucket.

36 Survivors being issued with emergency rations at one of the refugee assembly points.

37 Chalk messages appeared on many of the ruins, listing the whereabouts of those who used to live there. Some of them seem like gestures of defiance: *Wir leben* ('We are alive').

38 Ruined landscape. After the Gomorrah attacks Volksdorfer Strasse in Barmbek
was merely a pathway cleared through the rubble.

39 In Hamm only the façades of buildings still stand: everything else has been
turned to ash.

40 (*Above*) Life amongst the ruins: for the rest of the war, and for years afterwards, families were forced to live in the most basic of conditions wherever they could find shelter.

41 (*Left*) The memorial to the dead at Ohlsdorf depicts Charon ferrying the dead across the Styx. It stands in the centre of four mass-graves (*below*), where 36,918 bodies are buried. Thousands more were never recovered.

war crimes that were committed not by their parents, or even their grandparents, but by their great-grandparents. In the English-speaking world, feelings about the bomber war are even more complicated. While on the one hand there is a certain pride that they stood up to Hitler and rid the world of his particular brand of evil, on the other there is an unspoken sense of shame at the methods they were forced to use. There seems to be an underlying suspicion in the popular imagination that the RAF and the USAAF were only able to defeat the Nazis by descending, at least some of the way, to their level.

Two events encapsulate this discomfort. The first took place in central London, in May 1992, when hundreds of RAF veterans and their families attended a ceremony in honour of their old commander-in-chief, Sir Arthur Harris. The highlight of the day was to be the unveiling of a statue outside the church of St Clement Danes in the Strand, followed by a reception at the High Court. However, among the crowd a group of protesters had turned out to voice their disgust that the butcher of Hamburg, Dresden and countless other German cities should be so honoured. They hurled abuse at the RAF veterans, and even at the Queen Mother, who was performing the unveiling ceremony. That night the statue of Harris was daubed with red paint. This was cleaned off, but it was soon attacked again, and it has been defaced several times since.

The second event took place a year later, in Hamburg. The Lutheran Church marked the fiftieth anniversary of the firestorm by organizing a series of meetings and memorial services to commemorate the victims. On the whole these were gentle, sombre affairs, but during one service at the Michaeliskirche a group of students burst into the church and heckled the mourners. What had angered them was the all-inclusive nature of the commemoration. According to the students, the Church should have made a clear distinction between civilians and everyone else: the deaths of civilians should be mourned; the deaths of soldiers, or members of the Nazi Party, should not. After unfurling a banner with the slogan 'Operation Gomorrah – there's nothing to mourn', the demonstration finally became violent, and they had to be forcibly ejected from the church.[2]

Both events caused a furore at the time, not only because they represented a younger generation questioning the deeds of their grandparents, but because they highlighted some of the deep moral questions with which neither side has yet been able to come to terms. The Germans, to their credit, at least recognize that this is a subject they cannot avoid – they even have a specific word for it: *Vergangenheitsbewältigung* ('the process of coming to terms with the past'). Britain and America, however, seem much less prepared. They do their best to look back on the war in terms of black and white, good and evil, right and wrong – I am speaking not only of the veterans, but also of those who turn out to protest against the bomber war. When either group is confronted by the more ambiguous realities of bombing, few seem quite sure how to react.

★   ★   ★

The moral questions that surround the Allied bomber offensive are much deeper, and much more disturbing, than most people realize. During the course of my research for this book I have been asked repeatedly whether I thought the bombing of cities like Hamburg was justified. I have struggled to find an answer to this question, because it opens up so many difficult issues. Certainly it cannot be taken lightly: after all, if 'war's glorious art' is murder on a mass scale, then bombing is one of its most efficient weapons.

To begin with, I have very little problem with the *fact* that Hamburg was bombed. The city was a huge centre of industry, providing U-boats, aircraft, oil, chemicals and all kinds of other materials that were essential for the German war effort. It was imperative that the Western Allies did everything in their power to disrupt those industries, both for their own sake and for the sake of the Russians, who were dying in their millions on the Eastern Front. Britain and America lived in constant fear that the USSR would one day give up their titanic struggle by coming to some arrangement with Hitler. Bombing was the only way to prove that they were doing something to help, and successes like the devastation of Hamburg provided the Russians with a great morale boost. As Albert Speer pointed out after the war, the value of bombing cities like Hamburg lay not only in the disruption it caused to German industry but also in the huge resources it diverted away from the Russian Front.

A second issue is slightly more problematic. Towards the end of the war, and immediately after it, there was a great debate over whether the Allies were right to 'blanket' bomb German cities, or whether they should have concentrated more on the precision bombing of specific factories and military installations. Most people agreed that precision bombing was preferable, partly because it was much more efficient, but also because it was much less likely to involve civilian casualties.

While I wholeheartedly agree that precision bombing should always be chosen over area bombing wherever possible, in 1943 the RAF did not have the luxury of that choice. They had already tried precision bombing, and the results had been disastrous. Flying in daylight, the British planes were easy targets for German flak and fighters, and they were quickly decimated. Moreover, even during daylight, their equipment was so primitive and their accuracy so bad that they rarely hit what they were aiming for. In short, if they wanted to survive, and if they wanted to destroy specific targets, there was no choice but to go in during the night and bomb the entire area.

When the Americans joined the air war they went through much the same process. They began with a determination to fly by day, and to employ precision-bombing techniques. By the summer of 1943 they were paying for that decision with unsustainable losses. American planes were far less vulnerable to flak than British planes, and far better equipped to defend themselves against fighters – but during the battle of Hamburg their daytime flights meant that, in percentage terms, they were losing up to four times as many planes as the British. By the beginning of August their losses were so bad that they were forced to stop flying altogether. Their policy of flying by day was rescued only by the advent of long-range fighters, which finally began to escort them over Germany towards the end of the year.

It is tempting to view the Americans as the white knights of this particular story because, despite all the pressure to give up daylight bombing, they stuck to their convictions. One of the reasons they were so determined to do so was that they were convinced that the accuracy of their bombing made it worthwhile. The Americans were rightly proud of their Norden bomb sights, which were vastly superior to anything developed by either the Germans or the British, but this remarkable piece of equipment was only useful when the target was visible below. Whenever it was obscured by cloud or smoke, as it was at Hamburg, the Americans might as well have been flying by night.[3] So, for example, while they hit the Blohm & Voss shipyards on 25 July they also hit the historic city centre, the river, and a farmer's fields south of the city.[4] The only real difference that the people of Hamburg noticed between British bombs and American ones was that there were far fewer of the latter so they did less damage.

The American decision to stick to daylight bombing over Germany was an incredibly brave one. However, I do not think it gives them any right to claim the moral high ground – and not only for the reasons above. For all their protestations about blanket bombing they were not above employing this method when they thought it appropriate: indeed, their bombardiers on 26 July were told that if they could not locate the port they were to drop their bombs anywhere in the 'centre of the city'.[5] And while they may have exercised restraint in the European theatre of operations, their intentions were not nearly so exemplary in the Pacific. In fact, they used their time in Europe to study British methods of bombing so that they could apply them with equal success in Japan. Their firebombing of Tokyo in 1945 was every bit as devastating as what happened in Hamburg, and the civilian death toll even higher.

★   ★   ★

The final moral issue brought up by the bombing of Hamburg is by far the most difficult to justify. It concerns the intentions of those who created the firestorm. The British always claimed that they were aiming their bombs at Hamburg's docks and military installations: this was what they told the press, who dutifully reported that the aiming point for the RAF was the Blohm & Voss shipyard; it was also what many British crews were told during their briefings. But that was not the case. The largest concentration of purely 'military' targets, including the Blohm & Voss shipyards, was on the south shores of the river Elbe, yet this was the only area of Hamburg that the RAF did not aim for. Instead they went exclusively for the residential areas, to the north of the river. The targets of the bombs were not military installations at all, but civilians.

Some might argue that it makes no difference whether the RAF aimed at civilians or not. The vast area over which the bombs were dropped meant that the results were quite likely the same: the town was still flattened, the civilians still dead. But there is a huge moral gulf between bombing a suburban street by accident, and deliberately aiming for it. British planners justified this moral leap to themselves by pointing out that it was much more difficult to destroy factories than it was to kill the people who worked in them. As long as they destroyed the workforce it did not matter whether the Blohm & Voss shipyards were still intact – there would be nobody to build the U-boats.

This idea makes me extremely uncomfortable, but I have to admit that the people who planned the raids had a point. Why should there be any distinction between the German U-boat captain and the German factory worker who helped to build that U-boat? They were both working towards the same end, which was to kill British sailors. And since oil workers produced fuel for that U-boat, surely they were also legitimate targets. Farmers provided sustenance for soldiers at the front, textile workers produced their uniforms, and train drivers got them to and from the battlefield. In a 'total war' – and we must remember that it was the Germans who first proclaimed it as such – all of those people are considered fair game, as is anything else that supports the enemy's war economy.

The problem with this argument is that there is no clear place to draw the line. Can we also justify the killing of actors and musicians, since they contribute so much to the country's morale? And what about doctors and nurses, who heal soldiers' wounds so that they can go back to the battlefield? As I mentioned in chapter 7 some theorists even go so far as to say that women and children are a legitimate target. German soldiers believed they were fighting for their families, so by killing their wives and children one took away their incentive to fight. Under this kind of logic the Second World War was no longer a just and honourable struggle against an evil regime, but a war of annihilation.

The only thing that saves this policy from the charge of total immorality is that it was born from the best of intentions. Those who advocated bombing civilians sincerely believed they were trying to save lives rather than take them. Men like Harris, who had witnessed the terrible bloodbath of the First World War, saw bombing as the only way to spare British soldiers from total carnage. Fifty-five thousand RAF men and 26,000 USAAF men died during the course of the bombing war – a huge total, but only a tiny fraction of the number who suffered in the First World War trenches.[6] While the Russian Army was paying the butcher's bill on the Eastern Front, the Allied air forces were able to keep them on side by paying a far smaller share until the Allied armies were strong enough to launch a successful cross-Channel invasion.

Also, the theory went, it was not only Allied lives that would be spared. The British Air Ministry was convinced that bombing would save German lives, too, because it would shorten the war – in fact, after the destruction of Hamburg many in the government believed the war would be over before the end of 1943. Had the RAF achieved that, millions of people on both sides would have been saved.

This line of thinking must have seemed incredibly seductive at the time. But it is its very seductiveness that makes it so disturbing. The British were so caught up in the bomber dream that nobody seems to have considered what would happen if the policy did not work. In the search for the elusive knock-out blow the Allies launched attacks on civilian targets for several years. Before Hamburg they had bombed Lübeck, Rostock and Cologne. After Hamburg they bombed Mannheim, Kassel, Hanover, Munich, Berlin – the list of destroyed cities goes on and on. By May 1945 they had killed somewhere between 300,000 and 600,000 German civilians, most of whom had only tenuous links to the war.[7] The knock-out blow – the final strike that would end the war and so save lives – was never achieved.

Perhaps the worst aspect of this policy is that it removed all the traditional distinctions between combatants and civilians. There has to be some line over which military men will not cross, even if it is an arbitrary one. The problem with the Allied air strategy during the Second World War was that it removed the line without even attempting to draw a new one. The failure to do so opens the door to the nightmare of unlimited warfare, where anything is allowed provided it gets the job done – war without rules, without principles, without conscience. I hesitate to make the comparison with the amorality that led to the Holocaust, as several historians before me have done, because that would be going too far. But, ethically speaking at least, we are only a few steps away.

★ ★ ★

It would be reassuring to report that the British people of the time at least considered these issues before they lent their support to the bomber war, but this was by no means the case. Few people ever spoke out against the bombing of German cities like Hamburg. George Bell, the Bishop of Chichester, was one, as was the Labour politician Richard Stokes – but their speeches in Parliament were largely dismissed by the British press as unpatriotic. Basil Liddell Hart was another who objected: after writing enthusiastically about the theory of bombing he was much less enamoured with bombing in practice. As early as 1942 he claimed that it would be ironic if the so-called defenders of civilization could only defeat Hitler by depending on 'the most barbaric, and unskilled, way of winning a war that the modern world has seen'.[8]

Beyond those lone voices, however, the atmosphere was less

one of regretful determination than of pure triumph, with ever-increasing superlatives emblazoned across the front pages of all the newspapers. The men who flew the bombers were regarded as heroes: several British and American airmen have told me that they would often spend a night in a pub without ever having to buy a drink for themselves. Those who were recruited for morale-raising tours round British factories were treated like celebrities, and their descriptions of the huge fires created by Allied bombs were always greeted with enthusiastic cheers.[9]

By the end of the war, however, things had begun to change. Britain was already turning its back on the deeds of Bomber Command. After six long years of conflict the appetite for German blood was no longer what it had been in 1943, and nobody wanted to be associated with a policy that had killed hundreds of thousands of civilians. One by one, politicians, planners and even the Prime Minister distanced themselves from the decisions that had led to the 'blanket bombing' of German cities. The only senior figure who openly accepted responsibility for the policy was Sir Arthur Harris, who had always been its outspoken champion. At the end of the war he became something of a pariah, and there are numerous examples of how the political establishment tried to distance themselves from him.[10] Rightly or wrongly, his reputation remains severely tarnished to this day – as the defacing of his statue makes clear.

In the USA the tide was also turning. The American people had always opposed the wholesale bombing of cities, so their reaction to the supposedly indiscriminate bombing of Dresden in February 1945 was of outrage. Across the country front-page reports appeared claiming that American airmen were engaged in the 'deliberate terror bombing of great German population centres as a ruthless expedient to hasten Hitler's doom'.[11] The people, and the media, were not pacified until General Arnold stepped forward to insist that the USAAF had not departed from its strict policy of bombing only military targets. Unlike in Britain, this assertion was generally accepted, and the idea that American involvement in bombing Germany had been anything less than exemplary did not really resurface until the 1960s.[12] Even today, Americans tend to reserve their distaste either for the way the British conducted the air war, or for how they themselves acted in the subjugation of Japan.

As popular revulsion for bombing has grown, the men who flew the planes and dropped the bombs have gradually become the scapegoats for our communal sense of shame. And since it was the British whose bombing was apparently more indiscriminate, it is the RAF who have received most of the blame. Almost every British veteran I interviewed for this book expressed indignation over the way the world has come to judge their actions since 1945. Indeed, I have often found it difficult to secure interviews with them in the first place, because many were worried by my intentions. They assumed that my wish to show the German side of the story meant that I was likely to do what countless people have done: that is, to blame them *personally* for the suffering that British bombs caused ordinary Germans. In short, they were worried that I would treat them in the same way as the protesters treated them at the unveiling of Harris's statue.

This is one of the saddest legacies of the bomber war. While I admit that I have a small measure of sympathy for *some* of the beliefs held by those protesters, I deplore their abuse of Bomber Command veterans. If it is wrong to punish German civilians for the sins of their political leaders, then it is equally wrong to attack British airmen for the planning decisions of their superiors. British bomber crews were almost always told at briefing that they were attacking military or industrial targets. They were motivated by a sincere desire to help their country, and to rid the world of a profoundly evil regime. Whatever we think of the way the bomber war was conducted, those men, who faced death daily, and witnessed the deaths of countless friends and comrades, deserve our utmost respect.

It seems fitting here to record what the veterans themselves have to say about the part they played in the Hamburg bombings. Most of the men I have interviewed seem to have demonstrated an understandable lack of imagination while they were actually flying over Germany: they were young, some still in their teens, and they pursued war with all the enthusiasm of youth. As they flew over the fires at Hamburg the typical reaction was not 'Oh, those poor devils down there!' but 'Cor, this is a damn good show tonight!'[13] They rarely spared a thought for the people beneath the bombs, and even if they did it was usually only to register the notion that Germany had asked for it. For those who had lived through the Blitz on Britain, the Germans thoroughly deserved what they were getting.

Some of the veterans I have spoken to are unrepentant to this day. One who sees no reason to regret the part he played in the bombing says: 'I don't care about their cities. I was glad to see them burning . . . My only regret was that we got shot down when we did, because I would much rather have done a lot more.'[14]

Others seem to have softened over the years, if only to acknowledge the suffering of those who were, nevertheless, still legitimate targets. A few have taken the process further, and seem genuinely troubled by the thought of those who had to fight their way through the firestorm. In the years since the war they have had time to reflect on the terrible consequences of the fires, and even to question the part they played in events.

Colin Harrison of 467 Squadron is one such man. Some time after the war he came across a photograph of an old man and his wife, dead, on the street in Hamburg, and the image haunts him to this day. 'I often thought about those two old people,' he says. 'The street was clear – all the rubbish had been pushed to one side. There was no rubble on the road. And I often wondered whether they had anything to do with me . . . I wondered if I'd done it.'[15]

If we are ever to lay this painful subject to rest, we could do worse than take a leaf out of Colin Harrison's book. I do not wish to imply that he is right to feel any guilt for his part in the Hamburg bombings – far from it – only that his capacity for empathy is to be praised. The legacy of the last war will never be left behind until both sides learn to acknowledge the consequences of their actions, as he has done, regardless of whether or not we believe that those actions were justified.

*   *   *

And what of the people of Hamburg themselves? How do they view the ordeal they went through? Do they blame the British and Americans for the devastation that was wreaked upon their city? Are they angry? Whenever I have asked this question of anyone from Hamburg, I have invariably received the same answer, which exactly mirrors the sentiments of their enemies: 'We started it.' Or, even more tellingly, 'We deserved it.' Anger, resentment, indignation – even sadness – seem for most people to be irrelevant, because what *really* matters is that Germans are sorry.

Even during the war, many people in Hamburg realized that they were not blameless, and that, to a degree at least, they had brought the disaster upon themselves. Many saw the catastrophe as the logical consequence of the Luftwaffe's attacks on Britain; some even believed it to be just retribution for the way Hamburg had treated its Jews.[16] In any case, an unspoken sense of shame was already embedded in the German psyche long before the end of the war. As Hans Erich Nossack recorded shortly after the firestorm, it was difficult to view the Allies as anything other than the agents of some kind of divine justice:

I have not heard a single person curse the enemies or blame them for the destruction. When the newspapers published expressions like 'pirates of the air' and 'arsonists', we had no ears for that. A much deeper insight forbade us to think of an enemy who was supposed to have caused all this; for us, he too was at most an instrument of unknowable forces that wished to annihilate us.[17]

After the war, the sense that Germany had deserved this retribution grew, fuelled by the news of what had happened at Belsen, and Auschwitz, and Hamburg's own concentration camp at Neuengamme. The cold-bloodedness of the atrocities seemed to dwarf anything the Allied air forces might have done. As the

Nuremberg trials came and went, Hamburg's capacity for anger was smothered beneath a huge burden of communal guilt.

In such an atmosphere it was the Nazis, not the Allies, who were blamed for the catastrophe that had consumed the city in 1943. For example, when the famous memorial to the dead was unveiled at Ohlsdorf cemetery in 1952, the city's first post-war mayor, Max Brauer, gave a speech in which he denounced the 'inhuman dictatorship' that had led the people like lambs to the slaughter. 'This mass grave is a warning to us,' he said. 'We must recognize the danger [of extremism]. We must know that, in the end, as soon as mankind gives up its rights and freedoms it is stepping on to the road to self-destruction.'[18]

Those sentiments have been repeated in one form or another in every memorial since. On the fiftieth anniversary of the fire-storm, Elisabeth Kiausch, the president of the city council, implored her audience never to forget the horrors of war, and the 'sorrow that Nazism brought to innumerable people'.[19] That same day, even as the student demonstrators were clamouring outside her church, the Bishop of Hamburg was praying for forgiveness for the wrongs that Germany had committed in the past – particularly against eastern Europe, against the Jews and against Gypsies. Her sermon was primarily an appeal for world peace, but also a plea that we should never forget the time of the Third Reich, when the 'political blindness' of the German people had led to war and atrocity.[20]

However, there is a feeling in Germany that such attitudes might slowly be changing. While newspapers, politicians and community leaders maintain the official line that Germany herself was respon-sible for the firestorm and its aftermath, many privately hold different opinions. It is not only those who lived through the bombings – German society has always made concessions for *per-sonal* anger against the former Western Allies, so long as it is not voiced too loudly – there is now much more widespread resentment. A younger generation, which is not quite so intimately acquainted with German war guilt, has begun to question the readiness with which the Allies bombed civilians. Since 1989 there has also been an influx of ideas from the former East Germany. Understandably, the East Germans have never been quite so well disposed towards the way Britain and America bombed their country – an attitude that was encouraged by the country's Communist leaders for more than forty years.

Those feelings came to something of a head in 2002, when Jörg Friedrich published an extremely controversial history of the bombing war.[21] He claimed that the British insistence on area bombing made both Harris and Churchill no better than war criminals. Even more controversially, he deliberately described the bombings in terms usually reserved for Nazism and the Holocaust: so, for example, cellars are described as *Krematoria* ('crematoria'), cities as *Hinrichtungsstätten* ('places of execution') and the destruction of libraries as *Bücherverbrennung* ('book burning'). Needless to say, the book's publication created a media storm, both in Germany and abroad. It also created enormous concern because it appeared to strike such a chord with the German people: there were immediate worries that Germans were beginning to see themselves as the victims rather than the perpetrators of war crimes, and that such books might even become a clarion call for neo-Fascists.

While this last point seems unlikely, it is important to note that Germans seem to live in constant fear of a resurgence of right-wing extremism. Nowhere is this fear more prevalent than in Hamburg. In 1992 neo-Nazi violence provoked an anti-Fascist demonstration on the streets of Hamburg 400,000 strong. There were more demonstrations when the American neo-Nazi publisher Gary Lauck was tried and sentenced there in 1996. I myself experienced a hint of the city's anxieties when I first visited Hamburg in 2001, during a book tour. A complete stranger approached me and asked me to wear a badge bearing an anti-Fascist slogan: he had heard that I would be appearing on local television, and wanted his badge to appear with me. As I was unaware of Hamburg's political landscape at the time, I declined – but not without a measure of surprise at the strength of his feelings. It struck me then, as it has struck me many times since, how politically active Hamburgers seem to be when compared with my own countrymen. Sometimes it seems as though the city is vigilant to the point of paranoia when it comes to avoiding the political mistakes of the past.

⋆   ⋆   ⋆

It is against this background that the demonstration in the Michaeliskirche took place. The anti-nationalist students claimed to be protesting against the fact that churchgoers were mourning *all* of the deaths that took place during the catastrophe, rather than making a distinction between the guilty and the innocent. However, as they blew their whistles and sounded their horns, their objections seemed to go much further. Their banner claimed that there was no reason to mourn *whatsoever*, thus implying that every Hamburger who died in 1943 got what he or she deserved. Since all of Germany had stood by and allowed the Nazis to march to power, all of Germany was to blame.[22]

As an outsider, this strikes me as a bizarre form of self-flagellation. I find it shocking that a group of Germans will go so far as to deny their countrymen the right to mourn the deaths of thousands of undisputed civilians, simply in the name of expiating their guilt. Even the most hard-hearted proponents of British bombing expressed regret at what they felt forced to do. Even those theorists who claimed that women and children were a legitimate target recognized that bombing them was a horrific idea – indeed, they believed that the very horror of it would prevent civilized nations going to war in the first place. None of those groups would ever consider denying Hamburgers the right to mourn their dead. I doubt that such a denial would get much support in Germany either, but that a group like this can suggest it seems significant. If German war guilt has grown so great that it takes precedence over the city's capacity to mourn, it is unsurprising that there has been a right-wing backlash against it.

The more rational reasons behind the demonstration – that there should be a distinction between the civilian victims of the firestorm and those people who were legitimate targets for the bombs – are also much more interesting. *Should* such a distinction be made, or should we avoid distinctions, in the same way that the bombs did?

Since it is Christian doctrine to pray for *all* sinners, are churchgoers right to mourn the soldiers, arms manufacturers and Nazi Party members along with the housewives and children who were killed? And, further, is it possible to go so far as forgiveness, even for those who went enthusiastically to war in 1939? Or would this merely lend legitimacy to the atrocities the Nazis committed?

To consider these questions, the first thing we must do is to draw a distinction between public and private mourning. This is important because they are two very different acts. A private act of mourning is exactly that – something personal, unique to the individual who suffers through loss. A public act of mourning is a statement to the world, declaring openly the values that collectively we hold dear. The same person, commemorating the same event, can profess very different sentiments, perhaps even conflicting ones, depending on whether he is acting in a private or a public capacity.

Privately, of course, any individual has a right to mourn whomsoever they choose. A mother will naturally mourn her son even if he turned out to be a murderer. A husband might forgive his wife things in death that he could never forgive her while she was alive. Love, as Nietzsche wrote, is beyond good and evil; mourning for a loved one, therefore, takes no account of whether they were worthy of that mourning or not.

The same is true of Christian love for one's neighbour, whoever that neighbour might be – a civilian, a soldier, or even a Nazi. A storm trooper in the firestorm was no less human than a Hamburg housewife, and also deserves some empathy – if not for the *fact* of his death then at least for the *manner* of it. A Nazi prison guard might have committed countless crimes during his lifetime, and might even have intended to commit more, but at the point of death he was merely a human being undergoing a form of hell, and for this he, too, can be pitied. From a Christian point of view it is every individual's *duty* to try to forgive others, even those who have committed the most heinous crimes.

In a public ceremony, however, this duty dissolves into the background. The whole point of a public commemoration is, first, to remember what happened, second, to explain why it happened, and third, to show the world what you have lost. When commemorating an event as huge as the Hamburg firestorm, the ceremony is as much about the loss of ideals as it is about the loss of human life. In the years since the war, the firestorm has come to be symbolic of an even greater tragedy: the fact that civilians, not only in Hamburg but all over Europe, should involuntarily have found themselves caught up in the fury of aerial bombardment. The loss that is being commemorated, therefore, is not simply human life, but *innocent* human life.

During a ceremony like the one that took place at the Michaeliskirche in 1993, the Church authorities have to walk a fine line: on the one hand they need to provide a venue in which people feel able to express their private grief at what happened; but on the other they have an obligation to present the tragedy of the firestorm in terms of the public symbol it has become. If the firestorm is to be seen as a tragedy for the innocent, they cannot also include the guilty in their prayers. In short, a distinction must be made.

Furthermore, it is the duty of the Church to direct the moral values of the community it leads. In an atmosphere where there is already a widespread fear of a resurgence of neo-Nazi activity, any public forgiveness of the sins committed by the Nazis during the Second World War is unthinkable. Indeed, anything that goes even a tiny way towards an implied acceptance of Nazi crimes must be vigorously shunned. These things are important not only for those Hamburgers who happened to be present at the commemoration, but for the whole city, and indeed the whole of German society. Such ceremonies are a template for the way the German people think about themselves, and for the way they remember both what they did during the war and what they suffered.

For these reasons, I believe the protesters at the Michaeliskirche were right to demand a distinction between those who should be publicly mourned and those who should not (although I am less sympathetic to the methods they used to get their point across). One would never consider having a ceremony devoted *only* to those militant Nazis who died in the firestorm – so why include them in a ceremony that should have been devoted to the innocents? I have argued that the Allies should have drawn a line between combatants and non-combatants, even if it was an arbitrary one; likewise it is fitting for the Germans to draw a line between those who should be mourned, and those who should not.

However, *where* that line should be drawn is extremely problematic. Some people believe that all the genuinely innocent victims of the firestorm should be painstakingly named, in the same way that Berlin's Jews were listed for the Holocaust Museum, so that any future commemoration will be for them and them only. They argue very passionately that this is the only way to avoid the cloudy thinking that mixes the guilty with the innocent, and thereby devalues any commemoration of Hamburg's tragedy.[23]

I do not believe this is the answer. If such a register were ever created, it would necessarily have to include many people who do not fit with the spirit of the idea. For example, there were countless men and women in Hamburg who supported Hitler, who believed in 'final victory' and who hated Jews, but who were never required to do anything active for the Nazi Party. It would make me very uncomfortable if such people were included among the innocent victims of the firestorm, but how could they possibly be excluded? Freedom of speech and freedom of political association are two of the cornerstones of democratic society – by this token even the most ardent supporter of Nazism must be deemed innocent if they have not committed any actual crime.

Equally, some people for whom such a register seems designed might easily find themselves left off. Many soldiers privately hated the war, and despised Nazi policies yet still took up arms for their country. Hans Scholl is a perfect example. As the founder of the White Rose movement, he was executed for printing anti-Nazi leaflets – yet he had also served as a soldier in the German Army. Most Germans would say that Scholl was a victim of the Nazi regime rather than one of its perpetrators. But if he had been killed by a bomb before he had had the chance to print his leaflets, or while he was still in the army, would he have ended up on the other side of the dividing line?

The problem with listing the innocent is that everyone not listed then becomes guilty by default. The distress that this would cause countless families in Hamburg is surely too high a price to pay. In any case, I doubt that a register of the innocent would remove all ambiguity: disputes would inevitably arise, causing yet more distress, and in the absence of absolute proof it would be impossible to make a decision one way or the other. Guilt and innocence are rarely clear-cut concepts, no matter how much we would like them to be, and we must be prepared to allow for a rather broad grey area between the two.

If a line must be drawn, it should therefore be a broad conceptual one. Those people who both supported the Nazi Party and actively involved themselves in furthering its goals cannot, *must* not, be mourned publicly. Those who resisted the Nazis both in thought and deed should be remembered in our prayers. Everyone else should be left to God, in the faith that He will know His own.

★   ★   ★

I have written here about blame, about guilt, about morality, but in the end this book is not about any of those things. My main intention has never been to judge the events of the past, only to offer a reminder that they happened. One can always argue about who should be commemorated, and how, but in the end the most important thing is that a commemoration takes place at all: otherwise these terrible events will be forgotten. The world is already beginning to forget. Once the generation that lived through them has gone, there will be nobody left to tell the story first hand. That is perhaps the most dangerous thing of all. When the power of their direct experience is lost there will be little to prevent us stumbling into exactly the same mistakes all over again.

The purpose of this book, therefore, has been to try to give an impression of what bombing means to those unlucky enough to be caught up in it. There was nothing particularly special about any of the people whose experiences are recorded here. Those who flew the Allied bombers or the German night fighters were perfectly ordinary young men – a fairly typical cross-section of the societies from which they came. The people of Hamburg were also ordinary people, trying to go about their daily business in the same way they always had. And yet they were forced to live through some of the most terrible events the world has ever seen, simply because they happened to be born in the wrong time and place. In another time it could have been any of us.

Despite this, there are many who continue to harbour grudges – on the one side towards the Allied airmen who unleashed their bombs on Germany, and on the other side towards the German system, the German war generation, even Germany itself.

To those who continue to blame the Allies, and particularly the RAF veterans, for the way they conducted the war, I would say this: do not be too quick to judge history with the benefit of hindsight. What might seem obviously wrong to us today was not nearly so clear-cut in 1943. Their commanders might have made errors of judgement, but on the whole the men themselves acted honourably, and selflessly, at a time when civilization itself stood on the brink of the abyss. For this, if nothing else, subsequent generations owe them a debt of gratitude.

Likewise, for those who still harbour prejudices towards Germany, I have just one thing left to say. The bombs left their mark not only on Germany's cities, but also on its population. In the aftermath of the firestorm the German appetite for war quickly began to crumble, not only in Hamburg but across the country, and by the summer of 1945 it had disappeared. It has never really returned since. A nation that was once proud of its martial tradition is now one of the most pacifist countries in Europe, and one that is quick to admonish others for rushing into war.[24]

It is this innate pacifism that is perhaps the most lasting single effect of the bombing war. Since 1945, Germany has deployed its troops only in peace-keeping operations. This is in marked contrast to the USA, Britain, France and the USSR, who between them have waged wars in almost every corner of the planet. Hamburg has returned to its traditional role as a city of commerce, and its many newspapers and television companies remain fervently anti-war. The old U–boat yards at Blohm & Voss now work only in the repair and conversion of trade ships and passenger liners. Whatever else can be said about Germany – and much is still said – it cannot be denied that her people have learned their lesson.

Appendix A
Chronology of Hamburg

Year	Date	Events and description
808		Charlemagne begins building a fortress called Hammaburg at the point where Alster meets the Elbe.
831		Franconian emperor Ludwig the Pious sends Benedictine monk Ansgar to pitch tents on Elbe and appoints him bishop.
845		Viking marauders reduce Hammaburg to rubble.
9th–13th C		Reign of Schauenburg counts allows city to flourish and expand to south of the Elbe.
1186–7		Adolf III von Schauenburg parcels out wasteland to west of old town, and a mercantile settlement and harbour are constructed. This becomes Neustadt.
1189	7 May	According to tradition, Emperor Frederick Barbarossa grants Adolf III the right to duty-free trade all along the Lower Elbe to the point where it flows into the North Sea.
1190		Inhabitants revolt and try to free themselves from aristocratic rulers.
1201		Hamburg is invaded by Danes.
1227		Danes expelled by Adolf III's son, Count Adolf IV.
1235		Alster is dammed.
1250		Population 5,000.
1265		'Barbarossa's Charter' drawn up formally.
13th C		Hamburg joins Hanseatic League.

1400	Population 7,500.
early 1400s	Klaus Stoertebeker and Godeke Michels, Hamburg's equivalent of Robin Hood, wage buccaneer war against Hanseatic fleet.
1510	Emperor Maximillian I declares Hamburg an Imperial City – an important step in gaining emancipation from Danes.
1558	Founding of Hamburg Stock Exchange. Population around 20,000.
16th C	Lutheran reformation in city carried through by Johannes Bugenhagen. Influx of Protestants to city to avoid persecution elsewhere.
early 17th C	Influx of Sephardic Jews from Portugal and Spain to avoid persecution.
1619	Founding of Bank of Hamburg.
1800	Population 130,000.
1806	Napoleon invades Hamburg.
1814	Napoleon's troops repelled.
1815	Congress of Vienna guarantees freedom of the city.
1842	The Great Fire.
1847	Founding of HAPAG (Hamburg-Amerikanische-Packetfahrt-Actien-Gesellschaft), to become the biggest ship business in Germany.
1867	Hamburg joins North German League.
1871	Integration into German Reich under Bismarck.
1872	Opening of rail bridge across Elbe – followed by New Elbe Bridge for road traffic in 1887.
1881–88	Erection of Speicherstadt, a harbour storage city district.
1888	Hamburg joins German Customs Union. 'Free port' established, enabling Hamburg

		to become one of the largest storage locations for coffee, cocoa, spices and carpets.
1892		Cholera epidemic kills 8,000.
1895		Construction of Baltic–North Sea Canal.
1897		Inauguration of new *Rathaus*.
1900		Population passes 1 million.
1912		Hamburg becomes the third largest port in the world, after London and New York.
1914–18		40,000 citizens die in First World War.
1918		Revolution starts with mutiny of sailors in Kiel, and quickly spreads to Hamburg. On 6 November they form 'Workers and Soldiers Council', and seize political power. After elections the following spring, they hand over power to city council on 16 March 1919.
1919		University of Hamburg founded. Treaty of Versailles requires coastal towns to hand over majority of merchant fleets.
1923		Hyperinflation cripples Hamburg.
1927		Links with UK and US help Hamburg to recover quicker than most of Germany. Blue-collar workers' pay reaches pre-war levels again at last. White-collar workers pay would be the same by 1929.
1929–30		World slump hits Hamburg hard. Companies go bankrupt. City's welfare expenditure spirals out of control.
1932		Unemployment almost 40 per cent – radicalism returns.
1933	30 January	Hamburg's senate implements persecutions ordered by Nazis, so as not to give new government any pretext to intervene in the running of the city.
	28 February	Orders issued to carry out arrests.

	1 March	Seventy-five Communist Party functionaries arrested, to be followed by Social Democrats, trade unionists and other opponents of National Socialism.
	5 March	Nazi vote in Hamburg rises by 100,000, giving them 38.8 per cent of vote.
	14 October	Hamburg's city council, is dissolved.
1935	1 January	Nazi Party has 46,500 members in Hamburg, 3.8 per cent of population. Air-raid training begins.
1937		Greater Hamburg Act (Gross Hamburg Gesetz) incorporates Altona, Wandsbek, Harburg and twenty-seven other municipalities under Prussian control until then. As a result Hamburg nearly doubles in size, and population rises 41 per cent to 1.68 million inhabitants. Hamburg–Lübeck *Autobahn* completed. Black-out drills started.
1938	1 April	Merger of Hamburg and other towns comes into being.
	December	Neuengamme concentration camp is completed.
1939	July	Air-raid shelters start to be built – 108 completed by September 1942, but still only enough for 10 per cent of population.
1940	18 May	Hamburg bombed for the first time.
1943	20 April	Hamburg leaders draw up a disaster plan in case of heavy air raids.
	27 May	Sir Arthur Harris unveils plans to destroy Hamburg.
	19/20 June	Hamburg defences carry out rehearsal for their disaster plan in Altona. Their worst-case scenario involves some 3,000 dead, 1,000 wounded and 110,000 homeless.
	25 June	USAAF fly on Hamburg for the first time.

		They fail to reach the city, and lose eighteen planes.
	6–12 July	A week of consultation by Hamburg's leaders over the city's disaster plan, concluding in another rehearsal.
	27 July	Firestorm (see Appendix C).
	August	Goering, Goebbels, Frick and others visit the stricken city, but Hitler refuses to come.
1944	end	Anti-tank obstacles erected in streets, and territorial army of old men and adolescents called up.
1945	29 April	Commanding officer Brigadier-General Alwin Wolz establishes contact with British troops outside Hamburg.
	3 May	Wolz signs unconditional surrender. British troops enter the city.
1946–7	winter	Severe and sustained freeze sees temperatures drop to −28°C. Famine in the city.
1949		Hamburg becomes a federal state in Federal Republic of Germany.
1962		Storm causes flooding, which ruins old town and kills 300 people.
1993	24 July	Student protesters interrupt the fiftieth anniversary commemoration of the Firestorm, proclaiming 'there is nothing to mourn'.
2003		The British ambassador addresses sixtieth anniversary commemoration expressing regret at events of 1943.

Appendix B
Chronology of the Second World War

Before the war

5 March 1933	The Nazis win the German elections.
October 1933	Hitler withdraws from the World Disarmament Conference and the League of Nations.
16 March 1935	Germany denounces the Treaty of Versailles.
June 1935	The Luftwaffe is re-created, with Hermann Goering at its head.
7 March 1936	Germany reoccupies the Rhineland, taken from it by the Treaty of Versailles.
July 1936–March 1939	The Spanish Civil War.
26 April 1937	The Basque town of Guernica is destroyed by German bombers.
12 March 1938	German Army marches into Austria, a day ahead of the *Anschluss*.
1 October 1938	With French and British agreement, German troops march into the Sudetenland in Czechoslovakia.
10–16 March 1936	Germany annexes Bohemia and Moravia.
23 August 1939	Germany and Russia sign a 'non-aggression' pact.

1939

1 September	Germany begins the invasion of Poland.
3 September	Britain and France declare war.
17 September	Soviets invade Poland from the east.

13–26 September	Warsaw is bombed.
29 November	Soviets attack Finland.

1940

9 April	Germans begin the invasion of Denmark and Norway.
10 May	Winston Churchill becomes Britain's Prime Minister.
	German invasion of Belgium, Luxembourg, Holland and France begins.
14 May	Rotterdam is bombed.
15 May	RAF begins strategic bombing offensive with attacks on oil and transport targets in the Ruhr.
18 May	Hamburg bombed for the first time.
26 May	The evacuation of British forces at Dunkirk begins.
31 May	Roosevelt introduces a massive rearmament programme for the USA.
8 August	Battle of Britain begins.
24 August	Luftwaffe accidentally bombs central London.
25 August	In retaliation, Churchill orders bombing raid against Berlin.
17 September	After failing to win air supremacy, Hitler is forced to postpone the invasion of Britain indefinitely: the RAF has effectively won the battle of Britain.
30 September	Germany switches tactics to night bombing.
14/15 November	Bombing of Coventry devastates the city.

1941

24 March	Rommel begins advance in North Africa.
5–6 April	Germany invades Yugoslavia and Greece.
10/11 May	The final heavy bombing raid on London marks the end of the battle of Britain.
22 June	Germany begins Operation 'Barbarossa': the invasion of Russia.
7 December	Pearl Harbor is bombed by the Japanese.
11 December	Hitler declares war against the USA.
December–May 1942	Japanese army sweeps across South East Asia, taking Hong Kong, the Philippines, Malaya, Singapore, Burma and the East Indies.

1942

January–May	The Japanese army sweeps across South East Asia.
22 February	Sir Arthur Harris becomes C-in-C RAF Bomber Command.
23–26 March	RAF devastate Rostock.
28/29 March	RAF firebomb Lübeck, destroying 60 per cent of the old city.
30/31 May	RAF attack Cologne with their first 1,000-bomber raid.
4 July	USAAF fly their first mission in Europe, against German airfields in Holland.
4 November	The 'end of the beginning' of the war: the British win their first major land victory against the Germans at El Alamein.

1943

14–26 January	The Casablanca Conference, where Churchill and Roosevelt outline their bombing strategy. They agree on a policy of accepting nothing less than unconditional surrender from the Axis powers.
27 January	First USAAF raid against a German target: Wilhelmshaven.
2 February	The surrounded German army at Stalingrad finally surrenders.
18 February	Reichspropagandaminister Goebbels declares 'total war'.
20 April	Hamburg leaders draw up a disaster plan in case of heavy air raids.
27 May	Sir Arthur Harris unveils plans to destroy Hamburg.
10 June	Pointblank Directive is issued, and the 'Combined Bomber Offensive' against Germany begins: the USAAF bombing by day, the RAF by night.
19/20 June	Hamburg defences carry out rehearsal for their disaster plan in Altona. Their worst-case scenario involves some 3,000 dead, 1,000 wounded and 110,000 homeless.
25 June	USAAF fly on Hamburg, but never reach the city; eighteen planes are shot down.
5–13 July	The last German counter-offensive in the east fails at Kursk.
6–12 July	A week of consultation by Hamburg's leaders over the city's disaster plan, concluding in another rehearsal.
10 July	British and American troops land in Sicily.
24 July–2 August	Operation Gomorrah destroys Hamburg (see Appendix C).

25 July	Mussolini is deposed.
1 August	Goebbels orders the evacuation of women and children from Berlin.
6 August	Goering visits the ruins of Hamburg.
17 August	Goebbels, Interior Minister Frick and half a dozen gauleiters visit Hamburg.
	Disastrous USAAF attack on Schweinfurt and Regensburg, in which they lose sixty aircraft.
	Hans Jeschonnek, Luftwaffe Chief of Staff, commits suicide.
3 September	The Allies begin the invasion of the Italian mainland. Italy surrenders unconditionally.
13 October	Italy swaps sides, and declares war on Germany.
14 November	RAF begins the 'Battle of Berlin'.

1944

6 June	D–Day: the Allies land on the beaches of Normandy.
13 June	The Germans launch their first V-1 flying bombs on London.
20 July	Hitler survives assassination attempt.
8 September	The first V-2 rocket hits London.
16 October	Soviet forces enter East Prussia.
6 November	President Roosevelt is re-elected for a fourth term despite failing health.
16 December	Opening of the German Ardennes counter–offensive.

1945

26 January	Soviet troops liberate Auschwitz.
3 February	Berlin suffers its worst air raid of the war

	when 1,500 USAAF bombers drop more than 2,000 tons of bombs on the city.
4 February	Yalta Conference begins.
13–15 February	Dresden is bombed, killing tens of thousands in a firestorm similar to that at Hamburg.
7 March	The Americans cross the Rhine into Germany.
9/10 March	Tokyo is firebombed, destroying sixteen square miles of the city and killing almost 90,000 people.
18 March	RAF drop an incredible 4,000 tons of bombs on Berlin.
11 April	Concentration camp at Buchenwald is liberated by the Americans.
12 April	President Roosevelt dies.
13 April	Concentration camp at Belsen is liberated by the British.
16 April	Russians begin their final push across the river Oder towards Berlin.
30 April	Hitler commits suicide.
3 May	Hamburg surrenders to the Allies without a fight.
7 May	Unconditional German surrender.
8 May	VE Day.
6 August	The first atomic bomb is dropped on Hiroshima.
9 August	The second atomic bomb is dropped on Nagasaki.
15 August	The Japanese emperor informs his people that he will surrender.
2 September	VJ Day: the signing of the Japanese surrender brings the Second World War to an end.

After the war

30 September 1946	Nuremburg Tribunal on war crimes delivers its verdicts.
Winter 1945–6	Cold temperatures cause problems across occupied Germany.
Winter 1946–7	Severe and sustained freeze across Germany sees temperatures drop to −28°C.
27 May 1947	The British and American zones of control in Germany merge to form the 'Bizone'.
July 1947	Sixteen western European nations form the Committee for European Economic Co-operation. The Marshall Plan begins to take effect.
20–21 June 1948	The Deutschmark is introduced in Germany, signalling the beginning of the *Wirtschaftswunder*.

Appendix C
Chronology of 'Operation Gomorrah'

24 July

12.18	Public air-raid warning, set off by American B-17s heading for Norway.

Night of 24/25 July: first RAF raid

22.00	791 British aircraft set out for Hamburg.
00.19	Air-raid danger (thirty minutes) sounded.
00.30 approx	RAF begin dropping 'Window', creating confusion for German radar.
00.33	Main air-raid alarm.
00.57	Marker flares (*Tannenbaum*) rain down on western suburbs of Hamburg.
01.02	The first bombs begin to fall.
01.50	The last handful of 2,300 tons of bombs falls on the city.
03.01	The all-clear is sounded in Hamburg.

25 July: first USAAF raid

13.20	123 US B-17s take off for Hamburg.
16.15	Luftwaffe begin attacks on the US formations.
16.20	Main air-raid alarm sounded in Hamburg.
16.36	384th BG drop the first bombs on Howaldtswerke shipyards.
16.40	The last bombs drop on Hamburg.
17.10	381st BG, unable to locate Klöckner factory, drop

their bombs on Heide on the way home.

17.22	The all-clear sounds in Hamburg.
18.10	After almost two hours, the Luftwaffe finally stop harassing US formations.
20.00	The surviving B-17 crews return to base.

Night of 25/26 July

| 00.35 | Main air-raid warning in Hamburg. |
| 00.40 approx | 6 RAF Mosquitos bomb Hamburg in a nuisance raid. |

26 July: second USAAF raid

08.50	121 American B-17s take off for Hamburg; 379th BG and 384th BG abort mission, leaving only four bomb groups to do the job.
11.32	Main air raid alarm sounded in Hamburg.
11.59	Fifty-four B-17s drop their bombs on harbour district. The bombing lasts one minute.
12.50	All-clear sounds in Hamburg.
15.08	American bombers return to base.

Night of 26/27 July

00.20	Main air raid alarm sounded in Hamburg.
00.30 approx	Four RAF Mosquitos (of six dispatched) bomb Hamburg in nuisance raid.
00.55	All-clear sounds.

27 July

Five false alarms keep much of Hamburg in panic throughout the day.

Night of 27/28 July: second RAF raid

22.00	787 RAF bombers take off for Hamburg.
23.40	Main air-raid alarm sounds in the city.
00.55	RAF Pathfinders drop yellow markers.
01.00	First bombs begin to fall in the east of the city.
01.20	The firestorm begins to develop.
01.45	The last bombs fall.
02.00	Firestorm so strong that men outside main fire station can only crawl on their hands and knees against the wind.
02.40	All-clear sounds.
03.00–03.30	Climax of firestorm.
05.00 approx	British planes return to base.

28 July

Morning	Karl Kaufmann orders the evacuation of women and children. Almost a million people begin their exodus from the city.

Night of 28/29 July

00.15	Main air-raid alarm sounds.
00.25 approx	4 RAF Mosquitos bomb Hamburg on nuisance raid.
01.03	All-clear sounds.

Night of 29/30 July: third RAF raid

22.00	777 RAF planes take off for Hamburg.
23.58	Main air-raid alarm sounds in the city.
00.37	First marker flares fall on the city.
00.43	First bombs begin to fall.
01.30	The last bombs fall.
02.00	A second firestorm develops in the north-eastern suburb of Barmbek.
02.15	All-clear sounds.
04.30 approx	RAF bombers return to base.

Night of 2/3 August: fourth RAF raid

23.20	740 RAF bombers set out for Hamburg.
00.59	Main air-raid alarm sounds in the city.
01.30 approx	British force begins to encounter violent electrical storm.
02.07	Scattered bombing begins all over northern Germany.
02.10	Some marker flares fall over Hamburg, but most are misplaced or lost in cloud.
03.30	All-clear sounds.
06.00 approx	Battered RAF force returns to base.

Appendix D
Comparison of British, American and German Terms

1 *Air force units, 1943*

British (bombers)	American (bombers)	German (fighters)
RAF	USAAF	*Luftwaffe*
. . .	US Eighth Air Force	*Luftflotte*
Bomber Command	VIII Bomber Command	*Jagddivision*
Group (8–12 sqns)	Wing (6–9 groups)	*Geschwader* (3 *Gruppen* +1 *Stabschwarm*)
Squadron (3–4 flights)	Group (4 squadrons)	*Gruppe* (3 *Staffeln*)
Flight (6–7 aircraft)	Squadron (7 aircraft)	*Staffel* (9 aircraft)
. . .	. . .	[*Stabschwarm* (4 aircraft)]

NB The three air forces were very differently organized, and comparing them in this way is slightly problematic. For example, Allied bomber units are being compared to German fighter units. And, while RAF Bomber Command might have been similar to the American VIII Bomber Command, in 1943 the British organization was much larger than its American counterpart. The above is therefore only a very rough guide.

2 *Ranks*

British	American	German
Aircraftman	Private	*Flieger*
LAC	Corporal	*Obergefreiter*

British	*American*	*German*
Corporal	Staff Sergeant	*Unteroffizier*
Sergeant	Tech Sergeant	*Feldwebel*
Flight Sergeant	Master Sergeant	*Oberfeldwebel*
Warrant Officer	Warrant Officer	*Hauptfeldwebel*
Officer Cadet	Officer Cadet	*Fähnrich*
Pilot Officer	Second Lieutenant	*Leutnant*
Flying Officer	First Lieutenant	*Oberleutnant*
Flight Lieutenant	Captain	*Hauptmann*
Squadron Leader	Major	*Major*
Wing Commander	Lieutenant Colonel	*Oberstleutnant*
Group Captain	Colonel	*Oberst*
Air Commodore	Brigadier General	*Generalmajor*
Air Vice Marshal	Major General	*Generalleutnant*
Air Marshal	Lieutenant General	*General der Flieger*
Air Chief Marshal	General (four stars)	*Generaloberst*
Marshal of the RAF	General of the Army (five stars)	*Generalfeldmarschall*

Appendix E
British Order of Battle, 24 July 1943

RAF Bomber Command

1 Group (HQ Bawtry Hall)

Unit	Airfield	Type of Aircraft
12 Squadron	Wickenby	Lancaster
100 Squadron	Grimsby	Lancaster
101 Squadron	Ludford Magna	Lancaster
103 Squadron	Elsham Wolds	Lancaster
166 Squadron	Kirmington	Wellington
300 (Polish) Squadron	Ingham	Wellington
305 (Polish) Squadron	Ingham	Wellington
460 (RAAF) Squadron	Binbrook	Lancaster

3 Group (HQ Exning, Newmarket)

Unit	Airfield	Type of Aircraft
15 Squadron	Mildenhall	Stirling
75 (NZ) Squadron	Mepal	Stirling
90 Squadron	West Wickham	Stirling
115 Squadron	East Wretham	Lancaster
149 Squadron	Lakenheath	Stirling
214 (FMS) Squadron	Chedburgh	Stirling
218 Squadron	Downham Market	Stirling
620 Squadron	Chedburgh	Stirling

Special Operations

Unit	Airfield	Type of Aircraft
138 Squadron★	Tempsford	Halifax
161 Squadron★	Tempsford	Halifax, Hudson, Havoc, Lysander
192 Squadron	Feltwell	Halifax, Wellington, Mosquito

Non-operational

| 196 Squadron★ | Witchford | Wellington/Stirling |
| 199 Squadron★ | Lakenheath | Wellington/Stirling |

4 Group (HQ Heslington Hall)

10 Squadron	Melbourne	Halifax
51 Squadron	Snaith	Halifax
76 Squadron	Holme-on-Spalding-Moor	Halifax
77 Squadron	Elvington	Halifax
78 Squadron	Breighton	Halifax
102 Squadron	Pocklington	Halifax
158 Squadron	Lissett	Halifax
466 (RAAF) Squadron	Leconfield	Wellington

5 Group (HQ Morton Hall, Swinderby)

9 Squadron	Bardney	Lancaster
44 (Rhodesia) Squadron	Dunholme Lodge	Lancaster
49 Squadron	Fiskerton	Lancaster
50 Squadron	Skellingthorpe	Lancaster
57 Squadron	Scampton	Lancaster
61 Squadron	Syerston	Lancaster
106 Squadron	Syerston	Lancaster
207 Squadron	Langar	Lancaster
467 (RAAF) Squadron	Bottesford	Lancaster
617 Squadron★	Scampton	Lancaster
619 Squadron	Woodhall Spa	Lancaster

6 (Canadian) Group (HQ Allerton Park Castle, Knaresborough)

408 Squadron	Leeming	Halifax
419 Squadron	Middleton St George	Halifax
427 Squadron	Leeming	Halifax
428 Squadron	Middleton St George	Halifax

429 Squadron	East Moor	Wellington
432 Squadron	Skipton–on–Swale	Wellington

Non-operational

426 Squadron★	Linton-on-Ouse	Wellington/Halifax
431 Squadron★	Tholthorpe	Wellington/Halifax
434 Squadron★	Tholthorpe	Halifax

8 (Pathfinder) Group (HQ Castle Hill House, Huntingdon)

7 Squadron	Oakington	Stirling, Lancaster
35 Squadron	Graveley	Halifax
83 Squadron	Wyton	Lancaster
97 Squadron	Bourn	Lancaster
105 Squadron★	Marham	Oboe Mosquito
109 Squadron★	Marham	Oboe Mosquito
139 (Jamaica) Squadron	Wyton	Mosquito
156 Squadron	Warboys	Lancaster
405 (RCAF) Squadron	Gransden Lodge	Halifax
1409 (Meteorological) Flight	Wyton	Mosquito

RAF Fighter Command

Intruder Operations

10 Group

307 (Polish) Squadron★	Fairwood Common	Mosquito
456 (RAAF) Squadron★	Middle Wallop	Mosquito

11 Group

157 Squadron★	Hunsdon	Mosquito
418 (RCAF) Squadron★	Ford	Mosquito
605 Squadron★	Castle Camps	Mosquito

12 Group

25 Squadron★	Church Fenton	Mosquito
141 Squadron★	Wittering	Beaufighter
410 (RCAF) Squadron★	Coleby Grange	Mosquito

★ Not directly involved in bombing Hamburg, either because they were non-operational, or because they attacked other targets.

Appendix F
American Order of Battle, 24 July 1943

US Eighth Air Force

VIII Bomber Command (HQ Wickham Abbey)

1st Bombardment Wing (HQ Brampton Grange)

Unit	Airfield	Type of Aircraft
91st Bombardment Group	Bassingbourne	Boeing B-17
92nd Bombardment Group★	Alconbury	Boeing B-17
303rd Bombardment Group	Molesworth	Boeing B-17
305th Bombardment Group★	Chelveston	Boeing B-17
306th Bombardment Group★	Thurleigh	Boeing B-17
351st Bombardment Group	Polebrook	Boeing B-17
379th Bombardment Group	Kimbolton	Boeing B-17
381st Bombardment Group	Ridgewell	Boeing B-17
384th Bombardment Group	Grafton Underwood	Boeing B-17

4th Bombardment Wing (HQ Elveden Hall, Thetford)

94th Bombardment Group★	Bury St Edmunds	Boeing B-17
95th Bombardment Group★	Horham	Boeing B-17
96th Bombardment Group★	Snetterton Heath	Boeing B-17
100th Bombardment Group★	Thorpe Abbots	Boeing B-17
385th Bombardment Group★	Great Ashfield	Boeing B-17
388th Bombardment Group★	Knettishall	Boeing B-17

★ Detailed for other targets, and therefore not directly involved in the bombing of Hamburg.

Appendix G
Luftwaffe Order of Battle of Fighters in the West, 24 July 1943

1 Jagddivision (HQ Deelen, Holland)
Night fighters

Unit	Airfield	Type of aircraft
Stab NJG 1	Deelen	Me110 (a.k.a. Bf110)
I/NJG 1	Venlo	Me110
II/NJG 1	St Trond	Me110
III/NJG 1	Twenthe	Me110
IV/NJG 1	Leeuwarden	Me110

Day fighters

Stab JG 1	Deelen	Me109 (Bf109), FW190
I/JG 1	Deelen	FW190
II/JG 1	Woensdrecht, Schiphol	FW190
III/JG 1	Leeuwarden	Me109
I/JG 26	Grimbergen, Wevelghem	FW190
III/JG 54	Schiphol	Me109

2 Jagddivision (HQ Stade)

Stab NJG 3	Stade	
I/NJG 3	Vechta, Wittmundhafen	Do217, Ju88, Me110
II/NJG 3	Schleswig, Westerland	Do217, Ju88, Me110
III/NJG 3	Lüneburg, Wunstorf, Stade	Me110
IV/NJG 3	Grove, Kastrup	Do217, Ju88
NJ-Kommando 190	Aalborg	FW190
Stab JG 11	Jever	FW190

I/JG 11	Husum	FW190
II/JG 11	Jever	Me109
III/JG 11	Oldenburg	Me109
10 Staffel/JG 11	Aalborg	FW190
Jagdstaffel Heligoland	Heligoland	Me109
III/JG 26	Nordholz	Me109, FW190

3 Jagddivision (HQ Metz)

Stab NJG 4	Metz	Do217, Me110
I/NJG 4	Florennes	Do217, Me110
II/NJG 4	St Dizier	Do217, Me110
III/NJG 4	Juvincourt	Do217, Me110
Stab JG 26	Lille Nord	FW190
II/JG 26	Vitry-en-Artois	FW190
Stab JG 300 (Hajo Herrmann)		

NB This Order of Battle contains only units in western Europe between Denmark and northern France, and is the best estimate for 24 July 1943. Luftwaffe fighter units were moved around a great deal, and because of a lack of reliable documentation it is impossible to be completely certain where any one particular unit was on a given day. Those fighter groups that were too far from Hamburg to assist in its defence are not listed.

Appendix H
Air Force Casualties

First RAF raid, 24 July 1943

German losses

Unit	Aircraft	Losses
II/NJG 3	Ju88 C6, 360334	Lt W. Töpfer shot down into sea off Sylt by Mosquito of 25 Squadron. Two men killed.
	Do217N, 1414	Ofw. W. Ziegler shot down, probably by Halifax of 51 Squadron. Two men killed.

British losses

51 Squadron	Halifax II, HR940 MH-	Shot down by night fighter (Oblt Günter Köberich of IV/NJG3). Sgt W. J. Murray and six crew died.
75 Squadron	Stirling III, EE890 AA-L	Shot down by night fighter (Fw. Meissner of II/NJG3). Three survived as PoWs, but pilot W/O H. Nicol and three others died.
76 Squadron	Halifax V, DK187 MP-M	Lost over North Sea, probably by night fighter. Pilot F/O G. G. Such and seven crew died.
102 Squadron	Halifax II, JD316 DY-X	Shot down by night fighter. One survived as PoW (P/O F. G. Smith), but pilot F/L T. Bakewell and six others died.

103 Squadron	Lancaster I, ED389 PM-J2	Shot down by night fighter (Hptm. Rudolf Sigmund, IV/NJG1), crashed in North Sea. Pilot W/O G. E. B. Hardman and six crew died.
103 Squadron	Lancaster III, ED878 PM-V	Shot down by fighter (Oblt. Hermann Greiner, IV/NJG1). Pilot W/O F. F. O'Hanlon and six crew died.
103 Squadron	Lancaster III, JA886 PM-E	Lost without trace. Pilot F/S R. A. Moore and six crew died.
158 Squadron	Halifax II, HR941 NP-A	Shot down by night fighter (Lt Böttinger, II/NJG3), crashed near Schleswig. Pilot Sgt W. H. Bolam and six crew died.
166 Squadron	Wellington X, HZ314 AS-P	Hit by flak, crashed at Buchholz. Pilot W/O G. Ashplant and four crew killed.
214 Squadron	Stirling III, EE902 BU-P	Shot down by fighter and crashed at Barchel. Two survived as PoWs, but pilot P/O R. W. Belshaw and five others died.
218 Squadron	Stirling III, BF567 HA-P	Shot down by night fighter, crashed near Neumünster. One survived as PoW (F/O H. C. Eyre), but pilot W/C D. T. Saville and six others died.
460 Squadron	Lancaster III, W4987 AR-	Hit by flak and crashed near Cuxhaven. Pilot F/S A. G. Ashley and six crew died.

In addition one Halifax II (HR 803 TL-P) from 35 Squadron piloted by F/S N. J. Matich crash landed a minute after take-off, without any of the crew being hurt; and F/S S. M. Grzeskowiak's 305 Squadron Wellington X (HF472 SM-S) crash-landed because of insufficient fuel, but again no one was hurt.

First USAAF raid, 25 July 1943

German losses

III/JG 1	Me109 G-6, No. 207	Maj. K.-H. Leesmann shot down by unknown American bomb group.
II/JG 11	Me109 G-6, No. 20026	Lt W. Gloerfeld collided with stabilizer of 379th BG B-17 and crashed near Bliedersdorf. Pilot wounded.
	Me109 G-1, No.14147	Lt E. Kämpf shot down by B-17, possibly of 303rd BG. Crashed near Itzehoe. Pilot wounded.
	Me 109 G-1, No. 14125	Uffz. W. Riedmann shot down by B-17, crashed at Sauensiek. Pilot wounded.
III/JG 26	Me109 G-6, No. 16447	Pilot unknown. Crash-landed at Stade after combat, pilot unhurt.
IV/NJG 1	Me110 G-4, No. 6343	Night fighter of Oblt E. Gardiewski shot down into sea by B-17s of 303rd BG.

American losses

91st BG	B-17, 42–29813	Shot down by flak and fighters. One killed, but 2Lt Marshall L. Pilert and eight others survived as PoWs.

303rd BG	B-17, 42–29606	Shot down by flak and fighters, four killed (including pilot Lt John A. Van Wie), six survived as PoWs.
351st BG	B-17, 42–3272	Shot down by fighter, six killed, but four survived as PoWs (incl. pilot Lt Edwin S. Boyd).
379th BG	B-17, 42–23175	Shot down by fighter. All ten (incl. pilot Lt Frank A. Hildebrandt) survived as PoWs.
	B-17, 42–5917	Shot down by fighter: four killed, but six survived as PoWs (incl. pilot 2Lt Philip A. Mohr).
381st BG	B-17, 42–30013	Shot down by flak over Hamburg: four killed, but six survived as PoWs (incl. pilot Lt William R. Moore).
	B-17, 42–29976	Shot down by flak and fighters. All ten crew (incl. pilot Lt Jack H. Owen) survived as PoWs.
	B-17, 42–30153	Shot down by flak, crash-landed at Südmoor. All ten crew (incl. pilot Capt. Joe E. Alexander) survived as PoWs.
384th BG	B-17, 42–3122	Shot down by fighters. All ten crew (incl. pilot 2Lt Ralph J. Hall) survived as PoWs.
	B-17, 42–3069	Shot down by flak and fighters. All ten crew (incl. pilot Lt Gordon J. Hankinson) survived as PoWs.
	B-17, 42–3024	Shot down by flak and fighters:

seven killed, three PoWs (incl. pilot 2Lt P. J. Ward).

B-17, 42–3088   Shot down by fighters: five killed (incl. pilot Lt Clarence R. Christman), but five survived as PoWs.

B-17, 42–29670   Shot down by flak and fighters: two killed, but eight survived as PoWs (incl. pilot Lt Kelmer J. Hall).

B-17, 42–3075   Shot down by flak and fighters: seven killed, but three survived as PoWs (incl. pilot Lt. John M. Hegewald).

B-17, 42–5883   Shot down by fighters, crashed in sea. All ten (incl. pilot Lt Thomas J. Estes) were rescued by Danish fishing-boat and returned to England.

In addition Lt Willis C. Carlisle, Jr. of 379th BG was killed by a fighter – his crew brought the plane back safely.

2nd USAAF raid, 26 July 1943

American losses

91st BG   B-17, 42–3031   Shot down by flak and fighters: four killed, but six survived as PoWs (incl. pilot Lt James W. Rendall, Jr.).

B-17, 42–42709   Ditched in North Sea after fighter attack. All ten (incl. pilot Lt Jack A. Hargis) rescued and brought back.

In addition Lt Sidney Novell, a navigator with 381st BG, was killed when flak hit his B-17.

2nd RAF raid, 27 July 1943

British losses

12 Squadron	Lancaster III, EE142 PH-G	Shot down by night fighter (Oblt Willi Schmale of I/NJG3), crashed near Vechta. One survived as PoW (Sgt P. J. Bartlett), but pilot W/O W. Salthouse and five others killed.
15 Squadron	Stirling III, EH893 LS-J	Shot down by flak and fighter (Uffz. Lüschner, III/NJG3). One survived as PoW (Sgt E. Hurley), but pilot F/L J. R. Childs and six crew died.
50 Squadron	Lancaster I, R5687 VN-D	Shot down by flak over Bremerhaven. Pilot F/S N. P. I. Castells and six crew died.
78 Squadron	Halifax II, JD148 EY-A	Shot down by flak near Wilhelmshaven: four survived as PoWs but pilot Sgt L. E. Maidment and two others died.
100 Squadron	Lancaster III, EE169 HW-O	Lost without trace. W/O R. Gafford and six crew died.
101 Squadron	Lancaster III, JA863 SR-U2	Shot down over Hamburg by fighter (Maj. Hajo Herrmann, Stab/JG300). F/S D. P. Hurst and six crew died.
102 Squadron	Halifax II, JB864 DY-B	Shot down by fighter over Hamburg: three survived as

		PoWs, but pilot F/O G. McF. Clarke and three others died.
	Halifax 2, JD150 DY-A	Shot down by fighter (Fw. Hans Meissner, II/NJG3). Sgt G. H. Brown and six crew died.
106 Squadron	Lancaster I, ED303 ZN-	Lost without trace. Sgt E. G. McLeod and six crew died.
	Lancaster III, ED708 ZN-	Lost without trace. F/S J. B. Charters and six crew died.
156 Squadron	Lancaster III, EE178 GT-R	Shot down by fighter. At 13,500 feet the plane exploded, throwing pilot F/S G. W. Wilkins clear. All six others died.
	Lancaster III, JA709 GT-	Shot down into sea by fighter. F/O L. R. Crampton and six crew died.
207 Squadron	Lancaster I, W4962 EM-B Bar	Shot down by fighter (Maj. Walter Ehle, II/NJG1): two survived as PoWs, but pilot F/O C. Burne and four others died.
408 Squadron	Halifax II, DT749 EQ-O	Shot down by fighter (Lt Sachsenberg, II/NJG3): three survived as PoWs, but pilot F/L C. C. Stovel and four others died.
429 Squadron	Wellington X, JA114 AL-	Shot down by fighter near Neumünster. Pilot W/C J. A. Piddington and two others died, but two survived as PoWs.
467 Squadron	Lancaster I, W4946 PO-U	Shot down by fighter (Hptm. Hans Joachim Jabs, IV/NJG1), and crashed into sea. F/S J. T.

		Buchanan and six crew died.
Lancaster III, W5003 PO-H		Shot down by fighter: two survived as PoWs, but pilot P/O J. L. Carrington and four others died.

In addition four aircraft crashed in England:

7 Squadron	Stirling III, EF369 MG-Z	Lost power and crashed into a tree while preparing to land. Pilot P/O G. R. Wood and six crew all slightly injured.
15 Squadron	Stirling III, EF437 LS-Z	Hit by flak, and on return both engines cut out. Hit trees near airfield and crashed. Sgt D. Jackson and six crew injured, but not seriously.
76 Squadron	Halifax V, DK188 MP-J	Badly damaged by fighters, killing one and wounding two of the crew. On reaching England four crew bailed out, but pilot P/O W. E. Elder crash-landed at Shipham.
90 Squadron	Stirling III, BK693 WP-A	Damaged by flak. On return it swung off runway and crashed into parked Stirling. P/O R. Whitworth and crew escaped injury.

The following aircraft was lost on operations in the same area:

139 Squadron	Mosquito IV, DZ458 XD-	F/O E. S. A. Sniders and S/L K. G. Price both survived to become PoWs.

3rd RAF raid, 29 July 1943

German losses

I/NJG 3	Me110 G-4, No.5468	Crashed at Stukenborg, possibly after combat with Stirling of 90 Squadron. Crew unhurt.
III/NJG 3	Me110 G-4, No.6277	Ofw. W. Kurrek shot down near Lüneburg by Mosquito of 605 Squadron. Two men killed.
II/JG 300	FW190	Hptm. F. Angermann shot down over Hamburg, probably by Lancaster of 467 Squadron. Pilot killed.
	Me109	Uffz. H. Fritz shot down near Oldenburg, possibly by Lancaster of 467 Squadron. Pilot killed.

British losses

7 Squadron	Stirling III, EF364 MG-X	Lost without trace. P/O A. L. Forbes and seven crew died.
9 Squadron	Lancaster III, JA692 WS-D	Hit by flak and crashed in Hamburg area. F/L C. W. Fox and seven crew died.
35 Squadron	Halifax II, HR851 TL-T	Shot down by flak and fighter: two survived as PoWs, but pilot F/L H. C. Pexton and four others died.
	Halifax II, HR906 TL-L	Shot down by fighter. F/L W. L. Breckell survived as PoW, but pilot F/S R. Spooner and five others died.

51 Squadron	Halifax II, JD309 MH–	Shot down by night fighter over the sea. F/S A. Fletcher and six crew died.
57 Squadron	Lancaster III, ED616 DX–	Shot down by flak, crashed north Hamburg. P/O G. A. N. Parker and six crew died.
	Lancaster III, ED931 DX–C	Shot down by fighter and crashed at Tostedt. F/O B. G. N. Kennedy survived as PoW, but pilot F/S E.F. Allwright and five others died.
61 Squadron	Lancaster III, ED782 QR–	Shot down by fighter, crashed into sea near Heligoland. P/O J. M. Phillips and six crew died.
76 Squadron	Halifax V, ED244 MP–X Bar	Shot down by flak and fighter, crashed near Oberndorf: five PoWs, but pilot Sgt A. R. Bjercke and F/O C. Daniel died.
77 Squadron	Halifax II, JB956 KN–O	Shot down by fighter (Oblt Gerhard Kath, II/NJG3). F/S G. H. Sutton and seven crew died.
78 Squadron	Halifax II, JB798 EY–P	Hit by flak, crashed at Bad Oldesloe. F/S P. A. Fraser and six crew died.
	Halifax II, JD252 EY–W	Lost over sea. Sgt P. F. Snape and six crew died.
97 Squadron	Lancaster III, ED862 OF–P	Lost without trace. P/O D. J. Marks and six crew died.
	Lancaster III, EE172 OF–O	Shot down by fighter. P/O C. Shnier and six crew died.
102 Squadron	Halifax II, W7883 DY–R	Shot down by fighter (Lt Sachsenberg, 2/NJG3), crashed at Todesfelde. F/S Macquarie

		and six crew died.
	Halifax II, HR711 DY-C	Crashed in sea near Heligoland. Sgt J. S. Gaston and six crew died.
156 Squadron	Lancaster III, ED598 GT-	Shot down by fighter. F/L B. F. Smith and six crew died.
	Lancaster III, ED822 GT-	Shot down by fighter. F/S M. T. Hall and six crew died.
158 Squadron	Halifax II, JD277 NP-G	Shot down by fighter (Oblt Gerhard Raht, II/NJG3). F/O A. H. Boyle survived as PoW, but pilot F/S N. R. McDonald and five others died.
166 Squadron	Wellington X, HE810 AS-Y	Lost without trace. P/O Birbeck and four crew died.
214 Squadron	Stirling III, EF407 BU-A	Shot down by fighter over sea. F/O H. P. Shann and six crew died.
218 Squadron	Stirling III, BF578 HA-A	Shot down by flak and fighter (Uffz. Walter Rohlfing, III/NJG3), crashing at Ahrenswohlde. Pilot Sgt R. S. Pickard and Sgt E. C. Bray died, but five others survived as PoWs.
	Stirling III, EE895 HA-S	Hit by flak and crashed in east Hamburg. Sgt J. Clark and six crew died.
428 Squadron	Halifax V, DK239 NA-Q	Shot down by fighter, and exploded near Lüneburg. Sgt P. Demcoe survived as PoW, but pilot Sgt D. H. Bates and five others died.
432 Squadron	Wellington X, LN294 QO-E	Shot down by fighter and crashed near Lüneburg. Sgt J. H. Smith survived as PoW,

		but pilot W/C H. W. Kerby and three others died.
460 Squadron	Lancaster III, ED535 AR-	Shot down by fighter (Hptm. Egmont Prinz zur Lippe-Weissenfeld, III/NJG1). F/O A. J. Johnson and six crew died.
	Lancaster III, JA689 AR-	Shot down by fighter (Uffz. Lovenich, II/JG300). F/S H. L. Fuhrmann and six crew died.
467 Squadron	Lancaster III, ED534 PO-R	Lost without trace. F/S R. W. Park and six crew died.

NB All the general RAF summaries of this operation claim only twenty-seven planes were lost that night, but the squadron records clearly list the twenty-eight above.

In addition the following planes crashed in England:

15 Squadron	Stirling I, EF339 LS-Y	Crash-landed at Coltishall on return due to engine failure. F/L G. Bould and crew unhurt.
50 Squadron	Lancaster III, ED468 VN-	Crashed on take-off, and caught fire. Sgt E. W. A. Clarke and crew escaped unhurt.
83 Squadron	Lancaster III, R5625	Hit by flak over Hamburg. On return P/O K. A. King mistook Sibson for Wittering airfield and crashed off v. short runway. Crew unhurt.
90 Squadron	Stirling III, EE916 WP-F	Crashed shortly after take-off. F/L C. G. Crew and crew escaped injury.

4th RAF raid, 2 August 1943

German losses

II/NJG 3	Do217, No. 1493	Hptm. H. Baer shot down (possibly by Mosquito of 418 Squadron), crash-landed near Westerland. Crew injured.
	Do217N, No.1419	Fw. Krauter crashed at Wiemerstedt, possibly after collision with British bomber.

British losses

9 Squadron	Lancaster III, ED493 WS-A	Shot down by fighter (Ofw. Karl-Heinz Scherfling, IV/NJG1), crashed into sea off Dutch coast. Sgt D. Mackenzie and six crew died.
12 Squadron	Lancaster III, DV224, PH-G	Shot down by flak over Hamburg. F/O S. Norris and six crew died.
35 Squadron	Halifax II, HR863 TL-V	Crashed due to severe icing. Sgt A. Stephen survived as PoW, but pilot Sgt E. Solomon and five others died.
44 Squadron	Lancaster I, W4778 KM-T	Shot down by fighter (Hptm. Hans Joachim Jabs, IV/NJG1), crashed in the Waddenzee. Sgt P. L. Swan was picked up by German boat, but pilot Sgt A. R. Moffatt and five others died.
51 Squadron	Halifax II, HR859 MH-	Lost without trace (possibly shot down by Maj. Radusch of II/NJG3). Sgt E. R. Sklarchuk and six crew died.

57 Squadron	Lancaster III, JA696 DX-J	Crashed at Nindorf. Sgt A. C. Browning and six crew died.
61 Squadron	Lancaster III, W5000 QR-B	Lost without trace (possibly shot down by Lt Leube of I/NJG3). F/O R. Lyon and six crew died.
	Lancaster III, JA873 QR-	Shot down by fighter, crashed near Lüneburg. F/L B. McM. Laing and seven crew died.
75 Squadron	Stirling III, BF577 JN-M	Collided in air with Do217 flown by Fw. Krauter of II/NJG3. Crashed at Kaiser-Wilhelm-Koog. F/S J. A. Couper and six crew died.
	Stirling III, EH928 AA-A	Shot down by fighter (Hptm. Hans Joachim Jabs, IV/NJG1) and crashed into sea off Terschelling. P/O C. P. Bailie and seven crew died.
76 Squadron	Halifax V, EB249 MP-E	Crashed into woods at Hesedorf. F/O S. I. Dillon and six crew died.
100 Squadron	Lancaster III, ED688 HW-A	Shot down by fighter (Oblt Hermann Greiner, IV/NJG1), crashing in sea off Frisian Islands. W/O A. R. Wilden and six crew died.
	Lancaster III, ED705 HW-C	Shot down by fighter and crashed in sea near Heligoland. F/L R. R. Howgill and six crew died.
103 Squadron	Lancaster III, ED645 PM-F	Crashed south of Harburg. W/O J. S. Stoneman and six crew died.

	Lancaster III, ED922 PM-C	Crashed into the Elbe, off Herrenfeld. W/O R. Dash and six crew died.
115 Squadron	Lancaster II, DS673 KO-V	Shot down by fighter, crashed into sea off Wilhelmshaven. Sgt R. W. Bennett and six crew died.
	Lancaster II, DS685 KO-A	Lost without trace. F/S C. Button and six crew died.
	Lancaster II, DS715 KO-Q	Struck by lightning, fell out of control, crashed near Harburg. P/O R. J. Mosen and six crew died.
158 Squadron	Halifax II, HR751 NP-J	Hit by flak, crashed in east Hamburg. Sgt C. K. Davie and six crew bailed out, but Sgt R. B. Farmery's parachute failed to open and he died. All others became PoWs.
166 Squadron	Wellington X, HE464 AS-W	Shot down by fighter (Oblt Hermann Greiner, IV/NJG1), crashed in Waddenzee. Sgt H. Nash and four crew died.
214 Squadron	Stirling III, EF409 BU-V	Iced up and crashed in sea off Wilhelmshaven. Pilot Sgt A. A. R. McGarvey and Sgt A. B. Grainger survived to become PoWs, five others died.
300 Squadron	Wellington X, HF605 BH-P	Hit by flak, and forced down by severe icing. Pilot F/O Smyk and P/O T. S. Skalisz both died, three others survived to become PoWs.
305 Squadron	Wellington X, HZ467 SM-C	Shot down by fighter, crashed Elksop. F/S Grzeskowiak and four crew died.

405 Squadron	Halifax II, HR849 LQ-E	Hit by flak over Bremen. Sgt A. F. Gregory and six crew died.
	Halifax II, HR871 LQ-B	Hit by flak and storm, and eventually abandoned over Swedish territory. Sgt J. A. Philips and six crew were interned.
	Halifax II, HR917 LQ-G	Lost without trace (possibly shot down by Do217 of Hptm. R. Schönert of II/NJG5). F/L H. W. J. Dare and six crew died.
419 Squadron	Halifax II, DT798 VR-T	Crashed due to heavy icing and storm: three survived as PoWs, but pilot Sgt J. S. Sobin and three others died.
428 Squadron	Halifax V, EB212 NA-U	Lost over sea. P/O V. T. Sylvester and seven crew died.
	Halifax V, EB274 NA-H	Lost without trace (possibly shot down by Hptm. H. Jabs IV/NJG1). Sgt M. Chepil and seven crew died.
432 Squadron	Wellington X, HE906 QO-H	Crashed in the sea. P/O D. R. C. McDonald and four crew died.

In addition the following planes crashed in England:

7 Squadron	Stirling I, R9260 MG-O	Returned to Oakington with serious misfire. While landing the undercarriage collapsed. Pilot P/O W. E. Stenhouse and Sgt G. Breedon were injured, five others unharmed.

10 Squadron	Halifax II, DT792 ZA-O Farouk	Badly damaged by fighter, crashed on return to base. F/O J. G. Jenkins and crew unharmed.
57 Squadron	Lancaster III, LM322 DX-X	Crashed on take-off and caught fire. F/O E. T. Hodgkinson and crew unharmed.
166 Squadron	Wellington X, HF455	Crashed shortly after take-off. W/O J. A. C. Newman and crew unharmed.
300 Squadron	Wellington X, HE807 BH-O	Developed engine trouble after take-off and crashed in field near Worksop, before bursting into flames. F/L J. Spychala and four crew injured.

The following plane crashed on another operation in the same area:

166 Squadron	Wellington X, HE578 AS-G	Laying mines in Elbe estuary when lost without trace. W/O R. R. Burton and four crew died.

Appendix I

Tables of Statistics

RAF statistics

Date	Sorties	a/c attacking		Abortive sorties		Missing	Damage to bombers			Interceptions		Bombs carried (tons)	Tons dropped on Hbg (approx figures only)
		Hamburg	alternative	Over enemy territory	Not over enemy territory		Flak	Fighter	Other	Attacked	Not attacked		
24/25 July	791	728	6	1	45	12	20	2	9	7	42	2411.3	2300
27/28 July	787	722	6	2	42	17	29	5	7	15	67	2433.3	2300
29/30 July	777	699	6	2	45	28*	23	6	14	22	72	2396.3	2200
2/3 August	740	393	197	14	106	30	37	5	9	11	38	2048.1	1000
Total	**3095**	**2542**	**215**	**19**	**238**	**87**	**109**	**18**	**39**	**55**	**219**	**9289**	**7800**

*Total given in RAF Summary reports is 27, but squadron records show 28 losses on 29 July (see Appendix H)

[Source: Bomber Command reports on night operations, UK National Archives, AIR 14/3410]

US Bomb Group statistics – 25 July

Original target	Bomb Group	planes despatched	aborted	planes effective before losses	no. of bombs	altitude	planes lost	planes dmged	KIA	WIA	MIA	Claims dstryd	Claims prob. dstryd	Claims dmged	Actual kills
B&V	**379***	21	0	21	200×500lb	27,600	2	12	1	0	20	15	2	4	
	303	20	0	20	200×500lb	29,220	1	11	0	2	10	6	1	8	
	384	21	3	18	176×250lb	27,000	7	10	0	2	70	10	1	13	
Klöckner	91*	18	1	17	170×500lb	28,000	1	14	0	0	10	1	0	0	
	351	20	3	17	680×100lb	26,550	1	13	0	0	10	4	2	1	
	381	23	7	16	170×500lb	29,100	3	7	0	1	30	2	0	1	
	Totals	**123**	**14**	**109**	**482,000lb**		**15**	**67****	**1**	**5**	**150**	**38**	**6**	**27**	**6**

*Lead group
**Of these 67, 9 had major damage
[Source: 1st Bombardment Wing Report of Operations, 25 July 1943; US National Archives]

US Bomb Group statistics – 26 July

Original target	Bomb Group	planes despatched	aborted	planes effective before losses	no. of bombs	altitude	planes lost	planes dmged	KIA	WIA	MIA	Claims			Actual kills
												dstryd	prob. dstryd	dmged	
Klöckner	379	19	19	0	388 × 500 GP +	27,000	2		0	0	0	0	0	0	0
	303*	20	5	15			0		0	0	0	4	0	0	0
	384	20	20	0			0		0	0	0	0	0	0	0
B&V	91	20	11	9	234 × 250 IB	28,800	0		0	1	10	0	0	1	0
	351	24	9	15			0		0	1	0	0	0	0	0
	381*	18	3(1e/a)†	15			0		1	1	0	1	0	0	0
	Totals	121	67	54	126.25 tons		2	15	1	3	10	5	0	1	0

*Lead group

†e/a = enemy action

[Source: Bomber Command Narrative of Operations, 26 July 1943; US National Archives]

Appendix J
Aircraft Specifications

British bombers used on Hamburg

Vickers WELLINGTON X

Engines	crew	length	height	wing-span	max loaded weight	ceiling	cruising speed	max speed	bomb load (with fuel for distance)	bomb load (with fuel for distance)	armament
2	6	64.6 ft	17 ft	86.2 ft	36,500 lb	22,000 ft	165 mph	255 mph	4,500 lb (1,200 miles)	1,000 lb (2,550 miles)	8 × .303 guns

Short STIRLING III

4	7	87 ft	22.75 ft	90 ft	70,000 lb	17,000 ft	200 mph	270 mph	14,000 lb (590 miles)	2010 lb (3575 miles)	8 × .303 guns

Handley Page HALIFAX III

4	7	70.1 ft	20.75 ft	104 ft	50,000 lb	20,000 ft	225 mph	277 mph	13,000 lb (980 miles)	6,250 lb (2,005 miles)	10 × .303 guns

Avro LANCASTER I and III

4	7	68.9 ft	19.5 ft	102 ft	68,000 lb	20,000 ft	216 mph	266 mph	14,000 lb (1,660 miles)	–	8 × .303 guns

De Havilland MOSQUITO Mk IV

2	2	40.5 ft	12.5 ft	54.17 ft	21,462 lb	33,000 ft	265 mph	362 mph	2,000 lb (1,620 miles)	–	none

American bombers used on Hamburg

Boeing B-17 'Flying Fortress'

Engines	crew	length	height	wing-span	max loaded weight	ceiling	cruising speed	max speed	bomb load (with fuel for distance)	bomb load (with fuel for distance)	armament
4	10	74.7 ft	19.2 ft	103.8 ft	56,500 lb	37,500 ft	266 mph	299 mph	6,000 lb (1,300 miles)	–	11 × 0.5 guns

German day fighters defending Hamburg

Messerschmitt Me 109 G (Bf 109 G)

Engines	crew	length	height	wing-span	normal take-off weight	ceiling	cruising speed	max speed	range	bomb load (with fuel for distance)	armament
1	1	29 ft	8.2 ft	32.5 ft	7,491 lb	37,890 ft	260 mph	386 mph	620 miles	–	1 × 20/30 mm cannon 2 × 13 mm machine-guns

Focke-Wulf 190 A3

Engines	crew	length	height	wing-span	normal take-off weight	ceiling	cruising speed	max speed	range	bomb load (with fuel for distance)	armament
1	1	28.9 ft	13 ft	34.4 ft	8,738 lb	37,400 ft	260 mph	416 mph	497 miles	–	4 × 20 mm cannon 2 × 7.9 mm machine-guns

German night fighters defending Hamburg

Messerschmitt Me 110G (Bf110G)

Engines	crew	length	height	wing-span	normal take-off weight	ceiling	cruising speed	max speed	range	–	armament
2	3	42.8 ft	13.7 ft	53.4 ft	21,800 lb	33,000 ft	250 mph	342 mph	1,305 miles		2 × 30 mm cannon 2 × 20 mm cannon 2 × 7.9 mm machine-guns

Junkers Ju88C

Engines	crew	length	height	wing-span	normal take-off weight	ceiling	cruising speed	max speed	range	–	armament
2	2 or 3	49.4 ft	16.6 ft	65.8 ft	27,225 lb	32,480 ft	263 mph	307 mph	1,230 miles		3 × 20 mm cannon 3 × 7.9 mm machine-guns 1 × 13 mm machine-gun

Dornier Do217

Engines	crew	length	height	wing-span	normal take-off weight	ceiling	cruising speed	max speed	range	–	armament
2	2	58.57 ft	16.24 ft	63.3 ft	29,101 lb	29,200 ft	260 mph	320 mph	1,553 miles		4 × 20 mm cannon 4 × 7.9 mm machine-guns 1 × 13 mm machine-gun

Appendix K
Financial Cost of the Hamburg Bombings

British and American

Aeroplanes lost

USAAF	14	@ $500,000	$7,000,000
RAF	87	@ $350,000	$30,000,000
		Total	$37,000,000

Crews lost

USAAF	13	@ $120,000	$1,560,000
RAF	87	@ $58,000 (approx)	$5,000,000
		Total	$6,560,000

Gasoline consumed

USAAF	375,000 gals	@ 23c	$86,250
RAF	3,095,000 gals	@ 23c	$711,850
		Total	$798,100

Bombs dropped

USAAF	998	500#G.P.	@ $94	$93,800
	416	250#inc.	@ $75	$31,200
	680	100#inc.	@ $50	$34,000
RAF	9478	2000#G.P. (or equiv)	@ $200	$1,895,600
			Total	$2,054,600
			Total cost	$46,412,700

[Source: 'Cost of Destruction of Hamburg', Statistical Control Division, Office of Management Control, 1 September 1943; Air Force Historical Research Agency, Maxwell Air Base, Alabama, Microfilm A1107, 1654–6]

German

Damage to public buildings	140,000,000RM
Damage to military structures	48,000,000RM
Damage to stations, post offices and telephone exchanges	19,000,000RM
Damage to major industrial plants	200,000,000RM
Damage to residential housing and smaller plants	22,643,000,000RM
Total	23,050,000,000RM

Equivalent in US dollars (1943) $9,220,000,000

[Source: United States Strategic Bombing Survey, Hamburg Report]

Notes

The following abbreviations have been used throughout:

BBSU	British Bombing Survey Unit
BG	Bombardment Group
FZH	Forschungsstelle für Zeitgeschichte in Hamburg
Hamburg Police Report	*Secret Report by the Police President of Hamburg (as local Air Protection Leader) on the heavy air raids on Hamburg in July/August 1943 [Geheim. Bericht des Polizeipräsidenten in Hamburg als Örtlicher Luftschutzleiter über die schweren Grossluftangriffe auf Hamburg in Juli/August 1943]*
IWM	Imperial War Museum
NSDAP	Nationalsozialistische Deutsche Arbeiterpartei: (National Socialist German Workers Party or Nazi Party)
SPD	Sozialdemokratische Partei: Deutschlands (Social Democratic Party of Germany)
USSBS	United States Strategic Bombing Survey

Introduction

1 Friedrich Nietzsche, *Beyond Good and Evil* (London, 2003), maxim no. 146, p. 102.
2 Hans Erich Nossack, *Der Untergang* (Hamburg, 1981), pp. 18–19. Nietzsche's idea of gazing into an abyss was used as a central theme in this classic account of the Hamburg firestorm.
3 For a much longer discussion of this German reaction to the war, including Stig Dagerman's observations, see W. G. Sebald, *On the Natural History of Destruction*, trans. Anthea Bell (London, 2004).
4 According to the BBSU, Dresden suffered 1,681 acres of destruction,

as compared to Berlin's 6,427. In Hamburg, a much smaller city than Berlin, 6,200 acres were completely destroyed during the course of the war – 75 per cent of the city's total built-up area.

5 Coventry was attacked dozens of times during the war, but the only major attack occurred on 14–15 November 1940, when 600 people were killed and 800 injured. Casualties at Hamburg were some seventy-five times greater.

6 The exception, of course, was the Cuban missile crisis of 1962 – a threat that, thankfully, never materialized. During the Second World War, however, Cuba was an American dependency; and at the time of writing, more than fifteen years since the end of the Cold War, Cuba's ability to pose a threat to the United States has been vastly reduced.

Part One

1 City on the River

1 According to Eckart Klessmann, *Geschichte der Stadt Hamburg* (Hamburg, 2002), p. 413.

2 Major fires struck Hamburg in 1284, 1684, 1842 and 1943. See *ibid.*, pp. 38, 170, 393–406, 545. For the Great Fire of 1842, see also Hans Brunswig, *Feuersturm über Hamburg* (Stuttgart, 2003), pp. 129–34.

3 While the Hanseatic League was based around western Germany and the Baltic, it also had offices in cities as far away as Bruges, Amsterdam, Antwerp, Staveren, London, Bergen and Novgorod. See Klessmann, *Geschichte der Stadt Hamburg*, pp. 45–8.

4 For descriptions of these three fires, see *ibid.*, pp. 38, 170 and 545.

5 See Anna Brenken, *Hamburg: Metropole an Alster und Elbe* (Hamburg, 2001), p. 24; and Klessman, *Geschichte der Stadt Hamburg*, p. 228.

2 The Anglophile City

1 Wilfred Owen, 'Strange Meeting'. In this poem Owen describes a descent into a subconscious 'hell', where a forbidden empathy between the German and British enemies can at last be voiced.

2 Joseph Goebbels, *Die Tagebücher von Joseph Goebbels*, ed. Elke Fröhlich (München, 1993), vol. II, 12 August 1943.

3 See Eckard Klessmann, *Geschichte der Stadt Hamburg* (Hamburg, 2002), pp. 157–8.

4 For a fuller account of the city's involvement in the Napoleonic Wars, see David Chandler, *The Campaigns of Napoleon* (London, 2002), vol. II, pp. 133–4; vol. III, pp. 61–2, 90, 142. See also Klessmann, *Geschichte der Stadt Hamburg*, pp. 312–17, 349.

5 Klessmann, *Geschichte der Stadt Hamburg*, p. 414.

6 It was not only the rich who had close ties with Britain. For example, when Hamburg's dock workers went on strike in 1896 to protest against their shocking working conditions, British-based dock workers sent 30,000 Marks to Hamburg to support them. See *ibid*, p. 481.

7 For conditions in the slum districts of Hamburg, and also figures on emigration to the United States, see *ibid.*, pp. 442–50.

8 HAPAG were founded in 1847 by August Bolten, and began steam services across the Atlantic in 1856. See Anna Brenken, *Hamburg: Metropole an Alster und Elbe* (Hamburg, 2001), pp. 68–9.

9 Hamburg's international airport at Fühlsbuttel became a civil airfield in July 1912. During the First World War it temporarily became the headquarters of the German Army's Airship Division, before a more permanent station was erected at nearby Nordholz. See Basil Clarke, *The History of Airships* (London, 1961), pp. 56, 92.

10 The Canadians followed Britain into the war against Germany in 1914, while the United States remained neutral. For a description of Canadian fears that German Americans would attack the Canadian capital at Ottawa, see Lee Kennett, *A History of Strategic Bombing* (New York, 1982), p. 37.

3 City of Rebellion

1 Karl Marx and Friedrich Engels, *The Communist Manifesto*, trans. Samuel Moore (Harmondsworth, 1967), p. 83.

2 For a summary of events in Hamburg during the November 1918 revolution, see the website of the Museum für Hamburgische

Geschichte at http://www.hamburgmuseum.de. See also Eckart
Klessmann, *Geschichte der Stadt Hamburg*, (Hamburg 2002), pp. 535–6.

3 Gerhard Schultze-Pfälzer, *Hindenburg: Peace – War – Aftermath*
(London, 1931), p. 175.

4 General Sir Leslie Hollis, KCB, KBE, *Random Reminiscences*,
typescript memoir, IWM Department of Documents, 86/47/1.

5 See Klessmann, *Geschichte der Stadt Hamburg*, p. 538.

6 See Richard Bessel, *Nazism and War* (London, 2004), pp. 9–14. See
also Robert G. L. Waite, *Vanguard of Nazism: The Free Corps Movement
in Postwar Germany 1918–1933* (Cambridge, Mass., 1952).

7 See Klessmann, *Geschichte der Stadt Hamburg*, p. 538.

8 By the terms of the treaty of Versailles, Hamburg was required to hand
over the bulk of its merchant fleet to the Allies as war reparations, and
its trading links with overseas countries were suspended. See *ibid.*,
p. 559.

4 The Rise of the Nazis

1 Hermann Okraß, *Hamburg bleibt rot* (Hamburg, 1934), p. 207.

2 *Ibid.*, p. 202. Okraß gives a full rendition of the legend of this beer-
hall battle, which took place in the Am Stadtpark pub (pp. 201–7). An
English translation is available on the German Propaganda Archive
website at http://www.calvin.edu/academic/cas/gpa/okrass.htm

3 Eckard Klessmann, *Geschichte der Stadt Hamburg* (Hamburg, 2002),
p. 539.

4 In 1932 the NSDAP had 51 seats, the SPD had 46, and the KPD
just 26. See *ibid.*, p. 539.

5 Victor Klemperer, *I Shall Bear Witness: The Diaries of Victor Klemperer
1933–1941*, trans. Martin Chalmers (London, 1998), p. 6 (10 March
1933).

6 While the Nazis received almost 44 per cent of the vote in the
elections of March 1933, the Nazi vote in Hamburg never exceeded
39 per cent. See Klessmann, *Geschichte der Stadt Hamburg*, p. 539.

7 On 1 January 1935 the NSDAP had 46,500 members in Hamburg,
or 3.8 per cent of the population. Many more Hamburgers were
members of the party's sub-organizations. See the website of the

Museum für Hamburgische Geschichte at http://www.
hamburgmuseum.de / e / htm_e / textversion / t-20jhd-1-10.html (last
viewed 30 March 2005).

8 See Klessmann, *Geschichte der Stadt Hamburg*, p. 587.

9 'Gesetz zur Behebung der Not von Volk und Reich,' v.23.3.1933
(RGB 1.IS.173), available at http://www.documentarchiv.de/
ns.html

10 See 'Hamburg Police Battalions during the Second World War',
by Struan Robertson, at http://www1.uni-hamburg.de/rz3a035//
police101.html (last visited 4 August 2006).

11 Wiebke Stammers interview, IWM Sound Archive 9089/07.

12 *Ibid.* For some examples of such textbooks see the German Propaganda Archive at http://www.calvin.edu/academic/cas/gpa/
ww2era.htm

13 For more on the persecuted Hamburg jazz and swing movement,
see Detlev J. K. Peukert, *Inside Nazi Germany: Conformity, Opposition
and Racism in Everyday Life* (London, 1989), pp. 166–7, 199–201; see
also Earl R. Beck, *Under the Bombs: The German Home Front 1942–45*
(Lexington, 1986), pp. 17, 52–3.

14 This law was officially named the 'Law for the Protection of German Blood and German Honour', and was passed on 15 September
1935.

15 See Richard Bessel, *Nazism and War* (London, 2004), pp. 70–71.

16 Klaus Behnken (ed.), *Deutschland-Berichte der Sozialdemokratischen Par-
tei Deutschlands (SOPADE) 1934–1940* (Frankfurt am Main, 1980),
vol. 5, pp. 1352ff. See also Detlev J. K. Peukert, *Inside Nazi Germany:
Conformity, Opposition and Racism in Everyday Life* (London, 1989),
p. 59.

17 In the years after political parties were banned, the Communists and
the SPD tried repeatedly to establish underground movements to help
the victims of persecution. They were almost invariably found out
and destroyed, and many of the members were executed beside the
Holstenglacis. See 'Persecution and resistance in the National Socialist state' on the Museum für Hamburgische Geschichte website.

18 Mathilde Wolff-Mönckeberg, *On the Other Side*, trans. and ed. Ruth
Evans (London, 1979), pp. 27–8.

19 Quoted by Richard Overy, *War and Economy in the Third Reich* (Oxford, 1994), p. 189.

20 See Werner Johe, 'Im Glanz der Macht: Hitler in Groß-Hamburg' in Heinrich Erdmann (ed.), *Hamburg und Dresden in Dritten Reich: Bombenkrieg und Kriegsende* (Hamburg, 2000), p. 15; and 'Towards a War Economy' on the Museum für Hamburgische Geschichte website.

21 Along with Altona, Wandsbek and Harburg-Wilhelmsburg came the municipalities of Bergstedt, Billstedt, Bramfeld, Duvenstedt, Hummelsbüttel, Lemsahl-Mellingstedt, Lohbrügge, Poppenbüttel, Rahlstedt, Sasel, Steilshoop, Wellingsbüttel, Lokstedt, Cranz, Alten-werder, Preussisch-Finkenwerder, Fischbek, Frankop, Gut Moor, Kirchenwerder, Langenbek, Marmstorf, Neuenfeld, Neugraben, Neuland, Rönneburg, Sinstorf and Curslack. Conversely, Hamburg handed over several of its traditional outlying properties to *Land* Prussia, such as Cuxhaven, which lay sixty miles away at the mouth of the Elbe.

22 Hitler took a special interest in the construction of a new Hamburg, but his plans were never completed. See Albert Speer, *Inside the Third Reich* (London, 1970), p. 407. Illustrations of the architect's models can be found in Johe, 'Im Glanz der Macht', pp. 13–25.

23 Between 1925 and 1939 he came here no fewer than thirty-three times. In the last three years before the war he made six visits. See *ibid.*, p. 13.

24 The *Robert Ley* was originally launched as a *Kraft durch Freude* (the Nazi leisure organization 'Strength through Joy') ship, but it was so constructed that it could easily be converted into a troop carrier, as it was in 1939. See *ibid.*, pp. 15–16.

25 Speech quoted in the *Hamburger Tageblatt*, 14 February 1939. See also *ibid.*, p. 23.

5 *Hamburg Prepares for War*

1 Bertolt Brecht, 'To Those Born Later', from *Poems 1913–56* (London, 1987).

2 See Ian Kershaw, *Hitler, 1936–1945: Nemesis* (London, 2000),

pp. 200–221. Kershaw quotes, for example, William Shirer, an American correspondent in Berlin, who wrote at the end of August 1939 that he doubted the Nazis would actually go to war 'with a population so dead set against it'.

3 Mathilde Wolff-Mönckeberg, *On the Other Side*, trans. and ed. Ruth Evans (London, 1979), p. 27.

4 These figures and the accompanying description of air-raid precautions in Hamburg are taken from the Hamburg Police Report, UK National Archives, AIR 20/7287, p. 2.

5 *Ibid.*, pp. 1–12.

6 *Ibid.*, p. 99.

7 Eva Erna Coombes interview, IWM Sound Archive 16789/2.

8 Joseph Goebbels, *The Goebbels Diaries*, trans. and ed. Louis P. Lochner (London, 1948), 16 May 1943, p. 301.

9 Wolff-Mönckeberg, *On the Other Side*, p. 37. Despite the many warnings, there had only been seventy raids up to this point; see Hans Brunswig, *Feuersturm über Hamburg* (Stuttgart, 2003), p. 451.

10 For the conscription of women, restriction of vacations and longer working hours see Earl R. Beck, *Under the Bombs: The German Home Front 1942–45* (Lexington, 1986), pp. 40, 45; and Goebbels, *Diaries*, 25 January and 11 December 1942, pp. 15, 178.

11 Goebbels, *Diaries*, 23 April 1942, p. 131.

12 Wiebke Stammers interview, IWM Sound Archive 9089/07.

13 *Ibid.*

14 Else Baker interview, IWM Sound Archive 18582.

15 Hannah Kelson interview, IWM Sound Archive 15550/5.

16 Goebbels, *Diaries*, 17 April 1943, pp. 258–9.

17 Beck, *Under the Bombs*, p. 53.

18 For example, when the Americans and British defeated Rommel and turned their attention to Sicily, Mathilde Wolff-Mönckeberg expressed the hope that the British and Americans would hurry up and win the war: *On the Other Side*, p. 66.

19 Between July 1942 and July 1943 there were only fourteen raids on the city; most were merely nuisance raids performed by a handful of bombers. See Brunswig, *Feuersturm*, pp. 453–4.

20 Hamburg Police Report, pp. 1, 97. It is possible that the chief of

police wanted to deflect any blame from himself and those acting under him but (with a few exceptions only) the air-raid protection measures in Hamburg were exemplary. See Brunswig, *Feuersturm*, pp. 165–86.

21 Fredy Borck, 'Feuersturm über Rothenburgsort 1943' in Kerstin Hof (ed.), *Rothenburgsort 27/28 Juli 1943* (unpublished booklet, produced by Stadtteilinitiative Hamm e.V.), p. 11. Although I have not found any British record of a mission to drop such leaflets on Hamburg, many other German accounts attest to it. See, for example, Ilse Grass-mann, *Ausgebombt: Ein Hausfrauen-Kriegstagebuch von Ilsa Grassmann*, (Hamburg, 2003), pp. 9–10 (diary entry for 25–26 June 1943); and Wolff-Mönckeberg, *On the Other Side*, p. 65.

Part Two

6 A Brief History of Bombing

1 Primo Levi, 'Give us', *Collected Poems* (London, 1988), p. 68.

2 H. G. Wells, *The War in the Air, and Particularly how Mr. Bert Smallways Fared While it Lasted* (Leipzig, 1909), p. 312.

3 *Ibid.*, p. 186.

4 Gustaf Janson, 'A Vision of the Future', in I. F. Clarke (ed.), *The Tale of the Next Great War 1871–1914: Fictions of Future Warfare and Battles Still-to-come* (Liverpool, 1995), p. 279.

5 See the many examples in Clarke, *Next Great War*; Michael Paris, *Winged Warfare: The Literature and Theory of Aerial Warfare in Britain 1859–1917* (Manchester, 1992); and Lee Kennett, *A History of Strategic Bombing* (New York, 1982).

6 See Kennett, *Strategic Bombing*, p. 14.

7 In 1899, at the first Hague Peace Conference, Britain's Lord Wolseley refused to agree to a motion to ban aerial bombing because he believed it would shorten future wars and so reduce the total numbers of casualties in any conflict. Not only that, but fear of the effects of bombing would make nations hesitate about going to war in the first place. (See Sven Lindqvist, *A History of Bombing*, trans.

Linda Haverty Rugg (London, 2001), 58.) These claims were repeated eight years later by American commentators, such as Major George Squier of the US Signal Corps, who claimed that once politicians realized that aircraft could bypass the battle zone altogether – that the politicians could now become the target – they would be deterred from going to war in the first place. See Major George Squier, 'Present status of military aeronautics' (1907), reprinted in *Flight*, vol. 1, no. 9 (27 February 1909), p. 304. See also Paris, *Winged Warfare*, p. 164.

8 B. H. Liddell Hart, *Paris, or the Future War* (London, 1925), pp. 45–6.

9 Quoted in Andrew Boyle, *Trenchard: Man of Vision* (London, 1962), p. 229.

10 Quoted in the *New York Times*, 14 October 1917.

11 Boyle, *Trenchard* (London, 1962), p. 312.

12 Quoted in Max Hastings, *Bomber Command* (London, 1979), p. 46.

13 Leon Daudet, *La Guerre Totale* (Paris, 1918). Daudet is reputed to have coined the phrase 'total war'.

14 Giulio Douhet, *The Command of the Air*, trans. Dino Ferrari (London, 1943), p. 151.

15 Cicely Hamilton, *Theodore Savage* (London, 1922), p. 75.

16 Desmond Shaw, *Ragnarok* (London, 1926), p. 349.

17 J. F. C. Fuller, *The Reformation of War* (London, 1923), p. 70.

18 Douhet, *Command of the Air*, p. 52.

19 See Kennett, *Strategic Bombing*, p. 38, for a description of the air-raid scares in Ottawa and New York in 1918; and Sir Arthur Harris, *Bomber Offensive* (London, 1947), pp. 65–6, for the scares in 1942.

20 J. M. Spaight, *Air Power and the Cities* (London, 1930), p. 162.

21 Sir Malcolm Campbell, *The Peril from the Air* (London, 1937), pp. 54–5.

22 For the reader who is interested in how the international community has tried to restrict the use of various weapons and military practices, I strongly recommend Michael Howard (ed.), *Restraints on War* (Oxford, 1979). See also James Brown Scott (ed.), *The Hague Conventions of 1899 and 1907* (London, 1915).

23 For a brief description of this international conference, see Philip S. Meilinger, 'Clipping the Bomber's Wings: The Geneva Disarmament

Conference and the Royal Air Force 1932–34', *War in History* (1999), vol. 6, no. 3. See also Lindqvist, *Bombing* (London, 2001), pp. 116 and 140.

24 See Richard Bessel, *Nazism and War* (London, 2004), whose main thesis is that 'The ideology of Nazism was an ideology of war, which regarded peace merely as a preparation for war' (p. 1).

25 UK National Archives, AIR 41/40, Appendix 4, Roosevelt message, 3 September 1939.

26 Prime Minister Neville Chamberlain's speech to the House of Commons, 14 September 1939.

27 See Hastings, *Bomber Command*, p. 59.

28 Quoted in Robin Neillands, *The Bomber War* (London, 2001), p. 41.

29 See Hastings, *Bomber Command*, p. 64.

30 For a description of this 'ruchloser Terrorangriff auf die Zivilbevölkerung', see Hans Brunswig, *Feuersturm über Hamburg* (Stuttgart, 2003), pp. 43–6.

31 See Cajus Bekker, *The Luftwaffe War Diaries* trans. Frank Ziegler (New York, 1994), p. 172.

32 Hitler's speech in the Berliner Sportpalast, 4 September 1940, quoted in Uwe Bahnsen and Kerstin von Stürmer, *Die Stadt, die sterben sollte: Hamburg im Bombenkrieg, Juli 1943* (Hamburg, 2003), p. 72.

33 Sir Charles Webster and Noble Frankland, *The Strategic Air Offensive against Germany, 1939–1945* (London, 1961), vol.1, p.157.

34 These statistics are taken from John Ray, *The Second World War* (London, 1999), p. 95; and Neillands, *Bomber War*, p. 44.

35 See, for example, Churchill's speech, 15 July 1941, claiming that the people of London would certainly wish to 'mete out to the Germans the measure, and more than the measure, that they have meted out to us'; quoted in A. C. Grayling, *Among the Dead Cities* (London, 2006), p. 187.

7 The Grand Alliance

1 During the German Blitz on London, Sir Arthur Harris claims that he stood on the roof of the Air Ministry watching the fires and said, in an echo of this Biblical quote, 'Well, they are sowing the wind.'

Portal also swore at this time that 'the enemy would get the same and more of it'. See Sir Arthur Harris, *Bomber Offensive* (London, 1947), pp. 51–2.

2 Stanley Baldwin's famous quote about the bomber always getting through did not account for the difficulties of navigating at night and over thick cloud, which meant that the target was often not even found, let alone bombed. When the Butt Report was published in September 1941 it showed that even when the bombers found their targets only a third managed to bomb within five miles of it. See, for example, Robin Neillands, *The Bomber War* (London, 2001), p. 58.

3 Professor Pat Blackett, quoted in Max Hastings, *Bomber Command* (London, 1979), p. 111.

4 Quoted in *ibid.*, p. 120.

5 See Harris, *Bomber Offensive*, pp. 9–69.

6 Quoted in Hastings, *Bomber Command*, p. 135. Harris's memoirs have the politer version – 'tanks that ate hay and thereafter made noises like a horse', p. 24.

7 Harris, *Bomber Offensive*, p. 66.

8 Quoted in Hastings, *Bomber Command*, p. 135.

9 *Ibid*, p. 135.

10 Harris, *Bomber Offensive*, p. 52.

11 Harris, quoted in Hastings, *Bomber Command*, p. 147. The figure of 60 per cent was a British estimate from reconnaissance photographs – see Neillands, *The Bomber War*, p. 112; German estimates directly after the attack were as high as 80 per cent – see Joseph Goebbels, *The Goebbels Diaries*, trans. and ed. Louis P. Lochner (London, Hamish Hamilton, 1948), 31 March 1942, p. 109.

12 Goebbels, *Diaries*, 28 April 1942, p. 142.

13 These figures are taken from Hastings, *Bomber Command*, p. 152.

14 Their policy as regarded the Japanese was very different. The fire-bombing of Tokyo in 1945 owed much to the lessons the Americans had learned from observing British area bombing, and probably resulted in more casualties than Hamburg and Dresden put together.

15 See Roger A. Freeman, *The Mighty Eighth* (London, 2000), p. 1.

16 Towards the end of the war the Americans themselves began to

realize that their 'pickle-barrel' accuracy was a myth for these very reasons. See *Summary Report of the United States Strategic Bombing Survey (European Theatre)*, p. 4, UK National Archives, DSIR 23/15754 and online at http://www.ibiblio.org/hyperwar/AAF/USSBS/ETO-Summary.html

17 Quoted in Hastings, *Bomber Command*, p. 182.

18 Quoted in Neillands, *Bomber War*, p. 201.

19 The German rumours are reported in Earl R. Beck, *Under the Bombs: The German Home Front 1942–45* (Lexington, 1986), p. 59; the actual figures are taken from Neillands, *Bomber War*, pp. 218–21.

20 Mathilde Wolff-Mönckeberg, *On the Other Side*, trans. and ed. Ruth Evans (London, 1979), p. 65.

21 UK National Archives, AIR 24/257.

22 UK National Archives, PREM 3/11/8.

23 UK National Archives, PREM 3/11/8.

8 The British Plan

1 Theodore W. Adorno, *Minima Moralia: Reflexionen aus dem beschädigten Leben* (Frankfurt am Main, 1962), chapter 19, p. 42. Adorno's philosophical work, written during the war, is about the annihilation of the individual by society. His argument that technology only serves to distance us from our humanity applies equally to the new weapons employed by the Allies during the next few days and the civilian technologies of everyday life.

2 See the descriptions of Sir Arthur Harris's 'morning prayers' in Max Hastings, *Bomber Command* (London, 1979), pp. 247–9; for the specific meeting that morning, see Martin Middlebrook, *The Battle of Hamburg* (London, 1980), pp. 97–8; and Gordon Musgrove, *Operation Gomorrah* (London, 1981), p. 1.

3 Bomber Command Intelligence Narrative of Operations No. 649, UK National Archives, AIR 24/257.

4 D Form, 24/25 July 1943, UK National Archives, AIR 24/257.

5 Report on German Flak Towers, Flak Disarmament Branch, Air Division BAFO (December 1946), UK National Archives, AIR 55/158.

6 See David Irving, *The Rise and Fall of the Luftwaffe* (Boston, 1973), pp. 213–14.

9 *The First Strike*

1 John Webster, *The Duchess of Malfi*, ed. C. Vaughan (London, 1913), IV, ii, 254–5.
2 Quoted by Kevin Wilson, *Bomber Boys* (London, 2005), p. 245.
3 The average age of British bomber crews in 1944 was twenty-three, which means that those entering training were still twenty-one (an oft-quoted figure: see, for example, http://www.specialforces.co.uk/ airgunners2.htm). In the event, many crew members were much younger. Colin Harrison of 467 Squadron was a perfect example: he joined up at eighteen, and was still only twenty when he was flying over Hamburg. 'One minute I was a schoolboy wearing a cap, next minute they called me a man and put me in an aeroplane, next minute I'm a flight sergeant.' Interview with the author, 8 December 2004.
4 Bill McCrea, interview with the author, 8 December 2003; as a pilot with 57 Squadron, he took part in all four Hamburg raids in July and August 1943. See also his book *A Chequer-Board of Nights* (Preston, 2003), pp. 77–85.
5 This speech was exactly the same in briefings across the country. The advent of Window was considered such an important innovation that each intelligence officer was given an identical document that they were told to read out verbatim at briefing. See UK National Archives, AIR 24/257.
6 Colin Harrison, pilot in 467 Squadron, interview with the author, 8 December 2004.
7 Bill McCrea, interview with the author, 8 December 2004.
8 Letter to the author, 1 December 2004. Kenneth Hills's first operation with 9 Squadron was on the next Hamburg raid, on the night of 27 July 1943.
9 Quoted in Max Hastings, *Bomber Command* (London, 1979), p. 161.
10 While this job was usually allocated to the flight engineer, in some crews it would be the bomb-aimer or wireless operator.

11 See Martin Middlebrook, *The Battle of Hamburg* (London, 1980), p. 126.

12 *Ibid.*, p. 120.

13 For exact times of all air-raid alarms, see the Hamburg Police Report, UK National Archives, AIR 20/7287, p. 13.

14 The German 2nd Fighter Division (*Jagddivision*) had fighters stationed at Stade, Vechta, Wittmundhafen, Schleswig, Westerland, Wunstorf, Lüneburg, Grove, Kastrup, Aalborg, Jever, Husum, Oldenburg, Heligoland and Nordholz.

15 See Adolf Galland, *The First and the Last*, trans. Mervyn Savill (London, 1955), p. 209; Hastings, *Bomber Command*, p. 234; and Neillands, *The Bomber War* (London, 2001), p. 147.

16 Wilhelm Johnen, *Duel Under the Stars* (London, 1957), pp. 62–3.

17 UK National Archives, AIR 27/492. See also Middlebrook, *Battle of Hamburg*, p. 131.

18 See Mathilde Wolff-Mönckeberg, *On the Other Side*, trans. and ed. Ruth Evans (London, 1979), p. 61.

19 Colin Harrison interview. His bomb-aimer used to do this.

20 Middlebrook, *Battle of Hamburg*, p. 84. Middlebrook does not reveal his source for this information, but his numbers are backed up by a German website, www.lostplaces.de/flakhamburg, which has a map displaying the positions of each of the flak batteries in and around Hamburg (last viewed 1 December 2004).

21 Leonard Cooper, interview with the author, 19 November 2004.

22 Ted Edwards, interview with the author, 12 November 2004.

23 Leonard Bradfield, interview with the author, 20 October 2004.

24 Leonard Bradfield, who was also interviewed by Kevin Wilson, is quoted here from Wilson's book, *Bomber Boys* (London, 2005), p. 248.

25 A Wellington, piloted by George Ashplant of 166 Squadron, was shot down over Hamburg, and Flight Sergeant A. G. Ashley's 460 Squadron Lancaster was also shot down by flak near Cuxhaven. See W. R. Chorley, *Bomber Command Losses*, vol. 4 (1943), (Hersham, 2004), pp. 239–40.

26 Email to the author, 22 June 2004. See also Mel Rolfe, *Gunning for*

the Enemy: Wallace McIntosh, DFC and Bar, DFM (London, 2003), p. 65.

27 See Interim Report on the Attack on Hamburg, 24/25 July 1943, UK National Archives, AIR 14/3012.

28 Leonard Bradfield, interview.

29 Trevor Timperley, pilot in 156 Squadron (PFF), interview with the author, 17 November 2004.

30 75 Sqn Operational Record Book, UK National Archives, AIR 27/646.

31 Operation Summary, 'Royal Air Force Operations Record Book: Appendices', UK National Archives, AIR 24/257.

32 Bomber Command Intelligence Narrative of Operations No 649, 'Royal Air Force Operations Record Book: Appendices', UK National Archives, AIR 24/257.

33 See Gordon Musgrove, *Operation Gomorrah* (London, 1981), p. 37.

34 Grzeskowiak went missing nine days later on another Hamburg raid. It was his second operation. See UK National Archives, AIR 27/1672.

35 Wallace McIntosh quoted in Rolfe, *Gunning for the Enemy*, p. 65.

10 The Devastation Begins

1 Text from propaganda leaflet dropped on Germany in 1943, with the caption 'Das war Hamburg', courtesy of Lishman Easby, 100 Squadron, RAF.

2 For rumours about the Ruhr, see Mathilde Wolff-Mönckeberg, *On the Other Side* (London, 1979), p. 65; for rumours about exploding fountain pens see Joseph Goebbels, *The Goebbels Diaries*, trans. and ed. Louis P. Lochner (London, 1948), 20 May 1943, pp. 304–5.

3 While it was illegal in Germany to tune in to the BBC many people in Hamburg no longer trusted Nazi propaganda, and preferred foreign broadcasts to their own. See, for example, Earl R. Beck, *Under the Bombs: The German Home Front 1942–5* (Lexington, 1986), p. 37; Hiltgunt Zassenhaus, in Volker Hage (ed.), *Hamburg 1943: Literarische Zeugnisse Zum Feuersturm* (Frunkfurt am Main, 2003),

p. 167; Wiebke Stammers interview, IWM Sound Archive 9089/07.

4 See, for example, 'Die Festung Europa hat kein Dach', leaflet dropped on northern Germany late July 1943, sent to the author by Lishman Easby, 100 Squadron RAF. While it appears that these leaflets were not dropped directly on Hamburg until the attacks, there were widespread rumours that the RAF had dropped leaflets specifically mentioning the coming devastation of Hamburg. See Wolff-Mönckeberg, *On the Other Side*, p. 65; and Ilse Grassmann, *Ausgebombt: Ein Hausfrauen-Kriegstagebuch von Ilse Grassmann* (Hamburg, 2003), 25–26 June 1943, pp. 9–10.

5 Wolff-Mönckeberg, *On the Other Side*, p. 66. For the country-wide drop in morale, see also Goebbels, *Diaries*, 22 May 1943, p. 307.

6 Wolff-Mönckeberg, *On the Other Side*, p. 65. This rumour is uncannily similar to the arguments given by Sir Henry Tizard for not bombing Hamburg – see the end of chapter 7.

7 It was not until after the attacks that Kaufmann was finally able to announce to Goebbels that Hamburg's anglophile attitude was a thing of the past. See Joseph Goebbels, *Die Tagebücher von Joseph Goebbels*, ed. Elke Fröhlich (München, 1993), 12 August 1943.

8 See Charles H. V. Ebert, 'The Meteorological Factor in the Hamburg Fire Storm', in *Weatherwise*, vol.16, no. 2 (April 1963), pp. 70–75. The gentle breeze described was instrumental in bringing about the eventual firestorm on the night of 27/28 July.

9 Volker Böge and Jutta Deide-Lüchow, *Eimsbüttler Jugend im Krieg* (Hamburg, 2000), p. 21; Ludwig Faupel's diary, FZH 292–8, A–F.

10 See 'Frau W.' in Monika Sigmund *et al.* (eds), '*Man versuchte längs zu kommen, und man lebt ja noch . . .*' (Hamburg, 1996), p. 29.

11 Hamburg Police Report, p. 1, UK National Archives AIR 20/7287; Hans Brunswig, *Feuersturm über Hamburg* (Stuttgart, 2003), p. 187.

12 Wanda Chantler (née Wanziunia Cieniewska-Radziwill), interview with the author, 5 July 2004.

13 Hannah Kelson interview, IWM Sound Archive 15550/5. Tonight, fortunately for her, she was on holiday in a village just outside Hamburg, so missed the full force of the raid, although the noise and commotion were still enough to rouse her from her bed.

14 Martha Bührick, quoted in Renate Hauschild-Thiessen, *Unternehmen Gomorrha* (Hamburg, 1993), p. 25.

15 See, for example, Hanni Paulsen's description of a bunker, in Martin Middlebrook, *The Battle of Hamburg* (London, 1980), pp. 149–50.

16 Hans Erich Nossack, *Der Untergang* (Hamburg, 1981), p. 17.

17 *Ibid.*, p. 19.

18 *Ibid.*, p. 13.

19 Broadcast according to Georg Ahrens's nephew, Hans Ahrens, quoted in Renate Hauschild-Thiessen, *Die Hamburger Katastrophe vom Sommer 1943 in Augenzeugenberichten* (Hamburg, 1993), p. 18.

20 Interview with Frau M., St Pauli Archiv, 26 February 1993.

21 Letter to the *Hamburger Abendblatt*, 1 August 2003.

22 Joseph Goebbels, *The Goebbels Diaries*, trans. and ed. Louis P. Lochner (London, 1948), pp. 215 and 224.

23 Rudolf Schurig, quoted in Rudolf Wolter, *Erinnerung an Gomorrha* (Hamburg, 2003), p. 122.

24 *Ibid.*, p. 122.

25 Johann Ingw. Johannsen, typescript account, c/o Marga Ramcke, Ottensen Geschichtswerkstatt.

26 Hiltgunt Zassenhaus, 'Feuer vom Himmel', in Hage (ed.), *Hamburg 1943* (Frankfurt am Main, 2003), pp. 156–7.

27 Henni Klank, 'Operation Gomorrha', http://www.seniorennet-hamburg.de/zeitzeugen/vergessen/klank1.htm (last viewed 1 September 2005).

28 Hiltgunt Zassenhaus, in Hage, *Hamburg 1943*, p. 157.

29 *Ibid.*

30 Paul Elingshausen, typescript account, FZH 292–8, A–F.

31 Wanda Chantler interview.

32 'Klöntreff "Eimsbüttel im Feuersturm"', unpublished transcript of local-history group conversation, Galerie Morgenland/Geschichtwerkstatt, p. 4.

33 Liselotte Gerke, interview with the author, 6 April 2005.

34 Hamburg Police Report, p. 15, UK National Archives, AIR 20/7287. Later estimates put the death toll for this raid much higher, but it is almost impossible to say with any accuracy how many people died in any one particular raid during this intense period of attack.

35 Brunswig, *Feuersturm*, pp. 162, 167 and 175.

36 Erwin Garvens, in Hauschild-Thiessen, *Die Hamburger Katastrophe*,
    p. 33.

37 Paul Elingshausen, FZH 292–8, A–F.

38 Hamburg Police Report, p. 15.

39 *Ibid.*

40 See Wolten, *Erinnerung*, p. 125.

41 History of Luftgaukommando XI by General Flieger Wolff, Bundes-
    archiv, RL 19/424. See Martin Middlebrook, *The Battle of Hamburg*
    (London, 1980), pp. 154 and 168.

42 The single Wellington shot down belonged to 166 Squadron. See
    W. R. Chorley (ed.), *Bomber Command Losses*, vol. 4 (1943),
    (Hersham, 2004), p. 239.

43 Johannsen account.

44 *Ibid.*

45 Rolf   Arnold,   http://www.seniorennet-hamburg.de/zeitzeugen/
    vergessen/arnold1.php (last viewed 1 September 2005).

46 Wolff-Möncheberg, *On the Other Side*, pp.68–9.

47 Johannsen account.

48 Liselotte Gerke interview.

49 Franz Termer, in Hauschild-Thiessen, *Die Hamburger Katastrophe*,
    p. 47.

50 Pastor Schoene, of the Christuskirche in Eimsbüttel, quoted in
    Volker Böge and Jutta Deide-Lüchow, *Eimsbüttler Jugend im Krieg*
    (Hamburg, 1992), p. 24.

51 Total Damage Report, UK National Archives, AIR 40/426.

52 Reconnaissance report on photographs taken by RAF 542 Squadron,
    at 1200 hours, 27 July 1943, UK National Archives, AIR 24/257;
    see also Franz Termer, in Hauschild-Thiessen, *Die Hamburger
    Katastrophe*, p. 47.

53 Ilse Grassmann, *Ausgebombt*, p. 20.

54 Wolff-Mönckeberg, *On the Other Side*, p. 69.

55 *Ibid.*

56 Total Damage Report, UK National Archives, AIR 40/426.

57 Wanda Chantler interview.

58 See *Hamburger Zeitung*, 25 July 1943: 'Das Verlassen des Lufschut-

zortes Hamburg ist bis auf weiteres nur mit einer besonderen Genehmigung gestattet.'

59 Wolff-Mönckeberg, *On the Other Side*, pp. 69–70.

11 The Americans Join the Fray

1 Speech at Columbus, Ohio, 11 August 1880, in the *Ohio State Journal*, 12 August 1880; a photostat of the published speech can be found in Lloyd Lewis, *Sherman, Fighting Prophet* (New York, 1932), p. 637.

2 In March 1944, faced with high losses among his men, he was quoted as saying that he would like to bomb 'those damn cities' until 'there won't be a damn house left'. See Ronald Schaffer, *Wings of Judgement: American Bombing in World War II* (New York, 1985), p. 68.

3 Anderson flew with Flight-Lieutenant Garvey of 83 Squadron; see UK National Archives, AIR 27/687.

4 The Casablanca conference in January had designated U-boat manufacturers as the highest-priority target, but by the time of the Pointblank Directive in June this had taken second place to German air-force targets, such as Klöckner, which were 'second to none in immediate importance'. See W. F. Craven and J. L. Cate, *The Army Air Forces in World War II*, vol. II (Chicago, 1949), p. 666.

5 Group leader's report on mission, 25 June 1943, US National Archives, RG18, E7, Box 728, Folder 2. See also Roger A. Freeman, *The Mighty Eighth* (London, 1986), p. 52.

6 For details of this meteorological flight, see UK National Archives, AIR 29/867.

7 For all these plans, see VIII Bomber Command Report of Operations; and 1st Bombardment Wing Report of Operations, US National Archives, RG18, E7, Box 941. See also Martin Middlebrook, *The Battle of Hamburg* (London, 1980), pp. 176–80; and Gordon Musgrove, *Operation Gomorrah* (London, 1981), p. 56.

8 351st BG had arrived in Britain at the end of April and had flown its first mission in mid-May on Courtai (14 May); 379th BG had arrived around the same time (first mission, St Nazaire, 29 May); 381st BG and 384th BG had both arrived in May/June (first mission,

Antwerp, 22 June). See Roger A. Freeman, *The Mighty Eighth War Diary* (London and New York, 1981).

9 I had the great pleasure of working with Pierre Clostermann on the English translation of the millennium edition of his classic book *The Big Show*. This was one of his favourite anecdotes about the Americans he met during the war.

10 Walter K. Davis, interview with the author, 28 July 2005.

11 John F. Homan interview, 25 July 2002, Tape 3, side A, Oral History Archives of World War II, Rutgers University.

12 Samuel P. Fleming, *Flying with the Hell's Angels* (Spartanburg, 1992), pp. 49–50. In July 1943 the combat tour was still twenty-five missions.

13 Joseph E. Mutz interview, 9 February 2000, Tape 1, Side A, Reichelt Oral History Program, Florida State University. Mutz flew as armourer/gunner for the 95th BG in the Warnemünde wing on 25 July 1943.

14 The US Army was, of course, already engaged in Sicily and North Africa, but with nothing like the numbers that would be deployed the following year.

15 W. Scott Buist interview, 27 September 1995, Tape 1, Side A, New Brunswick History Department, Oral History Archives of World War II, Rutgers University.

12 *The Luftwaffe Strikes Back*

1 This is the popular form of the quotation. The actual quotation is 'No plan of operations extends with any certainty beyond the first encounter with the main enemy force.' See 'Über Strategie' in Helmuth von Moltke, *Moltkes Militärische Werke*, vol. II (Berlin, 1900), p. 291.

2 Philip P. Dreiseszun, 381st BG website, http://www.381st.org/ stories_dreiseszun.html (last viewed 5 April 2006).

3 Ironically, the Klöckner factory had already evacuated before these raids took place, so it was a much less important target than the USAAF thought. The plant had become a repair shop, with some continued production of gears and screws. See USSBS, *Economic*

Effects of the Air Offensive against German Cities: A Detailed Study of the Effects of Area Bombing on Hamburg, Germany (November 1945) p. 45, UK National Archives, AIR 48/19.

4 Quote and estimate of AA guns from 303rd BG 'Mission to Hamburg, Germany: Estimate', US National Archives, RG18, E7, Box 678, Folder 9. Martin Middlebrook lists the numbers of heavy flak guns in the city as 88mm, 166, 105mm, 96, and 128mm, 16 guns although he does not reveal his source for this information; see *The Battle of Hamburg* (London, 1980), p. 84. His numbers are backed up by the website http://www.lostplaces.de/flakhamburg (last viewed 1 December 2004), which says that in addition twenty 128mm guns and forty-eight 105mm guns were brought in on seventeen railway flak batteries.

5 Howard L. Cromwell, quoted in Middlebrook, *Battle of Hamburg*, p. 183.

6 Philip P. Dreiseszun, 381st BG website.

7 Edward Piech interview, c/o Shaun Illingworth, Oral History Archive of World War II, Rutgers University. Piech flew on the second Hamburg mission the following day, but his comments are relevant to both missions.

8 Sometimes it took even longer. For example, the 91st BG took off at 1320 but did not finally cross the English coast until 1437. See 91st BG immediate narrative, 26 July 1943, US National Archives, RG18, E7, Box 541, Folder 11.

9 Donald Hillenmayer interview, Oral History Archives of World War II, 11 September 2003, Tape 1, Side B, Rutgers University.

10 See Philip Dreiseszun, 381st BG website.

11 Albert S. Porter Jr interview, 9 February 2004, Tape 2, Side A, Oral History Archives of World War II, Rutgers University.

12 Edward Piech interview.

13 Lieutenant Darrell Gust, quoted in Brian D. O'Neill, *303rd Bombardment Group* (Oxford, 2003), pp. 61–2.

14 See Donald L Caldwell, *The JG26 War Diary*, vol.II (London, 1998), p. 121.

15 *Ibid.*

16 Walter K. Davis, interview with the author 28 July 2005.

17 *Ibid.*

18 381st BG War Diary, 25 July 1943. See 381st BG website.

19 Charles R. Bigler, quoted in Frank L. Betz and Kenneth H. Cassens (eds), *379th BG Anthology* (Paducah, 2000), p. 17. Bigler mentions this as happening on the Sunday raid, but it appears these events took place on the Saturday; see Derwyn D. Robb, *Shades of Kimbolton: A Narrative of 379th Bombardment Group* (San Angelo, 1981), 25 July 1943.

20 Major Kirk Mitchell, quoted in message from 303rd BG to 1st Bombardment Wing, 25 July 1943, US National Archives, RG18, E7, Box 678, Folder 9. For Mitchell's more realistic estimate, see US National Archives, RG18, E7, Box 406, Folder 9.

21 Staff Sergeant F. C. Thurman, quoted in PRO Report, US National Archives, RG18, E7, Box 1081, Folder 8. As the lead group, the 379th BG was supposed to drop its bombs first, but it was not uncommon for whole squadrons or groups to drop their bombs slightly before or slightly after they were supposed to. For example, within 303rd BG, the 360th Squadron dropped its bombs about fifteen seconds before their own group leader (see 303rd BG's mission report, US National Archives, RG18, E7, Box 406, Folder 9).

22 VIII Bomber Command Report of Operations, US National Archives, RG18, E7, Box 941. As the lead group, 379th BG should have been the first to drop their bombs, but it appears that the low group (384th BG) dropped fractionally earlier on this occasion.

23 As always, accurate numbers are difficult to pin down: different sources say different things. I have chosen to use the Reports of Operations of VIII Bomber Command and 1st Bombardment Wing as my main references here, and have used Roger Freeman's *The Mighty Eighth War Diary* (London, 1990), the standard work on the US Eighth Air Force, to fill in any gaps. Out of the ninety-four B-17s that managed to bomb Hamburg and return home, forty-six sustained flak damage.

24 See intercepted German radio messages for 25 July, UK National Archives, AIR 40–425.

25 Enemy Aircraft Attack Data for 103rd Provisional Bombardment Combat Wing, Mission, 25 July 1943, US National Archives, RG18, E7, Box 678, Folder 9.

26 See the Report of Operations for VIII Bomber Command, and for the 1st Bombardment Wing, US National Archives, RG18, E7, Box 941; and especially the Enemy Aircraft Attack Data for 103rd Provisional Bombardment Combat Wing, Mission, 25 July 1943, US National Archives, RG18, E7, Box 678, Folder 9.

27 See pencil charts, detailing attacks on each individual aircraft in 384th BG, US National Archives, RG18, E7, Box 1081, Folder 8.

28 Brad Summers, quoted in Ken Decker, *Memories of the 384th Bomb Group* (New York, 2005), p. 15.

29 *Ibid.*, p. 16.

30 Philip Dreiseszun, 381st BG website.

31 *Ibid.*

32 Again, there are some slight discrepancies in the numbers. The 103rd Provisional Bombardment Wing data show that 379th BG was attacked only fifteen times, but the pencil charts prepared by the bomb group suggest that there were twenty attacks, US National Archives, RG18, E7, Box 940, Folder 14. Likewise, the 103rd Wing data show eighty attacks on 384th BG, but the bomb group records suggest that there were 122, US National Archives, RG18, E7, Box 1081, Folder 8. The lower estimate in each case is more likely, since there was a tendency for double-counting in the bomb groups.

33 While this legend cannot be confirmed, Robert C. King, a B-24 pilot with 485th BG, claims he witnessed an instance where an American bomber from another group did this, and 'from that mission on the Luftwaffe targeted that group and annihilated it'. See Robert C. King interview, 30 November 1994, Oral History Archives of World War II, Tape 1, Side B, Rutgers University.

34 This man was believed to be the navigator in aircraft 075, flown by Lieutenant Hegewald. See the story of the attack on aircraft 883, US National Archives, RG18, E7, Box 1081, Folder 8.

35 *Ibid.*

36 Staff Sergeant George Ursta, Story of Attack, US National Archives, RG18, E7, Box 1081, Folder 8.

37 Unteroffizier Friedrich Abromeit, IV/NJG I, quoted in Middlebrook, *Battle of Hamburg*, p. 215.

38 See the summary of intercepted German radio messages, 25 July, UK National Archives, AIR 40/425.

39 See the description of Mission no. 53 on 303rd Bomb Group Association's CDRom, *The Molesworth Story* (2nd edition). *Yankee Doodle Dandy* was Aircraft 42–5264.

40 *Ibid.* Grimm's DFC was awarded in 1992, forty-seven years after the paperwork requesting it had been lost.

41 According to Paul Gordy, quoted in Middlebrook, *Battle of Hamburg*, p. 219.

13 The Americans Again

1 William Mitchell, *Winged Defense: The Development and Possibilities of Modern Air Power – Economic and Military* (New York, 1925), p. 163. Mitchell argued that to face such dangers required extraordinary moral qualities, so the fledgling US Air Force should only accept men of the highest calibre.

2 For all the statistics in the following paragraphs, except where otherwise stated, see VIII Bomber Command Report of Operations, and the 1st Bombardment Wing Report of Operations, US National Archives, RG18, E7, Box 941. Statistics for missions other than those to Hamburg are taken from Roger A. Freeman, *The Mighty Eighth War Diary* (London, 1990).

3 As always, there is some discrepancy in the statistics. These numbers are taken from the 1st Bombardment Wing Report of Operations for 25 July; but the VIII Bomber Command 'Analysis of Enemy Aircraft Encounters' for the day lists forty-four destroyed, six probables and twenty-eight damaged (a copy of this is available in the UK National Archives, AIR 40/425). Either way, the figures are greatly exaggerated.

4 These figures for German fighters lost are Martin Middlebrook's, in *The Battle of Hamburg* (London, 1980), p. 218. His figures are not always reliable (for example, he says the Americans claimed forty-one enemy aircraft destroyed when the 1st Bombardment Wing Report of Operations lists thirty-eight), but the main point still stands: American claims were vastly inflated.

5 See Freeman, *Mighty Eighth War Diary*, pp. 78–83 for exact figures: between 24 and 31 July 1943, the USAAF despatched 1672 B-17s and 261 B-26s to twenty-three different target areas.

6 See 303rd BG Report on Mission, 26 July 1943, US National Archives, RG18, E7, Box 729, Folder 2. See also VIII Bomber Command Narrative of Operations, Mission No. 77, US National Archives, RG18, E7, Box 941, Folder 1; and Middlebrook, *Battle of Hamburg*, pp. 223–4.

7 See VIII Bomber Command Narrative of Operations, Mission No. 77, US National Archives, RG18, E7, Box 941, Folder 1.

8 See 1st Bombardment Wing Narrative of Operations, 26 July 1943, US National Archives, RG18, E7, Box 941, Folder 1. For 351st BG reasons for abortive missions, see their Mission Summary Report, US National Archives, RG18, E7, Box 1002, Folder 22.

9 The flak, though intense, was 'somewhat lighter than that experienced in the raid of 25 July'. In 351st BG, for example, only a quarter of the planes were damaged by flak, compared with three-quarters the day before. See Group Leader's Narrative, and Mission Summary Report, 351st BG, 26 July 1943, US National Archives, RG18, E7, Box 1002, Folder 22.

10 See Immediate Interpretation Report, No. S.A.417, UK National Archives, AIR 40/426.

11 Martin Middlebrook claims wrongly that this plane was called *Local Girl* by her crew (see *Battle of Hamburg*, p. 231), but the 91st BG website is adamant that it was called *Nitemare*. See Lowell L. Getz's 2001 article 'Mary Ruth Memories of Mobile . . . We Still Remember' on the 91st Group website:http://www.91stbombgroup.com/maryruth4.htm (last viewed 22 June 2005). The name is backed up by Roger Freeman and David Osborne, *The B-17 Flying Fortress Story* (London, 1998), p. 88.

12 See US Bomber Command Narrative of Operations, and 351st BG's Teletype Field Order No. 172 A, Narrative, US National Archives RG18, E7, Box 1002, Folder 22.

14 *The Eye of the Storm*

1 Clem McCarthy, radio commentator, describing boxer Max Schmeling seconds before the 'Brown Bomber', Joe Louis, knocked him out in the famous 1938 world heavyweight title fight; quoted by David Margolick, *Beyond Glory: Joe Louis vs. Max Schmeling, and a World on the Brink* (London, 2005), p. 298.

2 These are British reconnaissance observations; see Immediate Interpretation Report Nos S.A. 410, and S.A. 417, UK National Archives, AIR 24/257; and Supplement to Immediate Interpretation Report No. K.1626, UK National Archives, AIR 40/426. American intelligence reports agree, but are slightly less detailed: see US Immediate Interpretation Report Nos 9 and 10, US National Archives, RG18, E7, Box 1040, Folder 3.

3 Rudolf Schurig, quoted in Rudolf Wolter, *Erinnerung an Gomorrha* (Hamburg, 2003), p. 125.

4 Hiltgunt Zassenhaus, quoted in Volker Hage (ed.), *Hamburg 1943 : Literarische Zeugnisse Zum Feuersturm* (Frankfurt am Main, 2003), p. 165.

5 See Hamburg damage report, UK National Archives, AIR 40/426; Hans Brunswig, *Feuersturm über Hamburg* (Stuttgart, 2003), pp. 198–9, 202–6; Martin Middlebrook, *The Battle of Hamburg* (London, 1980), pp. 153 and 155–9. See also eyewitness reports by, among others, Ilse Grassmann, Mathilde Wolff-Mönckeberg; and Erwin Garvens, Heinrich Reincke, Franz Termer and Vilma Mönckeberg-Kollmar, in Renate Hauschild-Thiessen, *Die Hamburger Katastrophe vom Sommer 1943 in Augenzeugenberichten* (Hamburg, 1993).

6 Hamburg Police Report, pp. 32–3, UK National Archives, AIR 20/7287.

7 Hiltgunt Zassenhaus, in Hage (ed.), *Hamburg 1943*, p. 162.

8 *Ibid.*, pp. 161–2.

9 Franz Termer, in Hauschild-Thiessen, *Die Hamburger Katastrophe* pp. 51–2.

10 'Klöntreff "Eimsbüttel im Feuersturm"', unpublished transcript of local-history group conversation, Galerie Morgenland/Geschichtwerkstatt, Sprecherin 2, p. 12.

11 Indeed, Goebbels himself had insisted that taxes on cinema and theatre tickets would not be raised for this very reason. See Joseph Goebbels, *The Goebbels Diaries*, trans. and ed. Louis P. Lochner (London, 1948), 20 March 1943, p. 241.

12 Many eyewitness reports from the time attest to how much the loss of these buildings distressed people. See, for example, the testimonies by Franz Termer and Vilma Mönckeberg-Kollmar, in Hauschild-Thiessen, *Die Hamburger Katastrophe*, pp. 50–51 and 54.

13 Official report, 'Bericht über die Katastrophennacht am 25.7.43 im Tierpark Carl Hagenbeck', sent to the author by Klaus Gille, Hagenbeck Tierpark.

14 Middlebrook claims the animals were killed by American bombs (see *Battle of Hamburg*, p. 201), but he misinterprets the account in the Hamburg Police Report: when it says they died in the 'second attack', it means the second *large* attack – i.e., the British night raid of 27/28 July.

15 For witnesses to the destruction of these churches, see Ilse Grassmann, *Ausgebombt: Ein Hausfrauen Kriegstagebuch von Ilse Grassmann* (Hamburg, 2003), p. 22; and Otto Johns and Heinrich Reincke, in Hauschild-Thiessen, *Die Hamburger Katastrophe*, pp. 28 and 39.

16 Hauptpastor Simon Schöffel in Hauschild-Thiessen, *Die Hamburger Katastrophe*, p. 23.

17 Hiltgunt Zassenhaus, in Hage (ed.), *Hamburg 1943*, p. 166; Erwin Garvens, in Hauschild-Thiessen, *Die Hamburger Katastrophe*, p. 37.

18 Erwin Garvens, in Hauschild-Thiessen, *Die Hamburger Katastrophe*, p. 37.

19 In the chaos that followed the first night of attacks, all the city's newspapers had been forced to merge into one: the *Hamburger Zeitung*. However, since there was only enough paper to print this on a single sheet, it was really only an emergency organ for getting essential messages to the people about where they could find rations and water, who could leave the city, and so on.

20 Renate Hauschild-Thiessen, *Unternehmen Gomorrha* (Hamburg, 1993), p. 25.

21 Fredy Borck, in Kerstin Hof (ed), *Rothenburgsort 27/28 Juli 1943*, p. 10.

22 'Die Papierblättchen sind harmlos', *Hamburger Zeitung*, 26 July 1943.

23 'Gegen sinnlose Gerüchte', *ibid.*, 27 July 1943.

24 For this, and the rest of the disaster plan, see the Hamburg Police Report, pp. 70–86 and Appendix 7.

25 Wilhelm Küper, in Hauschild-Thiessen, *Die Hamburger Katastrophe*, p. 30.

26 Erwin Garvens, in *ibid.*, pp. 36–7.

27 See Hamburg Police Report, p. 4; and *Hamburger Zeitung*, 26 July 1943.

28 See 'Sonderzuteilung an die Bevölkerung', and 'Warmes Essen durch Großküchen', *Hamburger Zeitung*, 25 and 26 July 1943.

29 Hamburg Police Report, p. 70.

15 Concentrated Bombing

1 Giulio Douhet, *The Command of the Air*, trans. Dino Ferrari (London, 1943), p. 22.

2 See 139 Squadron Operational Record Book, UK National Archives, AIR 27/960. Such nuisance raids were extremely effective. Earlier in the year Joseph Goebbels had complained that 'ten nuisance planes drove fifteen to eighteen million people out of bed': Joseph Goebbels, *The Goebbels Diaries*, trans. and ed. P. Lochner (London, 1948), 16 May 1943, p. 301. On this occasion, some German fire-fighters and rescue workers were convinced that the nuisance raid was specifically aimed at preventing their work. The fact that so many fire-fighters were still concentrated in the west of the city on the following night contributed to the catastrophe.

3 Bomber Command Intelligence Narrative of Operations No. 651, UK National Archives, AIR 24/257.

4 For that night's plan, see D Form, 27 July, UK National Archives, AIR 24/257.

5 See Martin Middlebrook, *The Battle of Hamburg* (London, 1980), pp. 235 and 242. While some bombers might indeed have strayed over this city, it was by no means part of the plan: the actual route took the bomber stream some sixteen miles or so to the west of Lübeck. See the RAF Operational Summary, UK National Archives, AIR 24/257.

6 On 24 July 724 planes dropped 1349.6 tons of high explosive, and 932 tons of incendiaries on Hamburg. On 27 July 721 planes dropped 1104.4 tons of high explosive, and 1174 tons of incendiaries. In the second attack, therefore, approximately the same number of planes dropped 245 tons less of high explosive, and 242 tons more of incendiaries. See Operational Summaries, UK National Archives, AIR 24/257.

7 See Middlebrook, *Battle of Hamburg*, p. 235.

8 UK National Archives, AIR 24/257.

9 Group Captains H. I. Edwards VC, from Binbrook; S. C. Elworthy, from Waddington; H. L. Patch, from Coningsby: A. D. Ross, from Middleton St George; and A. H. Willets, from Oakington.

10 See UK National Archives, AIR 27/687, which mentions General Anderson's trip to Essen, but not his flight to Hamburg. However, Middlebrook, who corresponded with Anderson, is adamant that he did indeed fly to Hamburg on this raid; see *Battle of Hamburg*, p. 236.

11 The rendezvous point that night was at 54.30N 07.00E.

12 Herrmann himself later implied that it was his disregard for the dangers of flying into their own flak that gave the *Wilde Sau* tactics their name; see Hajo Herrmann, *Bewegtes Leben* (Stuttgart, 1984), p. 256.

13 For the early history of Herrmann's 'Wild Boars', including the attack on Hamburg, see *ibid.*, chapters 10 and 11, pp. 247–307.

14 *Ibid.*, p. 273.

15 See Middlebrook, *Battle of Hamburg*, p. 248 and Gordon Musgrove, *Operation Gomorrah* (London, 1981), p. 73. According to the RAF Operational Record Book for the Pathfinder Force, the original plan was for red TIs to be used if, and only if, crews were 100 per cent sure that they had identified the correct aiming point. However, the final report seems to indicate that red TIs were never used. See UK National Archives, AIR 25/156, AIR 14/3410.

16 Other historians give very different figures for the number of aeroplanes that bombed Hamburg on this night. Max Hastings says 722, Robin Neillands 735, Martin Middlebrook 729, the American historian Earl R. Beck 722, the German historian Uwe Bahnsen 739. While this might look to the layman like errors of research, it is quite

common to find different figures in different official documents. For example, the US Strategic Bombing Survey gives the number that bombed as 739, citing the RAF Operational Summary as its source. However, the RAF summary (issued eight days after the attack) gives 736. To further complicate matters, the appendices of the RAF Operations Summary claim that only 721 aircraft bombed the *primary* target – presumably indicating that fifteen aircraft dropped their bombs on targets other than Hamburg, see Bomber Command Intelligence Narrative of Operations No. 651, UK National Archives, AIR 24/257. There are occasionally different figures in other sources, and it is easy to get bogged down in such minor details. Here, therefore, as elsewhere, I have assumed that the final official intelligence report issued by the force that carried out the attack is most likely to be accurate, and have given their figure accordingly, UK National Archives, AIR 14/3410. All figures quoted in this chapter are from the same source, unless otherwise specified.

17 Colin Harrison, interview with the author, 8 December 2004.

18 Bill McCrea, interview with the author, 8 December 2004.

19 Trevor Timperley, interview with the author, 17 November 2004.

20 Leonard Cooper, telephone interview with the author, 19 November 2004.

21 For a fuller description of this engagement, see Musgrove, *Operation Gomorrah*, p. 76.

22 According to Middlebrook, *Battle of Hamburg*, p. 245. The general claims, though not the exact time and altitude, are backed up by Peter Hinchliffe, in *The Other Battle* (Shrewsbury, 2001), p. 157.

23 Quoted by Middlebrook, *Battle of Hamburg*, pp. 246–7.

24 Ted Groom, telephone interview with the author, 11 November 2004.

25 F. H. Quick, private manuscript diary sent to the author.

16 Firestorm

1 John Milton, *Paradise Lost*, ed. Alastair Fowler, Book II, lines 170–76 (London, 1968), pp. 97–8. These words are spoken by Belial in the

depths of hell, as he warns the rebel angels of the possible consequences of embarking upon a new war.

2 See Chapter 10, in particular the passages relating to notes 47 and
48.

3 For a discussion of the different types of firestorm, see Gordon
Musgrove, *Operation Gomorrah* (London, 1981), pp. 102–3.

4 According to Hans Brunswig, who was the senior fire engineer on
duty that night, the wind speeds probably reached 75 metres
per second and more; see his *Feuersturm über Hamburg* (Stuttgart,
2003), p. 266. Charles H. V. Ebert prefers a lower estimate of about
50 metres per second; see his 'The meteorological factor in the
Hamburg Firestorm', in *Weatherwise*, vol. 16, no. 2 (April 1963),
p. 73.

5 Ebert, *Weatherwise*. For an eyewitness account, see the situation report
given by the head of FE-Bereitschaft 3/X ('Fire Service Stand-by
Crew 3/X'), quoted in Brunswig, *Feuersturm*, p. 232: the whirlwind
at the junction of Vogelweide and Volksdorfer Strasse in Eilbek was
strong enough to lift large pieces of burning wood from a timber
merchant and send them hurtling down the street.

6 Police engineers in Hamburg estimated that general temperatures
were more likely around 800°C – see Horatio Bond, *Fire and the Air
War* (Boston, 1946), p. 116. Bond was a US adviser to the USSBS
in Hamburg after the war.

7 For a much more detailed analysis of how weather conditions contributed to this firestorm, see Ebert, *Weatherwise*, pp. 70–75. According to Ebert, this firestorm is 'unmatched in the records'.

8 See Musgrove, *Operation Gomorrah*, p. 109; and Brunswig, *Feuersturm*,
pp. 271–2.

9 Indeed, the Germans took great pains to keep their findings about
the meteorological factor in such firestorms secret. *Ibid.*, p. 270.

10 For contemporary theories on the relative effectiveness of incendiary
bombing over high explosives, see J. Enrique Zanetti, *Fire from the
Air: The ABC of Incendiaries* (New York, 1941), particularly
pp. 49–50.

11 See the British official history, Solly Zuckerman's *The Strategic Air*

War Against Germany 1939–45: Report of the British Bombing Survey Unit (London, 1998), p. 6: 'the technical lessons of the German attacks on our cities were beginning to be driven home, and it was becoming more and more recognized that, in order to destroy built-up areas, incendiary bombs, and medium-charge and high-charge HE bombs were preferable to the types of load that we were then employing.' For British and German experiments and development of incendiaries, see also Frederick Taylor, *Dresden* (London, 2004), pp. 113–15.

12 Hamburg Police Report, p.16, UK National Archives, AIR 20/ 7287. The original German is in Erhard Klöss (ed.), *Der Luftkrieg über Deutschland 1939–45: Deutsche Berichte und Pressestimmen des neutralen Auslands*, p. 41.

13 Fredy Borck, quoted in Kerstin Hof (ed.), *Rothenburgsort 27/28 Juli 1943* (unpublished booklet, produced by Stadtteilinitiative Hamm e. V.), pp. 13–14.

14 Herbert Wulff, typescript account, FZH 292–8, T–Z.

15 See Hamburg Police Report, pp. 7–12, for a description of the city's fire-protection service.

16 *Ibid.*, p. 19.

17 See Zanetti, *Fire from the Air*, p. 20: 'On boards, flooring, beams, and other combustible but not easily ignitable material, phosphorus is not only useless but, as a matter of fact, somewhat fire retardant, since it forms a glassy deposit of phosphoric acid on exposed combustible material, thus protecting it from ignition.' Thermite, on the other hand, which is a mixture of metallic aluminium and iron oxide, burns at much higher temperatures, creating 'a white hot fluid that flows like water, setting fire to all combustible matter which it comes into contact with', p. 34.

18 Henni Klank, internet account, http://www.seniorennet-hamburg. de/zeitzeugen/vergessen/klank1.htm (last viewed 1 September 2005).

19 *Ibid.*

20 Erich Titschak, in Renate Hauschild-Thiessen, *Die Hamburger Katas-trophe vom Sommer 1943 in Augenzeugenberichten* (Hamburg, 1993), p. 77.

21 Titschak, in *ibid.*, p. 77.

22 Hans Jedlicka, typescript account, FZH 292–8, G–Kra.

23 In June 1953 a reporter for North German Radio interviewed a man who claimed that he and his colleagues often had to force people out of their cellars 'with kicks and slaps': see Uwe Bahnsen and Kerstin von Stürmer, *Die Stadt, die sterben sollte: Hamburg im Bomberkrieg* (Hamburg, 2003), p. 34. Musgrove, *Operation Gomorrah*, p. 97, also quotes a Herr Bey, who had had repeatedly to stop a woman running back into the cellar from which he'd just rescued her.

24 Wolf Biermann interview, *Der Spiegel*, 25 July 2003.

25 *Ibid.*

26 Hamburg Police Report, p. 66. To be safe in an open space that night, the space had to be more than three hundred metres in diameter.

27 Manuscript account by 'Albert H.', quoted in Hamburg secondary school project, 'Als die Bomben fielen: Hamburg vor 40 Jahren', Museum für Hamburgische Geschichte, HaIII 68, pp. 134–43.

28 Günther Severin (ed.), *Briefe an einen Pastor* (unpublished), letter 12.

29 Brunswig, *Feuersturm*, pp. 233–4. According to the Hamburg Police Report, the spraying of water upon fugitives as a protective 'cloak' while they escaped from burning houses was one of the most important lessons learned that night (p.39).

30 Quoted in Brunswig, *Feuersturm*, p. 226.

31 Ludwig Faupel, typescript account, FZH 292–8, A–F.

32 *Ibid.*

33 *Ibid.*

34 *Ibid.*

35 Wolf Biermann interview, *Der Spiegel*, 25 July 2003.

36 Ernst-Günther Haberland, quoted in Hof (ed.), *Rothenburgsort 27/28 Juli 1943*, p. 80.

37 See, for example, Heinrich Johannsen's description of being knocked on to his face by flying timber: Hamburg Police Report, appendix 10. A German transcript of this account is available in Klöss (ed.), *Der Luftkrieg*, pp. 84–7.

38 Anonymous letter from 1 August 1943, reproduced by Marcus

Petersen, in 'Den Feuersturm in Hamburg überlebt', *Die Heimat*, vol. 94, no. 3/4, March/April 1987.

39 Erika Wilken's account appears in Appendix 10 of the Hamburg Police Report: see Carl F. Miller (ed.), *Appendixes 8 through 19 to the Hamburg Police President's Report on the Large Scale Air Attacks on Hamburg, Germany, in World War II* (Stanford, December 1968), pp. 82–3: this translation differs very slightly from my own. The original German account has been reproduced in Klöss (ed.), *Der Luftkrieg*, pp. 80–84.

40 Italian author Curzio Malaparte propagated a gruesome story in the late 1940s about hundreds of people swimming in the waterways, unable to extinguish the phosphorus burning on their skin, who had to be put out of their misery by German soldiers. The story has been repeated by later historians, most notably the American author Martin Caidin, in *The Night Hamburg Died* (New York, 1960), pp. 142–7. For a comprehensive refutation of this urban myth, see Martin Middlebrook, *The Battle of Hamburg* (London, 1980), pp. 328–9 (following Brunswig, *Feuersturm*, pp. 244–5). Caidin claimed to have found corroborating evidence for the story, but both Middlebrook and Brunswig find this very difficult to believe. See also Bond, *Fire and the Air War*, p. 121.

41 Ben Witter interview, *The World at War*, Thames TV, translated by Ben Shephard, IWM Sound Archives 2916/01.

42 Hamburg Police Report, p. 22; Klöss (ed.), *Der Luftkrieg*, p. 55.

43 Heinz Masuch's letter to his parents, 28 August 1943, in Hauschild-Thiessen, *Die Hamburger Katastrophe*, pp. 98–9.

44 Wolf Biermann interview, *Der Spiegel*, 25 July 2003.

45 Brunswig, *Feuersturm*, pp. 214 and 216.

46 *Ibid.*, p. 266.

47 See the Hamburg Police Report, p. 16; see also the Fire Department's chronology of events, reproduced in Brunswig, *Feuersturm*, pp. 214–17.

48 *Ibid.*, map on pp. 218–19.

49 See the 'Town Plan of Hamburg', drawn up by the War Office in 1943, sheet 2.

50 Max Kipke, quoted in Kerstin Rasmußen and Gunnar Wulf (eds), *Es war ein unterirdischer Bunker* (Hamburg, 1996), p. 22.

51 Ruth Schramm, in *ibid.*, p. 32.

52 Else Lohse's letter to Frau Schilske in Kerstin Rasmußen and Gunnar Wulf (eds.), *Juli 1943: Hamburg erinnern sich* (Hamburg, 2001), p. 36.

53 Traute Koch, quoted in Middlebrook, *Battle of Hamburg* (London, 1980), p. 274. The description of the bodies being like tailor's dummies is fairly common: see also, for example, Waltraut Ahrens, in Hof (ed.), *Rothenburgsort 27/28 Juli 1943*, p. 43.

54 Erich Titschak, in Hauschild-Thiessen, *Die Hamburger Katastrophe*, p. 79.

55 Manuscript account by 'Maria K.', quoted in 'Als die Bomben fielen: Hamburg vor 40 Jahren', p. 163.

56 Hans Jedlicka, typescript account, FZH 292–8, G–Kra.

57 Herbert Wulff, typescript account, FZH 292–8, T–Z.

58 USSBS *Economic Effects of the Air Offensive Against German Cities: A Detailed Study of the Effects of Area Bombing on Hamburg, Germany*, tables on pp. 7a and 7e, UK National Archives, AIR 48/19.

59 Hamburg Police Report, p. 18.

60 Early estimates put the death toll in Hammerbrook at about 36 per cent of the total population. See Hans Rumpf, *The Bombing of Germany*, trans. Edward Fitzgerald (London, 1963), pp. 83–4.

61 The exact figure quoted in the USSBS, *Economic Effects*, p. 7a, was 37,439. UK National Archives, AIR 48/19.

62 Hamburg Police Report, p. 22; Klöss (ed.) *Der Luftkrieg*, p. 56.

63 'Maria K.', quoted in 'Als die Bomben fielen: Hamburg vor 40 Jahren', p. 163.

64 See Horatio Bond, 'Fire Casualties of the German Attacks', in Bond, *Fire and the Air War*, pp. 112–121. See also Professor Siegfried Gräff, *Tod im Luftangriff* (Hamburg, 1955), quoted at length in Klöss (ed.), *Der Luftkrieg*, particularly the report on the state of the corpses by 'W.W.', a fifty-one-year-old air-raid warden, p. 110.

65 'N.N.', quoted in Hauschild-Thiessen, *Die Hamburger Katastrophe*, p. 92.

66 This was typical of a heavy incendiary attack. See Rumpf, *The Bombing of Germany*, p. 157.

67 These bodies became the subject of intense scrutiny by pathologists during and after the war. The Hamburg Police Report Appendixes contain pathologists' reports into the various causes of death in the firestorm (see Appendix 15, pp. 213–39). See also the exhaustive study made by Professor Siegfried Gräff, quoted in Klöss (ed.) *Der Luftkrieg*, pp. 122–63, particularly pp. 128–40, on corpses found in basements.

68 Herbert Wulff, typescript account, FZH 292–8, T–Z.

69 Erich Titschak, in Hauschild-Thiessen, *Die Hamburger Katastrophe*, p. 79; Hans Jedlicka, FZH 292–8 G–Ha; Else Lohse in Rasmußen and Wulf (eds.), *Juli 1943*, p. 37.

70 Erika Wilken, quoted in the Hamburg Police Report, Appendix 10. A transcript of her report is available in Klöss (ed.), *Der Luftkrieg*, p. 83.

71 Henni Klank, Internet account.

17 The 'Terror of Hamburg'

1 Adolf Galland, *The First and the Last* (London, 1955), p. 239.

2 Joseph Goebbels, *Die Tagebücher von Joseph Goebbels*, vol. II, ed. Elke Fröhlich (München, 1993), 6 August 1943.

3 *Ibid.*, 29 July 1943.

4 Albert Speer, *Inside the Third Reich*, trans. Richard and Clare Winston (London, 1970), p. 389.

5 Milch, quoted in David Irving, *The Rise and Fall of the Luftwaffe* (Boston, 1973), p. 232.

6 *Ibid.*

7 Speer, *Inside the Third Reich*, pp. 388–9. From the flurry of meetings that took place around this time, it seems that Hitler was far more concerned about the situation in Italy in the wake of Mussolini's resignation. See Goebbels, *Tagebücher*, 24–29 July 1943.

8 *The Times*, 29 July 1943, pp. 4 and 6.

9 *Daily Express*, 31 July 1943, p. 1.

10 *New York Times*, 31 July 1943, p. 6; *New York Herald Tribune*, 1 August 1943, p. 10; *Washington Post*, 26 July 1943, p. 2.

11 Propaganda leaflet G61, Royal Air Force Museum.

12 Herr K. St., quoted in Volker Böge and Jutta Deide-Lüchow, *Eimsbüttler Jugend im Krieg* (Hamburg, 1992), p. 28.

13 See, for example, unpublished transcript of local-history group conversation, Galerie Morgenland/Geschichtswerkstatt, 'Klöntreff "Eimsbüttel im Feuersturm"', Sprecher 6, p. 13: 'Das habe ich von Frontsoldaten gehört, die haben mehrmals gesagt, an der Front sei es nicht so schlimm.' Contemporary reports agree. Directly after the attacks, for example, a reporter for the *Stockholm Aftonbladet* claimed that 'what the German people have been experiencing . . . is an ordeal by fire without example in history, which, in certain respects, is more horrible than the gigantic fight on the Eastern Front', quoted in *Daily Express*, 2 August 1943, p. 1.

14 Martha Bührich, in Renate Hauschild-Thiessen, *Unternehmen Gomorrha* (Hamburg, 1993), p. 25. Significantly, the soldier was talking about the first British night raid, which was not nearly so devastating as the second. Others also compare Hamburg to Stalingrad: see 'N.N.' and Adolf Freydag's accounts in Renate Hauschild-Thiessen, *Die Hamburger Katastrophe vom Sommer 1943 in Augenzeugenberichten*, pp. 189 and 215.

15 Giulio Douhet, *The Command of the Air*, trans. Dino Ferrari (London, 1943), p. 159.

16 For the official description of the evacuation that follows see the Hamburg Police Report, pp. 62 and 70–72, and appendices 7 and 14. See also Martin Middlebrook, *The Battle of Hamburg* (London, 1980), p. 278.

17 These figures are Middlebrook's, but unfortunately he does not give his source. Goebbels says in his diary that 300,000 loaves of bread were sent from Berlin (29 July 1943), and Georg Ahrens claimed that as many as 1,600,000 loaves were handed out; see Hauschild-Thiessen, *Die Hamburger Katastrophe*, p. 226.

18 See, for example, Ilse Grassmann's description of trying to leave Hamburg, in *Ausgebombt: Ein Hausfrauen-Kriegstagebuch von Ilse*

Grassmann (Hamburg, 2003), pp. 43–6; and the story told by a woman who found it almost impossible to hitch a lift out of the city even though she was heavily pregnant, in Uwe Bahnsen and Kerstin von Stürmer, *Die Stadt, die sterben sollte: Hamburg in Bombenkrieg, Juli 1943* (Hamburg 2003), p.35.

19 Heino Merck, in Hauschild-Thiessen, *Die Hamburger Katastrophe*, pp. 114–16.

20 Grassmann, *Ausgebombt*, p. 48.

21 Letter to Pastor Jürgen Wehrmann, in Günther Severin (ed.), *Briefe an einen Pastor* (unpublished).

22 Helmuth Saß, FZH 292–8, Ri–S.

23 Hans J. Massaquoi, 'Operation Gomorrha', in Volker Hage (ed.), *Hamburg 1943: Literarische Zeugnisse zum Feuersturm* (Frankfurt am Main, 2003), p. 265.

24 *Ibid.*, p. 262.

25 Lore Bünger, 'Operation Gomorrha', in Claus Günther (ed.), *erlebt – erkannt – erinnert: Zeitzeugen schreiben Geschichte(n) 1932–1952* (Hamburg, 2003), p. 134.

26 Hans Erich Nossack, *Der Untergang* (Hamburg, 1981), pp. 63–4.

27 *Ibid.*, p. 64.

28 Galland, *The First and the Last*, p. 239.

29 Margret Klauß, in Uwe Bahnsen and Kerstin von Stürmer, *Die Stadt*, p. 60.

30 Hiltgunt Zassenhaus, in Hage (ed.), *Hamburg 1943*, p. 160.

31 Hannah Hyde (née Voss) interview, IWM Sound Archive 10380/5.

32 *New York Times*, 6 August 1943, p. 4.

33 Friedrich Reck, *Tagebuch eines Verzweifelten* (Frankfurt am Main, 1994), 20 August 1943, p. 216.

34 Ernst-Günter Haberland, in Kerstin Hof (ed.), *Rothenburgsort 27/28 Juli 1943* (unpublished booklet), Stadtteilinitiative Hamm e. V., p. 80.

35 See, for example, W. G. Sebald, *On the Natural History of Destruction* (London, 2003), p. 89. Sebald interviewed a woman who had been a volunteer helper at Stralsund railway station when a train full of refugees arrived. Several of the women on it brought their dead children with them.

36 Nossack, *Der Untergang*, p. 26.

37 For the difficult relationships that developed between refugees and their hosts, see *ibid.*, pp. 26–9. For an example of one of the rare exceptions to the general charity extended to refugees, see FZH 292–8, T–H: when Herbert Wulff and his family knocked on a door in Lauenburg to ask if they could have some water to brew coffee the door was slammed in their faces with the words 'We are not a hotel!'

38 Story recounted by Luise Solmitz, in Hauschild-Thiessen, *Die Hamburger Katastrophe*, p. 62.

39 Erich Titschak, in *ibid.*, pp. 78–9.

40 Nossack, *Der Untergang*, p. 62.

41 'Berlin Given "3 Weeks to Live" by U.S.', *Daily Mail*, 4 August 1943, p. 1; RAF press conference, in *New York Herald Tribune*, 6 August 1943, p. 3.

42 Quoted in *Daily Express*, 2 August 1943, p. 1. See also *Daily Mail*, 2 August 1943, pp. 1 and 4; *The Times*, 2 August 1943, p. 4; *New York Times*, 2 August 1943, pp. 1 and 3; *Washington Post*, 2 August 1943, pp. 1 and 2.

43 See, for example, 'Stampede Out of Berlin Is Reported', *Washington Post*, 7 August 1943, pp. 1 and 2; 'German Life is Badly Disrupted by Air War', *New York Times*, 8 August 1943, p. E3; 'Evacuation of Berlin', *Manchester Guardian*, 7 August 1943, p. 5; 'Berlin Evacuates: Official', *Daily Express*, 2 August 1943, pp. 1 and 4.

44 While Harris firmly believed that the key to winning the war was the destruction of the Reich capital, it seems he thought this would happen by bombing the target in isolation, rather than by destroying it in quick succession with other cities. See his letter to Churchill, 3 November 1943: 'We can wreck Berlin from end to end if the USA will come in on it. It will cost us between 400 and 500 aircraft. It will cost Germany the war.' Quoted in Sir Charles Webster and Noble Frankland, *The Strategic Air Offensive Against Germany, 1939–1945*, vol. II (London, 1961), p. 48.

45 See Sir Arthur Harris's own memoirs, *Bomber Offensive* (London, 1947), p. 180.

18 Coup de Grâce

1 William Shakespeare, *Complete Works*, ed. Peter Alexander (London 1951), *Macbeth*, III, iv, 136–8.

2 See Hamburg Police Report, p. 34; and Hans Brunswig, *Feuersturm über Hamburg* (Stuttgart, 2003), p. 248.

3 Statistics taken from Roger Freeman, *The Mighty Eighth* (London, 1986), p. 66, and Roger Freeman, *The Mighty Eighth War Diary* (London, 1990), pp. 80–82.

4 While Zero Hour that night was fifteen minutes earlier than before, at 0045, the slightly shorter route meant that take-off and return times did not vary much from previous operations on Hamburg. The first turning point was at 54.30N 07.00E, exactly as it had been on 27 July. The second was at 54.03N 09.44E, very close to that of 24 July (53.55N 09.45E), which meant that the approach into Hamburg was only slightly more northerly than it had been on that night. After leaving the target their next turning point was at 53.23N 09.38E, which was about midway between those used on the two previous attacks (53.15N 10.00E on 24 July, and 53.20N 09.30E on 27 July). Once out at sea again, their final turning point was identical to that used on Tuesday, 27 July: 54.20N 07.00E. See the various operational plans of attack in UK National Archives, AIR 24/257.

5 The decoys were dropped at 53.33N 07.33E, about thirty miles along the coast west from Cuxhaven. For the route of these four Mosquitos see Interceptions/Tactics document no. 155/43 for 29/30 July, UK National Archives, AIR 24/257.

6 UK National Archives, AIR 27/796.

7 For a discussion of how the advent of Window changed German nightfighter tactics, see Peter Hinchliffe, *The Other Battle* (Shrewsbury, 2001), pp. 154–61.

8 The Hamburg Police Report mentions a 'second strong wave of bombers approaching from the direction of Bremen'. Martin Middlebrook also mentions that one of the Mosquitos attracted the attention of a German night fighter, but there is no record of this in the official summary of combats and enemy aircraft encountered: Interceptions/Tactics document no. 155/43, 29/30 July, UK National Archives,

AIR 24/257. See Martin Middlebrook, *The Battle of Hamburg* (London, 1980), p. 286.

9 The losses around the route markers were as follows: a 78 Squadron Halifax piloted by Sergeant R. Snape, a 61 Squadron Lancaster (Phillips), a Halifax from 51 Squadron (Fletcher), and a Halifax from 102 Squadron (Gaston) went down in the sea (the last one a long way from the route markers, as far south as Heligoland); a 7 Squadron Stirling (Forbes) and a 467 Squadron Lancaster (Park) were lost without trace, presumably also at sea; a Halifax from 158 Squadron (MacDonald) was shot down just after crossing the coast.

10 See Interceptions/Tactics document no. 155/43, 29/30 July, UK National Archives, AIR 24/257.

11 UK National Archives, AIR 27/796. Middlebrook also interviewed Pickles's navigator on this operation: *The Battle of Hamburg*, pp. 285–6.

12 These were probably Sutton's Halifax from 77 Squadron, Macquarie's Halifax from 102 Squadron and Fraser's Halifax from 78 Squadron. See W. R. Chorley, *Bomber Command Losses vol. 4 (1943)* (Hersham, 2004), pp. 247–51.

13 These were: a 9 Squadron Lancaster piloted by Flight Lieutenant C. W. Fox, a Wellington of 166 Squadron (Birbeck), and a Lancaster of 57 Squadron (Parker), which was one of those that arrived late on the target (see p. 256).

14 Six bombers were shot down by fighters in this area: a 460 Squadron Lancaster piloted by Flight Sergeant H. L. Fuhrmann, a 428 Squadron Halifax (Bates), a 432 Squadron Wellingon (Kerby), a 35 Squadron Halifax (Spooner), a 97 Squadron Lancaster (Schnier) and a 57 Squadron Lancaster (Allwright, who arrived late on target – see p. 256). Those hit by both flak and fighters were a Stirling of 218 Squadron, piloted by Sergeant J. Clark, a Halifax of 35 Squadron (Pexton) and a Stirling of 218 Squadron (Pickard).

15 Quoted by Middlebrook, *Battle of Hamburg*, p. 289.

16 According to the 1 Group summary. Fifty-eight of 1 Group's Lancasters were in the final wave of the attack so saw the fires when they were approaching their brightest. See UK National Archives, AIR 24/257.

17 Bill McCrea, *A Chequer-Board of Nights* (Preston, 2003), pp. 80–81.

18 All statistics quoted are from the RAF Operations Record Book Appendices, UK National Archives, AIR 24/257. The last four planes to be destroyed were probably from 76 Squadron (Bjercke), 460 Squadron (Johnson), 214 Squadron (Shann) and 97 Squadron (Marks).

19 Generaloberst Weise was originally sceptical of the worth of Herrmann's *Wilde Sau* fighters, but was won over by their successes in this period. For a discussion of this, and for the text of his order on 30 July 1943, see Hinchliffe, *Other Battle*, pp. 131 and 159–160.

20 See Hamburg Police Report, pp. 17, 35–6; and Erhard Klöss (ed.), *Der Luftkrieg über Deutschland 1939–1945: Deutsche Berichte und Pressestimmen des neutralen Auslands* (München, 1963), p. 43. For a picture of which areas were hit, see Plot of Night Photographs No. 172, taken 29/30 July 1943, UK National Archives, AIR 24/257.

21 Helmuth Saß, FZH 292–8, Ri–S.

22 *Ibid.*

23 See Carl F. Miller (ed.), *Appendixes 8 through 19 to the Hamburg Police President's Report on the Large Scale Air Attacks on Hamburg, Germany, in World War II* (Stanford, December 1968), Appendix 19, sheet 28, pp. 405–7. See also Hans Brunswig, *Feuersturm über Hamburg* (Stuttgart, 2003), p. 257.

24 A monument to these 370 people stands today in the central reservation of Hamburgerstrasse, close to a huge new shopping centre.

25 In Günther Severin (ed.), *Briefe an einen Pastor* (unpublished), letter 43.

26 *Ibid.*

27 Hans J. Massaquoi, 'Operation Gomorrha', in Volker Hage (ed.), *Hamburg 1943: Literarische Zeugnisse Zum Feuersturm* (Frankfurt am Main, 2003), p. 261.

28 Horatio Bond, who handled fire-damage analysis for the Physical Damage Division of the USSBS, estimated 800 died – see his *Fire and the Air War* (Boston, 1946), p. 86. Uwe Bahnsen and Kerstin von Stürmer estimate 1,000–5,000, in *Die Stadt, die sterben sollte: Hamburg im Bombenkrieg, Juli 1943* (Hamburg 2003), p. 54.

29 Adolf Pauly, in Severin (ed.), *Briefe an einen Pastor*, Letter 43.

19 The Tempest

1 William Shakespeare, *Complete Works*, ed. Peter Alexander (London, 1951), *Julius Caesar*, I, iii, 46–52: Cassius tries to convince Casca that the terrible thunderstorm over Rome is a good omen.

2 Hans Erich Nossack, *Der Untergang* (Hamburg, 1981), p. 69.

3 See Hamburg Police Report, pp. 70–72. The four special hospital trains were destroyed in the night raid of 29 July.

4 Wanda Chantler (née Wanziunia Cieniewska-Radziwill), interview with the author, 5 July 2004.

5 Hamburg Police Report, p. 21. The German text is reproduced in Erhard Klöss (ed.), *Der Luftkrieg über Deutschland 1939–1945: Deutsche Berichte und Pressestimmen des neutralen Auslands* (München, 1963), p. 53.

6 Franz Termer, in Renate Hauschild-Thiessen, *Die Hamburger Katastrophe vom Sommer 1943 in Augenzeugenberichten* (Hamburg, 1993), p. 175.

7 On 30 July 1943 Harris split his force into three for raids on Turin and Genoa in northern Italy, and Remscheid in the Ruhr valley. The Italian raids were called off by the Air Ministry at short notice, so only the Remscheid raid went ahead. See UK National Archives, AIR 24/257.

8 Night Raid Report no. 391, UK National Archives, AIR 14/3410.

9 Operations Record Book of 1409 Met. Flight, UK National Archives, AIR 29/867.

10 Operations Record Book of 83 Squadron, Pathfinder Force, UK National Archives, AIR 27/687.

11 UK National Archives AIR 27/538.

12 These were a 7 Squadron Stirling, piloted by Pilot Officer W. E. Stenhouse, whose undercarriage collapsed on landing; and a 300 Squadron Wellington of the Polish Air Force, which burst into flames when Flight Lieutenant J. Spychala was forced to crash-land in a field in Nottinghamshire. See UK National Archives, AIR 27/1657 and AIR 27/100. See also W. R. Chorley, *Bomber Command Losses vol. 4 (1943)* (Hersham, 2004), pp. 254 and 258.

13 Bill McCrea, *A Chequer-Board of Nights* (Preston, 2003), p. 82.

14 Typescript diary of Major J. K. Christie, 2–3 August 1943, RAF Museum Hendon, MF10016/5. Christie's rank was a Norwegian one.

15 McCrea, *Chequer-Board*, p. 82.

16 Colin Harrison, interview with the author, 8 December 2004. James Sullivan, interview with the author, 9 December 2004.

17 Sergeant C. C. Leeming, 620 Squadron, quoted in Martin Middlebrook, *The Battle of Hamburg* (London, 1980), p. 310.

18 Ted Groom, 460 Squadron, interview with the author, 11 November 2004.

19 Manuscript diary of Sergeant Dennis George Eli Brookes, RAF Museum Hendon, X001–3536/010.

20 UK National Archives, AIR 27/203. See also Gordon Musgrove, *Operation Gomorrah* (London, 1981), p. 153.

21 Sergeant A. Stephen, in Middlebrook, *Battle of Hamburg*, pp. 312–13.

22 These were: a 35 Squadron Halifax, piloted by Sergeant E. Solomon (of which Sergeant Stephen was a crew member), a 214 Squadron Stirling (McGarvey), a 300 Squadron Wellington (Smyk), and a 419 Squadron Halifax (Sobin). All these planes had survivors to testify to the fact that ice brought them down. Several others were lost without trace, and it is likely that some were also victims of the conditions.

23 This was a Lancaster of 115 Squadron piloted by Pilot Officer R. J. Mosen. See Chorley, *Bomber Command Losses*, p. 257.

24 I.e. 3rd *Gruppe* of 1st Nachtjagdgeschwader. There are no accurate equivalents to German units in the RAF or the USAAF; however, this can be loosely translated into British terms as 3 Squadron of No. 1 Night Fighter Group, or in American terms as 3rd Group of 1st Bombardment Wing. See Appendix D, page 367.

25 Wilhelm Johnen, *Duel Under the Stars* (Manchester, 1994), p. 73.

26 There are several instances of this happening on that night. For example, Leonard Cooper's 7 Squadron plane was attacked five times by a pair of night fighters before his pilot managed to lose them (interview with the author, 19 November 2004); Flight Lieutenant C. M. Shannon's 76 Squadron plane was approached three times by the same Messerschmitt before losing it – see Gordon Musgrove, *Operation Gomorrah* (London, 1981), p. 151.

27 See Chorley, *Bomber Command Losses*, p. 256.

28 These four are: a 12 Squadron Lancaster piloted by Flight Officer
   S. Norris, a 158 Squadron Halifax (Davie), and two 405 Squadron
   Halifaxes (Phillips and Gregory). *Ibid.*, pp. 255–8.

29 Rudolf Schurig, quoted in Rudolf Wolter, *Erinnerung an Gomorrha*
   (Hamburg, 2003), pp. 125, 131–2; Schurig corroborates both the
   figures and the sentiments in Renate Hauschild-Thiessen's *Die Hamburger Katastrophe vom Sommer 1943 in Augenzeugenberichten* (Hamburg,
   1993), p. 200.

30 For Peter Swan's own description of his ordeal, see Kevin Wilson,
   Bomber Boys (London, 2005), pp. 276–8.

31 Trevor Timperley, interview with the author, 17 November 2004.

32 Colin Harrison, interview with the author, 8 December 2004.

33 Bill McCrea, interview with the author, 8 December 2004.

34 This figure does not include the 57 Squadron Lancaster written off
   on take-off, but it does include a Wellington of 166 Squadron
   (Burton) that was lost while laying mines in the Elbe estuary. See
   Chorley, *Bomber Command Losses*, pp. 254–9.

35 UK National Archives, AIR 14/3410.

36 Hamburg Police Report, p. 17; Klöss (ed.), *Der Luftkrieg*, pp. 43–4.

37 See, for example, Waldemar Hansen's, Friedrich Sparmann's, Helene
   Hadenfeldt's and N.N.'s accounts in Hauschild-Thiessen, *Die Hamburger Katastrophe*, pp. 169, 182, 183–4, 186–8.

38 Hamburg Police Report, pp. 36–7.

Part Three

20 City of the Dead

1 Dante Alighieri, *The Divine Comedy of Dante Alighieri*, vol I: Inferno,
  canto 28, lines 1–3, trans. and ed. Robert M. Durling (New York,
  1996). This canto describes the beginning of Dante's final descent
  through the ninth circle of hell to its frozen core. Dante goes on to
  say, 'It is no task to take in jest, that of describing the bottom of the
  universe' (canto 32, lines 7–8); sentiments that I could not help but
  keep with me as I wrote this chapter.

2 For statistics on damage to the harbour installations, see USSBS, *Economic Effects of the Air Offensive against German Cities: A Detailed study of the Effects of Area Bombing on Hamburg, Germany* (November 1945), p. 12.

3 Hamburg Police Report, p. 37.

4 Interview with Annegret Hennings, in Kerstin Rasmußen and Gunnar Wulf (eds), *Es war ja Krieg* (Hamburg, 1993), p. 94.

5 Gretl Büttner, in Carl F. Miller (ed.), *Appendixes 8 through 19 to the Hamburg Police President's Report on the Large Scale Attacks on Hamburg, Germany, in World War II* (Stanford, December 1968), Appendix 10, pp. 119–20, although my translation differs very slightly. Erhard Klöss (ed.) *Der Luftkrieg über Deutschland 1939–1945: Deutsche Berichte und Pressestimmen des neutralen Auslands* gives the original German, pp. 104–5.

6 Hamburg Police Report, p. 43.

7 *Ibid.*, pp. 72–3, 75.

8 Ludwig Faupel, typescript account, FZH 292–8, A–F, p. 8.

9 See Luise Solmitz's diary, 17 August 1943, in Renate Hauschild-Thiessen, *Die Hamburger Katastrophe vom Sommer 1943 in Augenzeugen-berichten* (Hamburg, 1993), p. 343; see also Hans Erich Nossack, *Der Untergang*, p. 99.

10 Hamburg Police Report, p. 74.

11 Jan Melsen, quoted in Ulrike Jureit and Beate Meyer (eds), *Verlet-zungen: Lebensgeschichtliche Verarbeitung von Kriegserfahrungen* (Ham-burg, 1994), pp. 149–50.

12 *Ibid.*, p. 150.

13 Hamburg Police Report, p. 22.

14 *Die Zeit*, 30 July 1993.

15 Ben Witter interview for Thames Television's *The World at War*, IWM Sound Archive 2916/01. This quote has been lightly edited, but only to remove repetition of the same phrases.

16 Jan Melsen, in Jureit and Meyer (eds), *Verletzungen*, p. 151.

17 Ben Witter interview for Thames Television's *The World at War*.

18 *Hamburger Zeitung*, 29 July, 1 August and 15 August 1943. See also Hamburg Police Report, pp. 4, 82–3; and Miller (ed.), *Appendixes*, Appendix 17.

19 See Hamburg Police Report, p. 82.

20 Mathilde Wolff-Mönckeberg, *On the Other Side*, pp. 76 and 80.

21 Nossack, *Der Untergang*, pp. 99–100.

22 See, for example, Herman Sieveking, in Hauschild-Thiessen, *Die Hamburger Katastrophe*, p. 299.

23 Gretl Büttner, in Miller (ed.) *Appendixes*, Appendix 10, p. 119. The original German account has been reproduced in Klöss (ed.), *Der Luftkrieg*, p. 104.

24 Nossack, *Der Untergang*, p. 68.

25 *Ibid.*, pp. 72–3.

26 Hamburg Police Report, p. 79.

27 *Ibid.*, p. 76.

28 USSBS, *Economic Effects*, p.7a.

29 See contemporary photographs of Gothenstrasse.

30 There is perhaps some truth in this rumour – the Hamburg Police Report mentions it, and Liselotte Gerke, whom I interviewed, said that this happened to her. She was convinced for months that it was a sort of divine punishment for entering the forbidden area.

31 Nossack, *Der Untergang*, p. 99. According to police pathologists this was unlikely to be true, at least in the early days (Miller (ed.), *Appendixes*, Appendix 15, p. 211), and I have not come across any first-hand accounts describing such scenes.

32 See Martin Caidin, *The Night Hamburg Died* (London, 1966), pp. 142–7, and the refutation of this myth in Martin Middlebrook, *The Battle of Hamburg* (London, 1980), pp. 328–9 and Hans Brunswig, *Feuersturm über Hamburg* (Stuttgart, 1983), pp. 244–5.

33 See Nossack, *Der Untergang*, p. 98 for rumours. See USSBS, *Economic Effects*, p. 7a for probable number of deaths.

21 Survival

1 The words of the angels to Lot, as they saved him from the destruction of Sodom and Gomorrah. Lot's wife did look back, and as a consequence was turned into a pillar of salt.

2 Hans Erich Nossack, *Der Untergang* (Hamburg, 1981), p. 136.

3 René Ratouis, *Mémoires de guerre d'un non-combattant* (Paris, 2003), p. 117.

4 According to the situation report of the head welfare officer at the end of September 1943, cellars everywhere were overflowing with people, and families were often forced to sleep six to a room. See Monika Sigmund et al. (eds), *'Man versuchte längs zu kommen, und man lebt ja noch . . .': Frauenalltag in St Pauli in Kriegs- und Nachkriegszeit* (Hamburg, 1996), p. 25.

5 Mathilde Wolff-Mönckeberg, *On the Other Side*, trans. and ed. Ruth Evans (London, 1979), p. 81.

6 To add to the huge destruction to the transport infrastructure, 600 of Hamburg's 1,600 tram cars were completely destroyed, and half of its underground trains either destroyed or very badly damaged. What few trams, buses and trains still existed were strictly rationed at rush-hour: even those who were permitted to use them often could not cram their way in, and were obliged to walk anyway. See Hamburg Police Report, p. 86; and USSBS, *Economic Effects of the Air Offensive Against German Cities: A Detailed Study of the Effects of Area Bombing on Hamburg, Germany* (November 1945), p. 24.

7 Wolff-Mönckeberg, *On the Other Side*, p. 81.

8 Johannes Schoene, in Renate Hauschild-Thiessen, *Die Hamburger Katastrophe*, p.304.

9 Ilse Grassmann, *Ausgebombt: Ein Hausfrauen-Kriegstagebuch von Ilse Grassmann* (Hamburg, 2003), p. 28.

10 Maria Bartels letter, 15 September 1943, in Hauschild-Thiessen, *Die Hamburger Katastrophe*, p. 314.

11 Maria Bartels, letter to her husband, 8 September 1943, in Hauschild-Thiessen, *Die Hamburger Katastrophe*, p. 312.

12 Uwe Bahnsen and Kerstin von Stürmer, *Die Stadt, die sterben sollte: Hamburg in Bombenkrieg, Juli 1943* (Hamburg, 2003), p. 67.

13 USSBS, *Economic Effects*, p. 22.

14 Hamburg Police Report, p. 84.

15 See USSBS, *Economic Effects*, pp. 23–4; and Hamburg Police Report, pp. 84 and 91; and Carl F. Miller (ed.), *Appendixes 8 through 19 to the Hamburg Police President's Report on the Large Scale Attacks on Hamburg, Germany, in World War II* (Stanford, December 1968), Appendix 18.

For restoration of phone lines, see also Kurt Ahrens and Friedrich Ruppel, in Hauschild–Thiessen, *Die Hamburger Katastrophe*, pp. 308 and 318.

16 USSBS, *Economic Effects*, pp. 44–6; Charts 15 and 16.

17 *Ibid.*, pp. 44–5; Chart 15.

18 Ratouis, *Mémoires de guerre*, p. 111.

19 Eberhard Rössler, *The U-boat* (London, 1981), p. 266; see also Bahnsen and von Stürmer, *Die Stadt*, p. 71. This U-boat, U-792, was finally commissioned on 16 November.

20 Hannah Kelson interview, IWM Sound Archive 15550/5.

21 In Günther Severin (ed.), *Briefe an einen Pastor* (unpublished), letter 161.

22 Ahrens, in Hauschild–Thiessen, *Die Hamburger Katastrophe*, pp. 225–8.

23 See, for example, Nossack, *Der Untergang*, p. 108; Hans Brunswig, *Feuersturm über Hamburg* (Hamburg, 2003), p. 305; Hauschild-Thiessen, *Die Hamburger Katastrophe*, p. 285; and Hiltgunt Zassenhaus, *Ein Baum blüht im November* (Hamburg, 1974), whose title refers to this event.

24 Gretl Büttner, in Miller (ed.), *Appendixes*, Appendix 10, p. 122. There are dozens of other accounts of this happening across the city.

22 Famine

1 Heinrich Böll, *The Silent Angel* (London, 1994), p. 75. Food, and its lack, is the central theme of this novel about the aftermath of war in Germany.

2 Figures according to Hans Brunswig, *Feuersturm über Hamburg* (Stuttgart, 2003), pp. 454–6.

3 Hermann Holthusen, diary account, 11 August 1943, in Renate Hauschild-Thiessen, *Die Hamburger Katastrophe vom Sommer 1943 in Augenzeugenberichten* (Hamburg, 1993), p. 235.

4 Mathilde Wolff-Mönckeberg, *On the Other Side*, trans. and ed. Ruth Evans (London, 1979), p. 88.

5 Adolf Hitler's political testament, 29 April 1945, in Hans-Adolf

Jacobsen, *1939–1945: Der zweite Weltkrieg in Chronik und Dokumenten* (Darmstadt, 1961), p. 531.

6 Tommy Wilmott, IWM Sound Archive 19806, reel 9.

7 Dr P. J. Horsey, typescript diary, IWM Department of Documents, Con Shelf.

8 *Ibid.*

9 Philip J. C. Dark, 'Look Back This Once: Prisoner of War in Germany in WWII', typescript account, IWM Department of Documents, 94/7/1. Professor Dark returned to his memories of Hamburg in an exhibition of his paintings at the Honolulu Academy of Arts in 1994.

10 Katherine Morris, 'Destination Hamburg', typescript account, IWM Department of Documents, 91/27/1, p. 3. Ruth Evans, a native of Hamburg, expressed much the same sentiments when she returned there after the war: 'would this town ever be rebuilt? I doubted that'. See Wolff-Mönckeberg, *On the Other Side*, translator's epilogue, p. 163.

11 Janet Flaner's description for the *New Yorker*, in W. G. Sebald, *On the Natural History of Destruction* (London, 2004), p. 31.

12 Herbert Conert, in Frederick Taylor, *Dresden* (New York, 2004), p. 396. The description of Dresden as moonscape comes from Kurt Vonnegut, *Slaughterhouse 5* (London, 1991), pp. 130–31.

13 Victor Klemperer, *To the Bitter End: The Diaries of Victor Klemperer 1942–45*, trans. Martin Chalmers (London, 1999), 22 May 1945, p. 596.

14 Harry Hopkins diary entry, in Hans Rumpf, *The Bombing of Germany*, trans. Edward Fitzgerald (London, 1963), p. 126.

15 This was the figure taken before Congress in 1947. The actual investment was somewhat less. See Gregory A. Fossedal, *Our Finest Hour: Will Clayton, the Marshall Plan and the Triumph of Democracy* (Stanford, 1993), p. 252.

16 Dr P. J. Horsey, typescript diary.

17 Victor Gollancz, *In Darkest Germany* (London, 1947), pp. 28–9, 53–5, and plate 143.

18 *Ibid.*, pp. 55–6.

19 *Ibid.*, p. 52.

20 Morris, 'Destination Hamburg', p. 15.

21 *Ibid.*, p. 31.

22 Quoted in Gollancz, *In Darkest Germany*, p. 93.

23 Morris, 'Destination Hamburg', p. 15.

24 According to the Food Committee of UNRRA (United Nations Relief and Rehabilitation Administration), a normal population required 2,650 calories per day to maintain health. Official rations provided only 1,550 calories, but were rarely delivered. In Belsen the rations provided 800 calories per day. See Gollancz, *In Darkest Germany*, pp. 28–9 and 35.

25 Undated newspaper clipping from 1946/7 kept by Katherine Morris: 'Death warning to food rioters: U.S. may invoke military law', IWM Department of Documents, 91/27/1.

26 Gollancz, *In Darkest Germany*, p. 29.

27 E. G. W. Ridgers, 'The Life of a Sapper in World War Two', typescript memoir, IWM Documents, 99/16/1, p. 32. For winter temperatures in 1946/7 and their effects see Eckart Klessmann, *Geschichte der Stadt Hamburg*, p. 595; and Nora Heather, 'Experiences with Control Commission in Germany immediately after World War Two', typescript account, IWM Documents 03/1/1 (Mrs Heather kept a diary of temperatures, and even includes an official contemporary temperature chart).

28 For power cuts, see Heather, *ibid.*; and Klessmann, *Geschichte der Stadt Hamburg*, pp. 594–5. For several stories of children raiding coal trains, see Monika Sigmund et al. (eds), *'Man versuchte längs zu kommen, und man lebt ja noch . . .': Frauenalltag in St Pauli in Kriegs- und Nachkriegszeit* (Hamburg, 1996), p. 21.

29 Only eighty-five deaths from 'exposure' were entered on official registers, but this is a hopelessly low figure and does not include those who died from other conditions related to the severe cold: see Klessmann, *Geschichte der Stadt Hamburg*, p. 595.

30 In February 1962 the city suffered a catastrophic flood which ruined the underground train network, caused hundreds of millions of Deutschmarks' worth of damage, and claimed 315 lives. Smaller floods occurred in 1976 and 1983.

31 In 2001 more than six thousand companies were involved in media

based in Hamburg, including 3,200 advertising firms, 1,600 publishers and printers, and 700 film companies. See Anna Brenken, *Hamburg: Metropole an Alster und Elbe* (Hamburg, 2001), p. 45.

32 Hildegard Huza's memorial to the 370 people who died in the shelter at Karstadt shopping centre, at the junction of Hamburger Strasse and Oberaltenallee in Barmbek.

33 Alfred Hrdlicka's anti-war memorial at Dammtor comprises one sculpture of the Hamburg firestorm, and one of the concentration-camp prisoners who died when Allied bombs sank the ship *Cap Arcona* that was transporting them in the last days of the war.

34 Gerhard Marcks's sculpture, *Fahrt über den Styx*, is a memorial to the 36,918 bodies that lie in the mass graves.

35 'Klöntreff "Eimsbüttel im Feuersturm"', unpublished transcript of local-history group conversation, Galerie Morgenland/Geschichts-werkstatt, p. 13.

36 Hans Jedlicka, FZH 292–8, G–Kra.

37 Wanda Chantler, interview with the author, 5 July 2004; and Jan Melsen, quoted by Karin Orth, 'Jan Melsen: "Hamburg beschäftigt mich emotional am meisten."': Erinnerungen eines KZ-Überleb-enden an den Hamburger Feuersturm' in Ulrike Jureit and Beate Meyer (eds), *Verletzungen: Lebensgeschichtliche Verarbeitung von Kriegser-fahrungen* (Hamburg, 1994), p. 153. Wanda Chantler suffered an immediate breakdown as a result of the horrible scenes she witnessed during the first night of bombing (see chapter 10), and years later she was to suffer psychotic episodes that saw her hospitalized. Jan Melsen, one of the concentration-camp inmates forced to clear dead bodies from cellars, also had a breakdown in 1971. This was not the result of the firestorm alone, but of years of abuse in Neuengamme; even so, the events that affected him most deeply were those he experienced in the aftermath of the firestorm: 'Hamburg damaged me the most emotionally. The work there saved my life, when I was practically dead before I went there – but on the other hand, after the war it was this that most weighed on my mind, especially the corpses of all the old and young people. The worst came back to me as a syndrome – then you have dreams as if it's happening all over again . . .'

23 The Reckoning

1 Though this quote refers to nuclear warfare, what happened at Hamburg fits better into a nuclear context than it does into the context of conventional bombing, as I will argue in this chapter. In 2003 Eisenhower's words were quoted during a debate on nuclear weapons in the US House of Representatives; see 'Notable Words: S&T Policy Quotations from 2003', in *FYI: The American Institute of Physics Bulletin of Science Policy News*, no. 2, 8 January 2004.

2 All statistics here and in the following paragraphs are taken from the USSBS, *Economic Effects of the Air Offensive against German Cities: A Detailed Study of the Effects of Area Bombing on Hamburg, Germany* (November 1945), pp. 7–10. The Hamburg Police Report also contains most of these figures (pp. 17–18), and by and large they agree. Where they do not, I have assumed that the compilers of the former document, who based many of their findings on data from the Hamburg Police Report, also had access to later, more accurate sources of information. The report of the BBSU is slightly less reliable, since the unit was run on a shoestring budget.

3 *Ibid.*, pp. 9–11. The Hamburg Police Report claims that 2,632 'commercial establishments' and 580 'industrial establishments' were destroyed, but this does not seem to square with the huge amount of damage done to residential property, or the figure given by the USSBS of around forty thousand industrial buildings lost.

4 Hamburg Police Report, pp. 17–18.

5 The figures for the number of dead, which had not yet been completed by the time the Hamburg Police Report was finished, are taken from the USSBS, Hamburg Report, pp. 1 and 7A. I have assumed that the majority of the two thousand reported 'missing' were also dead, since many bodies were completely incinerated, and corpses were still being discovered in rebuilding works as late as 1951. The Hamburg Police Report has the number of injured slightly lower at 37,214 (p. 17), but it is likely that the real figure was much higher than either estimate.

6 This figure does not include the many deaths in months and years to come from radiation poisoning. For a detailed discussion of casualty

estimates at Hiroshima and Nagasaki, see Richard B. Frank, *Downfall: The End of the Imperial Japanese Empire* (New York, 2001), pp. 285–7.

7 USSBS, *Economic Effects*, p. 33A. The percentage of industrial workers who still had not returned is slightly lower: of the city's 250,000 industrial workers, 75,000 (or 30 per cent) had still not returned by the end of 1943 (see USSBS, *Economic Effects*, p. 1).

8 This unrecoverable loss in production is estimated at about 11.6 per cent. See *ibid.*, p. 42.

9 *Ibid.*, p. 1.

10 USSBS, *Economic Effects*, Submarine Plant Report no. 2, p. 13. The BBSU put the estimate higher, at twenty-six or twenty-seven U-boats lost: see Sir Charles Webster and Noble Frankland, *The Strategic Air Offensive Against Germany 1939–1945* (London, 1961), p. 287.

11 Hamburg Police Report, p. 84.

12 Solly Zuckerman et al., *The Strategic Air War Against Germany, 1939–45: Report of the British Bombing Survey Unit* (London, 1998), p. 161. See also USSBS, *Economic Effects*, p. 2.

13 See for example, Max Hastings, *Bomber Command* (London, 1979), p. 241.

14 Quoted in *ibid.*, p. 241.

15 For a comprehensive analysis of the shortcomings of the Luftwaffe, as told by the Luftwaffe generals, see Harold Faber (ed.), *Luftwaffe: An Analysis by Former Luftwaffe Generals* (London, 1979).

16 Adolf Galland, *The First and the Last* (London, 1955), pp. 241–2.

17 *Ibid.*, p. 243. Cajus Bekker quotes Hitler as having made this same declaration at a situation conference on 25 July, directly after the first Hamburg raid, to his Luftwaffe adjutant, Major Christian: see Cajus Bekker, *The Luftwaffe War Diaries*, trans. Frank Ziegler (London, 1966), p. 312. It is quite possible that he said it on both occasions: it was a sentiment he had been repeating since 1940.

18 Galland, *First and Last*, pp. 252–3. In fact, Goering never took him up on this resignation, and Galland retained his post.

19 'Cost of destruction of Hamburg 24 July – 2 August 1943', according to US Statistical Control Division, Office of Management Control, 1 September 1943. This figure does not take into account the huge amount of time spent in planning, administration and so on. Air

Force Historical Research Agency, Maxwell, Alabama, film copy A1107, 1654–6.

20 Original figure taken from USSBS, *Economic Effects*. The website http://eh.net uses fairly reputable sources and has the historical exchange rate as 1 Reichmark to $0.40, and projects $1 in 1943 to be worth about $11.29 today. (Website last viewed 19 April 2006.)

21 This is A. J. P. Taylor's figure, in *The Second World War* (London, 1975), p. 129. While Webster and Frankland's *Strategic Air Offensive* claims that only 7 per cent of the nation's manpower was involved in keeping the bomber offensive going, this does not represent the true cost: the bomber offensive monopolized not only the skilled workforce but also the majority of scientific and technological institutions.

22 For reactions to the Butt Report, which showed the bombing war to be a huge drain on national resources for disappointing results, see Hastings, *Bomber Command*, pp. 108–15.

23 Quoted in F. H. Hinsey *et al.*, *British Intelligence in the Second World War* (London, 1979–90), vol. III, pt I (1984), p. 44.

24 Redemption

1 Agathon, quoted by Aristotle; see *The Nicomachaen Ethics*, trans. H. Rackman (London, 1926), VI.ii.6. This is a passage in which Aristotle defines the concept of 'choice'. It is particularly apt because he uses the sacking of Troy as his example of something that cannot be undone.

2 *Hamburger Abendblatt*, 24 July 1993.

3 Even in clear conditions their bombing was not as accurate as the Americans liked to believe. All bombardiers were supposed to drop their bombs at the same time as the formation leader, but if they were just a fraction of a second late it could mean that the bombs landed hundreds of yards from where they were supposed to. Cloudy or smoky conditions merely compounded this problem. Towards the end of the year, Hap Arnold finally accepted that precision bombing was rarely possible in the cloudy skies over Germany, and gave a general order instructing US bomber crews to use radar to

locate their targets whenever they were obscured – in other words, to employ exactly the same methods of 'blind bombing' that the British used. By the end of the following year around 80 per cent of *all* US bomber raids over Germany were conducted by means of blind bombing. See Eric Markusen and David Kopf (eds), *The Holocaust and Strategic Bombing: Genocide and Total War in the Twentieth Century* (Boulder, 1995), pp. 165–6.

4 See Immediate Interpretation Reports S.A.410 and S.A.417, UK National Archives, AIR 24/257.

5 See Bombardier's Log, 26 July 1943, 351st BG, US National Archives, RG18, E7, Box 1002, Folder 22.

6 For statistics on total war losses for the RAF and USAAF, see Robin Neillands, *The Bomber War* (London, 2001), p. 379.

7 Statistics from *ibid.*, p. 379. See also Max Hastings, *Bomber Command* (London, 1979), p. 11. The USSBS estimates casualties at the bottom end of this scale, but is probably overly conservative: see its *Economic Effects of the Air Offensive against German Cities: A Detailed Study of the Effects of Area Bombing on Hamburg, Germany* (November 1945), p. 1. Likewise, the BBSU estimates the total number of deaths at 305,000: see Sir Charles Webster and Noble Frankland, *The Strategic Air War Against Germany, 1939–45: Report of the British Bombing Survey Unit* (London, 1998), p. 69.

8 Quoted in Brian Bond, *Liddell Hart: A Study of His Military Thought* (London, 1977), p. 145. For further voices of dissent, see A. C. Grayling, *Among the Dead Cities* (London, 2006), pp. 179–208.

9 According to Kenneth McDonald of 78 Squadron, in Neillands, *Bomber War*, p. 389.

10 See Neillands, *Bomber War*, pp. 402–3. For Churchill's attempts to distance himself from Harris, see Frederick Taylor, *Dresden* (New York, 2004), pp. 375–9; and Hastings, *Bomber Command*, pp. 343–4.

11 Associated Press report, 16 February 1945, in Neillands, *Bomber War*, p. 368; and Taylor, *Dresden*, p. 361. There are slight differences in the wording between these two; I have favoured the latter, who cites his source more completely.

12 The huge popularity of anti-war novels like Joseph Heller's *Catch-*

22 and Kurt Vonnegut's *Slaughterhouse 5* did a great deal to acquaint America with the arbitrary nature of American bombing in Germany. However, such novels were arguably more about the war in Vietnam than they were about the Second World War. The American burden of shame over Vietnam is the closest equivalent to British shame for the RAF bomber offensive on Germany.

13 Ted Groom, interview with the author, 11 November 2004. Ted Groom's observation is borne out by all the contemporary diaries and logbooks I have come across.

14 Doug Fry, interview with the author, 16 November 2004. See also Doug Fry's interview for the Imperial War Museum Sound Archive, 27255, Reel 7.

15 Colin Harrison, interview with the author, 8 December 2004.

16 See Martin Middlebrook, *The Battle of Hamburg* (London, 1980), p. 352; see also Mathilde Wolff-Mönckeberg, *On the Other Side*, trans. and ed. Ruth Evans (London, 1979), p. 27.

17 Hans Erich Nossack, *Der Untergang* (Hamburg, 1981), p. 65.

18 Max Brauer, *Nüchternen Sinnes und heißen Herzens . . .: Reden und Ansprachen* (Hamburg, 1952), p. 430.

19 Bürgerschaft der Freien und Hansestadt Hamburg Parlaments-Dokumentation, Elisabeth Kiausch speech, 23 July 1993, p. 3.

20 Frau Bischöfin Maria Jepsen, 'Predigt am 23 Juli 1993 in der St Michaelis Kirche: "Gomorrha"'. Manuscript of the sermon by courtesy of the bishop herself. For an excellent analysis of the bishop's speech, see Mirko Hohmann's dissertation for the University of Hamburg, 'So wurde die Zerstörung ihres Lebens für uns alle zu einer furchtbaren Anklage': Die Juliangriffe auf Hamburg in der hamburgischen Errinerungskultur 1943 bis 1993 (University of Hamburg, 2003), pp. 97–9.

21 Jörg Friedrich, *Der Brand: Deutschland im Bombenkrieg 1940–1945* (Berlin, 2002).

22 Ironically, these sentiments were echoed in the speech of the bishop of Hamburg, who, unusually, laid the burden of guilt not with the Nazis but with the 'people' as a whole. See Jepsen, '"Gomorrha"', p. 3.

23 See, for example, Rainer Hering, 'Operation Gomorrha – Hamburg

remembers the Second World War', in *German History*, vol. 13, no. 1 (1995), p. 93.

24 The authors of the USSBS attributed the growth of German pacifism to the horrors they had witnessed during the bombing war: 'The city area raids have left their mark on the German people as well as on their cities. Far more than any other military action that preceded the occupation of Germany itself, these attacks left the German people with a solid lesson in the disadvantages of war. It is a terrible lesson; conceivably that lesson . . . could be the most lasting single effect of the air war.' USSBS, Summary Report (European Theatre), p. 4. In 2003 Germany was among the first to criticize Britain and America for their invasion of Iraq.

Archives Consulted

1 *Archives in Britain*

Imperial War Museum
National Archives
British Library
RAF Museum, Hendon

2 *Germany*

(a) *Local history archives (*Geschichtswerkstätten *and* Stadtteilarchive*)*

Altona:	Stadtteilarchiv Ottensen
Barmbek:	Geschichtswerkstatt Barmbek e. V.
Barmbek Süd:	Jarrestadt-Archiv
Bergedorf:	Kultur & Geschichtskontor der Initiative historischer Bauten
Dulsberg:	Geschichtsgruppe Dulsberg
Eimsbüttel:	Galerie Morgenland e. V.
Eppendorf:	Stadtteilarchiv Eppendorf
Fuhlsbüttel:	Willi-Bredel-Gesellschaft Geschichtswerkstatt e. V.
Hamm:	Stadtteilinitiative Hamm e. V.
	Bunker Museum
Harburg:	Honigfabrik
St Georg:	Geschichtswerkstatt St Georg
St Pauli:	St Pauli-Archiv e. V.
Wandsbek:	Stadtteilarchiv Bramfeld

(b) Other archives

Bundesarchiv

Bürgerschaft der Freien und Hansestadt Hamburg Parlaments-
Dokumentation

Carl Hagenback Archiv

Förderkreis 'Rettet die Nikolaikirche' e.V.: Dokumentenzentrum in the
cellar of the ruined church

Forschungsstelle für Zeitgeschichte in Hamburg (FZH), especially their
oral history project 'Werkstatt der Erinnerung'

Hamburg Staatsarchiv

Kirchenkreis Alt-Hamburg (Church Archives)

Museum für Hamburgische Geschichte, particularly their library

3 United States of America

Mighty Eighth Museum, Savannah, Georgia

National Archives

National Fire Protection Association

National Technical Information Service

Oral History Archive of World War II, Rutgers University

Reichelt Oral History Program at Florida State University

United States Air Force University, Alabama

4 Internet sites

http://www.91stbombgroup.com – Official USAAF 91st BG website

http://www.303rdbg.com – Official USAAF 303rd BG website

http://www.polebrook.com/history.htm – USAAF 351st BG website

http://freespace.virgin.net/ken.harbour – USAAF 351st BG history

http://www.379thbga.org – Official USAAF 379th BG website

http://www.381st.org – Official USAAF 381st BG website

http://www.384thbg.iwarp.com – Official USAAF 384th BG website http://fas-history.rutgers.edu/oralhistory – Rutgers University oral history online

http://www.calvin.edu/academic/cas/gpa/ww2era.htm – German Propaganda Archive

http://www.hamburgmuseum.de – website of the Museum für Hamburgische Geschichte

http://www.lostplaces.de – website listing flak positions and air-raid shelters in Hamburg

http://www.seniorennet-hamburg.de.zeitzeugen – website where Hamburg's senior citizens record their memories of the city

http://eh.net – website containing historical exchange rates

Select Bibliography

1 Published books and booklets

(a) Official Histories

Craven, W. F., and Cate, J. L., *The Army Air Forces in World War II* (Chicago, 1949)

Hinsey, F. H., et al., *British Intelligence in the Second World War* (London, 1979–1990)

Webster, Sir Charles, and Frankland, Noble, *The Strategic Air Offensive against Germany, 1939–1945* (London, 1961)

Zuckerman, Solly, et al., *The Strategic Air War Against Germany, 1939–45: Report of the British Bombing Survey Unit* (London, 1998)

(b) Unattributed booklets

Gnadenkirche Hamburg 1907–1987 (Hamburg, 1987)

(c) Attributed works

Aust, Alfred, *Der Ohlsdorfer Friedhof* (Hamburg, 1964)

Bahnsen, Uwe, and von Stürmer, Kerstin, *Die Stadt, die sterben sollte: Hamburg im Bombenkrieg, Juli 1943* (Hamburg, 2003)

Bajohr, Frank, and Szodrzynski, Joachim (eds), *Hamburg in der NS-Zeit* (Hamburg, 1995)

Beck, Earl R., *Under the Bombs: The German Home Front 1942–45* (Lexington, 1986)

Bekker, Cajus, *The Luftwaffe War Diaries*, trans. Frank Ziegler (London, 1966)

Bessel, Richard, *Nazism and War* (London, 2004)

Betz, Frank L., and Cassens, Kenneth H. (eds), *379th BG Anthology* (Paducah, 2000)

Böge, Volker, and Deide-Lüchow, Jutta, *Eimsbüttler Jugend im Krieg* (Hamburg, 2000)

Bond, Horatio, *Fire and the Air War* (Boston, 1946)

Boyle, Andrew, *Trenchard: Man of Vision* (London, 1962)

Brauer, Max, *Nüchternen Sinnes und heißen Herzens . . .: Reden und Ansprachen* (Hamburg, 1952)

Brenken, Anna, *Hamburg: Metropole an Alster und Elbe* (Hamburg, 2001)

Brunswig, Hans, *Feuersturm über Hamburg* (Stuttgart, 2003)

Büttner, Ursula, *Gomorrha: Hamburg im Bombenkrieg* (Hamburg, 1993)

Caidin, Martin, *The Night Hamburg Died* (New York, 1960)

Caldwell, Donald L., *The JG26 War Diary* (London, 1998)

Campbell, Sir Malcolm, *The Peril from the Air* (London, 1937)

Chorley, W. R., *Bomber Command Losses, vol. 4 (1943)* (Hersham, 2004)

Clarke, Basil, *The History of Airships* (London, 1961)

Clarke, I. F. (ed.), *The Tale of the Next Great War 1871–1914: Fictions of Future Warfare and Battles Still-to-come* (Liverpool, 1995)

Decker, Ken, *Memories of the 384th Bomb Group* (New York, 2005)

Diecks, Herbert, *Friedhof Ohlsdorf auf den Spuren von Naziherschaft und Widerstand* (Hamburg, 1992)

Dissen, Adolf, *75 Jahre Horne Martinskirche* (Hamburg, 1961)

Douhet, Giulio, *The Command of the Air*, trans. Dino Ferrari (London, 1943)

Erdmann, Heinrich (ed.), *Hamburg und Dresden in Dritten Reich: Bombenkrieg und Kriegsende* (Hamburg, 2000)

Faber, Harold (ed.), *Luftwaffe: An Analysis by Former Luftwaffe Generals* (London, 1979)

Fossedal, Gregory A., *Our Finest Hour: Will Clayton, the Marshall Plan and the Triumph of Democracy* (Stanford, 1993)

Freeman, Roger A., *The Mighty Eighth* (London, 2000)
 The Mighty Eighth War Diary (London, 1990)

Freeman, Roger, and Osborne, David, *The B-17 Flying Fortress Story* (London, 1998)

Friedrich, Jörg, *Der Brand: Deutschland im Bombenkrieg 1940–1945* (Berlin, 2002)

Fulbrook, Mary, *The Divided Nation: A History of Germany 1918–1990* (Oxford, 1992)

Fuller, J. F. C., *The Reformation of War* (London, 1923)

Galland, Adolf, *The First and the Last*, trans. Mervyn Savill (London, 1955)

Goebbels, Joseph, *Die Tagebücher von Joseph Goebbels*, ed. Elke Fröhlich (München, 1993)

  The Goebbels Diaries, trans. and ed. Louis P. Lochner (London, 1948)

Gollancz, Victor, *In Darkest Germany* (London, 1947)

Grassmann, Ilse, *Ausgebombt: Ein Hausfrauen-Kriegstagebuch von Ilse Grassmann, Hamburg 1943–1945* (Hamburg, 2003)

Grayling, A. C., *Among the Dead Cities* (London, 2006)

Groehlen, Olaf, *Der Bombenkrieg gegen Deutschland* (Berlin, 1990)

Günther, Claus (ed.), *erlebt – erkannt – erinnert: Zeitzeugen schrieben Geschichte(n) 1932–1952* (Hamburg, 2003)

Hage, Volker (ed.), *Hamburg 1943: Literarische Zeugnisse zum Feuersturm* (Frankfurt am Main, 2003)

Harris, Sir Arthur, *Bomber Offensive* (London, 1947)

Hastings, Max, *Bomber Command* (London, 1979)

Hauschild-Thiessen, Renate, *Unternehmen Gomorrha* (Hamburg, 1993)

  Die Hamburger Katastrophe vom Sommer 1943 in Augenzeugenberichten (Hamburg, 1993)

Herrmann, Hajo, *Bewegtes Leben* (Stuttgart, 1984)

Hinchliffe, Peter, *The Other Battle* (Shrewsbury, 1996)

Hof, Kerstin (ed.), *Rothenburgsort 27/28 Juli 1943* (Stadtteilinitiative Hamm e.V., no date)

Hoffman, Egbert A., *Als das Feuer vom Himmel fiel* (Hamburg, 1983)

Howard, Michael (ed.), *Restraints on War* (Oxford, 1979)

Irving, David, *The Rise and Fall of the Luftwaffe* (Boston, 1973)

Jacobsen, Hans-Adolf, *1939–1945: Der zweite Weltkrieg in Chronik und Dokumenten* (Darmstadt, 1961)

Johnen, Wilhelm, *Duel Under the Stars* (Manchester, 1994)

Jureit, Ulrike, and Meyer, Beate (eds), *Verletzungen: Lebensgeschichtliche Verarbeitung von Kriegserfahrungen* (Hamburg, 1994)

Kennett, Lee, *A History of Strategic Bombing* (New York, 1982)

Klemperer, Victor, *I Shall Bear Witness: The Diaries of Victor Klemperer 1933–1941*, trans. Martin Chalmers (London, 1998)

To the Bitter End: The Diaries of Victor Klemperer 1942–1945, trans. Martin Chalmers (London, 1999)

Klessmann, Eckart, *Geschichte der Stadt Hamburg* (Hamburg, 2002)

Klöss, Erhard (ed.), *Der Luftkrieg über Deutschland 1939–1945: Deutsche Berichte und Pressestimmen des neutralen Auslands* (München, 1963)

Kruse, A., *Aufestehungsgemeinde und Kirchgemeinde Nord-Barmbek* (Hamburg, 1995)

Liddell Hart, B. H., *Paris, or the Future War* (London, 1925)

Lindqvist, Sven, *A History of Bombing*, trans. Linda Haverty Rugg (London, 2001)

Ludendorff, Erich, *Der Totale Krieg*, trans. by A. S. Rappoport as *The Nation at War* (London, 1936)

Markusen, Eric, and Kopf, David (eds), *The Holocaust and Strategic Bombing: Genocide and Total War in the Twentieth Century* (Boulder, 1995)

McCrea, Bill, *A Chequer-Board of Nights* (Preston, 2003)

Middlebrook, Martin, *The Battle of Hamburg* (London, 1980)

Miller, Carl F. (ed.), *Summary of Damage Inflicted by Air Raids on the City of Hamburg in the Period July 25 to August 3, 1943* (Stanford, 1968)

Appendixes 1 through 7 to the Hamburg Police President's Report on the Large Scale Air Attacks on Hamburg, Germany, in World War II (Stanford, 1968)

Appendixes 8 through 19 to the Hamburg Police President's Report on the Large Scale Air Attacks on Hamburg, Germany, in World War II (Stanford, 1968)

Mitchell, William, *Winged Defense: The Development and Possibilities of Modern Air Power – Economic and Military* (New York, 1925)

Müller, Rolf-Dieter, *Der Bombenkrieg 1939–45* (Berlin, 2004)

Der letzte deutsche Krieg 1939–1945 (Stuttgart, 2005)

Musgrove, Gordon, *Operation Gomorrah* (London, 1981)

Neillands, Robin, *The Bomber War* (London, 2001)

Nossack, Hans Erich, *Der Untergang* (Hamburg, 1981)

O'Neill, Brian D., *303rd Bombardment Group* (Oxford, 2003)

Okraß, Hermann, *Hamburg bleibt rot* (Hamburg, 1934)

Overy, Richard, *War and Economy in the Third Reich* (Oxford, 1994)

Why the Allies Won: Explaining Victory in World War II (London, 1996)

Paris, Michael, *Winged Warfare: The Literature and Theory of Aerial Warfare in Britain 1859–1917* (Manchester, 1992)

Peukert, Detlev J. K., *Inside Nazi Germany: Conformity, Opposition and Racism in Everyday Life* (London, 1989)

Plagemann, Volker, '*Vaterstadt, Vaterland . . .*': *Denkmäler in Hamburg* (no date)

Rasmußen, Kerstin, *Veränderungen 1894–1994: Hamburg–Hamm im Spiegel erlebter Geschichte(n)* (Hamburg, 1994)

Rasmußen, Kerstin, and Wulf, Gunnar (eds), *Es war ja Krieg* (Hamburg 1993)

   Es war ein unterirdischer Bunker (Hamburg, 1996)

   Juli 1943: Hamburg erinnern sich (Hamburg, 2001)

   Wir zogen in die Hammer Landstraße (Hamburg, 2001)

Ratouis, René, *Mémoires de guerre d'un non-combattant* (Paris, 2003)

Ray, John, *The Second World War* (London, 1999)

Reichel, Peter, *Politik mit der Erinnerung* (Frankfurt, 2001)

   (ed.), *Das Gedächtnis der Stadt: Hamburg im Umgang mit seiner national-sozialistischen Vergangenheit* (Hamburg, 1997)

Reiker, Michael, *Hamburg–Hamm 1693–1993* (Kiel, 1993)

Robb, Derwyn D., *Shades of Kimbolton: A Narrative of 379th Bombardment Group* (San Angelo, 1981)

Rumpf, Hans, *The Bombing of Germany*, trans. Edward Fitzgerald (London, 1963)

Schaffer, Ronald, *Wings of Judgement: American Bombing in World War II* (New York, 1985)

Sebald, W. G., *On the Natural History of Destruction*, trans. Anthea Bell (London, 2003)

Sigmund, Monika, et al. (eds), '*Man versuchte längs zu kommen, und man lebt ja noch . . .*': *Frauenalltag in St Pauli in Kriegs- und Nachkriegszeit* (Hamburg, 1996)

Spaight, J. M., *Air Power and the Cities* (London, 1930)

Speer, Albert, *Inside the Third Reich*, trans. Richard and Clara Winston (London, 1970)

Taylor, A. J. P., *The Second World War* (London, 1975)

Taylor, Frederick, *Dresden* (London, 2004)

Wells, H. G., *The War in the Air, and Particularly how Mr Bert Smallways Fared While it Lasted* (Leipzig, 1909)

Wilson, Kevin, *Bomber Boys* (London, 2005)

Wolff-Mönckeberg, Mathilde, *On the Other Side*, trans. and ed. Ruth Evans (London, 1979)

Wolter, Rudolf, *Erinnerung an Gomorrha* (Hamburg, 2003)

Zanetti, J. Enrique, *Fire from the Air: The ABC of Incendiaries* (New York, 1941)

Zassenhaus, Hiltgunt, *Ein Baum blüht im November* (Hamburg, 1974)

Zuckerman, Solly, *From Apes to Warlords: The Autobiography (1904–1946) of Solly Zuckerman* (London: 1978)

2 Journals

Lutherische Monatshefte, vol. 32 (1993)

Die Heimat, March/April 1987

German History, vol. 13, no. 1 (1995)

Weatherwise, vol. 16, no. 2 (April 1963)

3 Newspapers and magazines

Der Alter Hammerbrooker, July–August 1953

Bild, 22 July 1965

Hamburger Abendblatt, 16/17 August 1952, 18 July–4 August 1953, 18 and 19 July 1963, 1–31 July 1983, 17–24 July 1993

Hamburger Anzeiger, 1943–1944

Hamburger Echo, 25–29 July 1953

Hamburger Fremdenblatt, 1943

Hamburger Morgenpost, 15–22 August 1952

Hamburger Tageblatt, 1943

Hamburger Zeitung, 25 July–14 August 1943

Memo, October 1993 (magazine produced by the Museum für Hamburgische Geschichte)

Der Spiegel, 25 July 2003

Uhlenhorster Warte, 7 July 1953

Die Welt, special edition, July 1993, 'Unternehmen Gomorrha'

4 *CDRoms*

The Molesworth Story (2nd edition) produced by 303rd Bomb Group
Association

5 *Unpublished material*

(a) Official reports

*Secret Report by the Police President of Hamburg (as local Air Protection Leader)
on the heavy air raids on Hamburg in July/August, 1943 [Geheim. Bericht
des Polizeipräsidenten in Hamburg als Örtlicher Luftschutzleiter über die
schweren Grossluftangriffe auf Hamburg im Juli/August 1943]*, translated
by the British Home Office, Civil Defence Department, Intelligence Branch, January 1946. This document is available in the UK
National Archives, AIR 20/7287. Alternatively, it can be bought
from US Department of Commerce, Technology Administration,
National Technical Information Service under the following title:
Carl F. Miller (ed.), *Summary of Damage Inflicted by Air raids on the
City of Hamburg in the Period July 25 to August 3, 1943* (Stanford, July
1968). The Hamburg Police Report Appendixes are also available
from the National Technical Information Service.

United States Strategic Bombing Survey, *Economic Effects of the Air Offensive against German Cities: A Detailed Study of the Effects of Area
Bombing on Hamburg, Germany* (November 1945), available from
the UK National Archives, AIR 48/19.

*Summary Report of the United States Strategic Bombing Survey (European
Theatre)*, available from the UK National Archives, DSIR 23/
15754.

(b) Speeches

Brauer, Max, 'Gedächtnisstätte für die Hamburger Bombenopfer', delivered 16 August 1952, in Max Brauer, *Nüchternen Sinnes und heißen Herzens . . .: Reden und Ansprachen* (Hamburg, 1952)

Ehlers, Hermann, speech on the opening of the memorial at the Ohlsdorfer Friedhof on 16 August 1952 (Staatarchiv, 141–20 Friedhof Ohlsdorf/Bombenopfer)

Giordano, Ralph, *Rede zur 60. Wiederkehr des Luftangriffes auf Hamburg an der Nikolaikirche*, typescript from Förderkreis archive

Jepsen, Frau Bischöfin Maria, 'Predigt am 23 Juli 1993 in der St Michaelis Kirche: "Gomorrha"' (provided by the Bishop's office)

Kiausch, Elisabeth, 'Wer es erlebt hat, wird es nie vergessen', delivered at 11.00 a.m. on 23 July 1993 in the Great Hall of the Hamburg Rathaus. From Bürgerschaft der Freien und Hansestadt Hamburg Parlaments-Dokumentation (Press and public relations document 66/91: 17.00 100/23.07.1993/1.03 Kiausch, Elisabeth)

Schönfelder, Adolf, speech given on 16 August 1952 at the Ohlsdorfer Friedhof (Staatsarchiv, 141–20 Friedhof Ohlsdorf/Bombenopfer)

Witter, Ben, *Speech 1993*, from Berichte und Dokumente 952 (27 September 1993), Staatliche Pressestelle, Hamburg

(c) Letters and diaries

Gerke, Liselotte: typescript account

Herr Schult, Letter to Pastor Kreyer

Hof, Kerstin (ed.), *Rothenburgsort 27/28 Juli 1943*, unpublished booklet, produced by Stadtteilinitiative Hamm e.V.

Severin, Günther (ed.), *Briefe an einen Pastor*, collection of letters written to Pastor Jürgen Wehrmann in Eilbek from his parishioners

(d) University theses

Hohmann Mirko, *'so wurde die Zerstörung ihres Lebens für uns alle zu einer furchtbaren Anklage': Die Juliangriffe auf Hamburg in der hamburgischen Erinnerungskultur 1943 bis 1993* (Hamburg, 2003)

(e) Unattributed

Hamburg secondary school project, 'Als die Bomben fielen: Hamburg vor 40 Jahren, Museum für Hamburgische Geschichte, HaIII 68

'Klöntreff "Eimsbüttel im Feuersturm"', unpublished transcript of local-history group conversation at Galerie Morgenland/Geschichtswerkstatt

Acknowledgements

I am extremely grateful to the staff at the many institutions that have become essential to the creation of a book like this. The most important of these were, in no particular order, the Air Force University in Alabama, the US National Archives in Washington, the Reichelt Oral History Program at Florida State University, Oral History Archive of World War Two at Rutgers University, the British Library, the Imperial War Museum in London, the Royal Air Force Museum, the UK National Archives, the Museum für Hamburgische Geschichte, and the Forschungsstelle für Zeitgeschichte in Hamburg. I have been consistently surprised at the knowledge and helpfulness of the staff in such institutions on both sides of the Atlantic, and am truly grateful for their existence.

Special mention must be made of the various Geschichtswerkstätten and Stadtteilarchive in Hamburg, most of which are run with extremely limited funds, and rely on the unbounded enthusiasm of the people who run them. I am particularly indebted to Grunhild Ohl-Hinz of the St Pauli-Archiv and Sielke Salomon of Galerie Morgenland Geschichtswerkstatt Eimsbüttel, both for giving me access to unpublished material and for introducing me to survivors of the firestorm. Tim Bottoms at the Mighty Eighth Museum, in Georgia, and Robin Sellers, at Florida State University, should also be mentioned for assistance above and beyond the call of duty. Also Klaus Gille of the Carl Hagenbeck Archiv, who kindly provided me with information about the destruction of Hamburg's zoo.

Where possible I have tried to restrict myself to quoting contemporary diaries and letters in this book, since the details they give are more likely to be accurate. However, stories told face to face have an immediacy that can sometimes be lacking in written accounts. I would therefore like to express my deep gratitude to the men and women who have both shared their diaries and consented to be interviewed for this book, especially: Leonard Bradfield, Wanda Chantler, Leonard Cooper, Walter

Davis, Lishman Easby, Ted Edwards, Doug Fry, Liselotte Gerke, Ted Groom, Colin Harrison, Kenneth Hills, Norman Jones, Beege Margot, Wallace McIntosh, Bill McCrea, Gordon Moulton-Barrett, Ted Neville, F. H. Quick, James Sullivan, Denys Teare, Trevor Timperley and Louis P. Wooldridge.

There are several individuals whom I must thank for their help with research. I could not have covered the German side of the story in nearly so much detail without the help of Malte Thießen and Mirko Hohmann. David Isby got me started on the American research, and Paul Wolf was an enormous help at the US National Archives. Harry D. Gobrecht was very helpful with information relating to the USAAF's 303rd BG. Although I did not have time to follow up all the leads they gave me, Penny Ash and Keith Hill were generous with their own lists of contacts. The irrepressible Peter Hart of the Imperial War Museum not only helped with oral history sources but kept me smiling as well. Thanks must also go to H. E. Batchelder of the RAF Ex-Prisoner of War Association, Nigel Parker of *Bomber Command News*, and Frank Haslam of the British & Commonwealth Air Unit Register, and Oliver Clutton-Brock. My wife, Liza, gave me excellent advice on ways to improve the manuscript, as did Ion Trewin, Ian Drury and Gary Sheffield. I must also thank Sonia Stammwitz, Jenny Piening and Sylvia Goulding for their help with translating some of the denser German documents.

As always, I am very grateful also to my agents: Simon Trewin and Claire Scott at PFD; Nicki Kennedy, Mary Esdaile and all at ILA; and Dan Mandel at Sanford J. Greenburger Associates.

Lastly I must thank all those at my publishers who have made this book possible. After working for several years in the publishing industry myself I know what an enormous amount of effort goes into the creation, publicizing and marketing of a book, and I am grateful to everyone at Penguin for all their hard work. In particular I must thank my editors Eleo Gordon and Hazel Orme for all their patience, their excellent advice and their constant enthusiasm for this book throughout the publishing process.

Index